JSOT/ASOR MONOGRAPH SERIES
7

JOURNAL FOR THE STUDY OF THE OLD TESTAMENT
SUPPLEMENT SERIES
123

JSOT Press
Sheffield

Judahite Burial Practices and Beliefs about the Dead

Elizabeth Bloch-Smith

Journal for the Study of the Old Testament
Supplement Series 123
JSOT/ASOR Monograph Series 7

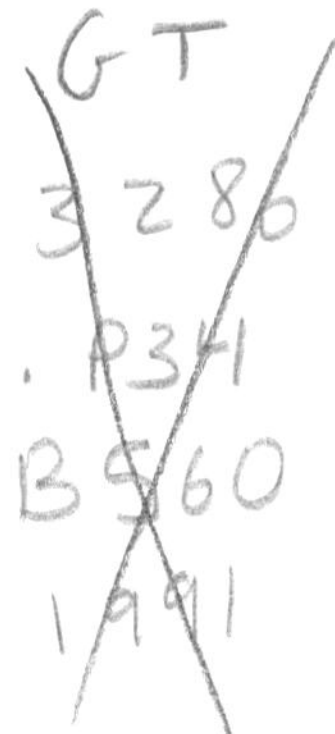

Published by JSOT Press
JSOT Press is an imprint of
Sheffield Academic Press Ltd
The University of Sheffield
343 Fulwood Road
Sheffield S10 3BP
England

Typeset by Sheffield Academic Press
and
Printed on acid-free paper in Great Britain
by Billing & Sons Ltd
Worcester

British Library Cataloguing in Publication Data

Bloch-Smith, Elizabeth
Judahite burial practices and beliefs about
the dead.—(Journal for the study of the Old
Testament. Supplement series. ISSN 0309-0787; 123)
I. Title II. Series
393.10933

ISSN 0309-0787
ISSN 0267-5684
ISBN 1-85075-335-0

CONTENTS

ACKNOWLEDGMENTS

I gratefully acknowledge the contributions of the following people. Professor Larry Stager is my mentor, the individual in whose (academic) image I was created. During my tenure as George A. Barton fellow at the W.F. Albright Institute of Archaeological Research in Jerusalem, Dr Sy Gitin provided a roof and guidance during the research and writing of this study. Professor Gabi Barkay of Tel Aviv University, a fellow 'dead head', generously shared his knowledge and enthusiasm in a subject considered morbid by many. Professor Gösta Ahlström's teachings and comments were very influential in shaping this work. Sadly, this work now serves as a memorial to his courageous and enduring contributions to the field of biblical studies. For a song and a dance, Tom Blenko generously brought the finished product to print. My children, Benjamin and Rachel, were able to complete their dissertations during a summer's digging season and couldn't understand why I didn't finish mine. Their youthful persistence served as a gentle chide. Most of all I would like to thank my parents, my father-in-law and especially my husband, Mark, without whose support, prodding and assistance the dead might have perished.

This book is dedicated to my husband Mark.

> *k*^{e}*tapûaḥ ba*$^{‘a}$*šṣê hayya‘ar kēn dôdî bên habbānîm*
> *b*^{e}*ṣillô ḥimmadtî w*^{e}*yāšabtî ûpiryô mātôq l*^{e}*ḥikî*

(Song of Songs 2.3)

List of Illustrations

Figure

LIST OF TABLES

ABBREVIATIONS

AASOR	Annual of the American Schools of Oriental Research
AB	Anchor Bible
ADAJ	*Annual of the Department of Antiquities of Jordan*
AfO	*Archiv für Orientforschung*
AJA	*American Journal of Archaeology*
AJBA	*Australian Journal of Biblical Archaeology*
AOAT	Alter Orient und Altes Testament
AOS	American Oriental Series
BA	*Biblical Archaeologist*
BARev	*Biblical Archaeology Review*
BASOR	*Bulletin of the American Schools of Oriental Research*
BIES	*Bulletin of the Israel Exploration Society*
BZAW	Beihefte zur *ZAW*
CAD	*The Assyrian Dictionary of the Oriental Institute of the University of Chicago* (ed. A. Leo Oppenheim; Chicago: Oriental Institute of the University of Chicago, 1956)
CBQ	*Catholic Biblical Quarterly*
CBQMS	*Catholic Biblical Quarterly*, Monograph Series
CTA	*Corpus des tablettes cuneiformes alphabetiques decouvertes a Ras Shamra-Ugarit de 1929 a 1939* (ed. A Herdner; Mission de Ras Shamra, 10; Paris: Imprimerie Nationale, 1963)
CTM	*Concordia Theological Monthly*
EncJud	*Encyclopaedia Judaica*
HSM	Harvard Semitic Monographs
HTR	*Harvard Theological Review*
HUCA	*Hebrew Union College Annual*
ICC	International Critical Commentary
IDBSup	*IDB*, Supplementary Volume
IEJ	*Israel Exploration Journal*
JAJ	*Journal of Anthropological Archaeology*
JAOS	*Journal of the American Oriental Society*
JBL	*Journal of Biblical Literature*
JCS	*Journal of Cuneiform Studies*
JEA	*Journal of Egyptian Archaeology*
JNES	*Journal of Near Eastern Studies*
JPOS	*Journal of the Palestine Oriental Society*

JSOTSup	*Journal for the Study of the Old Testament*, Supplement Series
JSS	*Journal of Semitic Studies*
KAI	H. Donner and W. Rollig, *Kanaanäische und aramäische Inschriften* (Wiesbaden: Otto Harrassowitz, 1964–68)
KTU	M. Dietrich, O. Loretz and J. Sanmartin, *Die keilalphabetischen Texte aus Ugarit einschliesslich der keilalphabetischen Texte ausserhalb Ugarits 1: Transkription* (AOAT, 24; Neukirchen–Vluyn: Neukirchener Verlag, 1976)
Or	*Orientalia*
OrAnt	*Oriens antiquus*
OTL	Old Testament Library
OTS	*Oudtestamentische Studiën*
PEFQS	*Palestine Exploration Fund, Quarterly Statement*
PEQ	*Palestine Exploration Quarterly*
PJ	*Palästina-Jahrbuch*
QDAP	*Quarterly of the Department of Antiquities in Palestine*
RArch	*Revue archéologique*
RB	*Revue biblique*
REJ	*Revue des études juives*
SBFLA	*Studii biblici franciscani liber annuus*
SBLDS	SBL Dissertation Series
StudOr	Studia orientalia
UF	*Ugarit-Forschungen*
VT	*Vetus Testamentun*
VTSup	*Vetus Testamentum*, Supplements
ZAW	*Zeitschrift für die alttestamentliche Wissenschaft*
ZDPV	*Zeitschrift des deutschen Palästina-Vereins*

INTRODUCTION

lôla el-ahyâ la-hilkat el-awmât

'Were it not for the living, the dead would have perished.'
—A Palestinian Muslim

Judahite mortuary practices and beliefs about the dead are the focuses of this study. The large number of uniform, reasonably well-preserved interments, when considered in conjunction with biblical testimony, enable reconstructing Judahite burial practices as well as clarifyng the recorded policy towards the dead and its implementation.

Based on the distribution of burial types, the territory of Judahite cultural hegemony appears to have been confined to the highlands. Biblical descriptions of the territories not conquered by Joshua (Josh. 13.2-4), together with the genealogy and settlement of the sons of Judah (1 Chron. 4) and Rehoboam's fortifications to the east and the west dating to the last quarter of the tenth century BCE (2 Chron. 11.5-10; cf. R. Cohen 1980; Herzog 1983; Meshel 1979)[1] delineate a state conforming to the territory where the Judahite burial type was in use. A common socio-economic adaptation to the highland terrain (Stager 1985a) and the distribution of the national, administrative *lammelek* stamp (Eshel 1989; Rosenbaum 1979) provide further archaeological evidence of the extent of Judahite hegemony. Philistine independence is attested in (First) Isaiah's cursing Philistia (Isa. 14.29-32) and in late eighth- and seventh-century BCE annals of the Assyrian kings Sargon II, Sennacherib and Ashurbanipal (Oppenheim 1969: 286-301).

Previous studies of Iron Age (1200–586 BCE) death and burial have tended to present or stress either the biblical[2] or the archaeological

1. For a different interpretation, see I. Finkelstein (1986b).

2. Some studies elucidate biblical references to death in light of literary evidence from Israel's predecessors and contemporaries. A. Heidel (1946) introduced relevant Mesopotamian literary and archaeological evidence. N. Tromp (1969), J. Healey

evidence.[1] The few synthetic treatments, primarily doctoral dissertations, have not fully utilized the archaeological evidence in support of

(1977) and T. Lewis (1986; 1989) explicated biblical references to death using Ugaritic materials. Tromp, writing of death but not the dead, concluded that Yahweh exercises complete control over death. Healey mentioned the Bible in passing in his doctoral dissertation, 'Death, Underworld and Afterlife in the Ugaritic Texts' (Healey 1977). According to Lewis, 'official' Yahwism condemned death cult practices, but 'a circumstantial case can be built for their existence in the popular religion' (Lewis 1986: Abstract).

K.-J. Illman, L. Bailey and H. Brichto studied death from the biblical perspective. Illman catalogued the formulas regarding all aspects of death to establish the commonly held view of death as the 'natural, inevitable and dreaded end of human life' (Illman 1979: 182). The studies by Bailey and Brichto provide frameworks for interpreting the isolated references to burial, to the dead and to the actions of the living towards the dead. These two works typify the two major scholarly positions regarding Israelite and Judahite practices. Bailey concluded that although the dead were attributed great knowledge in the pre-exilic period, necromancy was not regarded as efficacious, and 'to the extent that rites are performed for the dead they have been robbed of religious significance and reduced to custom' (Bailey 1979: 35). Brichto argued that Israelite treatment of the dead was not merely a matter of fossilized custom, but played a highly significant role in family, and hence national, survival. He reconstructed Israelite beliefs in analogy to an Indo-European model proposed by Fustel de Coulanges in his 1864 work, *The Ancient City*. The dead, endowed with attributes of sanctity and divinity, must be properly buried and their post-mortem needs attended to, thereby insuring an ongoing relationship with progeny and maintenance of the ancestral property (Brichto 1973).

1. Archaeologists have produced catalogues and tomb typologies which superficially incorporate the relevant literary evidence. S. Loffreda developed a typology of rock-cut tombs tailored to support the biblical account of Israelite conquest and settlement in Canaan (Loffreda 1968). R. Gonen's doctoral dissertation catalogued Late Bronze Age burials by types and noted changes in distribution as an indicator of change in Late Bronze Age settlement patterns (Gonen 1979). J. Abercrombie's doctoral dissertation, a computerized study of Iron Age burials, defined five types on the basis of method of interment, burial context and 'pottery pattern'. These five types were then shown to correlate with body treatment and geographical distribution (Abercrombie 1979). In both Gonen's and Abercrombie's works, the burying populations were not studied and the burial types not viewed within a larger cultural context. E. Meyers reviewed the evidence for secondary burial from the Neolithic through the Roman period in the area of modern-day Israel (Meyers 1970). L. Rahmani concentrated on the prevalent burial practices in Jerusalem from the third millennium BCE through the time of the Babylonian exile (Rahmani 1981).

their reconstructions.[1] The most recent books on the topic, K. Spronk's *Beatific Afterlife in Ancient Israel and in the Ancient Near East* (1986) and T. Lewis's *Cults of the Dead in Ancient Israel and Ugarit* (1989) both adopted a synchronic approach to the material.[2] Ignoring diachronic changes precluded distinguishing developments during the critical period of national and religious formation.

Building upon R. Gonen's work on Late Bronze Age burial practices (Gonen 1979), I propose a new categorization of Iron Age tomb types and burial remains designed to establish the Judahite form(s) of burial. The adopted approach to the material culture remains yields results that differ from those which were obtained in the previous study by J. Abercrombie (1979). The results of this study of the archaeological material will then be considered in conjunction with the biblical evidence, to preserve the integrity of the archaeological material rather than permitting the biblical material to dictate a historical reconstruction.

Anthropological studies indicate that all aspects of burial are significant and culturally determined.[3] Accepted as meaningful cultural

1. Southern Canaanite practices from the period of 1400–1100 BCE, as exemplified by the Dothan Tomb 1 remains, were the topic of R. Cooley's doctoral dissertation. Cooley summarized features of Middle and Late Bronze Age burials and concluded that the Canaanites believed the dead needed provisions for their long journey to the netherworld, a journey which was completed when decomposition had taken place. Once in the netherworld, the dead led a restful life completely removed from the world of the living (Cooley 1968). In his doctoral dissertation, J. Ribar began with a review of anthropological literature dating from early in this century arguing for the importance of the cult of the dead during the early stages of national and religious evolution. Ribar then surveyed the tomb evidence for feeding the dead dating from the Neolithic period through the Iron Age. On the basis of primarily archaeological evidence, he inferred that 'making offerings to the dead may have been characteristic of the pre-Israelite period in Palestine which was repressed to some degree or discontinued during the early Israelite period, especially Iron I and early Iron II, only to re-emerge. . . toward the end of Iron II'. Feeding the dead abated during the period when religious unity was of utmost importance—before the political unit stabilized—but increased under kings Manasseh and Amon and under Assyrian influence (Ribar 1973: 80-82). G. Heider addressed the questions of the extent of child sacrifice and the status of Molek (Heider 1985).

2. Spronk (1986) uncritically included archaeological evidence to support his thesis of beatific afterlife in the Hebrew Bible.

3. See the works of I. Hodder (1982: 9), R. Huntington and P. Metcalf (1979: 1)

expressions, the specifics of burial may be interpreted from a variety of different perspectives, such as economic, political, social, psychological or religious.[1] Ordinarily it is the documentation or the oral testimony of a people that enables interpretation of the patterned remains of burial. For Judah, the primary literary resource is a religious or theological document. The Hebrew Bible provides an understanding of the place of burial within the theological organization of the society. This then determines the framework for this study within which burial customs are interpreted.

Even though the burials will be interpreted within a theological framework, the form of burial was determined not by theological considerations alone, but by numerous other factors, both cultural and geological. For example, political considerations affected location of the burial, tomb plan and relative wealth. Kings and religious and administrative functionaries were not buried with their families on ancestral land, but in the capital city. These burials were not the usual family tomb designed to accommodate large numbers of individuals, but rather distinctive rock-cut tombs for only two or three persons. Gradations in wealth appeared among Jerusalem burials themselves no less than between burials in Jerusalem and those in the rest of the country. In Jerusalem, the finest tombs, constructed to accommodate a limited number of individuals, were hewn in proximity to the Temple and the palace precincts. Religious considerations shaped the

and S. Piggott (1969: 558). P. Ucko discusses the value of ethnographic study for interpreting burial remains, and sounds a cautionary note regarding the interpretation of tomb offerings (Ucko 1969: 262-80).

1. Death and burial have been interpreted from a primarily economic perspective in the works of M. Bloch (1982: 211-13), B. Fagan (1972), K. Flannery (1972), J. Goody (1962), P. Metcalf (1981: 564) and A. Saxe (1970: 119-20). Political perspectives are represented in the work of Huntington and Metcalf (1979: 122-81). Burials are most commonly presented from the social perspective, as in the works of B. Bartel (1982), L. Binford (1971), M. Bloch (1971; 1982: 217-20), M. Douglas (1973), W.A. Douglass (1969: 219), A. Fleming (1972), 'Flowers on Graves Don't Mean Much' (1986), R. Hertz (1960), S. Kuechler (1983), C. Renfrew (1978), N. Rothschild, (1979), D. Rupp (1985), A. Saxe (1970), T. Shay (1985) and S. Shennan (1975). The psychological perspective has been presented by M. Bloch and J. Parry (1982: 4), E. Durkheim (1915), A. van Gennep (1960), J. Goody (1962), R. Hertz (1960) and R. Steele (1977). The religious perspective was taken by P. Brown (1981), T. Canaan (1927), T. Gaster (1968), E. Leach (1977: 170), F. Reynolds and E. Waugh (1977) and R.H. Smith (1973).

conception of death and hence the design of the dwelling space for the deceased, the treatment accorded the body, and the mortuary goods provided. The belief in life after death found expression in situating the dead in a comfortable dwelling equipped with the essential material necessities for a continued existence.

Geological conditions were a consideration—but not the determining factor—in the development and choice of burial types. Certain burial plans were more easily executed and better preserved in particular soils or rock types. For this reason pit graves predominated in sandy regions, and caves or hewn tombs prevailed in the highlands, particularly in the softer rocks. However, there are sufficient examples of pit graves cut into bedrock and bench tombs hewn in kurkar with the addition of pillars to support the roof to demonstrate that geology was not the determining factor. Geological formations determined the major and local routes which affected the dissemination of ideas and practices concerning death and the dead, as well as the selection and availability of goods buried with the deceased. Geological factors also affected the feasibility of settlement in certain regions, and the likelihood that burials would be obscured by further accumulation such as in the swampy Sharon Plain or the Jerusalem Kidron Valley. For these reasons, the geological regions of Israel, Judah, Ammon and Moab with Iron Age settlements and burials will be detailed.

From west to east, the region is divided into three geological formations: the coastal plain, the highlands, and the Jordan rift valley which divides the highlands into east and west.

The coastal plain is itself divided into three geological formations: the shore and sand dunes, the kurkar ridges, and the resultant intermittent plains. The majority of simple burials, with inhumed or cremated remains placed directly in the ground or in jars, were cut along the shoreline from Tell er-Ruqeish in the south to Khaldé in the north. Simple burials were also cut into the soft alluvial deposits surrounding Jezreel, Beth Shan and Jordan River Valley sites, and isolated examples were carved into the bedrock at Megiddo, Tel Bira and Lachish. Kurkar, a relatively soft rock, is best suited for cutting simple pits for burial. However, bench tombs were hewn in the kurkar, with necessary adaptations, at the sites of Ashdod-Yam and Akhzib. Loose sand and sand overlying loess cover the kurkar ridges of the southern coast, obscuring the burials, as is the case at Deir el-Balah. Proceeding north along the coast, cliffs gradually rise in height, the dune belt shrinks and widespread swamps appear, rendering the Sharon plain virtually uninhabitable and obscuring burials. North of the Sharon plain, the westernmost kurkar ridge along the Carmel coast and the Acre plain have succumbed to waves, leaving small bays and a narrow strip of sand dunes in the south, and dunes and swamps in the north. Simple or pit graves prevailed along the sandy shore, but tombs were hewn at Akhzib.

East of the southern coastal plain, between the plain and the highlands, stretches the Shephelah, or 'lowlands', a broad expanse of Eocene limestone well suited to the carving of tombs. Coastal burial features spread through the Shephelah region, and were subsequently adopted in the highlands.

Hills occupy the central portion of the region from the Galilee in the north to the Negev in the south. The higher elevations are composed of relatively hard Cenomanian and Turonian limestone and dolomite, but the lower elevations are typically softer rocks better suited to carving out tombs. Most Iron Age cave, chamber, arcosolia and bench tombs occurred naturally or were hewn out of chalk. Chalks of the Senonian, Eocene, and occasionally Oliocene and Miocene periods are found in the northeastern Negev, the Judaean foothills and desert, the Nablus syncline and Menashe region of Samaria, the perimeter of the Galilaean hills, and on large portions of the Transjordanian plateau (Orni and Efrat 1971: 4). Particularly in the southern highlands of Judah, a thin hard crust called nari coats the chalk rocks, inhibiting vegetation growth and freeing the slopes for burial use.

The Jordan Rift Valley, together with a branch forming the Beth Shan, Harod and Jezreel Valleys, today consists of terraces of fertile, water-deposited lissan marl and alluvium. Most of this region is currently under cultivation which obscures or destroys burials; therefore reported interments are generally located on tell slopes, as at Megiddo and Tell es-Saidiyeh, or in cliffs bounding the valleys as at Pella.

Transjordanian geological formations correspond to those west of the Jordan River. Most preserved burials have been found in the lower elevations of the highlands of Moab and Ammon, between the river gorges of the Wadis Zered and Zerqa (Jabbok). Like the region west of the rift valley, the lower elevations of bedrock are composed of Senonian chalk and flint, and are generally more conducive to the hewing of tombs than the harder, upper elevations.

The geological formations and resulting routes determined the movement of peoples, ideas and goods. The coastal plain, valleys and gorges created by water flowing from the highlands down into the Mediterranean basin, plus the Jordan River and valleys cut by tributaries flowing into it, formed a continuous lowland region connected by the Via Maris and local routes. These interconnected, relatively fertile, lowland regions displayed a common cultural adaptation to the terrain and a common choice of burial types. Most of the roads which penetrated the highlands ran east–west, so that northern highland connections were with Phoenicia, while southern highland contacts were with Philistia. One important east–west route ran from the coast into the Jerusalem area and on to Rabbat-Ammon. This route facilitated relations between Jerusalem to the west and Amman to the east.[1]

The use of both literary evidence and archaeological data is problematic. Utilizing literary evidence, particularly the Bible, is complicated by difficulties in dating particular passages, questions of authorship, *Sitz im Leben*, genre and the host of other questions raised by higher criticism. These are formidable obstacles to determining the date and historicity of any text. In this study, archaeology provides chronological criteria for dating select biblical passages.

Archaeological data must also be interpreted with caution. Archaeological recovery is in large part arbitrary; the selection of sites, the preserved evidence and the published remains are each subject to a myriad of factors, some external to purely archaeological considerations. The various types of burial have different rates of preservation, recovery and recording, which usually favor the discovery and publication of the more wealthy examples. Tomb plan and location are always recorded, but the matrix into which the burial was cut, the full assemblage of mortuary goods and an analysis of the osteological, botanical, faunal and metallurgical remains are rarely included. Dating burials is particularly difficult because many have been used over extended periods of time, and only selected items from the assemblage have been pictured or described in the excavation report. The number of identified burials does not account for the estimated population, further supporting the contention that burial

1. For a full discussion of ancient routes and additional references, see Y. Aharoni (1967: 39-57) and D. Dorsey (1981).

recovery is selective. Numerous individuals must have received 'invisible' or informal disposal; in other words, burial in a manner that left little or no identifiable remains (Morris 1987: 105). Surveys in regions which were settled during this period, including the highlands of Ephraim and Manasseh, the Galilee and the Golan, have produced few, if any, burials. This paucity of recovered burials currently precludes generalizing about burial practices from the Kingdom of Israel. However, unless otherwise specified, the burials from the coast and major valley systems, Judah and Ammon are considered sufficiently numerous and representative to reflect Iron Age practices.

Excavations of over 850 burials from more than 60 Iron Age (1200–586 BCE) sites situated along the coast from Khaldé in the north to Tell er-Ruqeish in the south, and from the Mediterranean shore east to Amman, provide the specifics of burial location and plan, body treatment and selection of grave goods (fig. 15).[1] The difficulties in dating burials as well as the small numbers from any single region in any one century necessitated grouping the interments by historical periods. For Judah, the formation of the state, the fall of the northern kingdom of Israel and the conquest by the Babylonians were the historical events which shaped the country during the Iron Age. Accordingly, the burials are divided into chronological periods defined by these events: the twelfth and eleventh centuries BCE preceding the formation of the state, the tenth through the third quarter of the eighth century BCE from the rise of the united monarchy through the demise of the northern kingdom, and the last quarter of the eighth century BCE through 586 BCE or the first quarter of the sixth century BCE, i.e. down to the fall of Judah.

Late Bronze Age and twelfth- and eleventh-century BCE burials from throughout Canaan demonstrate the mortuary practices of the indigenous populations, and, of particular importance for this study, the distribution of practices later employed by the Judahites. The

1. Nearly half of these tombs were included in a computerized study, the results of which provide the basis for the discussion of Iron Age burials. Burials not computerized lacked either burial plan, human skeletal remains or some indication of burial goods. Of the burials included, many were incompletely excavated or published, or they showed signs of having been disturbed. The differing results obtained in the previous computerized study by J. Abercrombie (1979) may be due more to the organization of data and to the choice of burials included than to real differences.

proliferation of the bench tomb, the definitive Judahite form of burial by the eighth century BCE, began in the tenth century BCE. Mapping the distribution of tomb types by historical periods provides a striking picture of the adoption of the bench tomb in the southern highlands, in contrast to the variety of other burial types utilized by Judah's neighbors. These maps graphically delineate the parameters of Judahite cultural hegemony. The national or cultural affiliation of Judah's neighbors is conjectured on the basis of the distribution patterns of the burial types (including their mortuary provisions) and the biblical writers' perceptions of national and ethnic settlement. Tomb contents, including human and faunal remains, pottery, jewelry, personal items, tools and models, highlight the similarities and differences between Judahite burial customs and the practices of its neighbors. Changes in political and trade relations through the southern Levant are also revealed.

Finally, the results of a diachronic study of biblical references to burial and the dead will be considered in conjunction with the southern highland burial remains, and a reconstruction of Judahite mortuary practices will be offered. A picture emerges of a widespread, flourishing cult of the dead, practiced in Jerusalem as in the rest of the country, which persisted throughout the Iron Age. A 'cult of the dead' is here taken to mean that the Judahites believed the dead possessed powers and acted on that belief.

Chapter 1

Iron Age Burial Types from the Southern Levant and their Distribution

Tomb Types

Eight different burial types are distinguishable from among the approximately 850 burials reported from the southern Levant.[1] Body treatment, grave goods and the receptacle holding the body or—in the absence of a receptacle—the tomb plan are the primary determinants of the types. Strong correlations among the various factors enable labelling some types on the basis of the receptacle containing the body: jar, anthropoid coffin and bathtub coffin burials. Lacking such a vessel, the space designed to house the deceased characterizes the burial type: simple grave, cist grave, cave tomb and arcosolia or bench tomb. Cremation so differed from the other practices that it constitutes a distinctive type.

Simple Grave

Simple or pit graves were usually dug into coastal sand near a settlement, such as at Azor or Tell er-Ruqeish, or into debris around a tell, such as at Lachish or Megiddo. However, in some instances graves were hewn out of bedrock, notably Lachish 222 and Megiddo 17, 62 and 71 (fig. 1). Within cemeteries, most graves were oriented in the same direction, but from cemetery to cemetery the orientation differed. In Afula the heads were oriented towards the north–northwest, at Megiddo towards the southwest, at Azor generally towards the east, and at Tell es-Saidiyeh towards the west. In the Lachish graves most bodies were oriented north-south and at Deir el-Balah east–west. No

1. In 1979 J. Abercrombie produced a computerized catalogue of burials arranged alphabetically by site, including burial number, location, publication details, dating, method of interment, context, pottery pattern and other artifacts (Abercrombie 1979).

overall pattern(s) appears in the orientation of simple graves.

The Late Bronze Age practice of burial in simple graves continued unchanged into the Iron Age. The pit ordinarily accommodated one to three individuals in addition to the mortuary goods. Nearly three quarters of the burials contained a single individual who ranged in age from infant (Khaldé 165; Tell es-Saidiyeh 52, 135), child (Atlit iva; Azor 156; Tell el-Farah [S] 516; Tell es-Saidiyeh) or adolescent (Khaldé 1, 2, 166, 167; Tel Kishyon 2; Megiddo 17; Tell es-Saidiyeh; Tell Taanach) to adult (Afula 2, 4; Atlit i, vii; Azor; Khaldé 4, 21, 22, 23; Megiddo 62, 71, 237; Tell es-Saidiyeh). Multiple interments included varying combinations of adults (Tell Amal; Ashdod 1066; Azor; Khaldé; Tell es-Saidiyeh 118, 214); one or two adults with infants or children (Afula 1; Tell es-Saidiyeh); an adult, an adolescent female and an infant (Tell es-Saidiyeh 119); male and female adolescents (Ashdod 1122); and two children (Tell el-Farah [S] 222). Adults predominated in the Megiddo and Tell er-Ruqeish graves, with males most common at Tell er-Ruqeish. The multiple burial units may be categorized as family interments on the basis of sex and relative ages of individuals present. Preserved skeletal remains indicate that the usual body treatment and positioning was to have the individual lying extended, supine with hands outstretched along the sides or crossed on the chest or pelvis.

The quantity and quality of grave goods varied, but a bowl and jar were characteristically present, the same vessels typically found in Late Bronze Age simple burials. Late Bronze Age assemblages included two or three jars covered with inverted bowls, plus two or three jugs or juglets, plates, personal ornaments including jewelry, scarabs and amulets, and rarely tools or weapons (Cooley 1968: 104; Gonen 1979: III, 51).

Compared to other Iron Age burial types, the range of objects buried with the body was limited. In most twelfth- and eleventh-century BCE burials, the deceased were provided with ceramic vessels and a bead. The most elaborately provisioned burials contained beads, a scarab or faience piece, and metal bracelets, anklets, rings and earrings (Azor, Deir el-Balah, Tell el-Farah [S], Jericho, Tell es-Saidiyeh, Tell Taanach). These early burials contained a greater variety of mortuary objects than did the later burials, such as seals (Deir el-Balah, Tell el-Farah [S], Tell es-Saidiyeh), mirrors (Azor, Deir el-Balah, Tell es-Saidiyeh) and gaming pieces (Deir el-Balah,

Tell el-Farah [S]). Imported vessels including Egyptian, Cypriot and Mycenaean vessels, plus Philistine pottery, were present (Afula, Azor, Tell es-Saidiyeh). During the tenth and ninth centuries BCE, in addition to locally made ceramic vessels, simple graves contained beads, metal bracelets, anklets and rings (Tell el-Farah [S], Lachish), scarabs (Akhzib, Khaldé, Tell er-Ruqeish), scaraboids (Lachish) and imported Phoenician and Cypro-Phoenician vessels (Tell el-Ajjul, Akhzib, Ashdod, Atlit, Tell el-Farah [S], Khaldé, Lachish, Tell er-Ruqeish). From the eighth century BCE onwards, metals and beads (Akhzib, Ashdod, Atlit), Egyptian amulets, a scaraboid (Akhzib, Ashdod, Tell el-Farah [S]) and Assyrian wares (Tell Amal, Tel Dothan) were provided in burials. Megiddo and Taanach individuals were dressed in cloaks secured with a toggle pin and fibula respectively.

Throughout the Iron Age, simple or pit graves exhibited a strikingly limited distribution along the coast, through the alluvial valleys and at the highland sites of Lachish, Amman and Dhiban. Already in the Late Bronze Age simple graves displayed the same distribution: along the coast from Tell el-Farah (S) in the south to Sidon in the north, at the valley sites of Afula, Megiddo and Tell es-Saidiyeh and at the highland site of Lachish (Gonen 1979: map 1) (fig. 19). During the twelfth and eleventh centuries BCE, simple graves were cut at the southern site of Tell el-Farah (S) (and Ritma?), at the coastal sites of Deir el-Balah and Azor, and through the Jezreel, Beth Shan and Jordan River Valleys at Megiddo, Afula, Tel Kishyon, Tell Taanach, Tell es-Saidiyeh and Jericho (fig. 16). Beginning in the tenth century BCE, simple graves remained in use at southern coastal and northern valley sites, but they were also employed at Lachish in significant numbers, and they proliferated at northern coastal sites from Tell Bira north to Khaldé (figs. 17, 18).

Simple burial has been commonly assumed to be the prevalent practice among people without the means for more elaborate arrangements. Extensive surveying by archaeologists and grave robbers has surprisingly yielded no known examples of Iron Age simple burials in the Cisjordanian highlands. The fact that this type of burial displayed such a consistent distribution in lowland regions throughout the Iron Age supports the contention that simple burial was not practiced in highland Judah. However, references to a communal burial ground in the Jerusalem Kidron Valley (2 Kgs 23.6; Jer. 26.23), presumed to consist of simple graves, suggest that there were burial fields which have not yet been located.

Is it possible to identify the population which buried their dead in simple graves? Simple and cist burial was employed along the coast and through the lowlands from the Late Bronze Age through the Iron Age. Fourteenth- and thirteenth-century BCE letters from Ugarit (Rainey 1963) and the late thirteenth-century BCE Hymn of Victory of Merenptah (J. Wilson 1971: 375-78; Ahlström and Edelman 1985; Stager 1985b) situated the Canaanites in the southern Levant. Although biblical descriptions of the inhabitants of Canaan are often general and formulaic, several passages specify the Canaanites as the population living along the coast and through the Jezreel, Beth Shan and Jordan River Valleys. While some of these descriptions may date from as early as the tenth century BCE, most are incorporated into seventh-century BCE and later reworkings of the texts. A sweeping reference to the people living west of the Jordan River mentions 'all the kings of the Amorites on the western side of the Jordan, and all the kings of the Canaanites near the Sea' (Josh. 5.1).[1] Two verses in Joshua and Judges, both early descriptions preserved in Deuteronomic recensions, detail the land not conquered by the Israelites. These verses locate the Canaanites along the littoral from the Range of Lebanon in the north to Gaza in the south (Josh. 13.2-5; Judg. 3.3; also Zeph. 2.5; Boling 1975: 30; Soggin 1972: 151). Several passages relate the Israelites' failure to oust the Canaanites living in the cities of the Jezreel and Beth Shan Valleys (Josh. 17.11-12, 16; Judg. 1.27, although 'Canaanite' is also used in the general sense in this chapter, as in v. 9). Two verses locate the Canaanites in the Jordan Valley. In Num. 13.29 the spies report that 'Amalekites dwell in the Negeb region; Hittites, Jebusites and Amorites inhabit the hill country; and Canaanites dwell by the sea and along the Jordan'.[2] A similar view is presented in Josh. 11.3, also considered seventh century BCE Deuteronomistic material: 'to the Canaanites in the east and the west; to the Amorites, Hittites, Perizzites and Jebusites in the hill country; and to the Hivites at the foot of Hermon, in the land of Mizpah'.

As will be demonstrated in detailing the other burial types with

1. Josh. 5.1 is considered an ancient liturgy shaped by the Deuteronomist (Soggin 1972: 67).

2. M. Noth considered this verse a Deuteronomistic addition into earlier material (Noth 1968: 101, 107).

their associated mortuary provisions, these specific uses of the term 'Canaanite' refer to regions settled throughout the Iron Age by a population culturally distinct from the Judahites (figs. 16–18). Adherents of this coastal-lowland culture, including the population which buried its dead in simple graves, were collectively referred to by the biblical writers as 'Canaanites'. Therefore, biblical references to Canaanites in seventh-century BCE recensions need not be considered fabrications or anachronisms (so Noth 1968: 101, 107; Boling 1975: 30).

In the Ashdod Stratum III late eighth-century BCE industrial quarter of the city, pits cut into courtyards accommodated primary burials (loci 1005, 1029, 1050, 1051, 1052, 1060, 1066, 1121), secondary burials (loci 1006, 1114), decapitated bodies or skulls (loci 1113, 1115, 1052 [?], 1121 [?]) and animal bones (loci 1011, 1055, 1158). Loci 1113 and 1121, very large intramural pits containing hundreds of bodies, consisted of layers of bones covered by offerings and then dirt followed by a second sequence of bones and offerings before the floor was plastered over. More than 2,434 individuals were buried in Building 2 courtyard locus 1113. Perhaps the pits were a simplified version of large, stone-lined cists (see below) created in response to a cataclysmic number of deaths. Locus 1066 held the skulls and post-cranial skeletons of a man, two women, six cats and the foreparts or upper jaws of six donkeys (M. Dothan 1971: 92-103, 212-13). Skull burial is a radical departure from the indigenous burial practice of primary inhumation. All examples were found along the southern coast from Azor south to Tell er-Ruqeish and at the site of Tell es-Saidiyeh. These interments of skulls, decapitated bodies and animals may preserve distinctive Philistine, Phoenician or Sea Peoples burial practices.

Cist Grave

To construct a cist, a rectangular space roughly two meters long and one meter wide was lined with stones or mudbricks, and occasionally the floor was paved with cobbles and a superstructure erected (fig. 2). Stone-gabled roofs were preserved on Akhzib cists (possibly akin to the gabled-ceiling tombs of Silwan) and mudbrick roofs (vaults?) on Tell es-Saidiyeh and Azor (?) cists. Intact examples of Syro-Palestinian mudbrick-lined and vaulted cist tombs have been excavated at the Middle Bronze II Egyptian delta sites of Tell ed-Daba (van den Brink 1982: 20-25) and Tell el-Maskhuta (Redmount 1989) (fig. 3). In the extensive Tell es-Saidiyeh cemetery, 14 different variations of cists were constructed: fully or partially stone-lined pits; fully or partially mudbrick-lined pits; a rectangular grave with an inner clay kerb; mudbrick and stone-lined pits; a pit partially lined with stones and sherds; a burial on two mudbrick slabs; mudbrick-lined pits with mudbrick floors; a pit with a mudbrick and stone covering; brick-lined and covered pits; mudbrick-walled tombs; a partially stone-built tomb; brick-built tombs; stone and mudbrick-built tombs; and mudbrick-walled and roofed tombs (172, 188A/B [?], 191A/B, 246). Like simple burials, cist tombs displayed no overall pattern of orientation, but they were consistently aligned within cemeteries. Cists from Akhzib were oriented north–south, from Tell Zeror northwest–southeast and from Tell es-Saidiyeh and Azor east–west.

Like simple burials, cist graves ordinarily contained one to three primary inhumations, and, in the case of multiple interments, one of the individuals was frequently an infant or child. Large stone-lined cists were constructed for numerous individuals and for repeated use. In Tell Zeror V, dating from the middle of the eleventh through the middle of the tenth century BCE, the remains of four bodies and accompanying objects were overlaid by at least five bodies with their provisions. The tenth- to ninth-century BCE Azor D79 contained at least four layers of burials, and the tenth-century BCE Tell el-Farah (S) 201 yielded 116 adults and 6 children. It was suggested above that the Ashdod intramural pits with over 2000 bodies may have been an expedient version of the stone-lined cist devised to accommodate a cataclysmic number of dead. Cist graves with large numbers of individuals have been grouped with their smaller counterparts because they were identical in construction and positioned side-by-side.

In addition to an assortment of local wares, offerings in cist tombs included imported vessels and metal artifacts such as a dagger or blade, or a bronze wine set (Tell Abu Qudeis; Akhzib; Tell el-Farah [S] 201; Tell es-Saidiyeh 24, 32, 34, 41, 46, 101, 102, 159, 191A, 232, 246, 282; Tell Zeror I, III, IV, V, VI, VII, VIII). No particular items appear to have been characteristically supplied in cist burials. As in simple graves, Philistine, Mycenaean, Cypriot and Egyptian pots were provided in thirteenth- and twelfth-century BCE cists (Azor, Deir el-Balah, Tell el-Farah [S], Tell es-Saidiyeh) and Phoenician and Cypro-Phoenician vessels in later burials (Tell Abu Qudeis, Azor, Tell el-Farah [S], Khaldé, Palmachim, Tell Zeror).

The distribution of cist graves is similar to that of simple graves:

near settlements along the coast, through the Jezreel, Beth Shan and Jordan River Valleys, and through the Besor River Valley. However, unlike simple graves, cist graves have not yet been uncovered at highland sites. During the Late Bronze Age, cist graves occurred exclusively along the coast in the cemeteries of Tell Ridan, Dhahrat el-Humraiya, Palmachim, Tell Abu Hawam and Gesher Haziv (Gonen 1979: map 1; Ory 1948: 87) (fig. 19). Thirteenth- and twelfth-century BCE examples were excavated at the coastal and lowland sites of Azor, Deir el-Balah, Tell el-Farah (S), Tell es-Saidiyeh and Tell Zeror (fig. 16). Cist tombs were built throughout the Iron Age, but they exhibited their greatest popularity in the twelfth and eleventh centuries BCE and decreased in use through the succeeding centuries (figs. 17, 18).

In some cases simple graves may have sufficed as a simplified version of a cist tomb. The two types occurred together at Akhzib, Azor, Deir el-Balah and Tell es-Saidiyeh. At Tell es-Saidiyeh, in the best-documented examples of simple and cist graves occurring together, the cist graves contained aesthetically finer and more precious items than did the neighboring simple interments.

Some of the cist graves may have been Egyptian or Egyptianizing burials. Egyptian features of the Tell es-Saidiyeh burials included the east–west orientation (with heads usually to the west), a mudbrick superstructure, burial markers, Egyptian linen body wrappings, bitumen covering the body, unusually high incidences of metal artifacts, imported pottery, a large number of jars including alabaster and calcite examples and the absence of bowls and lamps. These tombs are clearly reminiscent of the Middle Bronze II Canaanite cist tombs at the Egyptian delta sites of Tell ed-Daba and Tell el-Maskhuta.

The population burying their dead in cist tombs—perhaps descendants of the Hyksos who returned to Canaan from the Egyptian delta at the end of the Middle Bronze Age, or individuals who could afford and desired this particular Egyptianizing style of burial—were part of the cultural group collectively referred to by the biblical writers as 'Canaanites'.

Jar Burial

For jar or pithoi burials, the vessel neck was removed to facilitate inserting the body, the contents were added, and then the vessel was frequently capped with a bowl, a stone or the base of another jar. A single jar usually sufficed for an infant or child (Tel Dothan, Tell el-Mazar,

Tell es-Saidiyeh, Tell Zeror), whereas two jars placed mouth-to-mouth or unusually large jars were necessary to encase an adult (Amman—Jebel el-Qusur, Kfar Yehoshua, Mt Nebo, Tell es-Saidiyeh) (fig. 4). At Tell es-Saidiyeh, a double pithos burial contained one partially articulated adult, a disarticulated infant, three additional skulls and a jumble of bones (76), and a double storejar burial held the skull and long bones of a single disarticulated infant (151). Two cooking pots stacked one on top of the other were employed for burial in Azor D60. The earliest jar burials usually consisted of a single vessel interred in a pit in the ground (Azor, Tell el-Farah [S], Kfar Yehoshua, Tell es-Saidiyeh, Tell Zeror). Tell es-Saidiyeh 35 and Azor D91 were set in mudbrick and stone-lined cists respectively. In two later burials, a vessel containing infant or child bones was placed in a cave or bench tomb among the remains of other individuals (Beth Shemesh 8; Sahab 1).

The majority of jar burials contained primary inhumations of infants (Afula, Azor, Tel Dothan, Megiddo, Sahab, Tell es-Saidiyeh), children (Beth Shemesh, Tell el-Farah [S], Megiddo, Tell es-Saidiyeh) or both (Azor, Tell Zeror). A single example from Kfar Yehoshua held an adolescent male, and four Tell es-Saidiyeh jars encased juveniles (209, 238, 277, 278). Except for a Sahab infant whose bones displayed a 'burnt effect,' jar burials held non-cremated inhumations. From Azor, M. Dothan reported five twelfth- to eleventh-century BCE jar burials which contained only skulls. Preserved skeletal remains displayed no consistent body position.

Burial provisions typically included a bowl and—with decreasing frequency—a lamp and a jug, plus a number of diminutive objects. Philistine pottery was found in the Azor burials and Egyptian pottery in the child's burial Tell es-Saidiyeh 126. Many of the infants, children and even adults were buried without provisions or with no more than a bowl or lamp, and beads, rings, bracelets or shells (Tel Dothan, Tell el-Farah [S], Megiddo, Tell es-Saidiyeh). Several of the Tell es-Saidiyeh deceased were relatively well-provisioned. A basalt quern and grinder were buried with an infant in Tell es-Saidiyeh 243. The juvenile in grave 209, adorned with a gold earring and an iron anklet, was cloaked as demonstrated by the bronze toggle pin, and provided with two jugs. The upper torso of an adult provided with three ceramic bowls, a bonze bowl and a bronze dagger, Tell es-Saidiyeh 228, was encased in facing pithoi set in a brick-lined pit. Both Tell es-Saidiyeh and Azor deceased were equipped with pyxides. The Azor and Kfar Yehoshua individuals were interred with similar provisions including bowls, craters, chalices, pilgrim flasks and scarabs.

The distribution of jar burials was similar to that of simple and cist graves: along the coast, in the Galilee (Tell el-Oremé), through the Jezreel, Beth Shan and Jordan River Valleys, and on the Transjordanian plateau (figs. 16–18). Jar burial continued to be practiced from the Late Bronze Age through the Iron Age. The Tell Abu Hawam, Azor, Tell el-Farah (N) (Gonen 1979: 138-39, VI, map 3), Kfar Yehoshua (Druks 1966) and Tell Zeror (Ohata 1970: 72) burials may date from late in the thirteenth century BCE. As with other Late Bronze Age burial types, jar burial was most widely attested in the twelfth and eleventh centuries BCE and much less so in subsequent centuries. Jar burials, like anthropoid coffin burials, another Late Bronze Age burial type, exhibited a shift in distribution. The earliest burials were concentrated in the northern and coastal regions of the country, but the later examples were concentrated on the Transjordanian plateau (figs. 16–18, 21).

A. Druks has summarized the evidence favoring a Hittite or north Syrian origin for the practice of jar burials in this region (Druks 1966: 216-17).[1] Druks' hypothesis is supported by the restricted distribution of jar burials through the northern half of Cisjordan and Transjordan. The selection of burial provisions, including scarabs, Philistine pottery, metal artifacts, pyxides, craters and pilgrim flasks is typical of other coastal-lowland burial types (see below).

Anthropoid, Wooden and Stone Coffin Burials

Anthropoid coffins consisted of a ceramic box, approximately two meters long and tapered at one or both ends, with a modelled lid depicting a human face and upper body (fig. 5). The lid depictions have been characterized as 'naturalistic' or 'grotesque', depending on whether the features were produced by moulding or appliqué. In most cases, all the facial features including protruding ears and a pronounced chin were present, framed above by an Egyptian wig with a hat or headgear (Beth Shan, Deir el-Balah) and below by a beard (Tell el-Farah [S], Lachish). Arms lay across the chest. The later Transjordanian examples from Amman, Sahab and Dhiban were

1. J. Free attributed the intramural, infant jar burials in Dothan level I to the Assyrians (Free 1960: 9).

further simplified with suggestive features, handles as ears and arms extending along the sides of the coffin. Undisturbed anthropoid coffin burials have been recovered from pit graves and stone-lined cists cut into the kurkar at Deir el-Balah. Other identifiable fragments have been found on a tell surface (Tell Midrass) and in cave and bench tombs (Beth Shan, Dhiban, Tell el-Farah [S], Lachish).

Skeletal remains from Deir el-Balah attest to primary inhumations in the coffins. Each coffin held the articulated remains of two to six individuals, at least one of whom was an adult male. Tomb 114 held an adult male, a second adult, an 18 to 25-year-old and a three- to four-year-old child. In Tomb 116 the man was accompanied by an adolescent male or young female, a third individual and the teeth from two older adults and an adolescent. Tomb 118 held a 25 to 40-year-old man and a 25 to 30-year-old woman. The Amman Royal Palace tomb coffins held the remains of two to three individuals.

The objects present in the earlier coffin burials included a high percentage of Egyptian imported or inspired vessels, scarabs and other amulets, and jewelry. Other distinctive items found with coffins included blades, spearheads, a javelin head, stamps and seals, *ushwabti* figurines, and gaming boards. Mycenaean, Cypriot and Philistine vessels accompanied the locally-made wares (table 1).

	Amman	*Beth Shan*	*Deir el-Balah*	*Dhiban*	*Tell el-Farah (S)*	*Lachish*	*Mt Nebo*
stamp/seal	+	+	+	+			+
javelin head					+		
spear head		+			+		
blade			+		+		
imported pottery		+	+		+		
Egyptian amulet		+	+	+	+	+	+
Egyptian vessel			+		+		
imitation Egyptian pottery		+					

Table 1. Anthropoid Coffin Burial Contents.[1]

1. A plus sign (+) indicates presence.

During the thirteenth to the eleventh century BCE, the distribution of anthropoid coffin burials was limited to the southern sites of Deir el-Balah, Tell el-Farah [S], Tell er-Ruqeish and Lachish, and the northern sites of Beth Shan, Tell Midrass and Pella (figs. 16, 21). Tenth- through early sixth-century BCE examples from the Transjordanian sites of Amman, Sahab, Mt Nebo and Dhiban represent the final, simplified expression of a practice introduced several hundred years earlier (figs. 17, 18).

The Egyptian origin of anthropoid coffin burial is conclusively demonstrated by its occurrence in Egypt proper, such as at the site of Qôm Abou Billou 70 km northeast of Cairo (Leclant 1971: 227-28), and in Transjordan and Cisjordan solely at sites at which an Egyptian presence is suggested. Further evidence of Egyptian origin is provided by the Egyptian character of the heads depicted on the coffin lids, a hieroglyphic inscription on a Lachish coffin, and the high incidence of accompanying Egyptian imported and inspired vessels. E. Oren has proposed identifying the individuals buried in the Beth Shan tombs 66 and 90 (coffins with 'grotesque' lids) as Denyen mercenaries on the basis of the headgear depicted on the coffin lids and of the architectural renovations to the tombs (Oren 1973: 138-39). The fact that an adult male was always present, at least in the Deir el-Balah tombs, together with the high incidence of metal blades and weapons, supports the hypothesis that administrative or military personnel were buried in at least some of these coffins. However, their identification remains tentative. The Deir el-Balah burials with women and children may have been the burials of Egyptian administrative or military personnel with their family members.

Deir el-Balah has thus far yielded a single sarcophagus made of local limestone. Unfortunately, the head end of the lid was broken away. This unique find was devoid of contents, but 'Egyptian type sherds' and scattered bones lay nearby. Like the other coffins from this site, it may date from the end of the Late Bronze Age. In a Middle Bronze II example from Tell ed-Daba Stratum F, a Canaanite in a contracted position equipped with a Syro-Palestinian battle axe and a bronze dagger had been buried in a limestone coffin. Several additional examples were also reported from the site (van den Brink 1982: 5, 25-26, 37-38).

Two carbonized wooden coffins were preserved in Sahab Area C Tomb 1. Their relative date is supplied by a level of primary inhumations lying below and four levels of burials above, the uppermost of which were jar burials. All of the burials were deposited in the tomb between 1200 and 1100 BCE. One coffin contained an infant, and the second held a 'warrior' identified on the basis of the accompanying dagger, bronze anklet and iron bracelet (Ibrahim 1972: 32).

Bathtub Coffin Burial

Bathtub coffins are named for their characteristic shape, a deep bathtub-shaped ceramic vessel approximately one meter long, with one round and one straight end, and handles around the sides (fig. 6). The Tell el-Mazar and Tel Dothan coffins contained one and two skulls respectively among other bones, and the Tel Dothan example also held ceramic vessels. Like other burial receptacles, bathtub coffins were found in a simple grave (Tell el-Mazar) and in a rock-cut tomb (Amman, Jerusalem), but they were also found inside domestic structures and palaces (Tell Abu Hawam, Tel Dothan level $1A^b$, Tell el-Farah [N], Megiddo).

Bathtub coffin burial was well-attested in Assyria proper. The introduction of this burial type into the southern Levant in the late eighth century BCE, its distribution at northern valley sites in addition to the capital cities of Jerusalem and Amman, the unusual burial context, and the accompanying Assyrian Palace Ware (Amman, Tel Dothan)—all these factors indicate the introduction of bathtub coffin burial into the region by the Assyrians (Stern 1982: 85) (figs. 17, 18). While the majority of bathtub coffin burials were found in the north, two undated examples from the Jerusalem vicinity and one from Khirbet el-Qôm demonstrate that this Assyrian style of burial was also practiced in Judah (G. Barkay, private communication 1984; 1986: 105).

Cave, Chamber and Shaft Tombs

Cave tombs consisted of bodies and accompanying objects deposited in natural or hewn caves (fig. 7). The caves were usually located in the tell slopes or wadi cliffs, in outcrops of soft chalk or limestone.

In undisturbed examples, individuals lay extended on their backs, with objects positioned around their bodies near the center of the cave. Jumbled bones and objects around the cave periphery suggest that bodies were later moved to the sides to clear a space for additional burials—primary inhumation with subsequent secondary deposition.

Secondary burial may also have been practiced. J. Abercrombie cited Lachish 223 as 'the most conclusive evidence in favor of fractional [secondary] burial'. The skeleton was missing arm and chest bones, and the skull had been placed in the pelvis (Abercrombie 1979: 41-42 n. 34). Excavation reports rarely stipulate minimum number of individuals. One exception is the twelfth- to middle-eleventh-century BCE Baqah Valley Cave A4, where 225 individuals were distinguished, the majority in secondary heaps. This tomb provided one of the two reported instances of separating men from women and children. Men, outnumbering women by a 2:1 ratio, were placed in the cave to the north and women and children to the south. Cave tombs were the only burial type which yielded greater proportions of infants than children and adolescents. This corresponds to relative infant and child mortality rates (Goodman and Armelagos 1989: 225-27), suggesting that the families using caves for burial were most likely to inter all family members together.

In nine tombs, dating from the twelfth through the seventh century BCE, skulls were separated from the remaining bones (Aitun C1; Baqah Valley A4; Jericho A85, WH1, WH2; Lachish 120, 224; Nahshonim [?]; Tell en-Nasbeh 54). In Baqah Valley tomb A4, dated from the twelfth to the first half of the eleventh century BCE, 12 crania were stacked in a row along the western cave wall. Seven skulls and a body surrounded by beads and sherds lay in the undisturbed loculus 4 of the twelfth- to tenth-century BCE Aitun C1. Two tenth century BCE burials preserved groups of skulls; Jericho A85 held 12 skulls stacked one on top of the other and Tell en-Nasbeh housed 32 mandibles. Eight skulls were reported from Lachish 224, dated to the second half of the ninth century BCE. In Jericho tombs WH1 and WH2, in use from the late eighth through the seventh century BCE, 146 and 17 skulls respectively were piled against the left-hand wall. Lachish 120 was unique in containing the remains of more than 1500 individuals with their separated skulls, covered by charred animal bones, primarily pig.

In three caves, large quantities of animal bones were deposited with the human bones (Gezer 8I; Lachish 107, 120). In the earliest example initiated in Late Bronze II, Gezer 8I, stones covered a pile of mixed human, sheep, goat and cow bones. Lachish Tombs 107 and 120 were distinctive in containing human bones covered by charred animal bones, primarily pig. Both Lachish tombs were cut in the Bronze Age, used for habitation or mortuary purposes around 900 and finally employed for burial in the seventh century BCE.

Burned and calcined human bones were interred in Jericho 11, Lachish 120 and 1002, and Mt Nebo UCV-20 and UCV-84. In Jericho 11, dated to approximately 1200 BCE, 'partially cremated remains' were associated with a large number of bronze and iron armlets, a scarab with the name of Tuthmosis III, and a scarab depicting Hadad standing on the back of an animal. Some of the bones from Lachish 120 were said to show signs of burning similar to bones in Tomb 1002. D. Risdon's analysis of the burnt and calcined skulls and bones from the sixth-century BCE Tomb 1002 revealed that the individuals 'died in a catastrophe of a kind in which fires were involved'. Perhaps, as J. Starkey first suggested, these were victims of an Assyrian attack (Ussishkin 1982: 56). J. Saller excavated 'cremation strata' throughout Mt Nebo UCV-20 and in one large area in Mt Nebo UCV-84 chamber 2 (Saller 1966). At Jericho and Mt Nebo, either an unintentional tomb fire or spontaneous combustion could have occurred producing 'partially cremated' remains or 'cremation strata'.

Due to the small number of recorded cave tombs with men and women separated, with decapitated bodies and/or skull burials, with large quantities of animal bones, or with cremated remains, it is impossible to interpret these practices or to attribute them to a particular population.

A commensurate number of gifts accompanied the large numbers of individuals buried in cave tombs. Locally-made bowls, lamps, jars, jugs and juglets predominated, with a wide assortment of other ceramic forms, household items and personal possessions. Virtually every thirteenth-to eleventh-century BCE burial yielded imported pottery (Beth Shan, Tel Dothan, Irbed, Lachish), scarabs and other Egyptian amulets (Azor [?], Baqah Valley, Beth Shan, Beth Shemesh, Tel Dothan, Gezer, Gibeon, Lachish, Sahab), blades, spearheads, arrowheads, needles, spindle whorls and jewelry. Lamps were most numerous in the Tel Dothan and Gibeon tomb assemblages, and bowls predominated at Lachish and Irbed. In tenth- through sixth-century BCE burials, Cypriot (Gezer, Lachish, Tell en-Nasbeh), Phoenician (Tell Abu Hawam, Amman, Samaria), Cypro-Phoenician (Tell Abu Hawam, Tell Bira, Madeba, Tell en-Nasbeh, Mt Nebo, Tambourit), Greek (Tambourit) and Assyrian (Amman) imported wares were present. Beginning in the tenth century BCE, the jug, juglet and dipper juglet were supplied with the greatest frequency (Aitun A1; Amman C, Jebel Jofeh esh-Sharqi; Ein Sarin; Lachish 120, 218; Tell en-Nasbeh 32, 54). The bowl's popularity increased as demonstrated by its inclusion as the predominant form in scattered tombs (Tell Abu Hawam II; Beth Shemesh 1; Lachish 223; Madeba B; Khirbet Rabud; Samaria 103). The lamp prevailed solely in the Mt Nebo tombs. Jewelry, toggle pins and fibulae, scarabs, blades, arrowheads, rattles and female pillar figurines were also commonly provided at burial.

The distribution of cave tombs was primarily restricted to the soft chalk and limestone outcrops of the foothills and highlands east and west of the Jordan River. Burial in caves was the predominant highland type in the Late Bronze Age (Gonen 1979)[1] and on into the first centuries of the Iron Age (figs. 16, 20). Beginning in the tenth century BCE, increased highland settlement resulted in a greater number of sites employing cave tombs. However, in succeeding centuries, as the bench tomb gained in popularity in the western foothills and highlands and on the Transjordanian plateau, a decreasing number of sites utilized cave tombs. At Lachish, Beth Shemesh, Gezer and Tell en-Nasbeh, the cave tomb was the only form of burial in the twelfth and eleventh centuries BCE. From the tenth to the eighth century BCE, the bench tomb was introduced and used side-by-side with the cave tomb. Cave tombs were initiated during the tenth through the sixth century BCE at the eastern Cisjordanian foothill and highland sites of Khirbet Beit Lei, Bethlehem, Lachish, Tell Judeidah, Ras-et-Tawil, Khirbet Rabud and Ez Zahariyah, and at Amman and Mt Nebo in Transjordan (figs. 17, 18).

The continued but decreasing use of the cave tomb may be explained in two ways. Burial in caves was the practice of the indigenous Bronze Age highland population. Two biblical passages attributed to the Deuteronomist, mentioned above in connection with the Canaanites, identify the highland population as Hittites, Amorites and Jebusites (Num. 13.29; Josh. 11.3).[2] One possibility is that adherents

1. The Transjordanian Baqah Valley caves A2 and B3 provide well-preserved and documented examples of Late Bronze Age cave burials (McGovern 1982a: 122-24; 1982b: 46-53).

2. For the biblical writers, the Hittites, Amorites and Jebusites were three of the more significant groups among the highland settlers. The Deuteronomistic full list of highland dwellers includes the Amorites, Girgashites, Arvadites, Perizzites, Hivites, Horites and others.

of the Late Bronze Age highland culture, the Amorites and others, lived among and in the highlands to the east of the bench tomb burying population (later the Judahites), and continued to bury in caves. In this case, from the tenth century BCE onwards, burial in a cave tomb was an expression of non-Judahite/non-Yahwistic affiliation. A second possibility is that some Judahites buried their dead in caves because it required less investment of time and labor than did hewing a bench tomb. Both cave and bench tomb burials appear to have been similarly conceived of as ancestral dwellings, and the socio-economic adaptation to the highland terrain shared by those burying in the two tomb types probably gave rise to the similar mortuary provisions deemed necessary for the deceased.

Chamber and some shaft tombs are classified with cave tombs, for they differed only in regularity of plan and method of access. Both caves and chambers may be hewn. Whereas a cave has rounded or irregularly-shaped cavities, the cavities in a chamber tomb appear more like rooms, due to their rectangular plan, corners, or orderly arrangement. In some cases, topographical limitations may have necessitated a shaft entrance. For tombs hewn in flat-lying bedrock, a shaft provided both access into the tomb and a means of closing off the entrance. Shaft entrances were employed for bench tombs as well. Like cave tombs, chamber and shaft tombs spanned the entire Iron Age. They were hewn along the coast (Akhzib, Tel Mevorakh), in the north (Megiddo, Nazareth, Tubas, Tekoa), in the Shephelah and the southern highlands (Aitun, Khirbet Beit Lei, Bethlehem, Ez Zahariyah, Jerusalem, Lachish, Manahat, Khirbet Za'aq), at Jericho, Tell el-Farah (S) and in Transjordan (Dhiban, Sahab).[1] As regards numbers of individuals, body treatment, pottery and other mortuary goods, chamber tombs are indistinguishable from cave tombs.

The Akhzib southern cemetery chamber tombs, in use from the eleventh to the end of the eighth century BCE, are so far unique in having a square or rectangular opening cut into the roof to accommodate a superstructure which purportedly served as a platform for an altar. B. Mazar reconstructed the tombs in the Jerusalem Tyropoeon Valley

1. The gabled-ceiling tombs in the Silwan cemetery could also be considered chamber tombs rather than bench tombs, for many have trough-niches in which to repose the dead, rather than benches. They will, however, be presented below with arcosolia and bench tombs.

opposite the Temple Mount on a similar plan with an opening in the roof to support an altar. Secondary use as cisterns and additional cuttings have obliterated the Tyropoeon Valley tombs to the extent that it is impossible to ascertain their original form. In recent excavations at Akhzib, E. Mazar has excavated gabled-ceiling tombs constructed of ashlar masonry (E. Mazar, private communication 1988). The quality of workmanship displayed by these tombs far exceeds that of most tombs in Judah. It is possible that additional shaft tombs not published in detail, such as the Tel Mevorakh tombs, together with the Akhzib, Silwan and Tyropoeon Valley tombs, constituted a distinctive type. These tombs were constructed of ashlar blocks or were hewn from the bedrock with square chambers and flat or gabled ceilings. Such fine workmanship is usually attributed to Phoenician craftsmen.

Arcosolia and Bench Tombs

Arcosolia and bench tombs are often difficult to distinguish from one another on the basis of published descriptions and photographs, but the distinction will be maintained wherever possible. Arcosolia and loculi were intended for single permanent burials, whereas benches accommodated single or multiple burials which in turn could be relocated and replaced with new burials. R. Gonen drew this distinction among Late Bronze Age burials (Gonen 1979: 108).

Iron Age arcosolia and bench tombs were of similar plan. The main chamber was entered through a square or rectangular doorway in a rock-cut facade. A stepped dromos outside the door or, later, one or two steps inside the door led down into a rounded (Ashdod-Yam) or square to rectangular (Aitun) chamber. Arcosolia or loculi radiated out from the center (Tubas [?]) or most commonly were cut into the walls parallel to the sides of the chamber (Aitun). Benches, hewn from the rock or built of stone, extended around the chamber periphery parallel to the chamber walls (fig. 8). Stone troughs or sarcophagi carved from the bedrock served as an elaborate form of arcosolia burial, a designated place for a single individual (Gibeon; Jerusalem—Old City walls, St Etienne, Silwan). These sarcophagi may have evolved from the earlier Canaanite-Egyptian stone coffins, such as the example found at Deir el-Balah.

In the En Hanasiv burials, a shaft opened onto a ledge where ordinarily a single body and accompanying pottery and metal gifts were placed. This is a unique form of burial which has been published only in preliminary form. It has been included with bench tombs, since the body was laid out on a bench-like projection.

Benches were already a feature of fourteenth- and thirteenth-century BCE tombs. In some examples, crude and irregularly-shaped benches were hewn from the rock (Aitun, Gezer, Sarafend); in others, the benches were constructed of stones around the periphery of the tomb (Aitun; Gezer 10A). In one Aitun tomb, benches were hewn from the rock on either side of a natural cave. Flat stones covered the central portion of the cave floor between the benches, and large stones—perhaps closing stones—lay outside the tomb on the north side near the entrance (Gonen 1979: 113). In a late thirteenth-century BCE example from Aitun, a stone bench was constructed in a possibly recessed area in a natural cave (V. Tzaferis, private communication 1984).

Over the centuries bench tombs were provided with a wide array of functional and decorative features. Decorative details included imitation sunken wooden panels (Jerusalem—St Etienne), gabled ceilings (Akhzib, Jerusalem—Silwan), right-angled cornices (Jerusalem—Ketef Hinnom, St Etienne, Silwan) and pillars carved with animal heads (Akhzib [?], Aitun). Among the additions for the comfort and convenience of the dead were lamp niches (Aitun, Tell Beit Mirsim, Gibeon, Tell Halif, Lachish, Tell en-Nasbeh, Khirbet el-Qôm), parapets along the exposed edge of the bench (Aitun; Gibeon; Tell Halif; Tell Ira; Jerusalem—St Etienne, Suleiman Street), molded niches to support the body (Jerusalem—Silwan, Khirbet el-Qôm), molded depressions shaped to support the head called 'headrests' (Aitun; Gibeon; Tell Halif; Tell Ira; Jerusalem—Ketef Hinnom, Old City walls, St Andrews, St Etienne, Silwan, Suleiman St., Wadi er-Rabibi; Khirbet el-Qôm; Zuba), and stone 'pillows' (Tell Halif, Tell Ira, Jerusalem—Silwan). Other architectural features included repository pits or niches (Abu Ghosh, Aitun, Beth Shemesh, Dhiban, Tell el-Farah [S], Gezer, Gibeon, Tell Halif, Jerusalem, Lachish, Motza, Tell en-Nasbeh, Khirbet el-Qôm, Zuba),[1] centrally located pillars to

1. As S. Loffreda found, repositories occurred most frequently in seventh- and sixth-century BCE tombs. Loffreda noted the tenth- to ninth-century BCE Tell en-Nasbeh 3 and Kefira 3 repositories, and the Dhiban J1 and J3, Gezer 142 and Tell en-Nasbeh 5 pits which he distinguished from repositories. Repositories in the shape of circular and square pits have since been found in the twelfth- to eleventh-century

support the roof (Ashdod-Yam, Tell Beit Mirsim, Gezer), pits in the floor (Tell Beit Mirsim, Dhiban, Gezer, Tell Halif, Motza, Mt Nebo, Samaria), holes in the ceiling (interpreted as funnels for periodically provisioning the dead) (Akhzib, Beth Shemesh, Gezer, Sahab, Samaria), and shaft entrances (Abu Ghosh, Akhzib, Ashdod-Yam, Tell Beit Mirsim, Tell el-Farah [S], Tell Halif, Lachish, Meqabelein).

D. Ussishkin distinguished three distinct types of ninth- to late eighth-century BCE rock-cut tombs in the Silwan cemetery: tombs with gabled ceilings, tombs with flat ceilings, and above-ground monolithic tombs with pyramid-shaped roofs. Flat-ceiling tombs were the norm throughout Judah. Other gabled-ceiling tombs have thus far been found in another section of the Kidron Valley cliffs and at Akhzib. The monolithic tombs (3, 28, 34, 35) remain unique. These consisted of a cube-shaped tomb carved out from the bedrock on three or four sides. A projecting margin or Egyptian cornice was carved out along the upper edge of the facade and a pyramid-shaped roof was constructed of blocks on top of the cube. Three of the four tombs bore burial inscriptions in the facade near the doorway. The Silwan tombs resembled classic bench tombs: a single square-rectangular chamber was augmented by burial places along the sides or in the back. They differed from standard bench tombs in that most had burial places for only one or two individuals, and no repository. While benches occurred only in flat-ceiling tombs, not all flat-ceiling tombs had benches. In Tombs 15 and 24, benches were carved next to and parallel to trough-niches. Tomb 24 and possibly Tombs 20 and 35 had benches in niches. The remaining tombs were provided with covered troughs in niches, uncovered troughs in niches, or stone coffins/troughs, and where none of these were detected wooden benches, troughs or basins are presumed (Ussishkin 1986).

In his search for parallels to the Silwan tombs, Ussishkin mustered examples of architecturally similar tombs from throughout the eastern Mediterranean basin. Tombs from Ararat and Cyprus clearly demonstrated that the gabled ceilings were skeumorphs of wooden beam gabled ceilings. Ussishkin's findings support the contention that bench tombs were designed to resemble residences. While functional and

BCE tombs Aitun Cl and 2, in the tenth-century tombs BCE Tell Halif 3, 4, 6 and the tomb excavated by A. Biran and R. Gophna in 1965, and in the ninth-century tombs BCE Aitun 1, 2, 4 and A2.

decorative details such as margins, imitation sunken wooden panels, lamp niches, pillows and parapets have not been identified in excavation, the tombs may preserve stone skeumorphs of these features. As will be argued below, Judahites believed in life after death. The rapid spread of the bench tomb through Judah demonstrates that it was culturally compatible with ideas of life after death and conceptually acceptable as a residence design.

S. Loffreda devised a typology of Iron Age rock-cut tomb plans (Loffreda 1968). He distinguished eight types which generally increased in elaboration with their introduction. Types 'T' (trapezoidal chamber), 'TT' (trapezoidal chamber with subsidiary chamber), 'C' (circular chamber with oval recesses) and 'CC' (circular chamber with benches), in use during the twelfth and eleventh centuries BCE, were all Late Bronze Age tomb plans or modifications of Late Bronze Age plans. Loffreda attributed these tombs to the Philistines and Canaanites. Types 'R' (rectangular chamber usually with benches) and 'RR' (rectangular chamber with subsidiary chambers) appeared in the tenth century BCE at sites occupied by Israelites. By the seventh and sixth centuries BCE, Type 'S' (square chamber with benches on three sides) constituted the standardized plan and Type 'M' (rectangular chamber with side Type 'S' chambers) had evolved from the earlier Type 'RR'. As J. Abercrombie noted in 1979, new data necessitated only minor refinements in Loffreda's typology. Types 'RR' and 'M' were subdivided to accommodate and better organize the expanded tomb repertoire (Abercrombie 1979: 49-50). Loffreda's dating and Abercrombie's acceptance were perhaps dictated by the desire to attribute a new tomb type to the recently established Israelites and Judahites. While the typology is useful for describing and comparing tomb plans, new data alter the scheme and allow a different historical reconstruction.

Bench tombs were present by the end of the Late Bronze Age and the beginning of the Iron Age at coastal sites (Tell el-Ajjul, Sidon) and at sites linked to the coast and lowlands (Aitun, Tell el-Farah [S], Gezer, Lachish, Pella) (Gonen 1979: Map 3). All the examples were rock-cut chambers with benches, arcosolia or recesses along the side or back walls, or chambers with subsidiary rooms and benches. Iron II bench tombs evolved from two different plans already in use in the region by approximately 1200 BCE: the Middle and Late Bronze Age circular chambers with recesses still in use at Gezer and Lachish, and the square to rectangular bench tombs of Tell el-Farah (S). A third plan exemplified by the Aitun tombs was not adopted in Judah (fig. 10).

One plan, Loffreda's Types 'C' and 'CC', had roughly circular chambers with recesses or benches around the walls. Most examples of this tomb type were originally cut in the Middle or Late Bronze Age and reused during the Iron Age. Lachish Caves 4002 and 4005 and Gezer Tomb 59, dated from the Middle and Late Bronze Ages respectively, were utilized for burial into the tenth century BCE, and, in the case of Lachish 4005, employed again in the sixth century BCE. Very few Iron Age tombs followed this plan; it was a Bronze Age plan which was not adopted in the Iron Age. The Ashdod-Yam tomb from the first half of the twelfth century BCE, Aitun A1 from 850–750 BCE and Tell Ira 16 from the seventh century BCE were fashioned according to this plan.

Tell el-Farah (S) Tombs 902, 905 and 914, dated to approximately 1200 BCE, already possessed the essential elements of Loffreda's Types 'R' and 'S'. In this second plan, a stepped dromos or shaft led into a square or rectangular chamber with one or more steps down to the chamber floor and benches along three sides of the chamber. Nearly identical tombs were cut at the northern coastal sites of Akhzib in the eastern and southern cemeteries beginning late in the eleventh century BCE and Tell Bira in the eleventh to the tenth century BCE. The twelfth- to eleventh-century BCE examples were from coastal sites, but during the tenth and through the third quarter of the eighth century BCE, this plan was adopted at sites in the Shephelah, the central highlands and Transjordan (Dhiban J1, J3; Gezer 142; Kefira 7; Lachish 116; Tell en-Nasbeh 3). Although the circular pit repository was already present in the late eleventh-century BCE Aitun Tomb 2, the pit between the back wall and back bench in the Gezer and Dhiban tombs was an innovative form of repository. During the eighth and seventh centuries BCE this plan was used at the coastal site of Tell el-Rechidiyeh and at the Jerusalem corridor sites of Abu Ghosh, Manahat and Motza. By the seventh to the sixth century BCE, the standardized plan consisted of a square chamber with steps down to the chamber floor, benches on three sides, and a repository pit or niche often cut in one of the far corners (Abu Ghosh; Beth Shemesh 14; Gibeon 1, 4; Khirbet Kufin 4; Meqabelein), very similar to the Tell el-Farah (S) tombs dating from 1200 BCE. Parapets, pillows and lamp niches were present but not common.

There were three variations of the second plan described above. One variation consisted of a single, rectangular chamber with an entrance in a short side and benches along the two long sides. Tell el-Farah (S) Tomb 544 from c. 1200 BCE, Lachish Tomb 521 from c. 1000 BCE and Gibeon Tombs 2 and 7 were hewn on this plan. A second variation, which first appeared late in the eighth century BCE, consisted of two square/rectangular chambers, either one behind the other (Tell Ira 5; Jerusalem—Suleiman St. 2; Motza VII), or side-by-side (Jerusalem—Mt Zion; Zuba). The first chamber had benches along two walls and an entrance in the third wall into the second chamber. Benches typically lined the three walls of the second chamber. With the exception of Tell Ira Tomb 5 which was not well-preserved, all these tombs had repositories, and all but the Motza tomb had parapets and pillows or headrests. A seventh- to sixth-century BCE variation consisted of a round or rectangular central chamber which provided access to subsidiary, square/rectangular chambers with benches. The prototype was Gezer Tomb 9, a Late Bronze II tomb in use through the early ninth century BCE, consisting of a roughly circular central chamber with two benches, plus two subsidiary rooms, each with a single bench. This expandable plan was perhaps designed to accommodate aggregate burials. In Aitun A2, used from 850–750 BCE, three chambers opened off a central court. The best-preserved burial chamber followed the common plan of a square/rectangular chamber with three benches lining the walls and a repository pit, in this case between the back bench and the back wall similar to Gezer 142 and Dhiban J1 and J3. The eighth- to seventh-century BCE tombs Beth Shemesh 5–9 and Suleiman St. 2 in Jerusalem employed this plan, as did the seventh- to sixth-century BCE tombs Lachish 105 and 106 and Khirbet Beit Lei 1. Khirbet el-Qôm 1 and the Jerusalem—St Etienne tombs were the most elaborate tombs cut on this plan with regularly-shaped chambers symmetrically arranged around the central court. However, even Khirbet el-Qôm 1 gives the impression that it was prepared to accommodate additional chambers, and the St Etienne 1 back chamber with a trough may have been a later addition.

The Aitun tomb plan was not adopted in Judah. This configuration may have developed from Bronze Age tombs such as Gezer 59 and Lachish 4002, circular chambers with five benches or recesses (Types

'C' and 'CC'). The Aitun examples consisted of a rectangular chamber with five (or three) arcosolia , two (or one) on each long side and one on the far short side. In the twelfth- and late eleventh-century BCE Tombs C1 and 2, the latter already possessed a circular pit repository. During the tenth to the eighth century BCE, this plan was adopted for Tell en-Nasbeh 5 and Tell Halif 6. The Tell Halif tomb is currently the earliest example with pillows, parapets and lamp niches. Aitun Tombs 1, 2, 3 and 4, in use from 850–750 BCE, also incorporated these elements. The northern site of Tubas produced a tomb of strikingly similar plan, but the preserved tomb incorporates Byzantine period alterations. A shaft entrance opened into the short side of a rectangular chamber with five loculi arranged two in each long side and one in the short side. This plan with a rectangular chamber and symmetrically arranged arcosolia or benches was not adopted. The only subsequent example may be the butterfly-shaped eighth- to seventh-century BCE Khirbet el-Qôm II, with a rounded rectangular chamber and two lateral, waist-high chambers to each side.

This rock-cut tomb plan typology demonstrates that all the elements of the standard Iron II bench tomb plan were already present in coastal and Shephelah tombs by the beginning of the twelfth century BCE. The bench tomb plan adopted and adapted for use in Judah derived from the plans of reused Bronze Age tombs at the sites of Gezer and Lachish, the bench tombs cut at Tell el-Farah (S), and perhaps the Tell Bira and Akhzib tombs, once the plans can be verified. This reconstruction supports W. Stiebing's contention that Iron Age bench tombs developed from local Bronze Age prototypes (Stiebing 1970), as opposed to J. Waldbaum's argument for a foreign introduction (Waldbaum 1966). Unfortunately, very few twelfth- and eleventh-century BCE bench tombs have been found that demonstrate the continuity between the 1200 BCE Tell el-Farah (S) tombs and the tenth-century BCE examples. The Gezer and Lachish tombs remained in use through the tenth century BCE providing continuity. The early Aitun tomb plan, though not adopted in Judah, provided a model for general spatial arrangement and the cutting of parapets, pillows, lamp niches and repositories.

Adoption of the bench tomb at Transjordanian plateau sites paralleled the process in Cisjordan. Throughout the Iron Age, bench tombs east and west of the Jordan River were similar in plan. However, they were always more numerous in Cisjordan than in Transjordan. While the bench tomb may have been introduced onto the Transjordanian plateau from local Late Bronze Age examples such as the Pella tombs, its continued use is perhaps to be attributed to its widespread adoption in Judah. Sahab was the only site with a bench tomb dating from the twelfth to the eleventh century BCE (fig. 16). In this earliest example, the benches were natural rock shelves within a cave, similar to Middle and Late Bronze Age tombs west of the Jordan River. Beginning in the tenth century BCE, bench tombs were reported from Irbed and Dhiban as well as Sahab (fig. 17). The Dhiban examples were similar to contemporary Gezer bench tombs. From the last centuries of the Iron Age, bench tombs have been uncovered in the Amman vicinity and at Dhiban (fig. 18). Throughout the Iron Age, highland settlers in Ammon and Moab employed a variety of burial practices: jar, anthropoid coffin, bathtub coffin, cave and bench tomb burial. Some of these interments may be attributed to foreign militia, administrators or merchants. The bench tomb, like the cave tomb before it, was probably adopted because it was compatible with cultural concepts of death.

In the vast majority of bench and arcosolia tombs, individuals were laid out supine and extended on benches, with their heads on stone pillows or headrests when provided (Aitun no number, 4; Gibeon; Tell Halif 6; Tell Ira; Jerusalem—Ketef Hinnom 25, Sultan Suleiman St. 2, St Etienne 1; Khirbet el-Qôm I; Sahab C1; Zuba). When additional space was required, the deceased and accompanying gifts were moved to a repository usually cut under a bench or in the rear of the tomb. Tombs varied considerably in the number of individuals they housed. Tombs in use for 50 to 100 years held 15 to 100 bodies, while the Akhzib tombs, reportedly utilized over 300-year periods, contained as many as 400 bodies. Only two publications specified the age and sex of the deceased. In a Khirbet Beit Lei tomb, one child, three adolescents including one male, and four adults, three of whom were women, were buried together. The Jerusalem tomb on Mt Zion held ten children, eight adolescents, five women and thirteen men. This is the only Iron Age burial for which the excavators state that at least some of the individuals belonged to the same family. However, there was no mention of family relations in the osteological report (Arensburg and Rak 1985). Published reports record no consistency in bones saved or discarded upon moving skeletal remains aside or into the repositories, but in several instances the presence of skulls was particularly noted (Ira 5, 14; Jerusalem—Mt Zion; Lachish 106; Nahshonim; Sahab B). Only at Akhzib were cremated remains interred in a bench tomb.

The collected burials do not account for the conjectured number of inhabitants of Judah. Bench tomb burial may have been the practice of the wealthy and those considered by society to be deserving of such treatment upon burial. Others, unable to afford a bench tomb, may have been buried in simple or cist graves (though none have been found) or in communal burial fields (Jer. 26.23; 2 Kgs 23.4-6). Aside from the Silwan tombs for civic (and religious?) officials, there are no indications of deviancy, either desirable or undesirable, other than relative wealth reflected in burial.[1] Both sexes and all ages were buried together in bench tombs, indicating that family relations (attested in biblical references but not yet demonstrated archaeologically), rather than achieved status or affiliation in social units, determined one's place in burial.

Grave goods were similar to those found in contemporary cave tombs: local and imported pottery, household items and personal possessions. Lamps, bowls and jugs were the most common ceramic forms, followed in frequency by jars and juglets. Similar assemblages were characteristically provided in Late Bronze Age bench tombs as well. Describing a thirteenth-century BCE Aitun tomb, V. Tzaferis distinguished two levels of burials with skeletons and bone piles accompanied by locally-made and imported Cypriot pottery including bilbils, lamps, jars, bowls and dipper juglets. He concluded that this was probably a family tomb used over approximately one century (V. Tzaferis, private communication 1984). A bench tomb in Pella, Tabakat Fahel, with anthropoid coffins dating from the end of the Late Bronze Age or early Iron Age, contained a particularly rich assemblage of grave goods including Mycenaean IIIA2 and IIIB pottery, Egyptian common wares, scarabs, jewelry, beads and alabaster objects of Egyptian origin (J. Balensi, private communication 1984; Yassine 1975: 60-62).

In twelfth- and eleventh-century BCE bench tombs, the lamp was the predominant form in Aitun C1, while the bowl was the most commonly recovered vessel in Ashdod-Yam, Tell el-Farah (S) 532, 542 and 552, and Lachish 521. Pilgrim flasks, craters and chalices were

1. See T. Shay for a discussion of deviancy in burial (Shay 1985).

also frequently provided. The early tombs contained a high incidence of imported Egyptian (Tell el-Farah [S] 552, 562, 905), Mycenaean (Gezer 9U, 58U; Lachish 4002; Sahab C) and Cypriot vessels (Tell el-Farah [S] 905; Gezer 9U, 58U), as well as Philistine pottery (Aitun C1; Tell el-Farah [S] 532, 542, 552, 562, 914; Gezer 59). Accompanying the ceramic vessels, the most common and noteworthy objects were rattles (Tell el-Farah [S] 905; Sahab C), figurines (Sahab C), bangles, rings, beads, toggle pins (Aitun C1; Tell el-Farah [S] 562, 914; Sahab C), scarabs (Aitun C1; Tell el-Farah [S] 532, 542, 552, 562, 905, 914, 960; Sahab C1), blades (Tell el-Farah [S] 542, 552, 562, 914; Gezer 31, 58U; Lachish 4002; Sahab C, C1) and arrowheads (Aitun C1; Gezer 9U, 59; Sahab C, C1a).

Beginning in the tenth century BCE, a change occurred in mortuary assemblages. The predominant items found in tombs were lamps (Dhiban J3; Lachish 106; Tell en-Nasbeh 3, 5; Mt Nebo UCV-84) and bowls (Abu Ghosh; Aitun A2; Beth Shemesh 7; Meqabelein; Motza I, VII; Sahab B; Samaria 103), as in the previous two centuries, but with the addition of jars (Ein Aruv), juglets (Halif 1965, 6; Jerusalem—Mt Zion) and dipper juglets (Beth Shemesh 2, 4; Lachish 116, 1006). Several new forms were introduced for the preparation, serving and storing of foodstuffs and wine: cooking pots (Aitun, Bethlehem, Gezer), plates or platters (Bethlehem, Beth Shemesh, Halif, Jerusalem, Motza), wine decanters (Abu Ghosh, Jerusalem, Manahat, Motza, Tell en-Nasbeh) and storejars (Abu Ghosh, Aitun, Beth Shemesh, Ez Zahariyah, Gezer, Jerusalem, Lachish). Tenth-century BCE and later tombs yielded fewer imported wares, but included Cypriot (Akhzib; Amman A), Phoenician (Akhzib; Gezer 96; Samaria 1968, 103), Cypro-Phoenician (Tell Bira; Halif; Mt Nebo UCV-84; Samaria) and Assyrian vessels (Meqabelein). The model repertoire expanded from rattles (Beth Shemesh 8; Lachish 106; Khirbet el-Qôm I; Samaria 103) to include a throne (Lachish 106), a shrine (Amman A), horse figurines (Beth Shemesh 2; Lachish 106; Mt Nebo UCV-84; Sahab B), horse and rider figurines (Amman A; Beth Shemesh 8; Lachish 106; Khirbet el-Qôm I; Meqabelein), a male figurine (Beth Shemesh 8), a female tambourine player (?) (Mt Nebo UCV-84) and female pillar figurines with 'beak' and moulded faces (Abu Ghosh; Beth Shemesh 5, 8; Lachish 106; Khirbet el-Qôm I). Toggle pins persisted (Gezer 142; Lachish 106), but they were gradually replaced by fibulae (Abu Ghosh; Beth Shemesh 2, 4, 5; Gezer 142; Meqabelein; Sahab B;

Samaria 1968, 103). Seals and stamps were recovered (Amman A; Halif; Jerusalem; Lachish 116; Meqabelein; Motza I; Samaria) as were scarabs, arrowheads and blades, but in proportionately fewer numbers than in the early Iron Age tombs. The repeated and extended use of bench tombs accounts for the wide assortment and numbers of retrieved mortuary goods.

Like cave tombs, bench tombs (thus far sought and located) were characteristically hewn in proximity to the settlement, in the tell slope or nearby cliffs, or in a cemetery distant from the site (Aitun). Their distribution was limited to a parent rock capable of sustaining the structure. For this reason the vast majority of bench and arcosolia tombs were hewn in the chalks and limestones of the hills and foothills east and west of the Jordan River. However, there are important exceptions, such as the tombs hewn in the coastal kurkar at Akhzib and Ashdod-Yam.

Bench and arcosolia tombs display the most intriguing change in distribution of all the burial types. In the Late Bronze Age, loculi/ arcosolia burials were identified at Megiddo (3, 77, 78, 80), Lachish (536, 3019, 4002-3, 4013) and Tell el-Ajjul (406, 407, 411). Bench tombs were cut at the coastal and Shephelah sites of Sarafend, Gezer (9, 10A, 58), Lachish (502, 536 [?], 4010) and Aitun, and at Tell el-Farah (S) (518, 529, 902, 914, 920, 921, 934, 936, 960) and Pella (Baramki 1956–58; Gonen 1979: 108-219, map 3) (fig. 21). With the onset of the Iron Age, bench and arcosolia tombs appeared at eleven sites: Ashdod-Yam, Tell Bira and Akhzib along the coast; Tell el-Farah (S); Aitun, Lachish and Gezer in the Shephelah; Megiddo and Tel Dothan in the north; and Sahab in Transjordan (fig. 16). Their use subsequently spread through the foothills and up into the highlands from west to east, from the Jerusalem area south and through Transjordan (fig. 17). From the end of the eighth century BCE until the fall of the kingdom of Judah in the sixth century BCE, the bench tomb constituted the overwhelming southern highland preference, as illustrated by examples from 23 different sites. Additional examples occurred at Nahshonim, Akhzib and Tell el-Rechidiyeh along the coast, and at Amman, Meqabelein, Sahab and Dhiban in Transjordan (fig. 18).

By the eighth century BCE, the bench tomb (and perhaps the cave tomb) constituted the standard Judahite form of burial (fig. 18). It is unclear how early the bench tomb was adopted by the Judahites or when the bench tomb burying population in the southern highlands first identified itself as Judahite. Therefore, for the twelfth and eleventh centuries BCE, the burial evidence illustrates only that the cultural group burying in bench tombs was concentrated in the Tell Aitun to Tell Halif region of the Shephelah. Other features of Judahite burial, including female pillar figurines, were also introduced into Judah from the Shephelah (see below). With the fall of the northern kingdom the bench tomb burying population, now conclusively identified as Judahite (and Israelite), swelled in numbers and settled throughout the southern highlands of Judah.

Unfortunately, very few burials have been located and excavated in the territory of the northern kingdom of Israel. Surprisingly, the surveys of M. Kochavi (1972), Z. Gal (1982) and I. Finkelstein (1986, 1988) in the highlands of Ephraim and Manasseh and in the Golan failed to locate even a single burial, even though Iron Age settlements were plentiful. The absence may be attributed in part to survey techniques, but the possibility should be entertained of an alternate 'invisible' form of burial which left no material remains (perhaps simple or cist graves, or a common burial pit as referred to in 2 Kgs 23.4-6 or Jer. 26.23).

Cremation Burial

Cremation burials have been uncovered in three forms: cremated remains inserted into ceramic vessels interred in the sand (fig. 9), pyre burials in the sand, both from primarily coastal sites, and partially cremated remains or cremation strata in cave tombs. This unusual treatment of corporeal remains, the preponderance of Phoenician and Cypro-Phoenician vessels, and the distribution of this burial type demonstrate that cremation burial was introduced into the region by the Phoenicians.[1]

The urns, amphoras and jars in which the cremated remains were interred were decorated with red slip and burnish (Tell er-Ruqeish), red and black painted bands (Khaldé), or Black-on-Red treatment (Akhzib). An inverted bowl capped the vessel to secure the contents. These vessels have been uncovered in a variety of different settings. Azor and perhaps Akhzib provided the only examples of urns buried

1. For the Hittite or Aegean origin, see respectively P. Bienkowski (1982) and W. Culican (1982).

in their own small, stone cist or frame. Some vessels were interred in cists, caves or bench tombs, often with inhumation burials (Akhzib, Tell el-Farah [S], Khaldé, Tell el-Rechidiyeh, Tambourit). However, the majority were simply placed in pits dug in the sand (Tell el-Ajjul, Akhzib, Tell el-Farah [S], Khaldé, Qasmieh, Tell er-Ruqeish).

Individuals of all ages and both sexes were cremated.[1] At Atlit and Tell er-Ruqeish, the pyre on which the body and accompanying goods were burned left traces in the sand. Most urns contained the calcined bones of not more than two individuals, one an infant or child. Recent analysis of the Tell er-Ruqeish cremations revealed no fixed selection or deposition of bones in the receptacle, except that the skull was always present and placed in the upper part of the vessel. All the Tell er-Ruqeish examples studied contained adults: three 40-year-old males, one 30-year-old individual of indeterminate, sex and an 18 to 25-year-old woman perhaps with a fetus. The Senior Medical Officer of the Jerusalem District during the British Mandate Period identified the cremated remains of children and adolescents in addition to those of adults in Tell er-Ruqeish burials. Azor Grave D63 held the remains of a 40 to 45-year-old man and an adolescent, in addition to the bones of birds and other domestic animals, including pig. Five Megiddo urns contained children's remains.

In the Tell el-Farah (S), Khaldé and Tell er-Ruqeish cemeteries, there were open cremation burials lying in the sand among urns and inhumation burials.[2] At Tell er-Ruqeish, a stele stood over an ash layer with a burned skeleton and nearby burned animal bones. Not far from the stele were skulls, a burial urn and a primary inhumation. One possible explanation for the occurrence of open cremation and urn burials together is that urn burial was a form of secondary interment for cremated individuals who could not be buried immediately. The sample is insufficiently documented to determine if age, sex, relative social status or other factors accounted for the differential treatment.[3]

1. J. Abercrombie (1979: 33-34) details age and sex of the cremated individuals and the accompanying grave goods.

2. J. Abercrombie (1979: 42 n. 38) suggested that Tell el-Farah (S) Tomb 135 'might also be a pyre burial or at least related to pyre burials, since it lacked a cinerary urn'.

3. In the Bible certain sexual crimes were punishable by burning the individuals involved: Tamar was suspected of harlotry and so threatened (Gen. 38.24), if a man

The earliest example of cremation burial in the region, the Azor urn, was dated by the excavator M. Dothan to the second half of the eleventh century BCE (fig. 16). The majority of cremation burials dated from the middle of the tenth through the end of the eighth or beginning of the seventh century BCE (Tell el-Ajjul, Akhzib, Tell el-Farah [S], Qasmieh) (figs. 17, 18). The Khaldé and Tambourit cemeteries were founded in the second half of the ninth century BCE, Atlit in the eighth century BCE, and Tell el-Rechidiyeh late in the Iron Age. Only the Tell er-Ruqeish cemetery continued in use into the Persian period.

Recovered goods were scant. Red-slipped, Samaria Ware, Cypro-Phoenician and locally-made bowls, jugs and juglets were the most common ceramic forms. Additional items included scarabs and other Egyptian amulets (Tell el-Ajjul, Akhzib, Tell el-Farah [S], Khaldé, Tell er-Ruqeish), jewelry, a gold mouthpiece (Azor) and arrowheads (Tell el-Ajjul, Tell el-Farah [S]).

Cave tombs at Jericho, Lachish and Mt Nebo contained calcined human bone. The Jericho and Mt Nebo tombs dated from the twelfth century BCE and the Lachish tombs from the end of the ninth century BCE. These geographically disparate sites yielded 'cremated' remains from different times, with no apparent uniformity in the treatment of calcined remains or accompanying goods. The fact that cremation strata were found in two tombs at both Lachish and Mt Nebo suggests that these were intentional cremations, but an unintentional tomb fire or spontaneous combustion in the tomb should not be ruled out. In Jericho Tomb 11, dated from approximately 1200 BCE, 'partially cremated remains' were accompanied by a large number of bronze and iron armlets, a scarab inscribed with the name Tuthmosis III, and a scarab depicting Hadad mounted on the back of an animal. Mt Nebo Tombs UCV-20 and UCV-84, in use through the Iron II period, were

married a woman and her mother all were threatened with burning (Lev. 20.14) and a priest's daughter who defiled herself through harlotry defiled her father as well so she was to be burned (Lev. 21.9). Burning may also have served as a symbol of reproach; the Moabites burned the bones of the king of Edom to lime (Amos 2.1). There is no indication, however, in the story of Saul and his sons, that their cremation was in any way a reproof or punishment. The inhabitants of Jabesh-Gilead retrieved the desecrated bodies of Saul and his sons, burned them and buried the bones under a tamarisk tree in Jabesh (1 Sam. 31.11-13). Perhaps the population of Jabesh-Gilead was Phoenician.

cave tombs with jar burials, anthropoid coffin burials and secondary burials on benches as well as cremation burials. 'Cremation strata' were reported throughout Tomb 20 and in one large area in Tomb 84 chamber 2. From the published report, particular goods could not be ascribed to the cremation burials. The Lachish cave tombs 120 and 1002 also contained burnt bone. In Tomb 120, more than 1500 individuals were buried and covered with a layer of animal bones, primarily pig. Some of the human bones showed signs of burning. In Cave 1002 secondary burials 'were affected by fire before they were reburied'.

Distribution of Burial Types

The various burial types, identified by a constellation of features and named for the receptacle or the space housing the body, were suggested to be the practice of different cultural groups known through biblical or extrabiblical texts to have inhabited the region. Simple and cist burial was practiced by the inhabitants of the coastal and lowland regions (including the Jezreel, Beth Shan and Jordan River Valleys) who were collectively referred to in the Bible as 'Canaanites'. Jar burial was introduced into the region from the north, and all examples were from sites along the central and northern coast, the contiguous northern valleys and the Transjordanian plateau. Egyptians interred their dead in pit graves, cist graves and anthropoid coffins at Egyptian occupied sites. Assyrians buried their dead in bathtub coffins. Phoenicians cremated and inhumed their dead at sites along the coast from Khaldé in the north to Tell er-Ruqeish in the south and at Tell el-Farah (S). The indigenous highland population, identified in the Bible as Amorites and others, buried their dead in caves, and by the eighth century BCE the Judahites buried their dead in bench tombs. The correlation between the distribution patterns of the various burial types and the settlement of different cultural groups known from the Bible, extra-biblical texts and inscriptions is very high.

The sites of Azor, Lachish, and, to a lesser extent, Jerusalem, displayed an unusually large variety of burial types not otherwise found together. This diversity suggests that they were cosmopolitan centers where different cultural groups coexisted and interred their dead.

Although the heartland of Philistia has been conclusively identified, Philistine burial practices are not yet known. Following twelfth-century BCE Philistine settlement in the region, simple, cist and jar burial continued from the Late Bronze Age. In the eleventh century BCE the Phoenicians introduced urn burial. Other new burial forms included massive pit and cist graves (Ashdod, Azor, Palmachim, Tell Zeror), skull burials (Aitun, Ashdod, Azor, Tell el-Farah (S), Tell er-Ruqeish, also Tell es-Saidiyeh), interments of decapitated bodies (Ashdod, also Tell es-Saidiyeh) and animal burials (Ashdod).

Of the skull burials and interments with skulls added, the twelfth-century BCE Tell es-Saidiyeh examples were the earliest. These pit graves containing the skull, and frequently long bones of one or more individuals, were interpreted by the excavator, J. Tubb, as 'derived secondary burials'—'significant' remains of a burial indadvertently disturbed which were reburied in a small pit or added to a later grave. One body and seven skulls were interred in Aitun C1 locus 4. The Azor, Tell er-Ruqeish and Tell el-Farah (S) burials dated from the tenth century BCE, and the Ashdod and Nahshonim (?) examples began in the eighth and seventh centuries BCE respectively. Of the tenth-century BCE examples, Azor cist D79 held four articulated bodies plus nine additional skulls. Pit grave D56 consisted of a skull and vessels, but D55, situated immediately above, included skull and bone fragments in addition to sherds that joined with sherds in D56. The majority of examples were from Tell el-Farah (S), all stone-lined cists in the 200 Cemetery: 212 (11 skulls), 213 (26 skulls), 225 (6 skulls), 227 (20 skulls), 228 (13 or 25 skulls), 229 (80 skulls), 233 (12 skulls) and 237 (10 skulls). From Tell er-Ruqeish, W. Culican noted four unaccompanied skulls as the single exception to cremation burial in the sand (Culican 1973: 68), and in a 1974 report from the Department of Antiquities, skulls and a burial urn were mentioned in proximity to a stele (Tell er Ruqeish 1974: 6). The Ashdod skull burials all dated to the late eighth century BCE. Courtyard burial Locus 1114 contained more than 40 skulls arranged in groups of four or five. The narrow pit Locus 1115 held 10 skulls stacked one on top of the other. Six incomplete human skulls and four more skulls (?) were buried in Locus 1052. Pit grave Locus 1151 consisted of seven nearly complete post-cranial skeletons, buried in parallel rows. While most of these examples occurred in Philistine territory, only Tell es-Saidiyeh 108 and the questionable Azor D56 contained any Philistine pottery. Azor D79, the tenth- through eighth-century BCE Tell el-Farah (S) cists and the eighth-century BCE Ashdod burials contained locally-made vessels, Cypro-Phoenician imports, jewelry including scarabs and metal blades.

The skull burials are the most radical departure from the indigenous burial customs. All the examples were from the coastal region from Azor south to Tell er-Ruqeish and from Tell es-Saidiyeh. These interments of animals, decapitated bodies and skulls may preserve distinctive Philistine, Phoenician or Sea Peoples' burial practices.

The Iron Age burial types displayed two distinct distribution patterns. Some types have been uncovered throughout a territory settled by a cultural or political entity coinciding with a topographical region. Simple and cist graves were used from the Late Bronze Age through the Iron Age at sites along the coast and through the northern and Jordan River valleys. The distribution of jar burials resembled that of simple and cist graves, but it was confined to the northern half of the region. Jar burials have also been recovered from the Galilee and the Transjordanian plateau. Cave tombs and later bench tombs were employed in the highlands. Other burial types such as anthropoid coffins, bathtub coffins and cremation were foreign practices whose distribution was limited to sites where the respective nationals were buried. The bench tomb was the only burial type to undergo a change in its distribution pattern. The earliest Iron Age bench tomb attestations were in coastal-lowland regions, but the type later predominated in the highlands.

Some burial receptacles were deposited in a variety of different contexts, such as jars in simple graves, cist graves, caves and bench tombs; urns in simple graves, cist graves, caves and bench tombs; or anthropoid coffins in simple graves, cist graves, bench tombs and reused Bronze Age tombs. For jar, anthropoid coffin, bathtub coffin and urn burials, ultimate deposition of the receptacle was of secondary importance.

Certain types repeatedly occurred together: simple and cist graves, jar and anthropoid coffin burials, cremations and simple inhumations, and cave and bench tombs. Simple and cist graves occurring together at Tell es-Saidiyeh may reflect 'social persona' distinctions and societal indebtedness (Binford 1971: 17), with individuals of higher wealth or status accorded more elaborate burial in a more prestigious area of the cemetery. In some cases jar burials may have served as a simplified form of anthropoid coffin burial, as in the Amman Royal Palace and Dhiban bench tomb burials.

Cremation and simple inhumation burials sometimes occurred

together (Akhzib, Atlit, Tell el-Farah [S], Khaldé, Tell er-Ruqeish). In the Khaldé cist Tomb 121, a primary inhumation, an urn filled with non-calcined human bones and an urn with calcined bones lay side-by-side. At Tell er-Ruqeish, urns with cremated remains, pyre burials and simple inhumations were interred together in the sand. The repetition of this constellation of burial practices suggests that members of a single society received differential burial treatment. A study of the osteological remains might indicate whether physical conditions in life or cause of death affected the form of burial. Social, religious or political beliefs and practices as determinants of burial form should also be considered.

Cave tombs and bench tombs were occasionally employed at the same sites (Amman, Gezer, Jerusalem, Lachish, Tell en-Nasbeh). During the Iron Age, use of the bench tomb spread from the coast and contiguous valleys up into the geographically distinct highlands. At sites in the foothills and western highlands where cave tombs had previously been utilized, the bench tomb was adopted (Beth Shemesh, Gibeah, Gibeon, Khirbet Rabud). From the third quarter of the eighth century BCE onwards, cave tombs were employed in the eastern highlands and at Jericho. Both in Cisjordan and on the Transjordanian plateau, as the number of sites with bench tombs increased, the number of sites with cave tombs decreased. This rise in number and greater distribution of sites with bench tombs, coupled with the decrease in number and more limited distribution of sites with cave tombs, may reflect the employment of variant practices by a single culture. Perhaps burial in bench tombs was increasingly adopted as a more elaborate and fashionable version of family burial in caves. A second possibility is that burial in bench tombs was not determined by economic or status motives alone, but rather reflected a divergent cultural choice. An increasing number of families may have adopted bench tomb burial as an expression of Judahite or Yahwistic affiliation. In this case, the only attested variation in Judahite burials was in relative wealth. Alternative forms of burial for those unable to 'afford' the usual practice, or for those whose deviance in life precluded the usual form of burial, have not been identified. If this latter hypothesis is correct, then the newly apparent population in the eastern Cisjordanian highlands who buried their dead in cave tombs (there may have been previous settlers with 'invisible' burial practices) were the last adherents to the Late Bronze Age highland culture (compare fig. 16 with figs. 17 and 18).

It is noteworthy that the Late Bronze Age practices of cist burial, jar burial and anthropoid coffin burial continued in Transjordan after they ceased or were rarely used in Cisjordan.

Tables 2, 3 and 4 list the number of burials of each type from the twelfth through the first quarter of the sixth century BCE. Although only suggestive, given the vagaries of burial excavation and publication, the numbers of burials of each type arranged by region demonstrate the rising and waning popularity of particular burial types and changes in their distribution.

Every burial type except cave tombs demonstrated a marked increase or decrease in numbers over the centuries. Double the number of cave tombs were in use during the tenth through the third quarter of the eighth century BCE than during previous or subsequent centuries. The popular Late Bronze Age practices of cist, jar and anthropoid coffin burial decreased in numbers through the Iron Age. Cist burial never spread beyond coastal and Jordan River Valley sites. Jar burial continued in use at northern, coastal and Transjordanian plateau sites throughout the period, with a shift in concentration from the north and the coast to the Transjordanian plateau. All other burial types were increasingly used over the centuries: simple burial, bench tombs, bathtub coffins and cremation burial. Simple burials were initially concentrated at sites along the south coast, but, beginning in the tenth century BCE, additional inhumations have been reported from Lachish and six northern coastal sites from Tell Bira north to Khaldé. Bench tombs more than quadrupled in number during the Iron Age. The earliest bench tombs were cut along the coast from Tell el-Farah (S) north to Tell Bira and in the southern foothills. From the tenth century BCE onwards, the bench tomb was increasingly used in the Shephelah, the southern highlands and Transjordan. From the single eleventh-century BCE example, more than one hundred cremation burials have been unearthed along the coast dating from the late eighth through the early sixth century BCE.

	Simple grave	*Cist grave*	*Jar burial*	*Anthro-poid coffin*	*Bathtub coffin*	*Bench tomb*	*Cave tomb*	*Cremation burial*
North coast	-	11	+77	-	-	+15	-	1
	-	(2)	(2)	-	-	(3)	-	(1)
Israel	15	-	5	10	-	2	6	-
	(5)	-	(5)	(2)	-	(1)	(2)	-
South coast	+117	+33	19	6	-	17	-	-
	(3)	(3)	(2)	(2)	-	(2)	-	-
Shephelah	-	-	-	1	-	4	5	-
	-	-	-	(1)	-	(2)	(3)	-
Southern	-	+	-	-	-	+4	2	-
highlands	-	(1)	-	-	-	(2)	(2)	-
Jordan River	+117	+60	+23	-	-	-	1	1
Valley	(1)	(1)	(1)	-	-	-	(1)	(1)
Transjordanian	+1	-	2	-	-	2	8	-
plateau	(1)	-	(2)	-	-	(1)	(5)	-
Total number of burials	+249	+104	126	17	-	+44	22	2

Table 2. Number of Burials of Each Type by Region during the Twelfth and Eleventh Centuries BCE. Note: a plus sign (+) indicates an unspecified number of (additional) burials. The number of different sites in the region is given in parenthesis below the number of burials.

	Simple grave	*Cist grave*	*Jar burial*	*Anthro-poid coffin*	*Bathtub coffin*	*Bench tomb*	*Cave tomb*	*Cremation burial*
North coast	+100	+11	-	-	-	+3	+9	+14
	(6)	(3)	-	-	-	(2)	(3)	(7)
Israel	5	+	?	-	1	2	2	5
	(1)	(1)	(2)	-	(1)	(2)	(2)	(1)
South coast	+50	+28	17	-	-	-	-	73
	(4)	(4)	(1)	-	-	-	-	(3)
Shephelah	42	-	-	-	-	13	13	2
	(1)	-	-	-	-	(3)	(3)	(1)
Southern highlands	-	+	-	-	-	40	+10	-
	-	(1)	-	-	-	(8)	(8)	-
Jordan River Valley	-	-	-	-	-	-	1	-
	-	-	-	-	-	-	(1)	-
Transjordanian plateau	+2	-	?	16	-	5	17	2
	(2)	-	(3)	(4)	-	(4)	(8)	(1)
Total number of burials	+199	+39	17	16	1	+63	+52	+96

Table 3. Number of Burials of Each Type by Region from the Tenth through the Third Quarter of the Eighth Century BCE.
Note: a plus sign (+) indicates an unspecified number of (additional) burials. The number of different sites in the region is given in parenthesis below the number of burials.

	Simple grave	*Cist grave*	*Jar burial*	*Anthropoid coffin*	*Bathtub coffin*	*Bench tomb*	*Cave tomb*	*Cremation burial*
North coast	+100	1	-	-	1	+3	-	+34
	(5)	(1)	-	-	(1)	(2)	-	(8)
Israel	+8	-	6	-	6	-	2	-
	(3)	-	(1)	-	(4)	-	(2)	-
South coast	+33	1	-	-	-	1	-	73
	(3)	(1)	-	-	-	(1)	-	(3)
Shephelah	10	-	+1	-	-	10	+9	-
	(1)	-	(1)	-	-	(2)	(2)	-
Southern	-	-	-	-	3	+165	+8	-
highlands	-	-	-	-	(2)	(23)	(4)	-
Jordan River	61	3	1	-	1	-	2	-
Valley	(1)	(1)	(1)	-	(1)	-	(1)	-
Transjordanian	-	-	+10	+9	3	5	+8	2
plateau	-	-	(4)	(3)	(1)	(4)	(7)	(1)
Total number of burials	+212	5	+18	+9	14	+184	+29	+109

Table 4. Number of Burials of Each Type by Region during the Last Quarter of the Eighth through the First Quarter of the Sixth Century BCE. Note: a plus sign (+) indicates an unspecified number of (additional) burials. The number of different sites in the region is given in parenthesis below the number of burials.

Chapter 2

BURIAL CONTENTS

Burial contents belong to the categories of human remains, pottery, jewelry, personal items, tools, metal objects and models. Chronological changes in body treatment and mortuary provisioning are obscured by the fact that the majority of osteological remains and objects were found in cave and bench tombs which were used over extended periods of time, frequently rendering it nearly impossible to pinpoint the time when a body or object was placed in a tomb.

Tables 5 and 6 list the number of sites by region in which burials were initiated during 50-year periods from the second half of the thirteenth through the end of the tenth century BCE, and from the ninth through the seventh century BCE respectively. Several factors prejudice the results: (1) burial recovery and publication are highly selective, (2) only the more complete burials have been included in these tables, (3) limitations in pottery dating skew the results, and (4) tenth-century BCE and later burials were used for many generations. However, the figures do illustrate that burial features can be termed 'early', twelfth and eleventh century BCE, or 'late', tenth through the sixth century BCE. Burials from the second half of the thirteenth century BCE and the first half of the twelfth century BCE continued Late Bronze Age practices. With the dramatic drop in number of sites where burials were initiated between the second half of the twelfth and the end of the eleventh century BCE, Late Bronze Age practices died out. During the tenth century BCE, burials were initiated at sites throughout the region and new practices were introduced which would continue throughout the duration of the Iron Age. After a decrease in the number of sites where dead were interred during the ninth century BCE, the first half of the eighth century BCE witnessed an upsurge along the north coast, in the Shephelah and in the Judahite foothills and highlands. With the second half of the eighth century BCE, came the introduction of bathtub coffin burials in the territory of the former northern kingdom and bench tombs in Judah. During the seventh century BCE the majority of new burials were initiated in Judah.

	1250–1200	*1200–1150*	*1150–1100*	*1100–1050*	*1050–1000*	*1000–950*	*950–900*
North coast	1	2	2	1	1	4	-
Northern highlands	2	5	1	2	-	5	-
South coast	3	1	1	1	-	3	-
Shephelah	2	1	1	-	-	3	2
Southern highlands	-	3	-	1	1	6	1
Jordan River Valley	2	1	-	-	-	1	-
Transjordanian plateau	3	2	1	-	1	4	1
Total number of *different* sites by century	-	18		8		26	

Table 5. Number of Sites by Region with Burials Initiated over Fifty-Year Periods from the Second Half of the Thirteenth through the Tenth Century BCE.

	900–850	*850–800*	*800–750*	*750–700*	*700–650*	*650–600*
North coast	2	2	4	-	-	-
Northern high lands	1	2	1	6	-	1
South coast	1	1	1	-	2	-
Shephelah	1	2	3	1	1	-
Southern high lands	3	1	5	5	5	2
Jordan River Valley	-	-	1	1	-	1
Transjordanian plateau	-	-	1	1	1	2
Total number of *different* sites by century	16		27		12	

Table 6. Number of Sites by Region with Burial Initiated over Fifty-Year Periods from the Ninth through the Seventh Century BCE.

Human Remains

Given the large number of Iron Age burials excavated, only a very small number of the individuals interred have been analyzed for sex or age. In the 316 burials computerized for this study, plus 239 recently published Tell es-Saidiyeh burials, there were a total of 54 infants, 66 children, 8 adolescent men, 12 adolescent women, 50 juveniles and adolescents of undetermined sex, 27 adult men, 23 adult women, and 285 adults of undetermined sex. These small numbers render generalizations regarding sex and age distinctions extremely tentative.

Infants buried alone or with other individuals are attested in all burial types except bathtub coffins. In the few instances in which they were buried alone, they were interred in simple graves (Khaldé 165; Tell es-Saidiyeh 52, 135), jars (Tel Dothan; Megiddo 37C2; Sahab C1c; Tell es-Saidiyeh 40, 63, 76, 151, 156, 161, 226) and urns (Megiddo). They were most often buried with other children in jars (Tell Zeror) or an urn (Tell el-Farah [S]). Infants have also been identified with two adults in pit graves (Tell es-Saidiyeh 119, 136) and a bench tomb (Lachish 6006), with adult women (Tell es-Saidiyeh pit grave 123; Ruqeish urn burial), an adolescent female (Sahab cave C1a), an adolescent male (Sahab C1b), an adult (Afula 1), an adult woman and a child (Tell Ira 14), and two adults and a child (Deir el-Balah 114). Except for the urns with cremated remains, all infant burials were primary or secondary inhumations.

Of the very small number of infants buried alone, those buried in pits or an urn received no gifts, while those placed in jars were provided with bracelets and beads (Tel Dothan; Megiddo 37C2; Tell es-Saidiyeh 40, 63, 156, 161) or a ring (Sahab C1c). Chronological differences do not account for the variations; the societal context must be considered. Such modest burial provisions have been interpreted as indicating lack of achieved status, and of acquired and treasured possessions. The colored beads and metal bracelets, anklets and rings probably served a symbolic, protective (see below) as well as decorative function, and so constituted an important element of mortuary provisioning. Even infants required and benefitted from the amuletic powers of jewelry.

Children were attested in all burial types except bathtub coffins: in simple graves (Atlit iva; Azor 56; Tell el-Farah [S] 222; Tell es-Saidiyeh 23, 27, 104, 111, 112, 125, 127, 128, 131), a cist grave (Tell el-Farah [S] 201), jar burials (Beth Shemesh 8; Tell el-Farah [S] 516; Megiddo; Tell es-Saidiyeh 120, 121, 126; Tell Zeror), an anthropoid coffin (Deir el-Balah 114), urns (Azor 63; Tell el-Farah [S]), a cave (Tell Abu Hawam IV) and bench tombs (Khirbet Beit Lei 1, 2; Dhiban J3; Samaria 103). From the thirteenth through the eleventh century BCE children were buried in pit graves, jars, anthropoid coffins and urns (Azor, Deir el-Balah, Tell el-Farah [S], Tell es-Saidiyeh, Tell Zeror), but beginning in the tenth century BCE, they were interred increasingly in cave and bench tombs.

Cremated children were recorded from Atlit, Azor and Tell el-Farah (S), but all the rest were primary inhumations. Children were most often buried with adolescents and adults together (Khirbet Beit Lei 1, 2; Deir el-Balah 114, 116, 118; Dhiban J3; Jerusalem—Mt Zion), but they were also buried alone or with one or more adults (Azor; Tell el-Farah [S]; Tell es-Saidiyeh 23, 127, 128; Samaria 103), with an infant (Tell el-Farah [S]; Tell Zeror), and with an adult woman and an infant (Tell Ira 14).

Generalizing from the 13 individual child burials in which pottery vessels were present, a bowl was the most common provision for a child. Other goods for children included beads, metal jewelry (Beth Shemesh 8; Tell el-Farah [S] 222; Tell es-Saidiyeh 27, 104), a scarab, scaraboid or faience piece (Azor 56; Beth Shemesh 8; Tell el-Farah [S] 516; Tell es-Saidiyeh 104, 111, 112) and shells (Tell el-Farah [S] 516; Tell es-Saidiyeh 104). In the contemporary Tell es-Saidiyeh children's jar and pit burials, those interred in jars were supplied with a bowl, while those buried in pits received beads and often a scarab or faience piece. In the pit grave Tell es-Saidiyeh 27, a five-year-old was adorned with a necklace of silver, carnelian and stone beads, bead and bronze bracelets, rings of silver and of steatite, and a silver earring. In her hair was a bronze clasp, her cloak was secured by a bronze fibula, and placed in the grave were a stamp seal, a bronze weaving spindle and a zoomorphic pottery vessel. Only in this burial and in Tell el-Farah (S) cist grave 201 were children buried with such an array of prestige items.

The first half twelfth- to second half eleventh-century BCE jar burial from Kfar Yehoshua presents the single case of an adolescent male buried alone. Burial provisions included a crater, a bowl, a chalice, a pilgrim flask and a metal ring. In Sahab C1c an adolescent male and an infant were buried together with a bracelet and a blade. Since none of the infant burials contained blades, the piece was probably provided for the adolescent. Adolescent males were buried in a pit with other adolescents and adults (Ashdod 1122), in a stone cist with an adolescent female (Akhzib), in a cave with an infant (Sahab C1c), and in bench tombs with children, other adolescents and adults (Khirbet Beit Lei 1; Gezer 58U).

There were four examples of adolescent women buried alone, all dating from the twelfth and eleventh centuries BCE, and all in simple or cist graves (Tel Kishyon 2; Megiddo 17; Tell Taanach; Tell es-Saidiyeh 101). Of the two provided with metal and ceramic vessels, the bowl was the only common form (Megiddo 17; Tell es-Saidiyeh 101). Both the Tell es-Saidiyeh and Tell Taanach women wore beads. In addition, the Tell Taanach woman had a fibula and scarab, and the Tell es-Saidiyeh woman had a toggle pin and cosmetic accoutrements including an Egyptian ivory cosmetic spoon in the form of a woman with extended arms supporting the cup. In a Tell er-Ruqeish urn containing cremated infant and adolescent female remains, the provisions included beads and a scarab. Adolescent women were buried in a simple grave and cists with an adolescent male (Akhzib), with an infant and an adult (Tell es-Saidiyeh 119) and with two adult women (Ashdod 1122). They were also buried in an urn with an infant (Tell er-Ruqeish) and in cave, chamber and bench tombs with children, other adolescents and adults (Khirbet Beit Lei 2; Gezer 58U; Sahab C1a).

There were only two examples of adult males buried alone. In an urn burial from Tell er-Ruqeish, a man was buried with virtually the same gifts as a woman and infant cremated together at the same site: a jar, a juglet, a bowl, beads and a scarab (the woman and infant also had a jug). The man in the Azor D76 mudbrick cist had been provided with an assortment of ceramic vessels including a bowl and a pilgrim flask, plus a flint scraper. Men were buried in a pit grave (Ashdod 1066), an urn (Tell er-Ruqeish), anthropoid coffins (Deir el-Balah 114, 116, 118), and in cave, chamber and bench tombs (Khirbet Beit Lei 2; Gezer 58U; Gibeon; Jerusalem—Mt Zion; Lachish 6006). They were interred with an adolescent (Deir el-Balah 116), with adults (Lachish 521), and with adolescents and adults together (Gezer 58U). Burials of two to ten individuals (including men) usually contained a wide assortment and great number of ceramic vessels, jewelry, scarabs, stamps, seals (Deir el-Balah 116, 118; Gibeon), gaming pieces (Deir el-Balah 116; Lachish 521), blades and arrowheads (Deir el-Balah 118; Gezer 58U; Gibeon; Lachish 521, 6006).

There was no example of an adult female buried alone. In the single instance where a woman was accompanied by two infants, Tell es-Saidiyeh 123, the mortuary goods included common ceramic forms and an assortment of jewelry. The greatest number of women were buried with children, adolescents and other adults in cave and bench tombs (Khirbet Beit Lei 1, 2; Gibeon; Jerusalem—Mt Zion; Lachish 6006). Women were also buried in pits with infants (Tell es-Saidiyeh 123), men (Ashdod 1066) or other adults (Tell es-Saidiyeh 118), and in anthropoid coffins with men or adults of undetermined sex (Deir el-Balah 114, 118). In the Deir el-Balah burials, an assortment of pottery, jewelry, stamps, seals, scarabs and other Egyptian amulets, blades, and arrowheads were supplied, but specific goods could not be attributed to the women.

To summarize, infants and children were attested in all burial types, with the possible exception of bathtub coffins.[1] They were interred alone in jars or in simple graves, but more often they were buried with adolescents and adults. Whereas infants were buried without grave goods or with jewelry only, children were provisioned with jewelry and a bowl (in jar burials). Adolescents have also been identified in all burial types. They were provisioned as adults, with a variety of ceramic forms, jewelry, tools and personal items. Adults, attested in all burial types, received the full range of mortuary goods given to children and adolescents, plus stamps, seals and gaming pieces. Generally, adults were equipped with more goods (including objects of greater value) than were younger individuals.

Examining the incidence of individuals by age and sex among burial types is informative. The vast majority of individuals were classed neither by sex nor by age, and since mature bones preserve better than immature bones, the percentages provided in table 7 (below) are speculative. Pit graves contained infants and children with older individuals. Although the numbers are small, it may be observed that infants occurred with the least frequency, children and adolescents

1. None of the skeletal remains from bathtub coffins have been analyzed for sex or age.

were twice as common, and adults occurred seven times more frequently than infants. There were three times as many women (adolescents and adults) as men. From stone cist and mudbrick cist graves, very few skeletal remains were analyzed. However, the results correlate well with those from simple graves and so are presented. No cists contained only infants or children (with the exception of Tell el-Farah [S] 201): all held at least one adolescent or adult. Excluding the massive Tell el-Farah (S) stone cist 201, one infant, one child, four adolescents and twelve adults were buried in stone or mudbrick cists, with a 3:1 ratio of females to males. Adult males are poorly attested in pit and cist burials. Jar burials most frequently held infants or children, but there are examples of a single adolescent male (Kfar Yehoshua), and of adults (Amman-Jebel el-Qusur; Mt Nebo UCV-84; Tell es-Saidiyeh). The Deir el-Balah anthropoid coffins contained infants, children, adolescents and adults, with a 1:1 ratio of females to males. Cave tombs contained the fewest children and adolescents, twice as many infants, and nine times as many adults. Females to males exhibited a 1:1 ratio. Bench tombs divide into early and late examples, with no appreciable differences. There were a few bench tombs found to contain only adults (Halif 4; Irbed C; Lachish 4002; Ramot), but the vast majority housed varying combinations of infants, children, adolescents and adults. Adults were always present. Infants occurred in the smallest numbers, with approximately three times as many children and adolescents and more than four times as many adults. Adults and adolescents displayed a 3:2 ratio of men to women. The small number of analyzed cremated remains from urns suggests that all ages were buried in urns: infants alone, infants and children with adults, and single adults. Adults were more common than younger individuals.

With the exception of jar and cave burials, all of the burial types contained increasing numbers of infants, children, adolescents and then adults. Cists, followed by cave tombs housed the highest proportion of adults, while cave tombs, were the only type to have a higher incidence of infants than of children or adolescents. Given the high projected infant mortality rate (Goodman and Armelagos 1989: 225-27), infants and young children are under-represented in all burial types. As for male to female ratios, pit and cist tombs displayed a 1:3 ratio, the three examples of anthropoid coffins and cave tombs a 1:1 ratio, and bench tombs a 3:2 ratio.

The vast majority of individuals initially received primary inhumation. Body orientation was noted in 78 burials, primarily from simple and cist graves. Over 20 percent lay supine; the rest lay extended on a side or stomach, or, rarely, flexed. No pattern emerges regarding body position. Thirty-nine percent lay with their heads to the north, 39 percent to the west, 13 percent to the east and nine percent to the south. Graves frequently displayed a consistent orientation within a cemetery, so topography, site-specific custom, efficiency, and the need for an orderly arrangement for the dead may have been determining factors. In twelfth- and eleventh-century BCE burials, the majority of individuals buried at Tell Zeror and Tell es-Saidiyeh were buried with their heads to the west, which was the Egyptian practice. Megiddo displayed the greatest diversity in orientation, with individuals headed both south and east. From the tenth century BCE on, north became the primary choice for individuals buried at Khaldé and Lachish, with single examples oriented northwest from Atlit and Khirbet Beit Lei.

	Infants	*Children*	*Adolescents*	*Adults*	*Males:Females*
Pit Graves	8.3%	16.7%	16.7%	58.1%	1:3
Cist Graves	5.5%	5.5%	22.2%	66.7%	1:3
Jar Burials	*	*	+	+	
Anthropoid Coffin Burials	+	+	+	+	
Cave Tombs	15.4%	7.7%	7.7%	69.2%	1:1
Bench Tombs	8.3%	25.0%	25.0%	41.7%	3:2
Cremation Burials	+	+	+	*	

Table 7. Relative Percentages of Individuals by Age in the Various Iron Age Burial Types, with Male:Female Ratio.[1]

In the first half of this century, skulls were analyzed in an attempt to identify the interred population. This analysis has not proven useful. D. Ferembach identified a mediterranean-type woman and a brachycephalic adult male in Azor cist grave D79. The Azor urn burial D63 contained two individuals, a 40 to 45-five-year-old brachycephalic man and a 12 to 16-year-old. The majority of identified individuals buried at Azor, presumably Iron Age interments (though accompanying datable goods were frequently lacking), were identified

1. Note: a plus sign (+) indicates presence and an asterisk (*) indicates the highest percentage.

as brachycephalic. In D56 the skull of a four-year-old mesocephalic individual was accompanied by numerous ceramic vessels, most with Philistine decoration, bracelets, beads and a scarab. W. Shanklin and M. Ghantus found the Khaldé skulls to be a homogeneous group, similar to a thirteenth century BCE example from Byblos and seven specimens from Sidon, '...all with cranial indices in the dolio-cephalic and mesocephalic range. Not a single skull was observed in the brachycephalic group' (Shanklin and Ghantus 1966: 93). Skulls with African affinities were unearthed in an Ashdod-Yam bench tomb (Gophna and Meron 1970: *1), and a bench tomb cut into the west slope of Mt Zion held individuals of 'common Mediterranean stock' (Arensburg and Rak 1985: 30).

Unusual burial practices included separating men from women and children, and burying skulls or decapitated bodies alone. Men were separated from women and children in the twelfth- to eleventh-century BCE Baqah Valley Cave A4 and a seventh-century BCE tomb from Tel Ira. There were numerous examples of skull burials in simple graves, cist graves, jar burials, cave tombs and bench tombs. The earliest such burials were nine twelfth-century BCE Tell es-Saidiyeh simple graves (5, 57, 58, 105L, 146, 170, 206, 221, 237) and one cist grave (108), and five twelfth- to eleventh-century BCE Azor jar burials. Five decapitated individuals including one infant were buried in the Tell es-Saidiyeh cemetery (224, 241, 248, 269A, 279). Skull burial was later practiced at Ashdod, Azor, Tell el-Farah (S) and Tell er-Ruqeish, and decapitated bodies were buried at Ashdod. These interments of skulls and decapitated bodies may preserve Philistine, Phoenician or Sea Peoples burial practices. There are several examples of cave, chamber and bench tombs where skulls were separated from the other bones or where the excavator noted a number of skulls (or mandibles) without specifying if only skulls were found or if the number of skulls were cited to indicate the minimum number of individuals. Ashdod-Yam B with five skulls and some bones (and the Tel Dothan tomb) dated to the twelfth century BCE or earlier, but all the other examples dated from the tenth century BCE or later (Tel Dothan; Tell Ira 5; Jericho A85, WH 1, WH 2; Jerusalem—Mt Zion; Lachish 120, 224; Nahshonim [?]; Tell en-Nasbeh 54). Only in the Jericho and Lachish tombs were decapitated skeletons and skulls buried in separate locations in a single tomb.

Pottery

J. Abercrombie distinguished five pottery patterns defined by the prevalent forms and the presence of distinctive types—often imports (Abercrombie 1979: 56-159). This study yielded no such clear-cut, statistically based patterns. Since complete assemblages were in most cases neither preserved nor fully published, this pottery study is undertaken on the basis of relative proportions of pottery forms preserved and the full range of shapes included. Dividing the tombs into early (twelfth and eleventh century BCE) and late (tenth through the first quarter of the sixth century BCE) phases refines Abercrombie's results.

The following discussion of prevalent pottery forms is charted in Table 8. The listed forms were the most prevalent in that century, and they continued in use into succeeding centuries. Bowls, the best represented pottery form in tomb assemblages, occurred twice as frequently as lamps. In the twelfth and eleventh centuries BCE, bowls predominated in jar burials (Tell Abu Hawam; Tell el-Farah [S] 516; Tell es-Saidiyeh 161B, 163, 228), pit graves (Tell el-Farah [S] 222; Tell es-Saidiyeh 59, 70, 73, 99, 173B, 218A) and cave and bench tombs (Ashdod-Yam; Tell el-Farah [S] 532, 543, 552; Irbed A and B; Lachish 570) (*contra* Abercrombie 1979: 99). They were often accompanied by lamps and juglets, followed in frequency by jars and pilgrim flasks. Beginning in the tenth century BCE, the popularity of the bowl spread along the coast (Tell Abu Hawam II; Ashdod 1111, 1114; Khaldé 121), through the north (Samaria 103; Tubas A), into the Shephelah (Aitun A2; Beth Shemesh 1, 7; Lachish 197, 223, 521), into the central hills (Abu Ghosh; Ez Zahariyah; Motza I, VII; Khirbet Rabud), to Jericho and along the Transjordanian plateau (Madeba B; Meqabelein; Sahab B). Most were cave, bench or chamber tombs (*contra* Abercrombie 1979: 99), but bowls also predominated in a few pit and cist graves (Ashdod 1111, 1114; Khaldé 121; Lachish 197). In assemblages where the bowl predominated, the most commonly attested forms following bowls were lamps (*contra* Abercrombie 1979: 58), jugs, and then, with equal frequency, juglets, storejars and chalices.

Lamps predominated primarily in cave and bench tombs, but also in some Tell es-Saidiyeh graves. In the twelfth- and eleventh-century BCE Tell es-Saidiyeh cist grave 166, in jar burial 196, and in pit graves 203 and 249, single articulated and disarticulated adults were provided with only a lamp. In twelfth- and eleventh-century BCE cave and bench tomb burials (Aitun C1; Amman-Jebel Nuzha; Tel Dothan; Gibeon), lamps were most commonly accompanied by bowls, followed in frequency by pilgrim flasks and pyxides. In tenth- to sixth-century BCE cave and bench tombs (Dhiban J3, 5, 6, 7; Lachish 106; Mt Nebo UCV-20, UCV-84; Tell en-Nasbeh 3, 5) the lamps were accompanied by juglets and bowls, followed in decreasing frequency by jugs.

	12th c.	*11th c.*	*10th c.*	*9th c.*	*8th c.*
North coast	pilgrim flask		amphora		
	pyxide		bowl		
	crater		plate/platter	cooking pot	
			storejar		
			dipper juglet		
Israel	pilgrim flask		bowl		
	pyxide		plate/platter		
	crater		storejar	cooking pot	
			dipper juglet		
South coast	pilgrim flask				
	pyxide		amphora		
	crater		storejar	cooking pot	
	bowl		dipper juglet		
Shephelah	pilgrim flask				
	pyxide		bowl		
	crater	dipper juglet	storejar		
	lamp		cooking pot		
	chalice				
Southern highlands	lamp		bowl		
	chalice		storejar	cooking pot	
		dipper juglet	dipper juglet	wine decanter	
			plate/platter		
			juglet		
Jordan River Valley	pilgrim flask				
	pyxide		dipper juglet		
	crater				
Transjordanian plateau	pilgrim flask		bowl		
	pyxide	dipper juglet	storejar	cooking pot	
	crater		plate/platter	wine decanter	
	lamp				

Table 8. Prevalent Pottery Forms in Burials from the Twelfth through the Eighth Century BCE.

Bowls and lamps were conspicuous for their absence as a standard mortuary provision in some burial types. While they did occur in small numbers in Tell Abu Hawam and Tell el-Farah (S) burials, bowls were notably missing from cremation, jar, pit and cist graves at coastal sites (Tell el-Ajjul, Atlit, Azor, Tell Bira, Khaldé, Tell Zeror), northern valley sites (Afula, Tell Amal, Megiddo) and Tell el-Farah (S). Beginning in the tenth century BCE the bowl was increasingly included in both highland and lowland burial assemblages. Throughout the Iron Age, lamps were a standard feature of highland burial assemblages, but generally were not included among coastal and valley burial provisions. The Tell es-Saidiyeh examples are not a surprising exception, given their location between the Cisjordanian and Transjordanian highlands. In addition to all the sites where bowls were not present, lamps were absent from pit, cist, jar, anthropoid coffin and cremation burials at Akhzib, Ashdod, Deir el-Balah and Tell er-Ruqeish along the coast, and at Tell Abu Qudeis and Kfar Yehoshua in the north. Burials without lamps frequently contained Egyptian objects; one-third included a scarab or another Egyptian amulet.

Chalices, present in surprisingly consistent numbers throughout the Iron Age, were included in northern and coastal jar burials (Azor, Kfar Yehoshua), pit graves (Ashdod) and stone cist burials (Azor, Tell el-Farah [S]), but they were most frequently supplied in highland cave, chamber and bench tombs.

Pilgrim flasks, pyxides and craters were also conspicuous for their absence. Pilgrim flasks were popular throughout the Iron Age in pit, cist, jar, cave and bench tomb burials at Gibeon and Tell en-Nasbeh to the north, at sites throughout the Shephelah, in the Jordan River Valley and in Transjordan. Their absence from highland sites is striking. Pyxides displayed a similar distribution. Also present throughout the Iron Age, in the same burial types, they appeared in assemblages from the coast (Azor, Tambourit), the northern valleys (Tel Dothan, Megiddo), the Shephelah (Aitun, Gezer), Gibeon, Tell en-Nasbeh and sites in Transjordan (Madeba, Tell es-Saidiyeh), but not in the highland territory of Judah. Craters followed the same pattern; however, they were attested in a Jerusalem tomb on Mt Zion and in a burial from Tell Ira near the Judahite southern border. Each of these three forms, pilgrim flasks, pyxides and craters, in local and imported versions, occurred with a high incidence of Philistine pottery in the twelfth and eleventh centuries BCE, and with Phoenician and Cypro-Phoenician pottery in the tenth through the seventh centuries BCE.

Juglets and dipper juglets emerged as the prevalent form in the tenth century BCE in an urn burial (Tell el-Farah [S]) and pit graves (Atlit iv.a; Lachish 152, 160, 167, 182, 239, 1004), but most frequently in cave, chamber and bench tombs (Bethlehem; Beth Shemesh 2, 4; Ein Sarin; Halif 1968, 6; Jerusalem—Mt Zion; Lachish 116, 120, 218, 224, 6006; Tell en-Nasbeh 32, 54). Even in tombs where the juglet and dipper juglet predominated, the jug, bowl and lamp occurred with virtually the same frequency. The next most common form was the storejar. The popularity of the juglet and dipper juglet may be attributed in part to their aesthetic appeal, and in part to their functions as dippers for liquids in storejars and as vials for scented oils and aromatics in a period when tombs were repeatedly entered and bodies annointed (Stager 1983: 254 n. 11). These burials consistently included Cypriot, Phoenician and Cypro-Phoenician vessels (not infrequently the juglets or dipper juglets themselves), plus scarabs and scaraboids.

Jugs also superseded the lamp and bowl as the prevalent form beginning in the tenth century BCE. In pit graves (Ashdod 1066; Lachish 147) and cave tombs from disparate sites (Aitun A1; Amman C, Jebel esh-Sharqi; Lachish 1002), the jug predominated, most frequently accompanied by bowls, lamps and dipper juglets.

This study demonstrates that lamps predominated in cave and bench tombs. While bowls, juglets, dipper juglets and jugs outnumbered other forms in isolated pit, jar and cremation burials, the vast majority of assemblages in which they predominated were also from cave, chamber and bench tombs.[1]

Vessels for preparing, serving and storing food and wine, including cooking pots, plates, platters, wine decanters and amphoras, were added to burial assemblages in the tenth and ninth centuries BCE. Cooking pots first appeared in bench tombs in the Shephelah (Aitun, Gezer). They were subsequently included in pit graves on the coast

1. J. Abercrombie's correlations between the prevalent pottery form and burial type are not borne out in the cases of his Bowl, Juglet-1 and Juglet-2 patterns. His relative and statistical frequencies of presence of secondary forms were unsubstantiated for the Bowl, Lamp-1, Lamp-2 and Juglet-2 patterns (Abercrombie 1979: 57, 99, 104, 105, 109, 126). This study includes disturbed and incompletely published assemblages which may account for the discrepancies.

(Ashdod, Atlit) and cave and bench tombs in the Shephelah, the central highlands including Samaria in the north and Bethlehem in the south, Jericho and Transjordan. Except for two twelfth-century BCE examples (Megiddo 1101/2 and Tell es-Saidiyeh 129), plates or platters were found in burials whose initial use dated after the tenth century BCE. Simple graves (Atlit), cist graves (Khaldé), cave tombs (Amman, Mt Nebo), chamber tombs (Bethlehem, Tubas) and bench tombs (Akhzib, Beth Shemesh, Dhiban, Halif, Jerusalem, Motza, Mt Nebo, Samaria) contained plates and platters in their assemblages with an unusually high incidence of Phoenician and Cypro-Phoenician imported pottery—not infrequently the plates or platters themselves. Wine decanters and amphoras displayed unique distribution patterns. Wine decanters were added to tomb assemblages beginning late in the ninth century BCE. Except for examples from the Akhzib tombs and Tell Amal pit graves, all other occurrences were from cave or bench tombs in the Beth Shemesh–Jerusalem corridor (Abu Ghosh, Jerusalem, Manahat, Motza), Tell en-Nasbeh, and sites clustered in the Amman vicinity (Amman, Meqabelein, Sahab). Amphoras were found in the twelfth-century BCE Tell es-Saidiyeh mudbrick-walled tomb 41, and in Phoenician coastal simple graves dating from the tenth through the seventh century BCE (Akhzib, Atlit, Khaldé).

In the late thirteenth and twelfth centuries BCE, storejars were concentrated in burials from Egyptian administrative and military posts and from sites which may have served as Egyptian collection centers: Afula, Aitun, Deir el-Balah, Lachish, Megiddo and Tell es-Saidiyeh. Egyptian, Mycenaean and Philistine pottery frequently accompanied the storejars. However, beginning in the tenth century BCE, storejars were recorded in all burial types—with the exception of cremation burials and bathtub coffins—from sites throughout the region: along the coast (Tell Abu Hawam, Ashdod, Azor), in the north (Tell Abu Qudeis, Tel Dothan, Samaria), through the Shephelah (Aitun, Beth Shemesh, Gezer, Lachish), in the highlands (Abu Ghosh, Ez Zahariyah, Jerusalem), at Tell el-Farah (S) and at Dhiban in Transjordan. Cypriot, Phoenician and Cypro-Phoenician vessels replaced the earlier imports.

The distribution of dipper juglets paralleled that of storejars. In the thirteenth and twelfth centuries BCE they were provided in simple graves, anthropoid coffins and chamber tombs at Deir el-Balah, Lachish, Megiddo and Tell es-Saidiyeh. During the twelfth and eleventh centuries BCE they were included in assemblages from cave, arcosolia and chamber tombs at Gibeon, Gezer, Aitun and Madeba, and by the tenth century BCE they were widespread. The imported wares accompanying dipper juglets were similar to those found with storejars. This correlation between the distribution of storejars and dipper juglets suggests that in many instances the two functioned together; the storejars held liquids which were dispensed with the dipper juglet. In Aitun C1, a storejar was found with a dipper juglet still inside it.

Mortuary assemblages illustrate that particular ceramic vessel shapes were preferred at certain sites. Unfortunately, few sites had large numbers of well-preserved burials. From the surprisingly few examples of poorly equipped but reasonably well-preserved pit, cave and chamber burials excavated at Megiddo, the crater and bowl appeared as the most common pottery forms, followed in frequency by the storejar and the pilgrim flask. No associated pottery was reported from the jar burials, and the urn burial was provided with a totally different complement of vessels. At Lachish, the pit, cave and bench tomb interments from the late thirteenth and first half of the twelfth century BCE were accompanied by the lamp and bowl in the greatest numbers, followed by the dipper juglet and storejar. In the second half of the twelfth and in the eleventh century BCE, the jug increased in frequency while the lamp decreased. From the tenth century BCE onwards at Lachish, the dipper juglet, bowl, storejar and jug were the most commonly included ceramic forms, the dipper juglet and jug having replaced the lamp in the standard repertoire. Grouping the Lachish burials by type yields a further distinction. Pit graves consistently contained dipper juglets, bowls, storejars and jugs in decreasing order of frequency. Cave tombs primarily yielded lamps, followed by bowls and dipper juglets with equal frequency, while bench tombs produced dipper juglets and bowls with equal frequency, followed by lamps and storejars. The assemblages in cave and bench tombs were similar, although they showed a slight preference for one form over another. Pit graves, however, displayed a significant difference in the absence of lamps and the frequency of bowls. At Tell es-Saidiyeh, pyxides and bowls were the most commonly provided forms, followed by jars and jugs. Groups of Khaldé pit burials were provided with varying pottery assemblages. The tenth to ninth-century BCE burials 21, 22 and 165 contained jugs, bowls and amphoras, while 166 and 167 included strainer jugs, flasks and pilgrim flasks. In the ninth- to eighth-century BCE burials 1, 2, 3, 4 and 121, the bowl and flask were most common, one item from each of the earlier assemblages.

Tracing the introduction and distribution of imported pottery in burial assemblages illustrates avenues of cultural contacts and trade through the region (figs. 22, 23). Mycenaean, Egyptian, Philistine and Cypriot wares were found in twelfth- and eleventh-century BCE burials (fig. 22). Egyptian pottery was provided among mortuary goods through the thirteenth and twelfth centuries BCE, and perhaps into the early eleventh century BCE with some tenth century BCE examples from Beth Shemesh. The distribution was limited to simple, cist, jar and anthropoid coffin burials. Mycenaean imports were recorded from simple and cist graves, anthropoid coffin burials, and cave and bench tombs in use from the thirteenth through the early twelfth century BCE. Egyptian pottery was frequently accompanied by Mycenaean and Cypriot pottery, suggesting that the Egyptians may have had a part in its distribution. However, Mycenaean and Cypriot pottery also enjoyed a wider distribution than Egyptian pottery at coastal and lowland sites and on the Transjordanian plateau, demonstrating independent avenues of trade for these wares. Cypriot imports, found in tombs in use from the thirteenth through the seventh century BCE, were the only imported wares to begin in the Late Bronze Age and continue well down into the Iron Age. Cypriot pottery has been documented in cist graves (Azor, Deir el-Balah, Tell el-Farah [S], Tell es-Saidiyeh), in cave and chamber tombs (Akhzib, Beth Shemesh, Tel Dothan, Gezer, Irbed, Lachish, Tell en-Nasbeh), and in bench tombs (Akhzib, Amman, Tell el-Farah [S], Gezer), from coastal sites, Shephelah sites, Tel Dothan, Tell en-Nasbeh and sites on the Transjordanian plateau. This distribution was similar to that of Philistine wares, and later Phoenician and Cypro-Phoenician imports. The pottery assemblage in which Cypriot imports most commonly occurred differed from the Philistine repertoire in two ways: it did not include the chalice and crater, and it more closely resembled the Phoenician and Cypro-Phoenician assemblages with bowls, jugs, juglets, jars and lamps. The greatest concentration of twelfth- through tenth-century BCE Philistine pottery was in the region of Philistia and the foothills to the east (Aitun, Azor, Beth Shemesh, Tell el-Farah [S], Gezer, Lachish). However, Philistine vessels were provided in burials at Tell Zeror, Megiddo, Afula and Tell en-Nasbeh, indicating the extent of Philistine or Sea Peoples' settlement and the popularity and availability of their distinctive wares. Philistine wares occurred among an unique assemblage of pottery forms, most frequently including chalices, craters, bowls, lamps and jars, plus Egyptian pottery and scarabs.

Cypriot, Phoenician, Cypro-Phoenician and Assyrian wares were included in tenth- through sixth-century BCE burial assemblages. As mentioned above, Cypriot vessels were noted in cist graves, cave tombs and bench tombs in use from the Late Bronze Age through the seventh century BCE. Both Phoenician and Cypro-Phoenician vessels were provided in tenth- through seventh-century BCE burials, with Cypro-Phoenician imports exhibiting a wider distribution, particularly in the tenth and ninth centuries BCE (fig. 23). Both are attested in assemblages from simple graves, cist graves, cave tombs, bench tombs and cremation burials. Assyrian pottery was introduced into the region in the seventh century BCE. Its distribution was limited to a simple grave from Tell Amal, bathtub coffin burials in Tel Dothan and Amman (the Adoni-Nur tomb), and a bench tomb from Meqabelein on the Transjordan plateau. The Assyrian pottery occurred with a typical late Iron Age complement of ceramic forms including bowls, wine decanters, jugs, lamps and cups.

To summarize, Mycenaean, Cypriot and Egyptian pottery continued to be imported from the Late Bronze Age into the Iron Age. The imports were often found together, particularly at sites with an Egyptian presence. Mycenaean imports ceased at the beginning of the twelfth century BCE, but Egyptian and Cypriot wares continued in burial assemblages dating down to the end of the tenth century BCE and to the first half of the eighth century BCE, respectively. Distinctive Philistine painted pottery appeared as Mycenaean imports ceased in the beginning of the twelfth century BCE, and continued into the tenth century BCE. By the tenth century BCE, Mycenaean and Egyptian imports ceased, and Philistine and Cypriot wares dwindled in number. At this time Cypro-Phoenician and Phoenician vessels appeared. The distribution of Phoenician pottery was limited to burials along the northern coast, but Cypro-Phoenician pottery, primarily juglets, proliferated throughout the region. Cypro-Phoenician vessels displayed a relatively wide distribution—not surprising, given their aesthetic appeal and the multiple functions which juglets and dipper juglets served. In the eighth and seventh centuries BCE, as Cypriot, Cypro-Phoenician and Phoenician imports decreased and eventually ceased,

Assyrian wares appeared in the north and in Transjordan. Egyptian, Phoenician and Assyrian wares were limited in their distribution to regions and sites controlled by, or in the sphere of influence of, the respective nations.

Based on the distribution in burials of prevalent forms and pottery forms in general, on site preferences for particular vessels, and on the incidence of imported wares, three different assemblages are apparent. In the first assemblage, lamps and bowls were a standard feature. This assemblage was characteristically found in highland cave, chamber and bench tombs throughout the Iron Age. The second assemblage typically included pyxides, pilgrim flasks and craters. It was provided in simple, cist, jar and cremation burials dating throughout the Iron Age, situated along the coast, through the Shephelah and in the valleys. Egyptian, Philistine and Phoenician wares were frequently present. The third assemblage consisted of storejars, dipper juglets, and possibly also bowls often accompanied by Egyptian, Mycenaean, Cypriot and Philistine vessels. This assemblage typically occurred in burials at twelfth- and eleventh-century BCE Egyptian administrative/military sites.

During the tenth to ninth century BCE, the three earlier assemblages were replaced by two new ones, a highland and a lowland assemblage. These new pottery repertoires were less dissimilar than their predecessors had been. The inclusion of storejars, dipper juglets and bowls (initially an Egyptian custom) spread throughout both the highland and lowland regions. Beginning in the tenth century BCE, both highland and lowland assemblages were augmented with new pottery forms: locally-made cooking pots, plates, and platters. Amphoras appeared in Phoenician coastal burials beginning in the tenth century BCE, and wine decanters were provided in burials in the vicinity of the capital cities of Jerusalem and Amman beginning late in the ninth century BCE. The new Cisjordanian highland repertoire included lamps, bowls, chalices, jugs and juglets, with the addition of dipper juglets, storejars, plates and cooking pots in the tenth century BCE, and decanters in the ninth century BCE. Few Cypriot and Cypro-Phoenician vessels were included among highland mortuary provisions. The lowland assemblage included pilgrim flasks, pyxides, craters and chalices, and (from the tenth century BCE onwards) dipper juglets, storejars, plates and cooking pots. Mycenaean, Philistine, Cypriot, Phoenician, Cypro-Phoenician and Assyrian vessels typically were provided in this assemblage. Typical forms from both the highland and the lowland repertoires were provided in Transjordanian plateau burials.

Jewelry

Jewelry was a standard item of burial apparel in all burial types and regions throughout the Iron Age. The assortment included beads; metal bracelets, anklets, rings and earrings; bone and stone pendants; and Egyptian amulets often in the form of beads or pendants. A. Wilkinson noted of Egyptian jewelry in particular, although it aptly pertains to jewelry in general,

> There is no way to distinguish between amuletic and ornamental jewellery because so much of the jewellery had amuletic significance. . . people expected to go on living after death in the same manner as they had been living up to that moment, and that they would need not only the magical talismans to help them on their mystical journey but the ornaments they were accustomed to wear. . . Equally, the ornaments they wore during their life-time would often have had protective significance either in the materials or design, or both (Wilkinson 1971: 196).

The symbolic powers of protection and vivification of various colors and shapes were afforded the dead by burying them with colored jewelry, usually beads (Erikson 1969: 136; Brunner-Traut 1975).[1] Metal was also considered to have apotropaic powers, lending the metal bracelets, anklets, rings and earrings this power as well (Gaster 1973: 22; see references in Stager 1985a: 10). Most metal artifacts in Iron Age burials were articles of jewelry. Jewelry does not necessarily indicate the sex of the deceased. An adolescent female and a man wore beads, an adolescent male a ring, and a young girl bangles and earrings.

Beads were the single most common burial provision, appearing in over one third of all burials. The frequency with which beads were provided in burials argues for their inclusion as amulets as well as adornments. Infants (Tel Dothan; Tell es-Saidiyeh 40, 63, 70), children (Beth Shemesh 8; Tell el-Farah [S] 222, 516; Tell es-Saidiyeh 27,

1. In the Beth Shemesh excavation report, D. Mackenzie noted the power ascribed to carnelian: 'today in Palestine it is considered a great curative power against ophthalmia (conjunctivitis)' (Mackenzie 1912–13: 63).

33A, 51, 65, 104, 111, 112, 125, 152, 186, 236, 237, 242, 245, 282), adolescent females (Tell es-Saidiyeh 101; Taanach) and adults, including a man from Tell er-Ruqeish (Megiddo 62; Tell es-Saidiyeh 23, 24, 33, 41, 137, 142, 153B, 159, 174, 176, 187, 192A, 198A, 207, 213, 217, 218B, 225, 232, 249B, 250, 282), were buried with beads. All were cave or bench tombs with the exception of the Atlit pit grave, the Tell er-Ruqeish urn burial, and the simple, cist and jar burials at Tell es-Saidiyeh. The Tell es-Saidiyeh beads were fashioned from glass, limestone, frit, white paste, carnelian and stone. Bead necklaces were preserved on the infant in Tell es-Saidiyeh jar burial 40, on the five- to six-year-old girl buried in simple grave 27, and on the adult buried in cist grave 159. The girl in simple grave 27 and the adult in cist grave 159 also wore bead bracelets (Tubb 1988: 73-80). An eyebead is a round- to cube-shaped blue bead that has whitish eyes with a blackish iris arranged around the bead (fig. 11A). Seven Iron Age burials yielded eyebeads: Gezer cave 8I, dated from the eleventh into the tenth century BCE, and Atlit ii, Beth Shemesh 4, Jerusalem 25, Lachish 106, Meqabelein and Samaria 103, in use from the end of the eighth into the sixth century BCE. Eyebeads have a long history of being regarded as protection for the wearer against the powers of the evil eye (Erikson 1969: 139-40; Gifford 1958: 67-68).

Pendants were the least common article of jewelry. Dating throughout the Iron Age, they were found primarily in cave and bench tombs (Aitun C1; Baqah Valley A4; Bethlehem; Gezer 142; Megiddo 76; Jerusalem 25; Lachish 107, 116, 120, 218, 224, 1002; Mt Nebo UCV-84; Tell el-Rechidiyeh A; Samaria 103), but also in pit and cist graves (Azor D; Tell el-Farah [S] 222; Tell es-Saidiyeh 282). Of the three burials with pendants from which skeletal remains were studied, Tell el-Farah (S) 222 contained two children, Samaria 103 a child and three adults, and Tell es-Saidiyeh 282 seven adults and juveniles. Pendants occurred consistently with Philistine, Cypriot, Cypro-Phoenician and Phoenician imports. In their studies of Late Bronze Age and Iron Age jewelry, both P. McGovern and E. Platt argued for divine favor and protection as the purpose for wearing pendants (McGovern 1980: 305; Platt 1972: 46).

Metal jewelry in the form of bangles, rings and earrings was provided for individuals of all ages and both sexes, in all burial types throughout the Iron Age. Bangles, referring to bracelets or anklets, were the most common articles of metal jewelry. They were provided for infants (Tel Dothan; Megiddo 37B, C2; Tell es-Saidiyeh 63, 120, 161), children (Azor 56; Tell el-Farah [S] 222; Tell es-Saidiyeh 27, 33A, 51, 209, 247, 255) and adults (Tell Abu Hawam II; Azor D; Tell es-Saidiyeh 167, 176, 177, 213, 218A/B, 276).[1] Bangles have been recorded from all burial types except bathtub coffins (perhaps due to the small number of recovered bathtub coffin burials): in simple graves (Atlit, Azor, Tell el-Farah [S], Jericho, Lachish, Tell es-Saidiyeh), cist graves (Azor, Tell el-Farah [S], Tell es-Saidiyeh, Tell Zeror), jar burials (Tel Dothan, Megiddo, Sahab, Tell es-Saidiyeh), anthropoid coffins (Beth Shan, Dhiban), urn burials (Tell el-Farah [S]), cave and chamber tombs (Tell Abu Hawam, Amman, Baqah Valley, Beth Shemesh, Ein Sarin, Ez Zahariyah, Gibeon, Jericho, Lachish, Madeba, Megiddo, Tell en-Nasbeh, Sahab, Tubas) and bench tombs (Abu Ghosh, Beth Shemesh, Tell el-Farah [S], Gezer, Halif, Tell Ira, Lachish, Meqabelein, Khirbet el-Qôm, Sahab). Rings were found on an infant (Tell es-Saidiyeh 248), children including a five- to six-year-old girl (Tell el-Farah [S]; Tell es-Saidiyeh 27, 104), an adolescent male (Kfar Yehoshua) and adults (Tell Abu Hawam II; Megiddo 71). Earrings were also provided for infants (Tell es-Saidiyeh 40), children (Beth Shemesh 8; Tell es-Saidiyeh 27, 33A, 51, 53, 209, 242, 245, 254) and adults (Deir el-Balah 118; Gibeon; Tell es-Saidiyeh 108, 137; Tell Zeror VIII), throughout the Iron Age in all burial types except urn and bathtub coffin burials (figs. 24-26).

Several different Egyptian amulets were provided for the deceased at burial. Most were worn as jewelry, in the form of beads, pendants or pins, and so are included here rather than with models. While they are often dismissed as family heirlooms or merely decorative jewelry, their symbolic and prophylactic functions need to be considered within the burial context. Scarabs were by far the most prevalent amulet, and other common items included various forms of scaraboids, the Eye of Horus, Bes figurines and faience amulets. Many other figurines such as Isis, Sekhet, Bast and Ptah-Sokher were attested in small numbers or single instances.[2]

1. Isaiah 3.16 refers to bangles on women's feet: 'Because the daughters of Zion are so vain and walk with heads thrown back, with roving eye and with mincing gait, making a tinkling with their feet'.

2. For the collected references to Egyptian amulets in Late Bronze and early Iron Age burials, see P. McGovern (1980: 55-71).

The scarab was the Egyptian emblem of rebirth and renewal (Bianchi 1983; Petrie 1914: 22) (fig. 11E). In the twelfth and eleventh centuries BCE, scarabs could have been acquired directly from Egyptians; therefore, their symbolic power as well as that of other Egyptian amulets was probably well-known. Since the amulets appear to have been dispersed through intermediaries in succeeding centuries, their specific meaning in the Egyptian context may have been lost, but the general sense was surely retained. Throughout the Iron Age, scarabs were provided for children (Azor 56; Tell el-Farah [S] 516; Tell es-Saidiyeh 111), adolescents including a female from Taanach (Khaldé 2, 167; Taanach) and adults, including a male from Tell er-Ruqeish (Azor D; Tell er-Ruqeish; Tell es-Saidiyeh 240), but not for infants. From the twelfth through the first half of the eleventh century BCE, scarabs occurred in all extant burial types at sites along the coast (Ashdod, Azor, Deir el-Balah, Tell Zeror), in the northern and Jordan River valleys (Beth Shan, Tel Dothan, Jericho, Tell es-Saidiyeh, Taanach), at Jerusalem and Gibeon, through the Shephelah (Aitun, Beth Shemesh, Gezer, Lachish), at Tell el-Farah (S), and in Transjordan (Baqah Valley, Madeba, Sahab) (fig. 27). These scarabs were frequently found with Egyptian and Philistine pottery, and somewhat less often with Cypriot and Mycenaean imports. Scarabs were usually accompanied by other articles of jewelry, by terracotta rattles, by personal items (e.g. a toggle pin, fibula, stamp or seal), by a blade or arrowhead, and by an additional Egyptian gift, often a Bes or an Eye of Horus. Whereas in the earlier centuries scarabs were accompanied by Egyptian and Mycenaean pottery, beginning in the tenth century BCE they were provided along with Phoenician and Cypro-Phoenician vessels, and their distribution correlated with that of the imported pottery. Scarabs were included in tenth-century and later burials from several new coastal sites (Tell el-Ajjul, Akhzib, Khaldé, Tell el-Rechidiyeh, Tell er-Ruqeish), from Tell el-Farah (S), from new sites in the north (Samaria, Nazareth), from all the previous Shephelah and highland sites plus Tell en-Nasbeh, Halif and Khirbet el-Qôm, from Jericho, and from Dhiban, Madeba and Mt Nebo in Transjordan (fig. 27). All other accompanying goods continued as before, with female pillar figurines being added to the assemblages. The changes in distribution and accompanying imported wares suggest that, although scarabs and other Egyptian amulets initially spread through Egyptian contact or trade, these items spread through trade channels established for Cypro-Phoenician pottery from the tenth century BCE onwards.

The distribution of the Eye of Horus, Bes and 'faience' amulets was similar to that of scarabs, except that they have been recorded in far fewer numbers. The Eye of Horus was an Egyptian amulet designed to invoke good health and security, and it was a standard funerary provision as the symbol of life and the power and ability to conquer death (Borghouts 1973: 148; Budge 1961: 141-42; Gifford 1958: 67; Westendorf 1977) (fig. 13C). These amulets were found primarily in cave tombs in use from the thirteenth through the seventh century BCE (Beth Shemesh 1; Tel Dothan 1; Lachish 107, 224, 570, 571, 1002; Madeba B; Mt Nebo UCV-20), but they were also found in chamber tombs (Tell el-Farah [S] 934; Jericho WH1) and bench tombs (Beth Shemesh 5; Khirbet el-Qôm I). They were also listed among the items found at Deir el-Balah (T. Dothan 1973: 136). Unlike the Eye of Horus, Bes figurines and faience amulets were found in an urn burial (Akhzib 645), in pit and cist graves (Ashdod 1114; Tell el-Farah [S] 201; Tell es-Saidiyeh 104, 112, 117, 142), and in an anthropoid coffin burial (Deir el-Balah 118), as well as in cave, chamber and bench tombs (Beth Shan; Beth Shemesh 1, 5; Tel Dothan 1; Tell el-Farah [S] 914, 934; Jericho WH1; Lachish 107, 116, 224, 570, 1002; Madeba B; Mt Nebo UCV-20; Khirbet el-Qôm I; Samaria 103). The pit graves with 'faience' amulets (Ashdod 1114; Tell el-Farah [S] 201; Tell es-Saidiyeh 104, 112, 117, 142) were among the most poorly provisioned, with no models or personal items, rarely a tool, single items of jewelry—sometimes no more than a bead—and occasionally a scarab. Burials containing Bes figurines or an Eye of Horus were far better supplied, but they were predominantly cave and bench tombs which yielded richer assemblages as a result of their multiple interments. Imports were common, as were articles of jewelry, personal items, blades, arrowheads, and other Egyptian gifts. Virtually all of the cave, chamber and bench tombs contained terracotta models. The rattle was the most popular 'model' in twelfth- and eleventh-century BCE burials containing Egyptian amulets, and the rattle and the female pillar figurine came into their own from the tenth century BCE onwards. Bes was the Egyptian guardian of the dead (fig. 13B) whose second role was to safeguard mothers and their newborn children (Wilson 1975: 80-81). The presence of female pillar figurines (clearly associated with lactation and hence with infants' welfare—see below) correlates well with this second function. Bes was also associated with merriment and dance, which might in part explain why terracotta rattles were included as a mortuary item. Bes' roles as guardian of the dead and protector of newborns, children and their mothers, in conjunction with her involvement with dance, explain the popularity of Bes figurines among burial provisions.

Gold and silver, primarily worked into small pieces of jewelry such as earrings and rings, were found in twelfth- to tenth-century BCE burials along the coast (Azor, Deir el-Balah), at Tell el-Farah (S), in the Shephelah (Aitun, Halif, Lachish), through the northern and Jordan River valleys (Beth Shan, Kfar Yehoshua, Megiddo, Tell es-Saidiyeh), and at sites in Transjordan (Irbed, Sahab) (fig. 28).[1] Throughout the Iron Age, there was no correlation between the presence of gold or silver and the tomb type. After a tenth- to eighth-century BCE hiatus (which may be due to the small sample), gold and silver objects reappeared in seventh-century BCE burial contexts. They were reported from only two thirds as many sites as in the previous centuries. With the exception of Atlit on the coast, all gold and silver was found in Judahite tombs (Tell Ira, Jerusalem, Lachish) and Ammonite burials (Amman, Meqabelein, Mt Nebo, Sahab). Objects made of precious metals were provided for generally well-provisioned individuals, along with Phoenician, Cypro-Phoenician and Assyrian imported vessels, multiple articles of jewelry (including Egyptian amulets), personal items, and blades or arrowheads.

Personal Items

Articles of dress (toggle pin, fibula), grooming (comb, mirror, cosmetic palette, hair clasp), amusement (gaming piece) and individual identification (stamp, seal) are grouped together as personal items.

Toggle pins and fibulae were found in twelfth- to tenth-century BCE and tenth- to sixth-century BCE burials respectively. Most toggle pins were retrieved from cave and bench tombs (Aitun C1; Baqah Valley A4; Beth Shemesh 1; Tel Dothan 1; Tell el-Farah [S] 562, 914, 934; Gezer 142; Gibeon; Lachish 106; Madeba B; Megiddo 1101/2; Tell

1. Gold and silver are among the items most likely to have been removed from a rifled tomb, therefore these data are to be understood as representative and suggestive.

en-Nasbeh 32, 54; Sahab C), although individuals had been provided with toggle pins in Megiddo pit grave 62 and in Tell es-Saidiyeh mudbrick cist 101 and storejar burial 209 (fig. 11D). Virtually all of the fibulae were found in cave and bench tombs (Abu Ghosh; Tell Abu Hawam II; Akhzib; Amman-Adoni-Nur; Beth Shemesh 2, 4, 5; Tel Dothan 1; Gezer 84/5, 142; Gibeon; Jericho WH1; Jerusalem 25; Lachish 1002; Meqabelein, Tell en-Nasbeh 32; Mt Nebo UCV-20; Sahab B; Samaria no number,103; Tekoa). Fibulae were also unearthed in stone cists at Akhzib and Azor and in simple graves at Tell es-Saidiyeh and Taanach. In all but one of the burials from which the skeletons were studied, adolescents or adults were present. The single exception was the lavishly provisioned five- to six-year-old girl in Tell es-Saidiyeh 27. In the three cases where a single sex was identified, it was a female (Tell es-Saidiyeh 27, 101; Taanach). Toggle pins and fibulae consistently appeared in well-provisioned burials along with stamps or seals, scarabs and other Egyptian amulets, terracotta rattles and model horses. The assemblage was further augmented by imported Philistine, Egyptian and Cypriot pottery in the earlier centuries, and by Cypriot, Cypro-Phoenician Phoenician, and Assyrian pottery in the later centuries. These fasteners indicate that bodies were clothed upon burial. However, the small numbers preserved suggest (1) that there was a poor preservation and recovery record, (2) that only select individuals—the wealthy and elite including women—were buried with these fasteners, or (3) that they were used on cloaks or some other item of clothing not commonly worn at burial.[1]

Combs, mirrors, a hair clasp and cosmetic palettes, though few in number, were provided in Iron Age burials. A comb and Philistine pottery were among the provisions in the twelfth- to eleventh-century BCE bench tomb Gezer 59, and three combs and a fragment of a fourth were placed in the generously equipped twelfth-century BCE Tell es-Saidiyeh cist grave 46. Mirrors (fig. 11G) were accompanied by Egyptian, Philistine and Cypriot pottery in the thirteenth- to eleventh-century BCE Azor simple graves, in the mudbrick cist Tell es-Saidiyeh 119 and in the anthropoid coffin burial Deir el-Balah 118. Assyrian pottery was supplied along with the mirrors in the seventh- to sixth-century BCE Amman-Jebel esh-Sharqi cave tomb and in the

1. In 1 Sam. 28.14, the old woman of En Dor raises the dead Samuel who is seen wearing a cloak.

Meqabelein bench tomb. In the two instances in which skeletons were analyzed for age and sex, a female adolescent or adult was present (Deir el-Balah 118; Tell es-Saidiyeh 119). The individuals interred in the Amman-Jebel esh-Sharqi, Azor D and Tell es-Saidiyeh 119 burials were provisioned with a mirror and jewelry but little else. In the remaining examples of tombs with mirrors, Deir el-Balah 118 and the Meqabelein bench tomb, the deceased were more generously equipped. Cosmetic palettes were provided in five burials: the mid-thirteenth- to mid-twelfth-century BCE mudbrick cist Tell es-Saidiyeh 101 and the eighth- to seventh-century BCE cave and bench tombs Amman C, Khirbet el-Qôm I, Sahab B and Samaria 103. Osteological studies revealed that adolescents or adults were always present, with an adolescent female interred in the Tell es-Saidiyeh cist. The young woman was dressed in a garment secured with a toggle pin, lavishly bejewelled, and supplied with a selection of bronze and ceramic vessels. The five- to six-year-old girl in Tell es-Saidiyeh simple grave 27 had been lavishly adorned and provided for, including a bronze clasp in her hair. Osteological analysis has thus demonstrated that combs, mirrors, cosmetic accessories and hair clasps were provided for females at burial.

'Gaming pieces', probably astragali or small ceramic pieces, were recorded in twelfth- to eleventh-century BCE anthropoid coffin burials (Deir el-Balah 116; Beth Shan), a pit grave (Tell el-Farah [S] 222) and a bench tomb (Lachish 521), and from tenth-century BCE and later cave tombs (Lachish 219; Mt Nebo UCV-20, UCV-84; Samaria). The Tell el-Farah (S) grave contained only children (an unusually rich assemblage for children buried alone among the Tell el-Farah [S] burials), but in the two other burials from which skeletal remains were analyzed, only adults or an adult and an adolescent were present and in both cases one of the identified individuals was a male. The gaming pieces were provided in burials at Egyptian controlled or administered sites or with assemblages rich in Egyptian items.

The deceased were buried with stamps (fig. 11B) and seals (fig. 11F) in simple graves, cist graves, anthropoid coffin burials, cave tombs and bench tombs, throughout the Iron Age, in all areas except the remote highlands of Judah. Seals were fashioned from carnelian (Deir el-Balah), bronze (Azor), bone (Samaria), ivory (Amman), steatite (Motza) and chalcedony (Meqabelein). They were shaped into conical stamps (Amman, Tell es-Saidiyeh), button-shaped stamps

(Aitun, Beth Shemesh, Tell en-Nasbeh), rectangular stamps (Amman, Tell es-Saidiyeh), cylinders (Akhzib, Amman, Baqah Valley, Tell en-Nasbeh, Mt Nebo), scaraboids (Halif, Jerusalem—Mt Zion) and finger rings (Deir el-Balah, Sahab). A single example of an eight-sided seal still mounted on a fibula was preserved in a Meqabelein tomb. Both stamp and cylinder seals were deposited in burials throughout the Iron Age. In the twelfth and eleventh centuries BCE, stamps and seals were provided in burials at Egyptian centers and at major sites (Aitun, Azor, Baqah Valley, Beth Shan, Deir el-Balah, Tel Dothan, Tell el-Farah [S], Gibeon, Sahab, Tell es-Saidiyeh) with rich burial assemblages including Egyptian, Mycenaean, Cypriot and Philistine pottery, jewelry, personal items, scarabs and other Egyptian amulets, tools and an unusually high incidence of gold and silver (fig. 29). From the tenth century BCE onwards, stamps and seals continued in the same burial types, but proliferated spreading north along the coast to Azor and Akhzib; through the Shephelah to Gezer, Beth Shemesh, Lachish and Halif; through the Jerusalem region to Jerusalem, Motza and Tell en-Nasbeh; to Samaria in the north; and to the Transjordanian sites of Amman, Meqabelein and Mt Nebo (fig. 29). Only a few seals are attributable to late eighth- to early sixth-centuries BCE contexts, all in the vicinity of the capital cities of Judah and Amman: Jerusalem 25, Mt Zion and Motza burials all in the Jerusalem area, Amman-Adoni-Nur and a Meqabelein tomb in the Amman vicinity, and perhaps the Mt Nebo tombs. All other features continued as before except that the early Iron Age imports were replaced by the later Cypro-Phoenician, Phoenician and Assyrian wares. Stamps and seals appear to have been the prerogative of the wealthy and the societally esteemed: the lavishly provided for children in Tell el-Farah (S) 222, the richly equipped five- to six-year-old girl in Tell es-Saidiyeh 27, an adolescent at Samaria, the three individuals represented by their skulls in Tell es-Saidiyeh 90, and the men and women in Deir el-Balah 116 and 118, the Gibeon tomb, the Jerusalem—Mt Zion tomb and Tell es-Saidiyeh graves 33 and 118.

Personal items were included with less frequency than pottery, jewelry or Egyptian gifts, but with roughly equal the frequency of tools and household items. The small numbers may be due in part to poor preservation and recovery resulting from their small size and fragile nature, and in part to their attractiveness to purveyors of antiquities. However, the small numbers are probably best explained by two factors: they were expensive, and as items of dress, adornment, identification and amusement, they were not requisite for the sustenance or protection of the individual after death.

Tools

A variety of items are grouped together under the heading of tools: blades, spearheads, javelin heads, a chisel, flints, hooks, fishhooks, tongs, tweezers, pins, needles, loom weights, spindles, spindle whorls, a quern, grinding stones and weights. Relatively few tools have been recovered from burials, perhaps because they were not perceived as requisite for the sustenance or protection of the deceased. Assuming tools were included for functional reasons, rather than symbolic or emotional ones, the range of items suggests that the living expected the dead to continue performing daily chores to meet their physical needs after death. Relatively numerous and expensive objects accompanied metal blades, spearheads and javelin heads compared to the meager goods found with flints, spindle whorls, loom weights and other items requisite for domestic chores. These two assemblages document differences in wealth and status of the deceased; these are the burials of the wealthy or elite and of the subsistence workers (figs. 24-26, 30).

Although blades were the most commonly provided tool, they were present in only eight percent of the computed burials. Two-thirds of the examples were found in twelfth- and eleventh-century BCE burials located along the coast (Akhzib; Deir el-Balah 118; Tell Zeror I, III, IV, V, VI, VII, VIII), at Tell el-Farah (S) (542, 552, 562), in the north (Tel Dothan 1; Megiddo 1101/2), through the Shephelah (Aitun 2; Gezer 31, 58U; Lachish 521, 4002), and in Transjordan (Irbed D; Madeba B; Sahab C; Tell es-Saidiyeh 24, 34, 41, 60, 102, 113, 185A, 228, 282). At coastal and valley sites, the blades were all in pit or cist graves, and at the remaining sites they were found in cave, chamber and bench tombs. Nearly one-half were accompanied by Egyptian, Mycenaean, Cypriot or Philistine pottery. A dramatic change in distribution took place beginning in the tenth century BCE. Blades were reported from roughly half as many sites, with none from along the coast. Burials from Judahite foothill and highland sites (Gezer, Halif, Tell Ira, Jerusalem, Lachish, Khirbet el-Qôm, Tekoa), Tell el-Farah (S) and Meqabelein produced the blades. Few imports were recorded with the blades in tenth to sixth century BCE burials. Of the burials with analyzed skeletal remains, none contained only infants or children, all included adolescents or adults. Most frequently males and females were interred together. There were no recorded instances of just females, and only one case with just a male (Sahab C1b).[1] Throughout the Iron Age, blades were included in relatively well-provisioned burials, with jewelry, personal items, Egyptian gifts and occasionally additional tools. In the Tell es-Saidiyeh cist grave 34, the individual was buried with a pilgrim flask plus a bowl, an iron dagger and a scatter of ovicaprid bones overlying the body. Ceramic vessels with ovicaprid bones and a bronze knife were also provided in the Kfar Yehoshua jar burial and a Gezer tomb. These three burials demonstrate that while some blades were placed in tombs as weapons,[2] others most certainly were provided for eating purposes. Tell es-Saidiyeh simple grave 60 contained the single example of a bone blade.

Javelin heads were supplied only in twelfth- and eleventh-century BCE burials: Tell Zeror jar and cist burials (VI, VIII), Tell es-Saidiyeh simple and cist graves (159, 251) and Tell el-Farah (S) bench tombs (552, 960). Spearheads were also all found in twelfth- and eleventh-century BCE burial contexts, from Megiddo, Beth Shan, Gibeon, Tell es-Saidiyeh and Tell el-Farah (S), but none in coastal or Shephelah burials. Half of the assemblages with spearheads included Mycenaean or Philistine vessels, all had jewelry, and virtually all had personal items, Egyptian amulets and additional tools, either a blade or an arrowhead. An adult was interred with just a bronze chisel (fragment) in Tell es-Saidiyeh pit grave 230.

Unlike the previous items, arrowheads appeared more frequently in the tenth to sixth century BCE than they did in twelfth- and eleventh-century BCE burials. With the exception of two simple graves (Lachish 4007; Tell es-Saidiyeh 183), two cist graves (Tell es-Saidiyeh 91, 159) and two urn burials (Tell el-Ajjul; Tell el-Farah [S]), all arrowheads were reported from cave or bench tombs. The early

1. There is the danger of a circular argument: certain items are presumed to be sex-related, and then the item is taken as evidence for identifying the sex of the individual.

2. Ezek. 32.27 refers to fallen warriors buried in battle gear with their sword beneath their head.

examples were from interments at Aitun, Beth Shan, Gezer, Gibeon and Sahab. Beginning in the tenth century BCE, arrowheads were provided in coastal burials (Tell Abu Hawam, Tell el-Ajjul) as well as at a new configuration of sites in the former regions: Samaria in the north, Beth Shemesh, Jerusalem, Lachish, Tell en-Nasbeh and Khirbet el-Qôm in the Shephelah and the highlands, Tell el-Farah (S), and Meqabelein, Amman and Sahab in Transjordan. Arrowheads figured in typical cave and bench tomb assemblages, with the ubiquitous jewelry, a variety of terracotta models, personal items and (infrequently) Egyptian objects or other tools.

The changing distribution of metals demonstrates that what was once the prerogative of the lowland inhabitants was adopted by the highland population (fig. 24-26). The only region where metals were rarely if at all supplied in burials was Philistia. This is surprising given the Biblical reference to the advanced Philistine metallurgy (1 Sam. 13.19-21). Apparently it was not a Philistine custom to include metal objects other than bangles as mortuary goods.

The majority of objects mentioned in archaeological reports were of unspecified metal type. Of the identified items, bronze prevailed over iron throughout the Iron Age. Bronze was the preferred metal for jewelry (the most common item fashioned from metal), while iron was used for blades, small tools such as pins and arrowheads, as well as for jewelry. In twelfth- and eleventh-century BCE burials, a lead ring and steel jewelry were identified in a Tell el-Farah (S) burial and the Baqah Valley A4 cave tomb respectively. From the tenth through the middle of the eighth century BCE, the incidence of metal artifacts dropped markedly and the distribution shifted from the lowlands up into the highlands and to the Phoenician coast (fig. 25). Decreasing incidences of metal objects in burials continued through the sixth century BCE, such that, by the end of the Iron Age, isolated coastal and valley sites produced only single pieces of jewelry or blades, and a reduced number of highland sites east and west of the Jordan River yielded metal objects (fig. 26). Throughout the Iron Age there was no demonstrated correlation between the presence of bronze or iron and burial type.

The following items occurred so rarely that generalizations from their presence or absence are offered with hesitation: flints, grinding stones, spindle whorls, loom weights, pins, needles, hooks, fishhooks, tongs, tweezers and weights (fig. 30). With the exception of weights, all of these items appeared in relatively meagerly provisioned burials. Flints were supplied in simple graves (Lachish 4027; Megiddo 71), cist burials (Azor D; Tell Zeror IV), cave and chamber tombs (Baqah Valley A4; Megiddo 76, 221), and bench tombs (Gezer 58U, 59) dating from the twelfth through the eighth century BCE. The accompanying relatively paltry provisions included Mycenaean, Cypriot and Philistine vessels among the locally-made pottery, jewelry, and rarely any additional objects. At Tell es-Saidiyeh, a grinding stone and carnelian bead accompanied the disarticulated remains in simple grave 13, and a basalt quern and grinding stone and a bead were provided for the infant in storejar burial 243. Spindle whorls (fig. 11C) were reported from pit graves (Ashdod 1122; Lachish 189; Tell es-Saidiyeh 93A), cist graves (Tell es-Saidiyeh 45; Tell Zeror I, VII), cave tombs (Baqah Valley A4; Megiddo no number, 27; Mt Nebo UCV-20) and bench tombs (Abu Ghosh; Akhzib; Tell el-Farah [S] 905; Gezer 9U; Samaria 103). Their initial distribution included sites along the coast and in the north, Tell el-Farah (S), Gezer, Tell es-Saidiyeh and Baqah Valley. Later examples were recorded from additional coastal sites, Samaria, Abu Ghosh, Lachish and Mt Nebo. Spindle whorls were provided in Ashdod 1122 with six adolescents, two males, two females and two others, and in Tell es-Saidiyeh 27 for a five- to six-year-old girl. Given the general paucity of non-ceramic items placed in burials with spindle whorls (bracelets, beads and an occasional fibula or arrowhead), it is noteworthy that nearly two-thirds of the burials contained Cypriot, Phoenician or Cypro-Phoenician imported vessels. A 'bone spindle' was supplied in the richly equipped Tell es-Saidiyeh cist grave 46. Pins, needles, hooks, fishhooks, tongs and tweezers were recovered from cave and bench tombs in the Shephelah and the central highlands (Abu Ghosh; Beth Shemesh 5; Gezer; Gibeon; Halif; Jerusalem 25; Lachish 219, 521, 4027; Khirbet el-Qôm I; Tekoa), with isolated examples being recovered from burials along the coast (Tell Abu Hawam II; Tel Bira), at Megiddo, at Tell el-Farah (S) and in Transjordan (Dhiban J3; Sahab C1a). Weights were provided in the twelfth-century BCE Tell es-Saidiyeh mudbrick-lined and roofed cist grave 191A, the ninth- to eighth-century BCE chamber tomb Lachish 219, and the eighth- to seventh-century BCE bench tomb Khirbet el-Qôm 1.

Models

A variety of terracotta models and figurines were placed in Iron Age burials, although few occurred with any frequency. Human or deity figurines included hollow and solid female pillar figurines, imitation Mycenaean female figurines, male figurines, hermaphrodite figurines and figurines of indeterminate sex. From the animal kingdom, birds and dogs (or horses—the riderless figurine resembles either animal in this simplified form) were represented, as well as horse and rider ensembles. Model thrones, beds and shrines represented the realms of architecture and furnishings. The most common item was the rattle. With the possible exceptions of 'gaming pieces' and rattles for young children, frivolous or amusement items were not included in burial assemblages. Therefore, rather than dismiss these models as 'crude playthings or homely symbols of no intrinsic worth' (Tufnell 1953: 374), they should be regarded as cultural objects selected for inclusion among the limited mortuary repertoire to invoke sympathetic powers on behalf of the deceased and on behalf of their surviving family members. T. Holland argued for the presence of

> some close connections between the objects found in private houses [and tombs] and in definite cultic contexts. . . Most of the Jerusalem material [including many of the model types discussed here]. . . belongs to Iron Age II and is the outward expression of popular 'Israelite' religion derived from Canaanite prototypes (Holland 1975: 326).

Holland is referring to figurines retrieved from the eighth-century BCE Jerusalem Cave 1 and associated cult center, located in proximity to the Temple. The presence of figurines in a 'cult center' near the Temple indicates that either factions with different views on iconographic representations and the acceptability of invoking sympathetic magic coexisted in Jerusalem, or the use of such figurines for sympathetic magic was a practice accepted by all. This question will be addressed below.

Perhaps the most intriguing models to be found in burials are the human and deity figurines. The different types of anthropomorphic figurines exhibited distinctive chronological and geographical distributions. Late Bronze Age to early Iron Age figurines included female plaque figurines, Egyptian *ushwabtis*, Mycenaean figurines, Philistine figurines and a unique figurine found at Madeba (fig. 31).

Hermaphrodite figurines, females with a tambourine (?) and female pillar figurines were provided in burials beginning in the eighth century BCE, though examples were recorded as early as the tenth century BCE. There is lively debate as to the identity of the anthropomorphic figurines; the general tendency is to try to identify them with specific deities. It is noteworthy that P. Ucko's anthropological study of figurines buried in tombs demonstrates that they 'never appear to be deities or symbolic representations of deities', being made and buried for particular reasons or as 'vehicles for sympathetic magic' (Ucko 1962: 46).

Female plaque figurines (fig. 12A) were provided in the late thirteenth- to early twelfth-century BCE Lachish cave tomb 571, the eleventh- to tenth-century BCE Gezer cave tomb 8I and the eleventh- to late tenth-century BCE cist tomb Tell Zeror V. The females stood or lay supine and extended, clasping their breasts. The Lachish female sported a Hathor headdress-like hairstyle, with shoulder length hair curled up at the bottom. The only apparel was a pair of anklets on each leg. In addition to the plaque figurine, Lachish 571 contained Base Ring and Mycenaean imported wares, a storejar (an Egyptian feature in this period), a minipithos, a ring and two Egyptian amulets, Ptah Sokhar and a debased Taurt or a hippopotamus. The Gezer example was accompanied by 'commonplace pots and sherds', a pile of human and animal bones, female pillar figurines, an eyebead and a scarab. The Tell Zeror plaque lay on the bottom paving stones of a stone-lined cist oriented northwest–southeast with four skulls, a bronze bowl, bronze rings, three bronze bracelets and unspecified other items. Both the cist construction and the concentration of bronzes typified Egyptian burial. M. Tadmor has suggested that the women depicted in plaque figurines, usually painted red, were lying on beds in analogy with popular Egyptian New Kingdom sculptures of a person reclining on a bed. Noting a lack of divine symbolism, Tadmor concluded that the figurines represented humans rather than deities, and that their consistent association with burial demonstrated that they were 'in some way connected with funerary practices and customs' (Tadmor 1982: 145, 149). Figurines of females with and without divine symbols, grasping their breasts, were fashioned in Mesopotamia, Syria and the Levant from the second millennium through the Iron Age (Müller 1929: pl. 9 fig. 193). An interpretation will be offered below in the discussion of female pillar figurines.

Other twelfth- to tenth-century BCE figurines provided among mortuary goods included *ushwabtis*, Mycenaean female figurines, a Philistine painted head and a fertility goddess with sheep (?). An Egyptian *ushwabti* (fig. 13A) and four 'naturalistic imitations of stylized Mycenaean III terra-cotta figurines' (fig. 12F) were found together in a Beth Shan northern cemetery sarcophagus (Oren 1973: 123-24). The mold-made *ushwabti* represented a worker or servant destined for continued service in the next life. *Ushwabti* figurines were also provided in Deir el-Balah burials (T. Dothan 1973: 138). The Mycenaean female figurines were similar to examples from Philistine contexts at Azor and Tell Jemmeh (Oren 1973: 124). In the Greek world, such figurines were put in children's burials as 'blessing goddesses' and 'divine nurses' to protect the children during their journey to the nether world. When provided for adults they were interpreted as assuming an attitude of grief and despair (Iakovidis 1966: 45). Mourning women were also depicted on the end panels of the tenth century BCE sarcophagus of Ahiram (Chéhab 1970–71; Porada 1973). A Philistine painted grotesque head in the form of a spout (?) was retrieved from Gezer Tomb 59, a cave in use from the twelfth through the tenth century BCE. The unique figurine identified as a 'fertility goddess with sheep' was found in the cave tomb Madeba B, in use from the second half of the eleventh though the second half of the eighth century BCE (fig. 12C).

The remaining figurine types were not commonly included in burials until the eighth or seventh century BCE. A most distinctive figurine was the hermaphrodite deity in the eighth-century BCE cave tomb Amman A and probably also in Sahab C (fig. 12B). This figurine had a red-painted face with a black beard and mustache, plus breasts and a pregnant belly. There are no close parallels for the Amman hermaphrodite figurine (Holland 1975: 50). The excavator, G. Harding, proposed identifying it with the deity Ashtor-Chemosh (Harding 1951: 37-38).

Three figurines of women in robes or long dresses holding round objects commonly considered tambourines, but more likely to be hand-drums (C. Meyers 1991), were found in the cave and bench tombs Akhzib 60/6, Irbed A (?) and Mt Nebo UCV-84 (fig. 31). Writing of a mold found at Tell Taanach for the production of plaque figurines of women holding similar objects, D. Hillers suggested that these 'cheap sacred objects connected with private cult, with folk religion' depicted a goddess with a tambourine, and 'if not that, then it seems that at least this figurine shows a devotee of a goddess, a songstress or cult-prostitute in service of a shrine' (Hillers 1970: 608, 611). Unless the tambourine, also suggested to depict a loaf of bread, was a divine symbol, the statuette presented no indication of divinity. In her recent study, C. Meyers collected the biblical references to the *tōp* ('hand-drum/frame-drum') and concluded that these figurines represent the women drummers in the drum-dance-song performance who publicly celebrated 'the victory of the Israelite warriors and/or God over the enemies' (Exod. 15.20; Judg. 11.34; 1 Sam. 18.6; Jer. 31.4) (C. Meyers 1991: 21-22). The 'Tambourine Goddess' has a hollow, bell-shaped body and a molded head. A similar figurine with her arms positioned under her breasts rather than holding an object was provided in Mt Nebo UCV-84. The distribution of these figurines does not correlate with that of any other mortuary provision. Perhaps Phoenicians were responsible for the introduction and dissemination of this particular figurine in the region. A similar male figurine with a bell-shaped body and molded head was recorded from a Late Bronze Age sanctuary at Myrtou-Pigadhes on Cyprus (Taylor 1957: pl. VIIc). T. Holland noted the absence of this type of figurine from the Judahite highlands, and suggested a coastal point of origin, perhaps Philistia. He attributed their presence in Transjordan to trade or independent development (Holland 1975: 319; Holland 1977: 125). Functioning trade routes from the Phoenician coast into Transjordan are well-attested by the occurrences of Phoenician and Cypro-Phoenician imported wares, gold, silver, scarabs and other Egyptian amulets in tenth-century BCE and later Transjordanian burials. These figurines could have been transported along the routes established for the above-mentioned goods, or they could have been brought by former coastal inhabitants settling in Transjordan. The meaning of this particular figurine in burial contexts is probably better explained within a Phoenician cultural context than a Judahite context.

The most common figurines were female pillar figurines with solid or hollow conical bodies, hand-fashioned or molded heads, and prominent breasts emphasized by the arms encircling and supporting them. Those with crude, hand-molded faces were labelled 'beak-faced' figurines (fig. 14D) to distinguish them from the more stylish figurines with molded heads (fig. 14C). Although they have been found in domestic contexts in Israel and Judah, these figurines have been reported from tombs only within the territory of Judah. The earliest burial examples were from Shephelah tombs: the eleventh- to tenth-century BCE Gezer 8I, the tenth- to ninth-century BCE Beth Shemesh 1, and the late ninth- to eighth-century BCE Lachish 1002. By the eighth and seventh centuries BCE, these figurines were provided in burials at sites throughout the Judahite foothills and highlands, from Jerusalem in the north to Ez Zahariyah in the south (Abu Ghosh, Bethlehem, Dura, Ez Zahariyah, Gezer, Gibeah, Jerusalem, Lachish, Khirbet el-Qôm) (fig. 31). Beak-faced figurines, ordinarily female, were supplied in the foothill and highland burials of Gibeah, Lachish 106 and 1002 and Beth Shemesh 5 and 8. A beak-face was also modelled on an Ez Zahariyah anthropomorphic juglet. A male beak face figurine and the upper half of a female found together in Beth Shemesh 5 were dubbed a 'divine pair'. The more attractive molded head female pillar figurines, with finer features and short curled hair, were better represented in tomb assemblages. The molded head figurine in the seventh-century BCE tomb Lachish 120 (which contained the remains of more than 1500 individuals with their skulls separated and covered with a layer of animal bones) sported a Greek/Cypriot smile. Only in a seventh- to sixth-century BCE Abu Ghosh tomb were the associated skeletal remains categorized by age but not sex. The tomb contained a single female pillar figurine with the remains of five adults, unfortunately of unspecified sex. The prominent breasts of both the molded head and beak-face types suggest that the figurines' symbolic function was to beseech adequate lactation to sustain newborns and infants. The sympathetic magical powers were presumably invoked not on behalf of the dead but on behalf of their surviving childbearing family members. The presence in tombs of these figurines poignantly illustrates the eighth- and seventh-century BCE Judahites' concern for the welfare of newborns and infants in order to ensure the survival of the family line with its patrimony.

The identity of the female represented as a pillar figurine continues to be hotly debated. The prominent breasts are agreed to indicate a connection with fertility. Accordingly, the figurine has been identified with various ancient Near Eastern fertility goddesses and with mother nature herself: Astarte (Albright 1939; Petrie 1928: fig. 3), Asherah (Ahlström 1984: 136 as the Queen of Heaven; Engle 1979; Hestrin 1987b), Ishtar ('Amr 1988), and the mother goddess, *dea nutrix*

(Hillers 1970; May 1935: 29). Inconclusive evidence identifying the figurine with any particular goddess prompted J. Pritchard to suggest the figurine functioned as a 'talisman associated with child bearing' (Pritchard 1943: 87). The cylindrical body is evocative of a tree or a wooden pole, the biblical cult symbol known as the asherah for the goddess Asherah.[1] References to Asherah/asherah in the eighth-century BCE Kuntillat Ajrud pithos inscription (Meshel 1976), the Khirbet el-Qôm inscription dated to approximately 700 BCE, and the Bible (e.g. 2 Kgs 21.7) demonstrate her/its continued presence in Judah throughout the Iron Age. M.S. Smith mentions several cultic functions of Asherah/asherah, including representing 'the maternal and nurturing dimensions of the deity', divination, and healing (Smith 1990: 84-85). Perhaps, as Smith maintains, 'the symbol [tree, pole, pillar figurine] outlived the cult of the goddess who gave her name to it, and continued to hold a place in the cult of Yahweh' (Smith 1990: 94). It is possible that the figurines had a general rather than a particular cultic association in Judah. The form is evocative of a tree, long depicted in ancient Near Eastern art as a source of nourishment, but identified with different deities at different times and places. The tree, often flanked by feeding twin animals, appeared in Mesopotamian art (Frankfort 1970: 135-37), on the thirteenth-century BCE Lachish ewer (Hestrin 1987b), on the tenth-century BCE Taanach cult stand (Hestrin 1987a), and on an eighth-century BCE Kuntillat Ajrud pithos (Beck 1982: fig. 4). In the Bible, the tree was a symbol of immortality, as illustrated by the 'tree of life' in the Garden of Eden (Gen. 2.9) and a reference to a eunuch as a 'withered tree' (Isa. 56.3). The connection between nurturing female and tree was iconographically depicted on Late Bronze Age medallions from Tell el-Ajjul, Minet el-Beidha and Ugarit showing women sprouting branches between their navel and pubic triangle (Negbi 1976: 1661, 1664, 1680, 1685, 1688, 1692) and in an Egyptian tomb painting of Isis as a tree goddess suckling Tuthmosis III (Hestrin 1987b: 219). There are no divine symbols which identify the female pillar figurines with a particular goddess, except perhaps the conical body meant to evoke the asherah. This form, however, was also attested in Cyprus, where pillar figurines were often modeled to depict men (see below). Whether the

1. The biblical evidence is detailed by S. Olyan (1988), the iconographic evidence by R. Hestrin (1987b), and other literary evidence by M.S. Smith (1990).

figurines represented the goddess Asherah, the cult symbol asherah, an appeal to Yahweh's nurturing concerns (Yahweh having incorporated Asherah's functions into his cult), or simply a superstitious or folkloric practice not associated with any particular deity, their presence in tombs throughout Judah including Jerusalem indicates widespread concern for adequate lactation to nourish newborns and infants, and an acceptance of the use of figurines for sympathetic magic.

In a discussion of women's roles in ancient Israelite religion, P. Bird proposed that women fulfilled religious roles outside the male-defined 'rituals'. One such role was providing for and consulting the ancestors, the mediator between the generations (Bird 1990). The role of 'Mother of Generations' may also be symbolically represented by, and physically embodied in, the female pillar figurines.

Cyprus had a long and developed tradition of terracotta human and deity figurines. Of the large number of published figurines, there were surprisingly few pillar base examples, and they depicted males as well as females. From Enkômi, a latter half of the twelfth-century BCE hollow, female pillar figurine clasping her breasts was depicted with appliquéd features, and painted hair, eyebrows and female genitalia (fig. 14A). J.-C. Courtois noted Cretan parallels (Courtois 1984: 81, fig. 26.1). A male bell-shaped figurine from Myrtou-Pigadhes was mentioned above. The extensive Cypriot collection of figurines including Mycenaean-style women with upraised arms, pregnant women, priests and priestesses, warriors, and male and female deities underscores the limited repertoire of figurines found in Canaan, and thus the importance of the female pillar figurine's function. The figurine's introduction into the Judahite highlands from the Shephelah, a region with well-established trade links throughout the eastern Mediterranean including Cyprus, helps to explain the presence of similar figurines in contemporary Judahite and Cypriot contexts.

A mold and a figurine fragment, perhaps depicting figurines in a similar stance, were reported from the cave tombs Irbed B and Tell en-Nasbeh 54. The Irbed torso apparently belonged to a female with her hands behind her back (R. Dajani 1966a: 88). The Tell en-Nasbeh mold, preserved from the waist down, was said to form a bound male, though a pregnant female is also possible (McCown 1947: 246).

All the remaining types of models occurred primarily in tenth-century BCE or later cave and bench tombs from the Shephelah and Transjordan (fig. 32). Birds (fig. 12D) were provided in the late twelfth-century BCE Gezer 28, the tenth-century BCE Beth Shemesh 1, the tenth- through sixth-century BCE Mt Nebo UCV-84 and the late ninth- to eighth-century BCE Lachish 1002. Bird models were frequently accompanied by Philistine, Phoenician and Cypro-Phoenician vessels. The presence of these imported wares supports the argument that the birds depicted doves, the symbol of Astarte. From this time Astarte was attested as a Phoenician goddess in the Bible (1 Kgs 11.5), in a Tyrian treaty with Esarhaddon (Reiner 1971: 533-34), and in an inscription from Umm el-Amed (KAI 17.1) (Donner and Röllig 1971: 3).[1] However, birds featured in ancient Near Eastern conceptions of death and funerary provisions from Mesopotamia and Syria to Egypt, so that it is difficult to identify or establish the function of the few examples found in the Shephelah and Transjordan.[2]

Quadruped figurines identified as dogs or horses were found in the tenth-century BCE Beth Shemesh 1, the tenth- to sixth-century BCE Mt Nebo UCV-84, the ninth- to eighth-century BCE Aitun A1, and the eighth- to sixth-century BCE Beth Shemesh 2, Jericho WH1, Sahab B and Lachish 106, and perhaps also at Tell Abu Qudeis. A dog statuette might be found in a tomb since cuneiform documents record that dogs were used to ward off demons (Lichty 1971: 26). Horses figured in the sun-cult, a feature of the cult of Yahweh (2 Kgs 23.11; Ps. 68.18; Hab. 3.8, 15) (Ahlström 1984: 220),[3] and so may have been provided in burials. Horse and rider figurines (fig. 12E) were well-attested, so some of these quadrupeds may simply have been horses separated from their riders. Horse and rider figurines have been interpreted as iconographically capturing the arrival of horsemen from the northern steppes, or the Assyrian introduction of cavalry into the region (Tufnell 1953: 377). T. Holland recorded considerable numbers of

1. The bird continued to play a role in the Phoenician conception of death. Philo of Byblos described the rites of Adonis in the sanctuary of Aphrodite of Byblos: 'they first sacrifice to Adonis as if to a dead person, but then, on the next day they proclaim that he lives and send him into the air' (Attridge and Oden 1976: 13).

2. P. Matthaie mentioned the presence of bird figurines in the Ebla tombs at a conference held at Yale in 1982; for Ugarit, see B. Levine and J.-M. de Tarragon (1984: 651); in Egypt, a human-faced bird known as the 'ba' represented the spiritual element of the deceased (Wente 1982: 20). Throughout the Near East the dove served as a divine and a royal symbol (Ahlström 1984: 120).

3. For recent discussions of the solar cult, see M.S. Smith (1988) and J.G. Taylor (1989).

horse and rider figurines from lowland and Transjordanian sites (Holland 1977: fig.1). Only five have been found in burials, all dating from the eighth to the sixth century BCE: Beth Shemesh 8, Lachish 106 and Khirbet el-Qôm I in Cisjordan, and Amman A and Meqabelein in Transjordan.

Models depicting a throne or chair (fig. 13F) were supplied in the tenth-century BCE Beth Shemesh 1, the ninth- to eighth-century BCE Lachish 1002, and the eighth-century BCE and later Tekoa tomb and Lachish 106. The single example of a bed or couch model (fig. 13E) was in Lachish 1002. Furniture models were also found in the non-funerary 'cultic' assemblages of the Samaria trench Locus E207 and Jerusalem Cave 1. These models recall the Ashdoda figurine, a Mycenaean-style female figurine formed into a throne, which was found at Ashdod (M. Dothan 1971: 129, 193, fig. 91). Assuming a Philistine or Aegean origin or inspiration, the presence of these models in the early tombs at sites in proximity to Philistia is attributable to Philistine influence or trade.

A single example of a terracotta 'shrine' (fig. 11H) was placed in a latter half of the seventh-century BCE cave tomb located in the foot-hills of Jebel el-Jofeh esh-Sharqi (Amman). The oval cave contained an undistinguished assemblage of more than 150 objects: jugs, followed in frequency by lamps, typical Transjordanian items such as tripod cups, plus a bronze mirror. A similar model was found in Megiddo stratum VIIb. Perhaps the shrine was placed in the tomb as a representation of the dwelling-place on earth of the divine dead.

Terracotta rattles (fig. 13D) exhibited the widest distribution of the various types of models. They were reported from cave, chamber and bench tombs dating throughout the Iron Age: from thirteenth- and twelfth-century BCE tombs at Dothan, Jerusalem—Dominus Flevit, Tell el-Farah (S), Gezer and Sahab, and from tenth-century BCE and later tombs at Beth Shemesh, Lachish, Manahat, Khirbet el-Qôm and Samaria (fig. 32). In the two instances in which skeletal remains were analyzed, rattles were buried with a child and numerous unspecified individuals in Beth Shemesh 8, and with a child and three adults in Samaria 103. Generally they occurred in rich assemblages with an unusually high incidence of jewelry, arrowheads, scarabs, scaraboids, Eyes of Horus and Bes figurines. Toggle pins, fibulae, stamps, seals, cosmetic palettes and imported Mycenaean, Egyptian, Cypriot, Philistine, Phoenician and Cypro-Phoenician wares were frequently present. O. Tufnell noted that, at Lachish and Gezer, rattles were found exclusively in tombs, not in houses (Tufnell 1953: 376). It was suggested above that rattles may have been provided for purposes of merriment and dance in conjunction with Bes. However, given the limited osteological evidence, their inclusion as a child's toy is also possible.

Other Features of Burial: Stelae, Inscriptions, Animal Bones and Food Remains

Several burial features not included in the previous discussion are presented here. Stelae as burial markers were erected over thirteenth- and twelfth-century BCE Egyptian pit graves at Deir el-Balah and Tell es-Saidiyeh, and over late ninth- to sixth-century BCE Phoenician pit and urn burials at Akhzib and Tell er-Ruqeish. The Phoenicians may have adopted this custom from the Egyptians.[1]

In pit graves (Tell Amal; Khaldé 3, 22, 23), cave tombs (Tell Abu Hawam I, IV; Tel Bira; Tell el-Farah [S] 532; Mt Nebo UCV-84) and bench tombs (Tel Dothan 1; Gezer 8I) dating from the thirteenth through the first half of the eighth century BCE, sherds or small stones were placed over the body, perhaps as a restraint. From the tenth through the eighth century BCE, shaft tombs were cut at Tell Abu Hawam, Nazareth and perhaps the Akhzib eastern cemetery (Makhouly 1941) with a rectangular, grave-shaped pit in the floor to accommodate the body.

Inscriptions were carved into entrance facades and interior walls of five tombs. While most were funerary inscriptions naming the deceased and warning against desecrating the tomb and its contents, there is disagreement regarding some of the inscriptions about whether or not they were funerary inscriptions, about their exact readings, and about whether they were inscribed at the time of burial or at a later date.

A local resident testified to having seen writing on the walls of the

1. In the Bible, burial markers served to preserve the memory of the righteous and men without offspring. A *maṣṣēbâ* marked the grave of Rachel (Gen. 35.20), a *ṣiyyûn* the grave of the unnamed prophet (2 Kgs 23.17), and a *maṣṣēbâ* called *yād* the graves of the childless Absalom (2 Sam. 18.18) and a faithful eunuch (Isa. 56.5).

tomb in Saris and to having defaced it 'lest it [the inscription] should reveal the exact spot [of the treasure] to some more instructed and fortunate seeker' (Hanauer 1889: 184).

Three of the four above-ground monolithic tombs in the Silwan cemetery bore inscriptions: Tomb 3, the Tomb of Pharaoh's Daughter, Tomb 34, published by A. Reifenberg in 1946, and Tomb 35, the Tomb of the Royal Steward. After the doorway was heightened, all that remained of the Tomb 3 inscription were the final two letters, 'd/q/r' and 'r' (Ussishkin 1986: 60). The Tomb 34 inscription reads, '[This is the] burial of z...whoever op[ens] (this tomb)...' (Reifenberg 1948; Ussishkin 1986: 165-72, 217-20). Two inscriptions, the work of different individuals at roughly the same time, were carved in panels in the facade of Tomb 35. The longer inscription preserved over the doorway reads 'This is [the tomb of...] Yahu, who is over the house. There is no silver and no gold. Only his bones and the bones of his slave-wife with him. Cursed be the person who opens this.' After his recent excavations in the cemetery, D. Ussishkin proposed a new reading for the shorter inscription, 'the (burial) chamber beside the burial-chamber carved from the rock' (Ussishkin 1986: 173-84, 221-26). Both of the longer inscriptions were similar to roughly contemporary Phoenician and Aramaic burial inscriptions and have been dated paleographically to the end of the eighth century BCE.

Inscriptions were preserved on the walls of two second half of the eighth-century BCE tombs in Khirbet el-Qôm. The inscription in Tomb I identified the occupants as perhaps siblings: 'Belonging to Ophai, the son of Netanyahu (is) this tomb-chamber' and 'Belonging to Ophah, the daughter (or 'Uzzah the son') of Netanyahu'. The Tomb II inscription has been variously read and dated. W. Dever, who originally published the tomb, read, 'Belonging to Uriyahu. Be careful of his inscription! Blessed be Uriyahu by Yahweh. And cursed shall be the hand of whoever (defaces it!) (Written by) Oniyahu' (Dever 1978: 976). Subsequent translators, including J. Hadley (1987: 51), K. Spronk (1986: 308) and Z. Zevit (1984: 43), have followed J. Naveh in reading Asherah/asherah in the inscription, 'Uriyahu the governor wrote it. May Uriyahu be blessed by Yahweh my guardian and by his Asherah. Save him (save) Uriyahu' (Naveh 1979: 28-30, n. 10).

The inscriptions and graffiti found on the walls of Khirbet Beit Lei Tomb I are generally regarded as prayers borne of distress, inscribed at a later date. J. Naveh first reconstructed and translated the longer inscription to read, '(Yahweh) is the God of the whole earth; the mountains of Judah belong to Him, to the God of Jerusalem' (Naveh 1963b: 81).[1] The second long inscription has been translated, 'The (Mountain of) Moriah Thou hast favored, the dwelling of Yah, Yahweh' (Naveh 1963b: 86), and 'Absolve (us) O Merciful God! Absolve (us) O Yahweh' (Cross 1970: 302). While these prayers were probably not funerary inscriptions, it is significant that tomb walls were deemed an appropriate place for a divine invocation.

Animal bones have been identified in simple and cist graves, jar burials, a cremation burial, and cave and bench tombs. Additional faunal remains were undoubtedly not identified at the time of excavation, particularly in multiple burials containing large quantities of bone. L. Horwitz proposed seven criteria for distinguishing food offerings for the dead from chance animal bone deposits: close association with a tomb or with human remains, a narrow range of animal species, deliberate selection of particular parts of the body, body parts (such as limbs) in articulation, preference for one side of the body, age-based selection and sex-based selection (Horwitz 1987). Although most examples were not scientifically analyzed, the limited number of species represented (known from textual evidence to have been human fare) which were buried in association with human remains, sometimes even in a covered bowl with a knife, demonstrate that these animal remains should be considered food offerings or sacrifices. While food in cave or bench tombs could have been provided for the living who entered the tombs, provisions in simple, jar and urn burials demonstrate that food was intended for the dead.[2] Bowls, jars and jugs were ubiquitously provided, in all burial types throughout the Iron Age, demonstrating the perception that the dead required continued sustenance. Beginning in the tenth and ninth centuries BCE, new ceramic forms were added to tomb assemblages specifically for the preparation, serving and storing of foodstuffs, wine and other

1. See F.M. Cross for an alternate reading (Cross 1970: 301).

2. In the late eighth-century Ashdod locus 1066, two women, one man and skeletal fragments of an additional individual were buried with a jug, six cats and six foreparts of donkey upper jaws. Cat and donkey are nowhere attested as human fare. This offering deviates from all other attested animal remains, and it may be interpreted as a Philistine or Sea Peoples' practice.

liquids: cooking pots, plates, platters, storejars, dipper juglets, wine decanters and amphoras.

The earliest preserved food remains were from simple and cist graves, a jar burial, a cremation urn, and cave and chamber tombs. Four twelfth-century BCE Tell es-Saidiyeh graves contained animal bones. In the brick-lined cist, Tomb 32, an articulated adult lying west–east, together with the skulls and bones of four additional individuals, was buried with bones of a large animal, possibly a cow. In the mudbrick-lined pit, Tomb 34, a bronze bowl, an iron dagger and a scatter of ovicaprid bones overlay a single articulated individual oriented west–east (Tubb 1988: 74). A collection of ovicaprid bones lay next to an adult and child with their heads to the west in the simple grave Tomb 128 (Pritchard 1980: 24). The equid leg buried with a single, disarticulated individual in the simple grave Tomb 198A may or may not have been intended as food (Tubb 1988: 78). In a twelfth-century BCE Tell Kishyon pit grave, on top of the individual lay an upside-down bowl with animal bones in it (Amiran and Cohen, n.d.). The single jar burial from which animal remains were identified was that of an adolescent male buried at Kfar Yehoshua in the twelfth to eleventh century BCE. Ox and pig bones lay near the body, and a vase held ovicaprid bones and a bronze knife (Druks 1966: 214-15). In the earliest recorded cremation burial from the region, the late eleventh-century BCE Azor D63, calcined bones of a human, a bird and domestic animals including pig were interred together in the urn (M. Dothan, field notes). Olive pits, sheep bones, shellfish and fish vertebra were identified in the fourteenth- to twelfth-century BCE Tel Dothan cave tomb (Cooley 1968: 52). In the twelfth- to tenth-century BCE Gezer cave tomb 8I, Macalister noted a pile of human and animal bones (Macalister 1912: I, 81). Elsewhere in a summary discussion of Iron Age tombs, Macalister mentioned one tomb in which 'an earthenware bowl contained some decayed matter in which a few mutton bones were mingled. A bronze knife lay in the midst for cutting the meat and a second bowl was inverted over the deposit, as though to keep it warm until he for whom it was destined should have need of it' (Macalister 1925: 260).

Beginning in the tenth century BCE, most preserved food remains were in cave tombs, but there were also examples from simple graves and bench tombs. Traces of fire, soot and a thin grey deposit were detected in each of the arcosolia of the tenth- to eighth-century BCE

Aitun Tomb 1. Cooking pots and lamps were also blackened with soot, but none of the skeletal remains showed signs of burning (Ussishkin 1974: 125), suggesting that the ash resulted from cooking food, burning spices and lighting lamps. In Lachish cave tomb 218, dated to c. 900 BCE, human and animal bones were found throughout the tomb but concentrated in Room A (Tufnell 1953: 203). In the Akhzib southern cemetery, el Buq-baq, ninth-century BCE inhumations were grouped around a central quadrangle which yielded offerings and unspecified remains of meals (Prausnitz 1969: 86-87; 1975b: 27; 1982: 35). At nearby Tel Bira, bowls containing charred animal bones were deposited with individuals in the ninth- to eighth-century BCE rock-cut simple graves (Prausnitz 1962:143; 1975b). Two men and six others represented by skeletal fragments were provided with remains of small and large cattle in the intramural burial Ashdod Locus 1005 (Haas 1971: 212). In Samaria cave tomb 103, in use during the late eighth century BCE, six holes had been hewn in the floor, some of which had double-rimmed mouths to secure a cover and two of which were connected by a narrow, shallow channel. The holes opened into bottle-shaped rock-cut pits filled with artifacts of pottery, stone, bone and metal, plus ass and ovicaprid bones. The excavators considered these pits 'receptacles of offerings connected with the cult of the dead' (Crowfoot, Kenyon and Sukenik 1942: 21-22). A mass of broken animal bones was found in a recess cut in the far end of the seventh-century BCE cave tomb Amman A (Harding 1945: 67-68). In the latest phase of use, during the seventh century BCE, layers of human bones covered with layers of charred animal bones, mostly pig, were deposited in Lachish cave tombs 107 and 120 (Tufnell 1953: 187, 193-94). Biblical injunctions against eating pig (Lev. 11.7; Deut. 14.8) and Isaiah's rebuke of those 'who sit inside tombs and pass the night in secret places; who eat the flesh of swine, with broth of unclean things in their bowls' (Isa. 65.4) demonstrate that pig was considered human and perhaps divine fare. R. de Vaux concluded that pig was an offering to the chthonic deities or demons (de Vaux 1958: 250-65), a practice which persisted through the time of (Third) Isaiah (65.3-4) and into Roman times (Kennedy 1983:12-13). The Lachish deposits seem to indicate that the dead were to partake of the meal as well. Food was preserved in the seventh-century BCE bench tomb Beth Shemesh 2. Similar to what was found by Macalister at Gezer, a bowl containing sheep bones was covered by a second, inverted bowl (Mackenzie

1912–13: 67). Although there are relatively few instances of actual foodstuffs preserved in burials, the ubiquitous jar and bowl indicate that food and liquids were provided for the dead.[1]

1. Feeding the dead is attested among Israel's predecessors, contemporaries and successors. The Ugaritic text RS 34.126 (KTU 1.161) may speak of feeding the rephaim, the dead royal ancestors, as well as the participants in the ritual (Pardee and Boudreuil 1982; Levine and de Tarragon 1984; Lewis 1989: 5-46). Further examples of feeding the dead are provided by KTU 1.142, which refers to a 'sacrifice by *byy*, son of *sry* to '*ttr*[ ] who is in the grave', and by KTU 1.17: 'Let him have a son in his house, offspring in his palace, one who sets up the stelae of the ancestral gods in his sanctuary, the marjoram of his clan. . .' (see Spronk 1986: 146-51, for a discussion of offerings to the dead). According to C.F.-A. Schaeffer, fourteenth- and thirteenth-century BCE Ugaritic tombs were equipped with pipes leading from occupied and functioning structures directly into the tomb to facilitate replenishment (Contenson *et al.* 1974: 17-18, 21, 24; Margueron 1977: 175-77; Saliby 1979: 105-11; Schaeffer 1929: 285-93; Schaeffer 1931: 2-5; Schaeffer 1933: 96-115; Schaeffer 1934: 114-17; Schaeffer 1935: 146-52, 156-70; Schaeffer 1937: 134-35; Schaeffer 1938: 199-247; 1954: 64; Schaeffer and Armand 1951: 7-8, 16). The relief on the side of the Byblian sarcophagus of Ahiram, dated to approximately 1000 BC or thereafter, portrays the deceased king and before him a table arrayed with meat and bread (Chéhab 1970–71; Porada 1973: 360). The first half of the eighth-century BCE Panammu inscription (*KAI* 214) records the Aramean practice of providing nourishment for the deceased, 'May the soul of Panamu eat with you and may the soul of Panamu drink with you' (Donner and Röllig 1971: 38; Greenfield 1973). Ahiqar instructed his child, 'My son, pour out thy wine on the grave of the righteous/just, rather than drink it with evil men/ignorant contemptible people' (Ahiqar 2.10 [Arabic], 13 [Syriac] [Charles 1913: II, 730-31]) Fifth- to second-century BCE references to feeding the dead include: 'Be generous with bread and wine on the graves of virtuous men, but not for the sinner' (Tobit 4.17), the 'atonement sacrifice offered to the dead' (2 Macc. 12.45), and 'Good things lavished on a closed mouth are like food offerings put on a grave' (Eccl. 30.18). According to early Rabbinic literature, it was customary to provide the dead with food and necessities (Ṣem. 8.7), and 'Sprinkling oil and wine on the dead was tolerated by the rabbis, because of their odoriferous properties' (Ṣem. 7.9) (Lieberman 1965: 509 n. 20).

Chapter 3

BIBLICAL EVIDENCE BEARING ON THE INTERPRETATION OF THE MATERIAL REMAINS OF THE CULT OF THE DEAD

Biblical Names for the Dead

The dead are known by many names in the Bible: *'ᵃbārîm/'ōbrîm* ('those who pass over') (Ezek. 39.11, 14, 15),[1] *'ᵉlōhîm* ('divine ones') (1 Sam. 28.13; Isa. 8.19), *'iṭṭîm* ('mutterers') (Isa. 19.3),[2] *mētîm* ('dead ones') (Isa. 26.14; Ps. 106.28), *nepeš* ('being') (Lev. 19.28; Num. 5.2; Hag. 2.13),[3] *'ōbôt* ('ghosts') (Isa. 29.4) and *yiddᵉ'ōnîm* ('knowing ones') (Isa. 8.19),[4] *peger* ('corpse') (Isa. 14.19),[5] *qᵉdôšîm* ('holy ones') (Ps. 16.3), and *rᵉpā'îm* ('healers'[?]) (Isa. 14.9; 26.14; Ps. 88.11).

1. M. Pope, K. Spronk, and S. Ribichini and P. Xella consider them long-deceased heroes in light of Ugaritic evidence (Pope 1977a: 173; Ribichini and Xella 1979; Spronk 1986: 229-31).

2. The *'iṭṭîm* are understood as ghosts, related to the Akkadian *etemmu* (*CAD*, E, 397-401).

3. M. Seligson gathered the evidence for *nepeš* referring to corpse (Seligson 1951: 78), and H. Saggs revived the interpretation of *nepeš* as 'external soul' (Saggs 1974).

4. H. Rouillard and J. Tropper conclude that *'wb* and *yd'ny* are either 'den weissagenden Totengeist oder den Totenbeschwörer', depending on context. In Isa. 8.19 the dead may be referred to, but in 2 Kgs 23.24 Josiah burned the *'wb* and *yd'ny*, which suggests they were objects constructed of a combustible material (Rouillard and Tropper 1987b: 235-37).

5. See T. Lewis on KTU 6.13, 6.14 (the Dagan Stela) for a discussion of **pgr* as the deceased and the mortuary stela at which offerings were presented (Lewis 1989: 72-79).

Biblical Formulas Indicating Death

In formulaic usage, *wayyiškab* ('and he slept/lay down') applied to kings who died a natural, peaceful death (Driver 1962: 139; Tromp 1969: 169-71), and *wayyāmot* ('he died') to kings following Solomon who met a violent or unnatural death (Tibni, Azariah, Jehoahaz, Jehoram, Ahab, Josiah, Amaziah, Amon) (Driver 1962: 139). *Wayyāmot* was also cited for both Abraham and David, who died natural deaths (Gen. 25.8; 1 Chron. 29.28). *ne'esap 'el- 'ammāyw/ 'ᵃbôtayw* ('gathered to his kin/ancestors') (Gen. 25.8; 35.29; Num. 20.24; Judg. 2.10) has been variously interpreted as meaning depositing the bones of the deceased into the grave (Driver 1962: 141), the union of the deceased with his ancestors in Sheol (Alfrink 1948), having died an ideal, natural death with no reference to actual burial (Rosenberg 1980: 198-99), and (in later occurences), as a euphemism for death and burial (Illman 1979: 43-45). The formula is found exclusively in the so-called P source, and is generally considered related neither to physical death nor to interment. However, it certainly evokes the image of the deceased reunited with family members in the ancestral tomb. Abraham died, *wayyāmot*, and was gathered to his kin, *wayyē'āsep 'el-'ammāyw* (Gen. 25.8). Elsewhere, the formula is followed by *wᵉne'ᵉsaptā 'el-qibrōtêkā* ('you will be gathered to your grave') (2 Kgs 22.20). If these two are understood as parallel phrases, then 'ancestors' are being equated with the 'grave,' and so being gathered to the ancestors was tantamount to burial.

Biblical Forms of Interment and their Significance

Proper burial required interment in a *qeber* (Gen. 23.4; Exod. 14.11; Isa. 22.16) or *qᵉburâh* (Gen. 35.20; Deut. 34.6; Isa. 14.20), a 'burial place'. Tombs, such as Shebna's tomb (Isa. 22.16) and the royal sepulchres (2 Chron. 16.14), were hewn in rock cliffs (see also 2 Kgs 23.16 and Isa. 57.7). *qᵉbārîm* in which commoners (*bᵉnê hā'ām*) were buried are generally understood as pit graves rather than hewn tombs. A common burial field just outside the city gates in Jerusalem's Kidron Valley is mentioned in the stories of Josiah scattering the ashes of a burned asherah (2 Kgs 23.6), Jehoiakim casting out the body of the assassinated prophet Uriah (Jer. 26.23), the ultimate fate of King

Jehoiakim himself (Jer. 22.18-19), and Jeremiah's prophecies of doom (Jer. 7.32-33). The disdain for the locale and those consigned there may be attributed in part to the fact that burial in a simple grave precluded joining the ancestors (which implies a subsequent lack of family veneration and care), and in part to the sometimes objectionable cultic practices performed there, such as the Tophet rites.

The Bible records the burial locations of eponymous ancestors, judges, prophets, kings and other distinguished individuals—the principal players in Israel's theological history. Following death, these individuals were thought to possess special powers and to maintain intimate contact with Yahweh as they had during their lifetimes. Given the presumed posthumous powers of the dead, it was important for the supplicant to know the location of the burial in order to petition the deceased.[1]

Burial in an ancestral tomb served as a physical marker of the family claim to the land. Beginning with the conquest generation, burials were located on the family *naḥ^a^lâ* ('inheritance') (Josh. 24.30; Judg. 2.9). Sometimes burials functioned as territorial boundary markers, as in the cases of Rachel, *biḡbûl binyāmin* ('on the border of Benjamin'), (1 Sam. 10.2), and Joshua, *bigbûl naḥ^a^lātô* ('on the border of his inheritance') (Josh. 24.30) (Stager: 1985a.23).[2] The Decalogue

1. The mid-fourth-century CE Rabbi Pinḥas ben Ḥama said of the tombs of the patriarchs, that the 'occupants were "holy" because they made available to the faithful around their tombs on earth a measure of the power and mercy in which they might have taken their rest in the Above' (Brown 1981: 3).

2. Anthropological studies of the Mae Enga in Melanesia, the inhabitants of the Cycladic Island of Nisos, and the Merina of central Madagascar are just a few of the documented cultures in which religion strengthens the lineage which assures continued family ownership of land.

> Religious and lineage systems reinforce each other both directly and indirectly. . . relative scarcity of arable land among the Mae is a significant determinant of the rigidity of their lineage structure, and that the people emphasize the importance of the continuity of solidarity descent groups which can assert clear titles to the highly valued land. The popular religion is well designed to support these ends. On the one hand, rituals regularly reaffirm the cohesion and continuity of the patrilineal group; on the other, the dogma in itself implies a title to land by relating living members of the group to a founding ancestor who is believed to have first selected that locality for settlement (Meggitt 1965: 131).

commandment to honor (*kabēd*) your father and mother (Exod. 20.12; Deut. 5.16) may refer to the filial obligation to maintain ownership of family property with the ancestral tomb so as to provide 'honor' after death as well as in life (Brichto 1973: 20-32; Milgrom 1976: 338). In the book of Ruth, the *gō'ēl* ('redeemer') re-establishes family control of the patrimony (Ruth 4.5, 10, 14) and thereby assures post-mortem care of the ancestors.

According to the Bible, interment was accorded to all who served Yahweh; sinners were cursed with denial of burial or exhumation (Deut. 28.25-26; 1 Kgs 13.22; 14.10-11; Jer. 16.4), and certain sexual crimes were punishable by burning the individuals involved (Gen. 38.24; Lev. 20.14, 21.9). Most individuals were probably interred in a family tomb, but civic functionaries (such as Shebna) and kings were buried in their capital city (Isa. 22.16). Less fortunate individuals were consigned to the common burial field (2 Kgs 23.6).

The only other form of interment mentioned in the Bible is burial in the Tophet (Jer. 7.32-33). The practice of sacrificing children, 'passing his son through fire' (2 Kgs 21.6), has been verified through excavations in the sacrificial precinct in Carthage (Stager and Wolff 1984). P. Mosca persuasively argues that, taken together, the late eighth-century BCE prophets' knowledge of details of the procedure (Isa. 30.27-33), a reference to sacrificing the first-born (Mic. 6.7), and King Manasseh's sacrifice (2 Kgs 21.6) demonstrate the 'presence and acceptability of child sacrifice within the official Yahwism of the late eighth century' (Mosca 1975: 225).[1] It was not until the reign of Josiah in the second half of the seventh century BCE that the Tophet

On the island of Nisos,

> Houses and fields are passed on from parents to children, with particular items of property going to certain individuals because of the particular Christian names they were given. Ownership of this inherited property entails the duty to perform funeral and memorial ceremonies for the soul of the previous owner; that is, to ensure that the body is buried in the cemetery and is later exhumed for reinterment in an ossuary built beside the chapel whose saint watches over the family lands (Kenna 1976: 21).

For the Merina, see M. Bloch (1982: 211-13); for general theory, see K. Flannery (1972: 28-29) and L. Goldstien (1981).

1. While G. Heider and P. Mosca disagree on the meaning of *mlk*, both contend that the cult involved human sacrifice and that it was accepted practice until the time of the Josianic reforms (Heider 1985; Mosca 1975).

was defiled in compliance with the rediscovered 'Book of the Law' (2 Kgs 23.10). In the late seventh- and early sixth-century BCE writings of the prophet Jeremiah, Tophet sacrifices were attributed to Baal, disclaiming Yahweh's desire for such offerings (Jer. 7.31; 32.35) (Mosca 1975: 227). However, the perseverance of this practice, which was prohibited in the Holiness Code (Lev. 18.21; 20.2-5), is attested to in the Jeremiah references as well as in (Third) Isaiah's scorn for 'you...who slaughter children in the wadis, among the clefts of the rocks' (Isa. 57.5). Remains of this form of death and burial lie undetected under the silt which now fills the Kidron Valley.

Burial Markers

Visible burial markers are explicitly mentioned for righteous individuals and men without offspring. These memorial markers probably served as a locus for death cult activities such as consulting the dead, feeding the dead or offering sacrifices, and perhaps 'calling the name'. Rachel's grave was marked with a *maṣṣēbâ* ('pillar') (Gen. 35.20). On ancestral ground, *bêt 'ᵉlōhîm*, Jacob erected a *maṣṣēbâ* and poured oil on it (Gen. 28.17-18). An unnamed prophet from Judah was buried near the Bethel altar during the reign of King Jeroboam, and his burial marker, *ṣîyyûn*, was recognized three hundred years later in the time of King Josiah (1 Kgs 13.30; 2 Kgs 23.15-18). During his lifetime, Absalom erected a *maṣṣēbâ* called *yad 'abšālōm* ('Absalom's memorial monument') in the King's Valley (2 Sam. 18.18). Yahweh promised the faithful eunuch through his Temple and holy city 'a monument and name (*yād wāšēm*) better than sons and daughters, 'I will give them an everlasting name which shall not perish' (Isa. 56.5; see also 2 Sam. 14.7 and Neh. 2.20). A memorial monument called *yād* ('hand' and 'phallus'—the instrument enabling one's memory to be perpetuated through progeny) was also erected inside the tomb. In a play on words, in which *yād* is used in parallelism with *zikrônēk* ('your memorial'), Isaiah may be referring to illicit fertility rites (Isa. 57.8).

Perpetuating the name of the deceased to insure their post-mortem well being is a documented aspect of the Mesopotamian and Ugaritic death cults, and so has been sought in Israelite practice (Lewis 1989: 118-20; Spronk 1986: 191 n. 2). Absalom erected a marker 'to memorialize my name', *hazkîr šᵉmî* (2 Sam. 18.18). Referring to the dead, without reference to a marker, the author of Psalm 16 declared, 'I will have no part of their bloody libations; their names will not pass my lips' (Ps. 16.4) (Pope *apud* Cooper 1981: 457; Spronk 1986: 334-37).

The burials of Israel's enemies and those who challenged Yahweh's annointed were marked with a *gal-'ᵃbānîm* ('circle of stones'). In this way, Achan, the King of Ai, the five kings of the southern coalition and Absalom (Josh. 7.26; 8.29; 10.26; 2 Sam. 18.17-18) are chastised in perpetuity.

Biblical Descriptions of Burial

According to the stories about the patriarchs, family members were buried together in a cave located on family-owned land. With the exception of Rachel, the patriarchs and matriarchs were interred in the Cave of Machpelah purchased by Abraham (Gen. 49.29-31).[1] To comply with the wishes of Jacob and Joseph to be interred with family, their embalmed remains were carried from Egypt to Canaan for burial (Gen. 47.29-30; 50.2, 13, 25, 26;[2] Exod. 13.19).

Interment at the location of death in proximity to a tree was also attested in this period, as at the time of the United Monarchy. Rebekah's nurse, Deborah, was interred where she died near Bethel under an oak tree, *'allôn* (Gen. 35.8).[3] The cultic significance of the oak was recorded in prophetic admonitions against those who offered illicit sacrifices under the tree (Hos. 4.13) and used its wood to fashion idols (Isa. 44.14-17). Rachel was also buried where she died, on the way to Ephrathah in Benjamin (1 Sam. 10.2).[4] The people of Jabesh-Gilead cremated the bodies of Saul and his sons and then buried their

1. While it is assumed that Jacob was buried in the Cave of Machpelah, Joseph related to Pharaoh his father's wish to be buried 'in my tomb which I hewed out for myself in Canaan' (Gen. 50.5), which would not have been the Cave of Machpelah.

2. The relevant verses from Gen. 47 and 50 have been attributed to the so-called J and E sources (von Rad 1961: 425; Speiser 1964: 317, however verse 13 to P).

3. This description of burial is attributed to the so-called E source (Speiser 1964: 271).

4. P. McCarter explains the variant tradition locating Rachel's burial in the Bethlehem vicinity (Gen. 35.19-20) as a later attempt to associate her burial with Ephrathah in Judah, the ancestral home of David and the site of the present-day 'Tomb of Rachel' (McCarter 1980: 181).

bones under a tamarisk tree, *'ēšel* (1 Sam. 31.12-13). Interment under a tree situated the deceased at the god's shrine, the divine earthly abode. That the tree represented the divine presence was demonstrated by Abraham planting a tamarisk tree and calling on the name of Yahweh at the site where he had concluded a treaty with Abimelech and Phicol of the Philistines (Gen. 21.32-33). Burial under a tree also symbolically served to perpetuate the memory of the individual, for the tree was long associated with immortality as illustrated by the 'tree of life' in the Garden of Eden (Gen. 2.9; see Isa. 56.3—the eunuch as a 'withered tree').

Like Deborah and Rachel, members of the Exodus generation were buried where they died: Miriam in Kadesh (Num. 20.1), Aaron presumably on Mt Hor (Num. 33.39)[1] and Moses in Moab near Beth-peor (Deut. 34.6). Burial at the death locale deviates from the patriarchal practice of communal burial in an ancestral tomb on family-owned land. Perhaps Moses and his family as priestly descendants of Levi (Exod. 2.1) had no territorial claims in Canaan.

The burial sites of only three individuals of the 'settlement generation' have been recorded, one in southern Manasseh and two in Ephraim. According to the book of Joshua all were buried on their *naḥ^a^lâ* ('inheritance'), initiating family tombs which would insure and demonstrate a visible, perpetual claim to the land. Joshua himself was buried on the border of his inheritance in the hill country of Ephraim (Josh. 24.30), Joseph on family land in Shechem (Josh. 24.32), and Eleazar the son of Aaron in the hill country of Ephraim (Josh. 24.33). The only other burial from the 'conquest' period was that of the five Amorite kings killed by Joshua. After being hung from trees, their bodies were thrown into a cave at Makkedah, and the mouth of it was sealed with stones (Josh. 10.26).

By the period of the Judges, family tombs on inherited lands were well established, and so individuals were interred 'in their father's tomb' or 'in their home town'. For Gideon, Samson and Asahel, the Bible specifies that they were buried in their ancestral tomb on family land (Judg. 8.32; 16.31; 2 Sam. 2.32). Only the fact of burial locale is given for the remaining judges: Tola in Shamir, Ephraim (Judg. 10.2),

1. Inserted into the story of the Ten Commandments is a variant tradition describing Aaron's death and his son Eleazar's succession in the priesthood. In this version Aaron died and was buried in Moserah (Deut. 10.6).

Jair in Kamon, Gilead (Judg. 10.5), Jephthah in a town in Gilead (Judg. 12.7), Ibzan in Bethlehem, Zebulun (Judg. 12.10), Elon in Aijlon, Zebulun (Judg. 12.12), Abdon in Pirathon, Ephraim (Judg. 12.15), and Samuel in Ramah (1 Sam. 25.1; 28.3). The desecrated remains of Saul and his sons were retrieved by David and buried in their family tomb in Zelza, Benjamin (1 Sam. 31.8-13; 2 Sam. 21.6, 9, 14).

Beginning with David's reign, kings and probably religious and administrative high functionaries were buried in their capital cities (Isa. 22.15-16; 2 Chron. 24.15-16). David initiated a royal tomb in the City of David (1 Kgs 2.10) and was joined by his son Solomon (1 Kgs 11.43; 2 Chron. 9.31). There is no indication that other family members were buried with them. Burial in the royal tombs was a monarchic prerogative. Other recorded family burials from the period of the United Monarchy include Abner and the head of Ishbaal (Ishboshet) in Hebron (2 Sam. 3.32; 4.12), Ahitophel (2 Sam. 17.23), Barzillai in Gilead (2 Sam. 19.38) and Joab in the wilderness (1 Kgs 2.34).

Following the death of Solomon and the division of the country into Israel in the north and Judah in the south, the monarchs were buried in their capital cities of Tirzah or Samaria and Jerusalem respectively. Of kings and prophets it is recorded that they were sometimes buried near holy sites: prophets of Judah and Bethel (Cogan and Tadmor 1988: 290) in proximity to the Bethel altar (2 Kgs 23.17-18), and later Jerusalem kings adjacent to the Temple. Ezek. 43.7-8 is pertinent:

> The House of Israel and their kings must not again defile My holy name by their apostasy and by the corpses of their kings—at their death (*bāmôtām*). When they placed their threshold (*sippām*) next to My threshold and their doorpost (*m*^{e}*zûzātām*) next to My doorpost with only a wall between Me and them, they would defile My holy name by the abominations that they committed. . . [1]

The death and burial of the kings of Israel are recounted solely, and exceedingly briefly, in the books of Kings. With the exception of Joram/Jehoram and the last ruler Hoshea, for whom no sources are mentioned, the Annals of the Kings of Israel is cited as the source of information. Several kings, including Nadab, Elah, Zimri, Ahaziah, Zechariah and all subsequent kings, were murdered and no details of

1. The tomb doorpost (*hamm*^{e}*zûzâ*) is also mentioned in Isa. 57.8.

burial are cited (1 Kgs 15.28; 16.10, 18; 2 Kgs 1.17; 15.10). The remaining kings except Ahab died natural deaths and were buried in the royal city: Baasha in Tirzah (1 Kgs 16.6), and Omri, Ahab, Jehu, Jehoahaz, Joash and probably Jeroboam II in Samaria (1 Kgs 16.28; 22.37; 2 Kgs 10.35; 13.9, 13; 14.16, 29).

For the burial accounts of the kings of Judah, there are significant divergences between the records in Kings and Chronicles.[1] Kings consistently refers to the Chronicles of the Kings of Judah, whereas Chronicles cites the Books of Shemaiah the Prophet and Ido the Seer (2 Chron. 12.15; 13.22), the Book of Jehu son of Hanani (2 Chron. 20.34), the Book of the Kings (2 Chron. 24.27), the Book of the prophet Isaiah son of Amoz (2 Chron. 26.22; 32.32), the Chronicles of the Kings of Israel (2 Chron. 33.18), the Sayings of the Seers/Hozai (2 Chron. 33.19), the Book of the Kings of Israel and Judah (2 Chron. 27.7; 35.27; 36.8) and the Book of the Kings of Judah and Israel (2 Chron. 16.11; 25.26; 28.26; 32.32). The Chronicler's supplemental information has been discounted as glorifying favored kings and discrediting others. However, the Chronicler may have expressed judgment not through 'manufacturing' new material, but in choosing which references to include and which to delete (Rosenbaum 1979: 29). The consistency of the Kings account may be evidence of an attempt to fabricate a positive record for the Judahite kings in homage to the House of David. Ending the record of a king's reign with the fact of burial with his predecessors in the City of David emphasizes descent from David with its official divine sanction of maintaining the Davidic dynasty.

Judahite kings were buried in the Jerusalem City of David, a small ridge bounded by the Kidron, Hinnom and Tyropoeon Valleys. According to the account in Kings, all kings from Rehoboam through Ahaz were buried with their fathers in the City of David (1 Kgs 14.31, 15.8, 24, 22.51; 2 Kgs 8.24, 9.28, 12.22, 14.20, 15.7, 38, 16.20; Neh. 3.16). Subsequent kings were buried elsewhere, for example Manasseh and Amon in the household Garden of Uzza (2 Kgs 21.18, 26), and Josiah in his own tomb (2 Kgs 23.30).[2] No details of

1. For a discussion of the reliability of the Chronicler's account, see S. Japhet (1985).

2. While I. Provan concurs that the change in formulaic language regarding burial reflects a change in practice beginning with Hezekiah, he cites H.R. Macy who

burial were recorded for Hezekiah or Josiah's successors.

The Chronicles and Kings accounts differ on the burial location of several kings; according to the Chronicler not all kings merited burial in the royal tombs. The Chronicler admits that kings afflicted with illness, which was a divine punishment, were not buried with the others but in their own tombs. Such was the consequence of divine displeasure for Asa (2 Chron. 16.13-14), Jehoram (2 Chron. 21.20), the leprous Uzziah, who was interred in the royal burial field (2 Chron. 26.23),[1] and Ahaz, who was buried within Jerusalem but pointedly excluded from the royal tombs (2 Chron. 28.27). Murdered monarchs were also denied burial with their predecessors in the royal tombs: Ahaziah was simply buried (2 Chron. 22.9), Joash was interred in the City of David but not in the royal tombs (2 Chron. 24.25), Amaziah was buried in a family tomb in the city of Judah (2 Chron. 25.28), and Amnon's burial was not recorded. Josiah may have been buried in a royal tomb—'in the tomb of his fathers' (2 Chron. 35.24). All the remaining Judahite monarchs of whom the Chronicler approved, Rehoboam, Abijah, Jehoshaphat and Jotham, were accorded burial with their fathers in the City of David (2 Chron. 12.16; 13.23; 21.1; 27.9). For the two remaining kings, burial elsewhere is more likely due to cultic censure than to a lack of space. Hezekiah's burial *b^ema^{ʿa}lēh qibrê b^enê-dāwîd* should perhaps be translated as 'on the ascent to the Davidic tombs' (2 Chron. 32.33). He was honored with a *kābôd* by all the Judahites and the inhabitants of Jerusalem, even though he had sinned according to both the Deuteronomist and the Chronicler. His burial was not even mentioned in the Kings account (2 Kgs 20.21). Manasseh's return to Yahweh earned him the

attributes the variations in formulas not to a change in the place of burial, but to a change in scribal conventions of the Deuteronomistic school. Macy unconvincingly suggests that 'buried with his ancestors' was omitted for stylistic reasons, and that 'City of David' was deleted because of the new emphasis on Jerusalem as Yahweh's rather than David's city (Provan 1988: 136, 138).

1. The first-century BCE inscribed funerary tablet of Uzziah, which reads 'the bones of Uzziah, king of Judah, were brought hither; not to be opened' (Sukenik 1931), has been interpreted as further evidence of Uzziah's burial 'in the field [beside] the cemetery of the kings' (Myers 1965: 149, 154). No other king is said to have been buried 'in the burial field' (*biśdēh haqq^ebûrâ*), indicating he received distinctive treatment while still accorded honor and a place of burial 'with his fathers' (2 Chron. 26.23).

Chronicler's praise (2 Chron. 33.12-17), but not a place in the royal tombs. He was buried in his residence, or, according to the King's account, in the palace garden of Uzza (2 Chron. 33.20; 2 Kgs 21.18). G. Barkay locates the garden on the western slopes of Jerusalem, the name deriving from the spot where Uzza was struck down when he touched the ark during the procession into Jerusalem from Kiriat Yearim to the west (2 Sam. 6.6-7) (Barkay 1977: 76-78).[1] Ezekiel's reference to defiling the Temple with the corpses of kings may refer to these later burials on the palace grounds near the Temple (Ezek. 43.7-8). Jehoiadah the priest was also accorded burial with the kings in the City of David (2 Chron. 24.16).

The Chronicler's account preserves details of tomb architecture and funerary practices. Asa's mortuary preparations included laying the body 'in the resting-place (*miškāb*) which was filled with spices of all kinds, expertly blended; a very great fire was made in his honor' (2 Chron. 16.14). The 'very great fire' probably resembled in appearance and intent the burnt-offering sacrifices of sweet savor presented to Yahweh (Gen. 8.20-21; Lev. 1.9, 18). A. Heidel interpreted *m*ᵉ*sārpô* in Amos 6.10 as referring to burning the body as a protective measure against the spread of plague (Heidel 1946: 170). The recent Jewish Publication Society translation is preferable: 'And if someone's kinsman—who is to burn incense for him (*m*ᵉ*sārpô*)—comes to carry the remains [of the deceased] out of the house...' (Tanakh 1988: 1026). A *kābôd* ('honor') was prepared for Hezekiah (2 Chron. 32.33). *kābôd* refers generally to the honor accorded the dead, in this case a monarch. The honor certainly entailed lamenting (1 Kgs 13.30; Jer. 22.18) and offering sacrifices (Isa. 57.7; 2 Chron. 16.14). Subsequent services to satisfy the needs of the deceased and perpetuate their memory were probably also involved.

Isaiah described rock-cut tombs and mortuary practices in a condemnation of the cult of the dead. Isaiah 57, so-called 'Third Isaiah', is usually dated to the last quarter of the sixth century BCE. The text describes Jerusalem bench tombs which had attained their postexilic form by the seventh century BCE. Who was Isaiah addressing, and to whom was he referring? T. Lewis suggested that Isaiah was describing a royal death cult (Lewis 1987: 282). According to S. Ackerman,

1. For other suggestions regarding the location of the Garden of Uzza, see M. Cogan and H. Tadmor (1988: 20).

Isaiah was addressing the whole community of Israel, rather than just the leadership. She conceded that 'some of the worshippers in the community do seem to have considered a cult of the dead a legitimate part of their religious expression' (Ackerman 1987: 173, 236). Following Ackerman, Isaiah was addressing anyone who would listen in an effort to discredit those who consulted the dead and to establish himself as a legitimate prophet. The description need not refer solely to a royal death cult; feeding and consulting the dead were common practices.

The subject of Isaiah's diatribe is the living who perform services for the dead in order to receive the dead's services in return. Isaiah begins with a description of human sacrifice with drink and meal offerings in the wadi (Isa. 57.6) and then turns to rock-cut tombs (Isa. 57.7-8). Both S. Ackerman and T. Lewis, following M. Pope, noted Isaiah's use of fertility cult terminology and imagery, as reflected in Lewis' translation:

> 7: On a high and lofty mountain
> You have placed your bed/grave (*miškāb*).
>
> There too you have gone up
> To offer sacrifice.
>
> 8: Behind the door and doorpost
> You have put your indecent symbol/mortuary stela (*zikkārôn*).
>
> You have tried to discover (oracles) for me (by) bringing up (spirits)
> You have made wide your bed/grave (*miškāb*).
>
> You have made a pact for yourself with them [the dead of v.6]
> You have loved their bed/grave (*miškāb*),
> You have gazed on the indecent symbol/mortuary stela (*yād*).
>
> 9: You have lavished oil on the (dead?) king
> You multiplied your perfumes.
>
> You sent your envoys afar
> You sent them down to Sheol (Lewis 1989: 156).

These verses literally—not metaphorically (pace Hanson 1975: 198 and Ackerman 1987: 267)—describe a bench tomb similar to the Silwan tombs. The tombs were hewn high in the cliff. A framed door (*delet wᵉhammᵉzûzâ*) led into a chamber provided with a resting-place (*miškāb*) for the deceased. Memorial markers at which offerings were presented have not been preserved. However, food and other provisions are well attested in Judahite tombs. The perfume of verse nine is also specified in the *kābôd* ('honor') prepared for king Hezekiah (2 Chron. 16.14, see also Jer. 34.5).

Isa. 57.13 ties all these practices to the issue of inheritance (Ackerman 1987: 188). 'But whoever takes refuge in Me will inherit the land (*yinḥal-'ereṣ*) and will possess my holy mountain.' True inheritance passes not through the ancestral dead, but through Yahweh.

Powers of the Dead

Israelite and Judahite narrative and prophetic passages relate the dead's benevolent and malevolent powers to foretell the future, create life, revive life and exact vengeance. The repeated admonitions not to consult the dead attest to the prevalence of the practice. A wide array of intermediaries were avilable: *'ōbôt* ('diviners'), a *ba'^{a}lat-'ôb* (a woman who consults ghosts) (1 Sam. 28.7-14), *yidd^{e}'ōnîm* ('knowing ones') (Lev. 19.31), *dōrēš'el-hammētîm* ('seeker of the dead') (Deut. 18.11), *ḥōbēr ḥāber* ('magician') (Deut. 18.11) (M.S. Smith 1984), prophets (Isa. 8.19), and even priests (in 1 Sam. 1, Eli probably assisted Elqanah with the *zebaḥ hayyāmîm*). The prescient powers of the dead are best illustrated in the story of Saul and the woman of En-Dor (1 Sam. 28). At Saul's bidding, the woman raised the deceased Samuel, who predicted the Israelite defeat and the demise of Saul and his sons (1 Sam. 28.19). A second example of the dead's presumed prescient powers is preserved in the writings of (First) Isaiah. Yahweh warned Isaiah against those who counsel him to 'inquire of the ghosts (*'ōbôt*) and familiar spirits (*yidd^{e}'ōnîm*) that chirp and moan; for a people may inquire of its divine beings (*'^{e}lōhayw*)—of the dead on behalf of the living—for instruction and message' (Isa. 8.19-20a) (Tanakh 1988: 633). Those 'who sit inside tombs and pass the night in secret places' (Isa. 65.4) were continuing the earlier practice of inquiring of the dead.

Using a figurine for divination may have been preferable to disturbing the dead. Josiah burned *'ōbôt* and *yidd^{e}'ōnîm* along with *t^{e}rāpîm* (2 Kgs 23.24), suggesting they were all objects made of combustible materials, used for related purposes. On the basis of Mesopotamian evidence, K. van der Toorn interprets *t^{e}rāpîm* as ancestor figurines, used both at home and in the public cult for divination (van der Toorn 1990).

The powers of bestowing and reviving life were also attributed to the dead. The dead ancestors' ability to invoke fertility blessings on behalf of surviving family members may underlie the story of Elkanah and his family's annual sacrifice at Shiloh (1 Sam. 1). *zebaḥ hayyāmîm* ('annual sacrifice') (1 Sam. 1.21; 2.19; 20.6), also called a *zebaḥ mišpāḥâ* ('family sacrifice') (1 Sam. 20.29), is here accepted as a sacrifice for the ancestors (see further below).[1] On the occasion of this sacrifice, Elkanah's wife Hannah prayed for a child (1 Sam. 1.11). The dead's miraculous powers of revivification are demonstrated in a story about the prophet Elisha. When a band of marauding Moabites struck a funeral procession, the corpse was expediently thrown into Elisha's tomb. The moment the corpse touched Elisha's bones, the dead man miraculously revived (2 Kgs 13.20-21). Even after death, Elisha retained the power of revivification which he possessed while alive. 2 Kgs 4.17-37 relates how Elisha revived the dead son of the Shunammite woman.

The dead's presumed ability to exact vengeance explains why King David had the hands and feet cut off of Ishbaal's murderers whom he had put to death (2 Sam. 4.12) (Lods 1932: 220). R. Rosenberg detected an awareness of a prohibition against disturbing the dead's rest lest they become vengeful in 1 Sam. 28.15, 'Samuel said to Saul, "Why have you disturbed me and brought me up?"' (Rosenberg 1980: 197 n. 1).

Feeding the Dead

The dead were believed to continue living with benevolent and perhaps malevolent powers, therefore, it is not surprising that the living would want to appease the deceased, including providing nourishment. The most explicit reference to feeding the dead is in a Deuteronomic passage referring to tithed food. Upon presenting the tithe to Yahweh the Israelite vowed, *lō'-'ākaltî b^e'ōnî mimmennû w^elō'-bi'artî mimmennû b^eṭāmē' w^elō'-nātatî mimmennû l^emēt* ('I have not eaten of it while in mourning; I have not cleared out any of it while I was unclean, and I have not deposited any of it with the dead')

1. So J. Morgenstern (1966: 167-77 n. 286), A. Malamat (1968: 173 n. 29), M. Haran (1969a; 1969b; 1978: 304-16; Haran classifies these as 'cultic-familial, non-national observances' of unspecified purpose) and B. Halevi (1975: 108).

(Deut. 26.14). Offering consecrated food to the dead was sufficiently widespread to require a verbal disavowal (see Gen. 28.22, discussed below). The dead were 'divine beings' (*'ᵉlōhîm*), and so consecrated, tithed food was considered their due. This injunction specifies only tithed food; this is not a general injunction against feeding the dead.

Understanding *'ᵉlōhîm* and *'ᵉlōhê 'ābîw* ('gods of his father')[1] as divine ancestors, B. Halevi noted several additional examples of sacrifices to the ancestors. To conclude a covenant of mutual non-aggression, Jacob and Laban set up a stone boundary marker, swore on their ancestral gods and sacrificed to them, *'ᵉlōhê 'abrāhām wē'lōhê nāḥôr yišpᵉṭû bênênû 'ᵉlōhê 'ᵃbîhem* ('May the gods of Abraham and the gods of Nahor—their ancestral deities—judge between us') (Gen. 31.52-54) (Halevi 1975: 109). On the first night of Jacob's journey to Haran, on ancestral land, he dreamt that he was promised land, progeny and a safe trip (Gen. 28.13-15). Upon awakening, Jacob erected a stone as a *maṣṣēbâ* ('pillar') and poured oil on it (Gen. 28.17-18). He then vowed that, in thankfulness for a safe return, he would make a tithe offering at this marker, the *bēt 'ᵉlōhîm* (shrine to the deified ancestors) (Gen. 28.22)—precisely the tithe offering prohibited in Deuteronomy 26.14 (Halevi 1975: 114). Jacob's sacrifice to the god of his father Isaac at the onset of his journey to Egypt (Gen. 46.1) may be a similar case of appeasing the ancestors before undertaking a trip (since no one would be there to provide for and honor them). The ancestors needed progeny to guarantee ownership of the patrimony (with the family tomb), and so would protect them on their travels.

There are additional references to feeding the dead through sacrifices in narrative and prophetic texts and in the Psalms. As M. Pope has pointed out, while they were in Moab, the Israelites adopted local practices including eating the sacrifices of the dead: *wayyō'kᵉlû zibḥê mētîm* (Ps. 106.28b; see also Num. 25.2) (Pope 1977: 217). This explicit reference has been dated to the mid-eighth century BCE or later, and the Numbers account is considered later than that (for references, see Smith and Bloch-Smith 1988: 282 n. 15). Referring to the dead as, *qᵉdôšîm 'ᵃšer-bā'āreṣ* ('holy ones in the underworld'), Psalm 16.3-4 declares, 'I will have no part in their bloody libations',

1. Analogous to the Ugaritic *'il'ib* (*CTA* 17.1.27) (H. Cohen 1978: 73, n. 144).

which were sacrifices for the dead (Spronk 1986: 334-37). The *kābôd* accorded dead monarchs, and presumably others as well, consisted in part of burning sacrifices—a food offering to the dead (2 Chron. 16.14; 32.33; see also Isa. 57.7). (Third) Isaiah's condemnation of the leadership's evil ways included pouring libations and presenting offerings to children buried in the 'wadis' or 'tombs,' as well as sacrificing to those interred in chambers hewn high in the cliffs (Isa. 57.6-7) (Irwin 1967; Kennedy 1989).

The *zebaḥ hayyāmîm* ('annual sacrifice') (1 Sam. 1.21; 2.19; 20.6) and the *zebaḥ mišpāḥâ* ('family sacrifice') (1 Sam. 20.29), mentioned above, were family sacrifices which Elkanah offered annually at the local shrine, and David offered at the time of the new moon (1 Sam. 20.5-6) (Malamat 1968: 173 n. 29). The Codex Vaticanus of the Septuagint adds that Elkanah offered tithed products on the occasion of the *zebaḥ hayyāmîm*, 'Elkanah offered his annual sacrifice and his vows and all the tithes of this land' (1 Sam. 1.21) (McCarter 1984: 55). That tithed food was offered to the dead has been documented above. These sacrifices are here considered familial offerings to the ancestors on the basis of their similarity to the Mesopotamian *kispu*. The *kispu* consisted of invoking the name of the departed, presenting food offerings, and pouring a water libation on the first, sixteenth or twenty-ninth day of the month according to the regional practice. The purpose of the *kispu* was to placate hostile spirits and to invoke the deceased's intercession on behalf of the living to insure family prosperity, and to safeguard the family inheritance (*CAD* 1971: 425-27; J.J. Finkelstein 1966: 113-17).

In Mesopotamia the *paqidum* regularly provided food and drink offerings for a deceased father or relative (J.J. Finkelstein 1966: 115). T. Lewis noted a reflex of the Mesopotamian *paqidum* in the verb *piqdû* used in reference to Jezebel's remains (2 Kgs 9.34). Lewis claims the '*pqd* ritual' was a Canaanite practice introduced into Israelite society by the Omride rulers (Lewis 1989: 120-22). The following examples suggest that caring for the dead was not a foreign practice introduced into Israelite society in the first half of the ninth century BCE, but an integral aspect of the social organization. Moses denied proper post-mortem care to the accused Korahites: *wûpqudat kol-hā'ādām yippāqēd ʿᵃlêhem*, '[these men] are cared for as are all men' (Num. 16.29). In a play on words, David instructed Jonathan what to say should Saul note his absence in court, *'im-pāqōd yipqᵉdēnî 'ābîkā*) ('If your father should miss me'), Jonathan is to relate that David has returned home for a family ancestral sacrifice (1 Sam. 20.6).[1]

In an obscure passage, Yahweh enjoins Ezekiel not to mourn his wife's death, including refusing to eat the 'food of men', *leḥem 'ănāšîm* (Ezek. 24.17, 22). This is probably the *leḥem 'ônîm* of Hos. 9.4 (and probably also Jer. 16.7): 'It shall be for them like the food of mourners, all who partake of which are defiled.' Yahweh also forbids Jeremiah to mourn for his people: 'do not enter a *bêt marzēaḥ*, do not go to lament, and to condole with them' (Jer. 16.5). The *bêt marzēaḥ* appears to have been a fraternal drinking club where mourners sought companionship and consolation.[2]

Sacrifices to the ancestors were offered at various locales: on mountain tops, in wadis, at shrines, in tombs, at *bāmôt*,[3] on ancestral land, at any propitious spot, and perhaps at the *bêt marzēaḥ*. At the spot where his ancestors appeared to him, Jacob erected a stone and poured oil on it (Gen. 28.13-15). Jacob and his kin also sacrificed to their ancestral deities on a mountain and then partook of the meal

1. Ancient Greek sacrifices and rituals for the dead provide a model for studying ancient Israel and Judah (Jameson 1989). For the Greeks, a dead person with continuing power to affect the living was considered a hero. Sacrifices were offered to the dead and the great dead (heroes) to please them; the dead and heroes were invited as guests to full meals of cooked food. Petitioners also appeased the dead and heroes by performing 'powerful actions', sacrifices accompanying an oath or request. Sacrifices to dead and chthonic deities were related to but distinguished from sacrifices to the Olympian gods. Generally, sacrifices to Olympian gods were made on raised altars and worshippers partook of the offered foodstuffs. Sacrifices to the dead, heroes and underworld deities were made on low altars, in a hole in the ground or at a tomb, without the performers eating any of the offered food. The living did not partake of sacrifices to the dead.

Ritual prayer in the Greek cult may also provide a model for reconstructing Israelite practice. Priests controlled access to the deities at the shrines, but no priest was needed if a household invoked 'a household form of Zeus by means of sacrifice in his own courtyard' (Jameson 1989: 963).

2. See also Jer. 16.8 and Amos 6.7. M. Pope strongly advocated the funerary character of the *bêt marzēaḥ* (Pope 1981: 176-79). See K. Spronk (1986: 196-202) and T. Lewis (1989: 80-94) for a summary of the data and current interpretations.

3. W.F. Albright (1957: 246-47) and R. de Vaux (1965a: 58) advocate ancestral sacrifices at *bāmôt* ('high places'). P. Vaughan (1974), W. Barrick (1975) and M. Fowler (1982) critique Albright's view.

(Gen. 31.53). Elkanah and his family sacrificed and partook of food and strong drink at the shrine in Shiloh (1 Sam. 1.3). David's family celebration took place at an unspecified location in his home town (1 Sam. 20.29). Sacrifices in wadis and in tombs cut in the cliffs are recorded in Isa. 57.6, 7. In his study of 'high places', W.F. Albright insightfully concluded,

> Biblical references to veneration of heroic shrines (e.g. Rachel and Deborah), cult of departed spirits or divination with their aid, and high places in general add up to a much greater significance for popular Israelite belief in life after death and the cult of the dead than has hitherto appeared prudent to admit (Albright 1957: 257).

Death Cult Proscriptions[1]

Nowhere in the Bible are Israelites and Judahites forbidden to feed the dead. However, there was an important exception. The dead, though divine, were not to be offered tithed food (Deut. 26.14).

Consulting the dead directly is also not expressly forbidden in the Bible (depending on the identity of *'ōbôt* and *yidd*[e]*'ōnîm*). However, according to the Deuteronomic and Holiness Law Codes, priests, prophets and all Israel were denied the services of intermediaries who put them in contact with the dead. Recourse to the *šō'ēl 'ôb w*[e]*yidd*[e]*'ōnî w*[e]*dorēš 'el-hammētîm*, 'one who consults ghosts or familiar spirits or one who inquires of the dead', was forbidden to all priests (including the Levites) and prophets in the Deuteronomic Law Code (Deut. 18.10-11). In the Holiness Code, the entire people of Israel was instructed not to turn to the *'ōbôt* and *yidd*[e]*'ōnîm* ('ghosts' and 'familiar spirits') and thereby become impure, for Israel was a chosen, sanctified nation (Lev. 19.31). These prohibitions presuppose the powers of the dead. Necromancers were stoned to death (Lev. 20.27) and their clients cut off (**krt*) from the community (Lev. 20.6). In the Holiness Code, the verse following the admonition against consulting necromancers instructs the Israelite to 'rise before the aged, show deference to the old and revere your ancestors' (*w*[e]*yārē'tā mē'*[e]*lohêkā*) (Lev. 19.32). B. Halevi suggested the phrase 'you shall fear your ancestors' implies that fearing the dead brings

1. I am indebted to my husband M.S. Smith for guidance in preparing this and the following section. Expressed herein are not family views but my own.

protection for the living (Halevi 1975: 101-10).

Stories of the dead's powers were preserved in northern literary traditions. Rachel's and the unnamed prophet's burial markers were duly noted (Gen. 35.20; 1 Kgs 13.30). The woman of En-Dor conjured up the prescient Samuel (1 Sam. 28),[1] and the deceased Elisha miraculously revived a dead man (2 Kgs 13.20-21) (R. Wilson 1980: 192, 202-206).

The cult of the dead functioned in Judah as it did in Israel. Jacob offered ancestral sacrifices (Gen. 28.17-18). Absalom erected a burial marker in his lifetime (2 Sam. 18.18). In the second half of the eighth century BCE, prophets consulted the dead when Yahweh was 'hiding His face' (Isa. 8.19-20). The *kābôd* accorded the late eighth-century BCE King Hezekiah probably involved post-mortem activities. Hezekiah's son Manasseh was later denounced for his cultic practices, which included consulting necromancers. The lack of explicit references to a cult of the dead in Judah may be due to the limited number of narratives such as the Elijah–Elisha cycle, and the desire of later editors to create the impression of the apostasy of the north compared to the faithfulness of the south.

In the Bible, men, but not women, who enjoyed a special relationship with God during their lifetime were recorded as having been empowered upon death. These attributed post-mortem powers explain why biblical tradition preserved the burial location of judges, prophets and kings. David's crippling of Ishbaal's dead murderers (2 Sam. 4.12) and the presence of female pillar figurines in tombs (see above) suggest the possibility that commoners, perhaps even women, were also thought to be empowered upon death.

On the one hand, a cult of the dead appears to have been a significant and ongoing component of Israelite and Judahite society. The dead lay claim to the patrimony, counselled descendants and invoked fertility for offspring. On the other hand, the Bible includes legislation restricting contact with the dead through purity laws and prohibitions against offering tithed commodities to the dead. Necromancers are condemned to death, their clients banished, and proponents of the cult are ridiculed.

1. 1 Sam. 28.3 claiming Saul banished necromancers from the land was probably a Deuteronomic addition. For references, see M.S. Smith and E. Bloch-Smith (1988: 281 n. 12).

Purity laws distanced the living from the world of the dead by decreeing ritual impurity from physical contact with the dead. Touching a corpse, a human bone or a grave (Num. 19.11, 16), entering a tent following a death (Num. 19.14), physical contact with an unclean person (Num. 19.22), or killing or touching the slain in battle (Num. 31.19) rendered an individual impure. There were further restrictions for priests. According to the Holiness Code, a priest was permitted to contract impurity from a corpse only for an immediate family member (Lev. 21.1-3), but the High Priest was forbidden to defile himself by a corpse even for his parents (Lev. 21.11). The consecrated Nazirite was subject to the same law as the High Priest (Num. 6.6-7). These laws served a double function. They insured the purity of the highest religious functionaries, and, at the same time, for the high priest and the Nazirite they precluded the improper appearance of a priest consulting the dead.

Purification entailed being sprinkled on the third and seventh days with water mixed with hyssop and the ashes of a heifer sacrificed as a sin offering, and on the seventh day washing all garments and bathing in water to attain ritual purity at nightfall (Num. 19.9, 12, 17-19; 31.19). A priest was required to prepare the 'water of purification', but any clean individual could administer it. While these rituals were intended to provide cultic purification, their lengthy duration discouraged contact with the dead. The penalty for not undergoing the lengthy purification procedure was **krt*, 'being cut off' (Num. 19.13, 20). This section detailing the preparation and use of purification water following contact with the dead could be relatively old, since most societies perceived a need to mediate relations between the worlds of the living and the dead.[1]

**krt* was an ingenious punishment for those who consulted the dead through mediums or did not submit to the lengthy purification process after contact with the dead. 'Being cut off' meant severing family ties with the consequent loss of inheritance and a place in the family tomb.

1. Anthropological studies document the dead as 'polluted' (Bloch 1982: 215-17), and the meeting point of the living with the dead as a 'boundary between polarities' which is 'both ambiguous and sacred' (Leach 1977: 70). In anthropological terms, 'In the interstitial, interfacial realm of liminality. . . the dead are conceived as transformative agencies and as mediating between various domains normally classified as distinct' (Turner 1977: 38).

The loss of inherited lands deprived those who were cut off of any future contact with their ancestors thereby incurring ancestral wrath and perhaps vengeance. **krt* may also have precluded the possibility of future nourishment and honor from their own descendants.

The earliest opposition to the cult of the dead may be preserved in the northern Covenant Code, which mandates *ḥerem* ('proscription') for anyone sacrificing to divine beings other than Yahweh (Exod. 22.19). The dead are not specified in the Deuteronomic Law Code parallel section (Deut. 13.1-18). There the objectionable divinities are 'other gods, whom neither you nor your ancestors have known' (Deut. 13.7, see also v. 3).[1] Neither the Deuteronomic Law Code (Deut. 12–26) nor the Holiness Law Code (Lev. 17–26), which prohibits consulting necromancers, has been conclusively dated. Both attained a composite form in the second half of the seventh century BCE or later, but both probably incorporate earlier material (Alt 1968: 133-71; Boecker 1980: 187, 188; Haran 1971: 824; Knohl 1987; Noth 1965: 128). A late eighth- to seventh-century BCE date coincides with the first prophetic objections to mortuary cult activities and the Hezekian-Josianic reforms instituted after the fall of the north.

Prophetic and Deuteronomic objections to the cult of the dead began in the eighth and seventh centuries BCE. (First) Isaiah, an upper-class Jerusalemite prophet who served king Hezekiah (2 Kgs 19–20) (R. Wilson 1980: 215, 219, 270-71), provided the earliest explicit and datable objection to death cult activities. Yahweh warned him not to be tempted by those who propose that he seek his prophecies from the dead when Yahweh 'is hiding His face from the House of Jacob' (Isa. 8.17-20). This passage should be considered in conjunction with the Deuteronomic description of a true prophet: one who, among other things, does not consult the dead (Deut. 18). Isaiah was asserting his status as a 'true' prophet. On the subject of the *bêt marzēaḥ*, Jeremiah preached that Yahweh had withdrawn his favor from those who eat and drink in the house of mourning (Jer. 16.5-7). Two narrative passages prohibiting and condemning death cult activities have been attributed to the Deuteronomist(s). The Deuteronomist inserted a verse claiming Saul had banished necromancers from the land into the story of the king's consulting the necromancer at En-Dor (1 Sam. 28.3)

1. For a discussion of the relationship between the Covenant Code and the Deuteronomic Law Code see D. Patrick (1985: 85, 97, 107-109).

(Smith and Bloch-Smith 1988: 281-82). The Deuteronomist has also been credited with the recitation of Manasseh's deplorable cultic practices including consulting necromancers (2 Kgs 21.6) (Cross 1973: 285-86). The author of Psalm 16 (Ps 16.4) and (Third) Isaiah (Isa. 57.6, 13; 65.4) condemned those who went to the dead for their services.

A Historical Explanation for Judahite Yahwistic Opposition to the Cult of the Dead

Beginning in the latter half of the eighth and the seventh century BCE, death cult legislation was introduced or revived in Judah. What precipitated the change in attitude expressed by Isaiah, the Deuteronomic and Holiness Law Code promulgators and the author of Psalm 16? These authors and promulgators attempted to discourage contact with the dead and to invalidate those who attained knowledge from the dead by prohibiting priests and prophets from consulting the dead, by killing necromancers, by invalidating the dead's powers, and by ridiculing proponents of the cult and blaming the fall of Israel on such practices. While the legal regulations and proscriptions and prophetic rhetoric create the impression that 'official' circles were attempting to eradicate the cult of the dead, only certain facets of the cult were being suppressed. The Deuteronomic and Holiness Law Codes do not forbid consulting the dead directly, but only consulting the dead through intermediaries (Lev. 19.26, 31; 20.6, 27; Deut. 18.10-11). There is no general injunction against feeding the dead; however, diverting tithed food to the dead, while not legally prohibited, was discouraged (Deut. 26.14).

B. Lang has offered a historical reconstruction to account for changes in attitude towards the cult of the dead. Following Morton Smith, Lang postulated an eighth-century BCE prophetic movement which advocated the exclusive worship of Yahweh—the 'Yahweh-alone Party' (YAP). The true god, once acknowledged, was expected to intervene and save Israel. As part of their agenda, the YAP 'insisted on reducing, if not outlawing, the cult of the dead' (Lang 1988: 149). Following the Assyrian conquest of Israel, YAP advocates became more zealous in their cause and moved south into Judah. Their tenets were embodied in King Josiah's reforms, which promoted a centralized cult for the exclusive worship of Yahweh. Lang (1988: 150) claims:

> By taking the decisive step towards monotheism, the reform drastically reduced private worship, especially the ritual activities relating to the dead. The only ceremony still tolerated was the placing of food in or near the tomb as a funerary offering. What used to be a real sacrifice was now reduced to a simple gesture of convention. The dead may be fed and therefore kept alive, but any other contact was forbidden.

According to Lang's reconstruction, the northern traditions adopted in Jerusalem deemed sacrifices to the dead ineffectual, and they prohibited contact with the dead.

The evidence does not accord with Lang's reconstruction. The reasons for curtailing death cult activities were more complex than the emergence of a YAP. First of all, following the fall of the north, Judah, and especially Jerusalem, was beset by a refugee population (see below) including cultic personnel who needed to be integrated into or excluded from the Jerusalem cult. Secondly, the fall of the northern kingdom necessitated a theological response. The late eighth- to seventh-century BCE Hezekian–Josianic reforms were initiated to resanctify the people Israel and to centralize the Yahwistic cult in Jerusalem (Clements 1965; Weinfeld 1985). This policy blaming Israel's demise on its religious infidelity (2 Kgs 17.7-23) served to strengthen the Jerusalem Temple cult by defining what was proper behavior for the priest, the prophet and all Israel. As part of the effort to centralize both worship and cultic personnel, the dead were deemed an inappropriate source of knowledge. Formerly the dead could be consulted at various locales, either directly or with the aid of shrine or *bāmôt* personnel, prophets or necromancers. Towards achieving centralization and resanctification, necromancers had to be eliminated and true priests and prophets were identified as those who attained their knowledge not from the dead but from Yahweh alone 'in the place where He causes his name to dwell'.

Opposition to the cult of the dead involved religious, political and economic motives. Jerusalem priests and prophets hoped to purify and centralize the Temple cult, resanctify the people Israel and assert their status as faithful servants of Yahweh. In this way they would insure their livelihood as the only acceptable intermediaries of Yahweh and as beneficiaries of the tithe. Curtailing mortuary cults also served the interests of the central government. Breaking down clan fidelities, which were fostered by ancestral cults, would strengthen the central government. Rather than acting in the interests of the clan, individuals would pledge allegiance to the king empowered by the national god.

In Judahite culture, the dead were an integral part of the social organization. Individuals believed that their descendants would nourish and care for them following death, just as they had provided for their predecessors. Moreover, the legitimacy of land holdings was validated by the ancestral tomb, and the prosperity of the land may have been thought to be insured or blessed by benevolent ancestors. Disrupting the mortuary cult represented a radical move. Neither the existence of powerful dead nor the efficacy of necromancy could be negated. However, in the late eighth- seventh-century BCE Hezekian–Josian reforms, the promulgators of the Deuteronomic and Holiness Law Codes, together with prophets (notably Isaiah), adopted societal regulations and taboos regarding the dead, devised sanctions, and denounced mortuary activities in order to strengthen their own positions. The views which they advocated were designed to preserve the functions and holiness of prophecy and priesthood, and to protect the holiness and current practice in the Temple. According to this reconstruction of the biblical evidence, there was little or no change in attitude or practices among the inhabitants of Judah towards the dead. Rather, the legislation reflects a policy change initiated in the eighth and seventh centuries BCE by the palace and Jerusalem Temple Yahwistic cult authorities.

Chapter 4

SUMMARY AND CONCLUSIONS

Summary of Archaeological Evidence

Burial Types and Their Distribution

Burials from throughout the southern Levant have been studied here in an effort to define Judahite burial practices and to trace their origin and development. Eight different burial types were distinguished. Body treatment, mortuary goods and form of the receptacle or space housing the body were the determinants of the types. Strong correlations among all the features enable the labelling of seven of the types by the receptacle or the space housing the body. The eight types are (1) simple, (2) cist, (3) jar, (4) anthropoid coffin, (5) bathtub coffin, (6) cave and (7) bench tomb burial, and (8) cremation burial.

Simple or pit graves were ordinarily dug into the sand or loess, although some examples were hewn out of bedrock (fig. 1). The graves contained one to three inhumations; in the case of multiple interments, one was usually an infant or child. A bowl and jar were characteristically provided. Additional gifts included locally-made and imported pottery, beads, a scarab, and a metal bracelet, anklet, ring or earring. These graves exhibited a strikingly limited distribution in the Late Bronze Age and throughout the Iron Age: along the coast, through the continuous Jezreel, Beth Shan and Jordan River Valleys, and at the sites of Lachish, Amman and Dhiban (figs. 16–18). Simple graves were one of several burial types used by the population referred to by the biblical writers as 'Canaanite'. The persistence of this agglomeration of distinctive burial types including simple graves demonstrates that the population known as Canaanite remained culturally distinct throughout the Iron Age. The pit burials of animals, decapitated bodies and skulls at sites along the coast from Azor south to Tell er-Ruqeish and at Tell es-Saidiyeh in the Jordan River Valley may preserve Philistine or Sea Peoples' burial practices.

To construct a cist tomb, a rectangular space roughly two meters long and one meter wide was lined with stones or mudbricks, and occasionally the floor was paved with cobbles and a superstructure erected (figs. 2, 3). Like simple graves, cists ordinarily accommodated one to three inhumations, and in the case of multiple burials one of the inhumations was ordinarily an infant or child. Large stone-lined cists, constructed for multiple burials and repeated use, held bodies and their accompanying provisions stacked in layers. In addition to the mortuary goods supplied in simple burials, cist tombs yielded metal artifacts including daggers, blades and wine sets. Cist tombs, like simple graves, were used in lowland regions: along the coast and in valleys. Unlike simple graves, they have not been found at inland, highland sites (figs. 16–18). Cist tomb burial was practiced by the population referred to in the Bible as 'Canaanite'. Some cist graves may have been Egyptian or Egyptianizing burials. Among the Egyptian features of the Tell es-Saidiyeh burials were the west–east orientation, a mudbrick superstructure, burial markers, Egyptian linen body wrappings, bitumen encasing the body, unusually high incidences of metal artifacts, a large number of jars including alabaster and calcite examples, and the absence of bowls and lamps among the mortuary provisions.

For jar and pithoi burials, the vessel neck was removed to enable the body to be inserted. The filled vessel was then frequently capped with a bowl, a stone or the base of another jar (fig. 4). Ordinarily a single jar sufficed for an infant or child, and two jars placed mouth-to-mouth (or unusually large jars) accommodated adults. While most jars were set in pits in the ground, two examples were placed in mudbrick and stone-lined cists, and some later examples were deposited in tombs. The majority of jar burials contained infant inhumations, but children, adolescents and adults were also interred in jars. Infants were frequently buried without provisions or with only a shell. Older individuals' mortuary goods typically included a bowl, often a lamp and a jug, beads, rings, bracelets and shells. The distribution of jar burials was similar to that of simple and cist graves, but was confined to Transjordan and northern Cisjordan. Twelfth- and eleventh-century BCE burials followed the Late Bronze Age distribution: along the coast, through the valleys and in the Galilee. Later examples were concentrated on the Transjordanian plateau (figs. 16–18). Jar burial is generally considered to have been introduced into the region from Anatolia or northern Syria.

Anthropoid coffins consisted of an approximately two-meter-long ceramic box tapered at one or both ends, with a modelled lid depicting a human face and upper body (fig. 5). The Deir el-Balah coffins held from two to six inhumations, at least one of which was an adult male. Among the accompanying provisions were a high percentage of Egyptian vessels, pottery imitating or inspired by Egyptian types, Egyptian scarabs and other amulets, *ushwabti* figurines, and jewelry. Local and imported pottery, blades, spear heads, a javelin head, seals and gaming boards were also present. Undisturbed anthropoid coffin burials have been recovered from pit and cist graves as well as from cave and bench tombs. Evidence for the Egyptian origin of this practice includes their occurrence in Egypt proper, their limited distribution beginning in the late thirteenth century BCE at southern Levantine sites with an attested Egyptian presence (figs. 16–18), the Egyptian-style head depicted on some lids, an hieroglyphic inscription on a Lachish coffin, and the high incidence of Egyptian and Egyptianizing provisions. The Deir el-Balah multiple burials with women and children have been interpreted as interments of Egyptian administrative or military personnel with their families.

Two twelfth-century BCE wooden coffins were preserved in Sahab Tomb 1. The first coffin contained an infant and the second a warrior. Deir el-Balah provided a single example of a limestone coffin.

Bathtub coffins are named for their characteristic shape: a deep bathtub-shaped vessel approximately one meter long with one rounded end and one squared end (fig. 6). This burial type has been found in a simple grave, a rock-cut tomb and palace courtyards. Skulls, bones and ceramic vessels were the sole retrieved contents. The introduction of the type into the region in the late eighth century BCE, its distribution at northern valley sites and the capital cities of Jerusalem and Amman (fig. 18), together with the unusual burial context and accompanying Assyrian Palace Ware, demonstrate that the practice was introduced into the region and employed by Assyrians.

For cave tomb burials, bodies and accompanying objects were deposited in natural or hewn caves (fig. 7). The reported examples are most frequently located in the soft chalk and limestone outcrops of tell slopes or nearby wadi cliffs. The deceased was laid out near the center of the cave with the mortuary provisions positioned around the body.

When space was required for additional burials, individuals' skeletal remains and provisions were moved to the cave periphery. All ages and both sexes were buried together in caves. This is the only burial type in which the percentage of infants most closely resembles the conjectured infant mortality rate. Distinctive practices noted from isolated caves included the separating of skulls from the rest of the body, the depositing of large quantities of animal bones among or on top of human bones, and the burial of calcined bone. A commensurate number of goods accompanied the large numbers of individuals buried in cave tombs. Locally made bowls, lamps, jars, jugs and juglets predominated, with a wide assortment of other local and imported ceramic forms, tools, household items and personal possessions. Burial in caves was the predominant highland type in the Late Bronze Age and into the first centuries of the Iron Age (figs. 16, 20). Beginning in the tenth century BCE, with increased highland settlement the number of sites employing cave tombs grew. In succeeding centuries, as the bench tomb gained in popularity in the Cisjordanian and Transjordanian foothills and highlands, a decreasing number of sites utilized cave tombs. The continued but decreasing use of the cave tomb may be explained in two ways. One possibility is that some Judahites buried their dead in caves rather than bench tombs because they required less time and labor to prepare. A second possibility is that the indigenous highland population, identified in the Bible as Amorites and others, continued to live in and around the highlands to the east of the Judahites, and to bury their dead in caves. In this case, cave burial is an indicator of non-Judahite or Yahwistic affiliation.

The Akhzib, Silwan Village, and perhaps Tel Mevorakh and Tyropoeon Valley tombs may constitute a distinctive type. These chamber tombs were either constructed of ashlar blocks or hewn from bedrock with square chambers and flat or gabled ceilings. The exceptionally fine workmanship is usually credited to the Phoenicians.

Bench and arcosolia tombs were of similar plan. A square to rectangular doorway in a rock-cut facade led down into a chamber with arcosolia, loculi or benches arranged around the perimeter of the room. Occasionally, additional roughly square chambers were hewn with benches aligned along the walls. Individuals were laid out supine on the benches with their heads on stone pillows or headrests when provided. When space was required for another burial, a previous burial and at least some accompanying goods were moved to a repository pit usually cut under a bench or in the rear of the tomb. All the elements of this classic Iron II bench tomb plan were present in the region by c. 1200 BCE. The two different tomb plans which displayed the elements were the Middle and Late Bronze Age circular chambers with recesses still in use at Gezer and Lachish, and the square to rectangular bench tombs of Tell el-Farah (S). A third plan exemplified by the Aitun tombs was not adopted in Judah (fig. 10).

Of all the tomb types, bench/arcosolia tombs displayed the most noteworthy change in distribution. In the Late Bronze Age and at the onset of the Iron Age, such tombs were employed at coastal, lowland and Shephelah sites (figs. 16, 21). Their use subsequently spread from west to east through the southern foothills and up into the highlands, from the Jerusalem area south, and through Transjordan (fig. 17). From late in the eighth century BCE through the fall of the southern kingdom in 587/86 BCE, the bench tomb constituted the overwhelming preference for Judahite burials as illustrated by examples from twenty-three different sites (fig. 18). The identification of the bench tomb as the typical, official Judahite form of burial is confirmed by its distribution throughout the kingdom and by its virtually exclusive use in Jerusalem. It is unclear how early the bench tomb was adopted by the Judahites, or when the bench tomb burying population first identified itself as Judahite. Therefore, for the twelfth and eleventh centuries BCE the burial evidence illustrates that the cultural group burying their dead in bench tombs was concentrated in the Shephelah. Adoption of the bench tomb on the Transjordanian plateau paralleled the process in Cisjordan, but in Transjordan several different burial types were practiced contemporaneously in contrast to the virtually exclusive adoption of the bench tomb in Judah.

Grave goods were similar to those provided in contemporary cave tombs: local and imported pottery, household items and personal possessions. Lamps, bowls and jugs were the most common ceramic forms, followed in frequency by jars and juglets. A change in the repertoire of pottery forms and other provisions occurred in the tenth century BCE. At that time, several coastal-lowland and Egyptian objects and ceramic forms were added to the highland bench and cave tomb mortuary assemblage. The new pottery forms were all utilized in the preparation, serving and storage of foodstuffs and liquids.

Three forms of cremation burial have been uncovered: (1) pyre burials in the sand, (2) cremated bodies interred in urns, amphoras or jars (fig. 9), both primarily from coastal sites, and (3) partially cremated remains or cremation strata from inland cave tombs. One possible explanation for pyre and urn burials occurring side-by-side is that urn burial was a secondary form of interment for cremated individuals who could not be buried immediately. Infant, child, adolescent and adult remains have been identified in urns. Accompanying goods were scant. Scarabs and other Egyptian amulets, red-slipped and Samaria wares, Cypro-Phoenician vessels and locally-made bowls, jugs and juglets were the most commonly provided items. The earliest southern Levantine cremation burial was at Azor in the second half of the eleventh century BCE (fig. 16). The majority of cremation burials dated from the middle of the tenth through the beginning of the seventh century BCE (figs. 17, 18). This unusual treatment of corporeal remains, the preponderance of Phoenician and Cypro-Phoenician vessels, and the distribution of this burial type, collectively demonstrate that it was introduced into the region by the Phoenicians.

The large number of tombs excavated in Jerusalem provides a unique opportunity to examine the growth of the nation's capital. Bench tombs have now been found cut into hillsides encircling the Old City: to the east, the Mt Scopus tomb; to the southeast, the Silwan and Kidron Valley tombs; to the south and west, the tombs excavated by R.A.S. Macalister and C. Schick, and the tombs at St Andrew's Church, the Sultan's Pool, and those located under the present day Old City wall; and to the north, the tombs in the Coptic Church, in the Greek Praetorium on the Via Dolorosa, on Suleiman Street, on the grounds of the Monastery of the White Sisters and on the grounds of St Etienne, plus the Garden Tomb. Within the modern city of Jerusalem, tombs have been reported from Shimon Hazadiq Street to the north, Talpiot to the south, and the Knesset gardens and Mt Herzl to the west.[1]

A chronological ordering of the tombs demonstrates the growth of Jerusalem's population with the consequent need for new burial grounds. This discussion presumes that burials were extramural, with the exception of the royal interments. The Silwan tombs and the City of David tunnels were the earliest burials, dating from the ninth century BCE. This tomb evidence suggests that Jerusalem was still quite

1. M. Broshi, G. Barkai and S. Gibson provide a topographical map with the tomb locations marked (Broshi, Barkai and Gibson 1983: 32).

small and only the civil and religious authorities were buried in the capital, so the Silwan cemetery sufficed. As the population increased in the eighth and seventh centuries BCE, new burial grounds were designated as demonstrated by the tombs in the Church of the Holy Sepulchre, on Suleiman Street, on the White Sisters' grounds and on Nablus Road (the Garden Tomb) to the north, and by the tombs cut in the Tyropoeon Valley, on Mamilla Street (?), and under the present day Old City walls to the west. With the fall of the northern kingdom and the consequent population influx into Jerusalem, the city expanded north to the line of the present day northern Old City walls. The Wadi er-Rabibi/Ben Hinnom Valley and St Etienne tombs have been dated to the seventh century BCE, and the tombs at St Andrew's Church to the seventh or sixth century BCE. It was only in the seventh century BCE or slightly later that the southern and southwestern extents of the Ben Hinnom Valley began to be utilized for rock-cut burials. Perhaps this area, like the Kidron Valley, had previously been devoted to burial practices considered by some to be illicit. Perhaps the previous Jerusalem burial grounds were full. Jeremiah's denunciation of the Tophet ends with the curse of burial in the Tophet, *mē'ên māqôm*, literally, 'for lack of room' (Jer 7.32).[1]

The Jerusalem tombs were exceptional in the quality of their workmanship, the value of the provisions, the number of individuals accommodated, and the adoption of foreign features. Architectural details such as sunken panels and right-angled cornices, Hathor-wig and horseshoe-shaped headrests in place of the conventional pillow, and sculpted benches to cradle the reposed body were features found almost exclusively in Jerusalem tombs. Some of these tombs were intended for a limited number of individuals, as indicated by the stone sarcophagi carved from the bedrock and the small number of 'resting-places', with no repository for additional remains. These tombs accommodated the likes of Shebna (Isa. 22.15-16), who chose to be buried in the capital city with his slave-wife rather than with the generations in a family tomb. Jerusalem tombs also exhibited foreign burial features. Phoenician burial inscriptions and platforms with altars placed directly above the tomb and the imposing pyramid-shaped roofs were adopted in the Silwan and the Tyropoeon Valley tombs.

1. So R. Carroll (1986: 220), but W. McKane and Tanakh translate, 'until no room is left' (McKane 1986: 178; Tanakh 1988: 784).

Human Remains and Accompanying Provisions

The following generalizations regarding age- and sex-specific provisioning are based on a limited sample of primarily simple, cist and jar burials in which there was no doubt as to the recipient of the objects. Given that the selection of mortuary goods was culturally determined, these generalizations, which are based on primarily lowland burial assemblages, might not be true for highland cave and bench tomb burying populations.

Mortuary goods were differentiated on the basis of age, sex, social status and wealth. There were notable exceptions. Some young children were lavishly provisioned, but, in general, the relative wealth of the burial goods correlated with the age of the interred individual. The older the person buried, the greater the value of the accompanying objects. All ages and both sexes were interred in all burial types from which osteological remains have been studied. Infants were consistently the most minimally equipped, usually with no more than beads, a ring or a bracelet. These paltry provisions reflect perceived needs in the afterlife rather than family poverty. Children received the same gifts as their elders, but in fewer numbers: bowls and other vessels, beads, a scarab and tools. Rattles may also have been supplied for children. Both infants and children were interred singly in jars, in vessels placed in cave and bench tombs among other individuals, and with older individuals in simple graves, cist graves, anthropoid coffins, caves and bench tombs. Adolescent and adult males were frequently supplied with a blade or arrowhead; additionally the adult received a seal and, rarely, gaming pieces. Adolescent and adult females were provided with bowls and other vessels, beads, a scarab, cosmetic accoutrements, and occasionally a toggle pin or fibula. There were distinctions in relative wealth observable among mortuary assemblages. Elements of a poor assemblage included flints, spindle whorls, 'faience' and beads, but no metal jewelry. Lavish assemblages were equipped with metal vessels such as a wine set; imported ceramic wares; a rich assortment of jewelry; personal items, particularly seals; metal items such as toggle pins, fibulae, mirrors, blades, spearheads or javelin heads; and gold and silver. Metals and imported goods were the prestige items of the Iron Age.

Although the various burial types differed in conception (as reflected in multiple versus individual burial, inhumation versus cremation) and in the choice of specific goods provided for the deceased, they all contained the same categories of goods at comparable relative frequencies. Ceramic vessels and jewelry were most common, personal items and tools less so.

Nourishment in the afterlife was of paramount importance. An open vessel such as a bowl or crater for food, and a pilgrim flask, chalice or jar for liquids, were the most common forms, frequently accompanied in highland burials by a lamp for light. Beginning in the tenth century BCE, bowls, storejars with dipper juglets, plates/platters, cooking pots, wine decanters and amphoras were widely adopted into the mortuary repertoire. These new vessel forms functioned in the preparation, serving and storing of food and liquids. Two tombs contained a bowl containing sheep bones and a knife, with a second inverted bowl covering it. Numerous other examples of food remains preserved in tombs have been detailed above.

After ceramic vessels, jewelry was the second most common item provided in burials. The dead were perceived as vulnerable in their new condition, as they had been while alive, and perhaps even more so. For this reason, they were regarded as needing the sympathetic protective powers invested in the colors, materials and designs of jewelry. Beads, pendants, Egyptian amulets and metal jewelry served this purpose. The presence of the female pillar figurine in tombs is also best explained as an appeal to sympathetic powers. In this case the dead were thought to intercede on behalf of their surviving family members.

Personal items such as articles of grooming, dress, amusement or identification, household items and tools occurred with the least frequency in all burial types throughout the period. Economic considerations do not explain the relative incidence of different items, for although metal blades or seals may have been relatively expensive, readily available objects such as spindle whorls, flints and gaming pieces were also present only in small numbers. Perhaps the continued performance of daily chores was considered a matter of choice, or of necessity for the poor. For those buried in cave and bench tombs, personal identification and distinctive appearance may have been relinquished for a non-personal, familial identity. Personal items were regarded as extraneous, familiar objects not requisite for continued survival.

Lowland and Highland Burial Patterns

This study of mortuary practices demonstrates that two distinct cultural responses to death were expressed in the method of interment, body treatment, and mortuary provisioning. One pattern, consisting of an agglomeration of burial types, typically occurred in coastal, Shephelah and valley regions. This response was identified in the Bible with the cosmopolitan, technologically advanced (at least in the realm of metallurgy according to Josh. 17.16-18 and 1 Sam. 13.19-20) Canaanite and Philistine cultures. The second, remarkably homogeneous response was confined to the highlands of Judah. Both lowland and highland burial practices were employed by Transjordanian plateau settlers. From the Bronze Age onwards, the population living along the coast and in contiguous valley systems maintained wider cultural contacts, or incorporated a wider variety of cultural and ethnic elements, than did the southern highland population. Therefore, it is not surprising that a wider range of items were found in lowland burials than in highland burials. During the twelfth and eleventh centuries BCE, the selection of objects found exclusively in the lowland assemblage included scarabs, metal blades, javelin heads, spearheads and arrowheads, combs, mirrors, cosmetic palettes, gaming pieces and female plaque figurines. Many of these items may be attributable to the Egyptian presence in the region. Only the lamp was characteristically more common in highland than in lowland burials of the twelfth and eleventh centuries BCE.

Both the lowland and the highland patterns underwent significant changes in the tenth century BCE. They were more dissimilar in the twelfth and eleventh centuries BCE (given the few number of Iron I highland burials) than in the tenth and succeeding centuries BCE (table 9). Of the lowland objects discontinued after the eleventh century BCE, metal blades and arrowheads were adopted into the highland assemblage, but javelin heads, spearheads and female plaque figurines disappeared from the repertoire of burial provisions. Beginning in the tenth century BCE, scarabs, which had been primarily a lowland feature, were supplied in highland mortuary assemblages. New figurine types included the 'Tambourine goddess' in northern coastal and Transjordanian interments, the hermaphrodite deity in Ammonite burials, the female pillar figurine in Judahite burials, and horse and rider figurines.

The critical interface between the highland and lowland assemblages was the Shephelah, the lowlands and foothills between Philistia to the west and Judah to the east. Several significant, characteristic features of Judahite burial initially appeared in Shephelah and Jerusalem corridor tombs: first and foremost the bench tomb plan, but also blades, arrowheads, spindle whorls, toggle pins, fibulae and the female pillar figurine. On the basis of 'visible' burial remains, the highlands appear to have been settled from precisely these boundary regions, the Shephelah and the Jerusalem corridor (figs. 16-18). Israelites and Judahites may have adopted more from Philistine culture than the biblical writers acknowledged.[1]

Very few burials have been located and excavated in the territory of the northern kingdom of Israel. The absence may be attributed in part to survey techniques, but the possibility should be entertained of an alternative 'invisible' form of burial. The few recorded interments indicate that burial practices in the territory of the northern kingdom diverged from those in the southern kingdom. Israel encompassed the Jezreel and Beth Shan valleys, whose populations employed coastal and northern forms of interment throughout the Iron Age: pit, cist, jar and urn burial. Similar to contemporary southern highland examples, bench and arcosolia tombs were cut at the Israelite highland sites of Samaria and Tubas. As was the case in Judah, either the indigenous highland dwellers adopted the bench tomb (from the neighboring site of Tel Dothan) or adherents of the bench tomb burying culture moved up into the highlands bringing the bench tomb with them (Josh. 17.15-18). Samaria bench tomb 103 exhibited a unique feature which has been compared to fourteenth- or thirteenth-century BCE Ugaritic antecedents (Sukenik 1940: 60-62). Cut into the tomb floor were six bottle-shaped pits, some of which had a double-rimmed mouth to carry a cover stone, and two of which were connected by a narrow and shallow channel. The excavators explained this configuration as 'receptacles of offerings connected with the cult of the dead as regularly practiced in ancient Israel in spite of the attacks of the prophets' (Crowfoot, Kenyon and Sukenik 1942: 22). It is possible that these pits and channels were added secondarily for non-mortuary purposes.

1. The stories of king David demonstrate ongoing relations between Judah and Philistia. The Judahite David (1 Sam. 16.1) fled from King Saul to Philistia where he served as a Philistine vassal in Ziklag (1 Sam. 27.6). Upon Saul's death, David returned from Philistia to the prominent Judahite city of Hebron where he was appointed king (2 Sam. 2.1-4).

	TWELFTH AND ELEVENTH CENTURIES BCE	
	Lowland Pattern	*Highland Pattern*
Burial Type	(anthropoid coffin), simple, cist, jar, bench, cremation	cave
Pottery Forms	pilgrim flask, pyxide, crater	lamp, chalice
Imported Pottery	(*Mycenaean*),(*Egyptian*), Cypriot	Cypriot
Jewelry	pendant, bangle, *ring*, earring, scarab, Bes, Eye of Horus, gold and silver beads	pendant, bangle, earring, Bes, Eye of Horus, faience
Tools	(*javelin head*), (*spearhead*), blade, arrowhead, spindle whorl flint, pin, needle	spindle whorl, flint, pin, needle, 'fishhook', tong, tweezer
Personal Items	toggle pin, fibula, seal, comb, *mirror*, *cosmetic palette*, *gaming piece*	toggle pin, fibula, seal
Models	(*female plaque figurine*), rattle	rattle
	TENTH THROUGH SIXTH CENTURY BCE	
	Lowland Pattern	*Highland Pattern*
Burial Type	simple, cist, jar, cremation	bench
Pottery Forms	bowl, storejar, dipper juglet, cooking pot, wine decanter, *amphora*, plate/platter	bowl, storejar, dipper juglet, cooking pot, wine decanter, jug
Imported Pottery	*Phoencian*, *Assyrian*, Cypro-Phoenician	Cypro-Phoenician
Jewelry		scarab
Tools		blade, arrowhead
Personal Items		
Models	tambourine goddess, horse and rider figurine	*female pillar figurine*

Table 9. A Comparison of Iron Age Cisjordanian Lowland and Highland Burial Patterns.[1]

No bench tombs have been recorded from the centuries following the fall of the northern kingdom, although cave tombs were reported from Samaria and Ein Sarin.

1. Note: Items in italics were found almost exclusively in that assemblage during those centuries. Enteries in parenthesis ( ) did not continue into succeeding centuries.

Burial Contents as Evidence for Foreign Relations

Changes in the incidence of imported pottery in burials reflect the vicissitudes of foreign trade, and foreign presence and control of the Iron Age southern Levant. Mycenaean and Egyptian vessels were found only in thirteenth- and twelfth-century BCE lowland assemblages. The extent of Philistine settlement and trade is illustrated by the presence of Philistine vessels in burials from Tell Zeror, Megiddo and Afula in the north; Beth Shemesh, Gezer and Lachish in the Shephelah; and Tell en-Nasbeh, situated approximately ten kilometers north of Jerusalem. Only Cypriot and Philistine vessels were provided in highland burial assemblages of the twelfth and eleventh centuries BCE. By the tenth century BCE, Mycenaean and Egyptian imports ceased, Cypriot wares dwindled in number, and Philistine vessels were no longer well defined. At this point, Phoenician and Cypro-Phoenician wares were introduced. Phoenician wares were confined to coastal burials, but Cypro-Phoenician vessels, primarily dipper juglets, were rapidly adopted as mortuary provisions throughout the region. The appearance of these imported vessels at highland and Transjordanian sites delineates the avenues and extent of trade (fig. 23). As expected, Assyrian wares appeared in burials in the territory of the former northern kingdom of Israel and in Transjordan following the Assyrian conquest and settlement in the late eighth and early seventh centuries BCE.

The distribution of tomb types and survey of objects found in tomb assemblages suggest other avenues of cultural contact not generally recognized. The first is the close connection of Jordan River Valley and Transjordanian plateau sites with the coastal–lowland culture. Trade items brought by land or sea to the region of Tell Abu Hawam on the coast were transported inland through the Jezreel and Beth Shan Valleys to Jordan River Valley sites such as Tell es-Saidiyeh and Tell el-Mazar, and from there up onto the plateau into the Amman vicinity. The distribution of simple, cist, jar, bathtub coffin and bench tomb burials, and Mycenaean and Cypriot pottery illustrate this avenue of trade and cultural contact (fig. 16-18, 22, 23). Eighth- to seventh-century BCE and earlier relations between the capital cities of Amman and Jerusalem help explain the use of the bench tomb in Ammon and common mortuary provisions such as lamps, seals, wine decanters, silver objects and eighth- to seventh-century BCE Cypro-Phoenician pottery.

This study also demonstrates Egyptian influence on burial customs throughout the Iron Age, and a possible continued Egyptian presence in the region. During the thirteenth and twelfth centuries BCE, anthropoid coffin burials and probably also some simple and cist burials, especially those with a stele or marker (Deir el-Balah, Tell es-Saidiyeh), were Egyptian burials. In addition to Egyptian vessels and amulets, Mycenaean pottery, storejars, dipper juglets, cosmetic palettes, gaming pieces, rattles, and large quantities of metal including vessels, wine sets and spearheads, may initially have been Egyptian mortuary provisions. From the tenth century BCE on, Phoenicians and other coastal entrepreneurs disseminated Egyptian goods through the region in conjunction with Cypro-Phoenician wares. However, the continued presence of Egyptians and their descendants is supported by D.L. Risdon's study of the osteological remains from Lachish which demonstrated a 'close racial resemblance to the population of Egypt at that time...the population of the town in 700 BCE was entirely, or almost entirely from Upper Egypt' (Ussishkin 1982: 56).

Summary of the Biblical Evidence

Biblical stories and prohibitions illustrate that the dead, called *'ᵉlōhîm*, 'divine ones', were regarded as posessing prescient powers (1 Sam. 28) and the ability to revivify (2 Kgs 13.20-21), fructify (1 Sam. 1.11), and perhaps harm the living (2 Sam. 4.12; Isa. 57.11). It is, therefore, understandable that the living would want to appease them by providing for their needs. Tithed food (Gen. 28.17-18; Deut. 26.14), oil (Gen. 28.17) and sacrifices (Gen. 31.53; 46.1; Isa. 57.6-7) were offered. The *zebaḥ hayyāmîm/zebaḥ mišpāḥâ* and **kbd* and **pqd* terminology probably also refer to care and sacrifices for ancestors and deceased royalty.

An ancestral tomb, whether located on inherited land or in the village cemetery, served as a physical, perpetual claim to the patrimony. Family proximity to the tomb facilitated caring for and venerating the dead. These functions of the tomb, in addition to the attributed powers of the deceased, made the cult of the dead an integral aspect of Israelite and Judahite society.

It has been suggested here that the earliest objections to feeding the dead tithed food and to consulting the dead through intermediaries were incorporated in the Hezekian–Josianic reforms dating from the eighth century BCE and in the later Deuteronomic and Holiness Law Codes and the writings of the prophet(s) Isaiah. In the face of an influx of refugee cultic personnel from the north, Jerusalem priests and prophets hoped to purify and centralize the Jerusalem Temple cult and assert their status as 'true' servants of Yahweh (Deut. 18). As the legitimate cultic functionaries, they were assured a ready clientele and sustenance in the form of the tithe. Towards this end, the dead were deemed an inappropriate source of knowledge. Necromancers were to be stoned to death, and true priests and prophets were identified as those who attained their knowledge and direction from Yahweh alone, not from the dead.

While priests, prophets and the Nazirite were forbidden to consult the dead (Lev. 21.1-4, 11; Num. 6.6-7; Deut. 18.19-22), ordinary citizens were nowhere forbidden to feed the dead (except for tithed food) or to consult them directly without intermediaries. **Krt*, literally 'cut off' from the religious community, as the consequence for those who consulted media or did not undergo the lengthy purification process following contact with the dead (Num. 19.11-20) was an ingenious punishment. Offenders' loss of inherited land forbade them (according to their presuppositions) any future contact with their ancestors, thereby incurring ancestral wrath and perhaps vengeance. This sanction also has the similarily ironic effect of precluding the possibility of future nourishment and honor from the offenders' own descendants. According to this reconstruction of the biblical evidence, there was little change in attitude or practices regarding the dead among the inhabitants of Judah; rather, a politically and religiously motivated change in policy was initiated by the Jerusalem national and religious authorities. Beginning in the eighth and seventh centuries BCE with the Hezekian–Josianic reforms, the cult of the dead was no longer an acceptable feature of the Jerusalem Temple Yahwistic cult. Breaking down clan fidelities, by undermining the family-oriented cult of the dead, will also have served the interests of the central government.

Judahite Burial Practices and Beliefs about the Dead

Mortuary remains, both from Jerusalem and throughout the kingdom, demonstrate that the Judahite conception of the tomb and the fate of the deceased remained consistent throughout the Iron Age. From Judah, the current totals of reported tombs from the tenth through the third quarter of the eighth century BCE are 24 cave tombs and 81 bench tombs, and from the third quarter of the eighth through the first quarter of the sixth century BCE 17 cave and 187 bench tombs. Each tomb contained multiple interments, so hundreds of individual burials constitute the sample.

The cave or bench tomb was the dwelling for individuals who were thought to continue a form of existence and so were provided with the basic necessities of life and some amenities: vessels with food and liquid, lamps for light, jewelry and amulets for protection, models to invoke sympathetic magic, personal items and tools. The only deviations reflected in burial were relative wealth and status for kings and civic and religious functionaries. According to the Bible all but one of the kings and Shebna and Jehoiadah the priest (Isa. 22.16; 2 Chron. 24.15-16) were buried, not in a family tomb associated with the patrimony, but in their capital city.

Bench tombs are assumed to have accommodated family burials, as recorded in the Bible (Gen. 49.29-31), though osteological evidence is lacking.[1] Infants, children, adolescents and adults were buried together. The patrimony with tombs as the physical claim to the land was maintained by the *bêt 'āb* ('lineage') and its constituent elements, extended or multiple families (Stager 1985: 22). Nuclear families most likely maintained single tombs, since most undisturbed burials housed from 15 to 30 individuals of varying ages, which would represent two to four generations. Multiple family households may have constructed aggregate tombs such as Beth Shemesh 5–9 or Gezer 9.

Archaeological and biblical evidence allow the following reconstruction of eighth-century BCE Judahite burial and mortuary activities. The body was dressed and adorned with jewelry including rings, earrings, necklaces and bangles. Select individuals, including women, were then wrapped in a cloak, as evidenced by Samuel's apparition and the presence of toggle pins and fibulae in burials. The attired body was then carried to the tomb on a bier (*miṭṭâ*) (2 Sam. 3.31). Assembled mourners rent their clothes, wore sackcloth, lamented and offered sacrifices including tithed commodities (Deut. 26.14; **kbd*, **pqd*). The majority of reported tombs were cut into rock outcrops of

1. The excavators D. Davis and A. Kloner claimed that family members were buried together in the Mt Zion tomb (Davis and Kloner 1978: 19), but there was no mention of familial relations in the osteological report (Arensburg and Rak 1985).

tell slopes (Tell Beit Mirsim, Lachish) or wadi cliffs (Silwan), because this is where archaeologists surveyed for tombs. A small, square to rectangular doorway cut in the facade, probably closed with a stone, opened into the tomb. One or two steps led down to the floor of the tomb chamber. The tomb, which usually measured roughly five meters square, consisted of a chamber with a continuous waist-high bench cut from the rock extending along the two sides and the back. A repository pit was usually hewn either under one of the benches or in a back corner of the chamber. Occasionally, a second chamber of similar plan was added. In aggregate tombs such as those at St Etienne or Beth Shemesh, the chambers opened off of a central court. The body of the deceased was laid supine, extended, on a bench, or (in certain Jerusalem and Gibeon tombs) in a 'resting-place' (sarcophagus or trough-niche). Stone pillows or headrests (molded depressions carved into the rock to support the head) were frequently carved into the bench or resting-place for the comfort of the deceased. Parapets to keep the deceased from falling and lamp niches were also commonly carved into tombs. Ceramic vessels provided for the dead included bowls and lamps; less frequently, jars, chalices, juglets, storejars and dipper juglets; and rarely, cooking pots and wine decanters. The lamps provided light, the jars held liquids, the bowls foodstuffs and the juglets scented oils. While most vessels were locally made, Cypriot and Cypro-Phoenician imports were also provided. Other common burial items included scarabs, blades, arrowheads, stamps, seals, rattles and female pillar figurines. Following interment, family members or others would offer sacrifices to propitiate the dead and beseech blessings, perhaps on a regular basis (*zebaḥ hayyāmmîm/zebaḥ mišpāḥâ*). Mourners could seek consolation at the *bêt marzēaḥ*.

Three dichotomies drawn with regard to Judahite treatment of the dead need to be re-examined: rich–poor, Canaanite–Israelite and official–folk/popular. The number of retrieved burials does not approximate the conjectured population of Judah, therefore it is assumed that select individuals were interred in bench tombs while 'most people received a simple interment' (Spronk 1986: 239; also de Vaux 1965a: 58). Biblical descriptions of the tomb burials of kings and powerful men such as Shebna (Isa. 22.15-16) reinforce this presupposition. Unfortunately the burials of commoners were not detailed so that assumption represents an argument from silence. Not a single simple grave has been found in eighth-century BCE or later Judah, except for at Lachish, which was an ethnically diverse settlement. However, the Bible does reproachfully record a common burial ground in the Kidron Valley outside of Jerusalem (2 Kgs 23.6). Family burial in the ancestral tomb was an integral aspect of Judahite social and economic organization. Interment in the family tomb guaranteed a continuous claim to the *naḥ*^{a}*lâ* or patrimony, and propitiatory post-mortem care for the ancestors with its consequent benefits for the living. Therefore, single burial would have constituted a deviation from basic Judahite-Yahwistic ideological tenets. Variation in relative wealth is attested in tombs. The Jerusalem tombs exhibited by far the finest workmanship and goods of greatest value, but exemplary tombs were also cut at Gibeon and Tell Judeidah. Bench tombs outside Jerusalem generally displayed inferior workmanship and the retrieved goods were of less value. Gradations in wealth were also evident among burial assemblages. Richer collections contained metal and imported objects, the prestige items of the Iron Age.

The Canaanite–Israelite and popular–official dichotomies are frequently synonymous. Regarding the cult of the dead, from the tenth century BCE onwards, an official Yahwistic-Judahite/'Israelite' position is conjectured in opposition to the popular practice which preserved 'Canaanite' or 'pagan' features (W. Dever quoted approvingly in Ackerman 1987: 357; Albright 1957; Brichto 1973: 49-50; Lewis 1986; Lewis 1989; Spronk 1986: 345). These dichotomies presume the existence of a tenth-century BCE Yahwistic religion which tolerated or forbade 'syncretistic' elements such as death cults. However, the cult of the dead, defined as the belief in the empowered dead with the attendant practices stemming from that belief, was a feature of Israelite praxis throughout the Iron Age. The promulgators of the Holiness and Deuteronomic Law Codes, the Deuteronomist and prophets (notably Isaiah), attempted to purify the Jerusalem Temple cult and the people and to safeguard their own prerogatives and roles. These moves to discredit the dead and those who attained their knowledge from the dead was the 'official' policy beginning late in the eighth century BCE. The injunctions appear to have been aimed at intermediaries, priests and prophets who consulted the dead, that is, at individuals who challenged the authority and usurped some of the roles of self-styled 'legitimate' priests and prophets by claiming access to transmundane knowledge. Judahite citizenry was enjoined not to offer tithed food to the dead and forbidden to consult the dead through intermediaries, but they were neither forbidden to provide for the needs of the dead nor to consult them personally. The fact that officialdom attempted to curtail but not suppress or halt death cult activities testifies to the degree that the cult was integrated into Judahite social, religious and economic fabric. The lack of change during this period in the material remains uncovered through archaeological field work, including in Jerusalem, supports the interpretation that there was no general shift in practices or attitudes regarding the dead. If common practice is to be labelled 'popular', then Jerusalem residents including Judahite national and religious authorities also followed 'popular' practice. The divine ancestors, *'ᵉlōhê 'ābîw*, continued as vital entities in Judahite religion and society as long as the kingdom existed.

Appendix

CATALOGUE OF IRON AGE BURIALS

Burials from the Twelfth and Eleventh Centuries BCE

Simple Graves
Afula. In the Afula Eastern Cemetery on the eastern slope of the tell, M. Dothan of the University of Haifa and the Israel Department of Antiquities excavated shallow, oblong-shaped graves cut into the Early Bronze Age debris. Four tombs, Tomb 4 from Stratum IIIB (1200–1150 BCE) and Tombs 1–3 from Stratum IIIA (1150–1050 BCE), each contained a single individual lying supine with its head to the north-northwest and pottery offerings on the western side of the burial, usually in proximity to the head. A storejar decorated with a seven-branched date palm, a dipper juglet and sherds were found in the earliest tomb, Tomb 4. A child jar burial had been placed in Tomb 1 (see below). Storejars, in some cases covered by small bowls and juglets, were retrieved from the later Tombs 1 and 2. One jug from Tomb 2 was described by T. Dothan as 'unique in shape and decoration' of 'the monochrome variant of Philistine pottery, which may reflect an early phase of Philistine pottery production' (M. Dothan 1955: 47-50; T. Dothan 1982: 81). Various sizes and shapes of bowls and a pilgrim flask were found between and above the tombs (M. Dothan 1955).

Azor. In the 1958 excavations in Azor Area D cemetery squares M9 and M10, M. Dothan of the University of Haifa and the Israel Department of Antiquities uncovered the remains of nine pit graves (D6, 8, 9, 14, 15, 20, 24, 29, 32) and seven skull burials (D17, 18, 23, 25, 26, 27, 34) dating to the twelfth and eleventh centuries BCE. The brachycephalic individuals lay supine, oriented east–west with their heads to the west. A few objects or some jewelry were found with each individual, usually near the head and the right hand. The goods included Philistine pottery forms such as pyxidoform vessels and bowls comparable to examples from Tell Qasile XII and XI. In a pocket of sand, burial D6, which had been disturbed by a later burial, yielded skull and skeletal fragments identified by D. Ferembach as belonging to a woman of more than fifty years. A Cypro-Phoenician Black-on-Red juglet, a black juglet, a spouted jar, a fragment of a bilbil handle and two beads (perhaps from a later burial) were found with the woman's body (M. Dothan field notes, photos 22073, 22080, 22082). Burial D8 consisted of a well-preserved skeleton lying supine in the sand, head to the west, with two Philistine bowl fragments and a bronze bracelet (M. Dothan field notes, photo 22101). In D9 an adult, probably a brachycephalic male, lay in earth blackened in several places by burning (?) with fragments of jars, bowls and a jug (M. Dothan field notes). All that remained in D14 were scattered fragments of a skull and spinal cord, a bowl, juglet, pilgrim flask, fragments of a chalice, a bronze bracelet and a scarab. The scarab reads 'born of Ra', and next to the inscription sits a youth holding a stick (M. Dothan field notes, photo 22126). In D15, one of the most deeply cut of the burials, were preserved a bronze mirror and stone bowl resting next to the skull, a Philistine bowl rim and body fragment decorated with spirals inside a metope, bowl and jug fragments, a silver and a bronze earring, a bronze needle and two beads (M. Dothan field notes). In burial D20, an inverted Philistine bowl with horizontal handles lay near the chest of a well-preserved skeleton oriented east–west (M. Dothan field notes, photos 22207, 22212). In the best preserved of all burials, D24, an inverted bowl rested over the hips of a supine young woman of Alpine type, oriented east–west. Near her right hand had been deposited two carinated bowls, a pyxis and a pilgrim flask (M. Dothan field notes, photos 22254, 22256, 22258, 22263). Burial D29 had been disturbed by a modern wall, but the Iron Age objects ascribed to the burial included a complete pilgrim flask and a white steatite scarab engraved with 'Ptah is truth' surrounded by a border of cotangent circles (M. Dothan field notes, photo 22269). In burial D32, a young woman approximately 20 years old of brachycephalic, Armenoid or dinarique type, lay supine, oriented east–west, with a carinated bowl with red slip and burnish inside and on the outer upper half of the vessel (M. Dothan field notes, photo 22294).

In seven instances the only skeletal material recovered was a skull, which may reflect the actual burial practice, or may in some cases be due to poor bone preservation and disturbances. The skull designated D17 had been provided with a large jar, a smaller jar, a chalice and a bronze bracelet, all fragmentary, and a blue faience bead (M. Dothan field notes). D18 will be presented below in the context of the stone enclosure in which it was found. A complete jug and fragments of a carinated bowl and a rounded bowl base plus a crater ring base lay in the vicinity of burial D23. D25 and D26 consisted of isolated skulls. The skull of burial D27 was accompanied by a single sherd from the body of a pilgrim flask. Two skulls, a body fragment of a pilgrim flask, and a Cypriot juglet comprised burial D34 (M. Dothan field notes).

S. Pipano conducted salvage operations on the southwestern part of the hill. He uncovered six tombs, all on an east–west axis, with most of the deceased positioned with their heads to the west. Unfortunately, only two were dated. The single well-published tomb, perhaps dating to this period, was Tomb A. This cist measuring 2.00 × 1.20 m was dug into kurkar, lined with rough kurkar blocks and roofed with a heavy slab supported by an arch constructed of medium-sized stones. Near the heads of the three interred individuals were a lamp, a bowl with a 'suspension' handle, a small pilgrim flask painted with black and red bands, and a jug. Tombs D, E and F were also lined with kurkar blocks, but so was Tomb B, which the excavator dated to no earlier than the Byzantine period (Pipano 1984).

Deir el-Balah.[1] The Deir el-Balah cemetery, in use during the late thirteenth and early twelfth centuries BCE, was excavated by T. Dothan of the Hebrew University in Jerusalem. Among the anthropoid coffin burials which Dothan uncovered were simple and cist graves of adults and children (Tombs 100, 107, 108, 110, 112, 115). All burials at Deir el-Balah were oriented east–west. Grave goods included Egyptian and locally-made bowls and storejars. A standing storejar with a bowl as a lid and a dipper juglet was a common configuration (Beit-Arieh 1985a; T. Dothan 1972: 65, 68).

Dhiban. A.D. Tushingham excavated simple graves and elaborate rock-cut tombs in the city cemetery, designated Area J. One grave was explicitly mentioned though not detailed, and the hillside was presumed to have been where individual graves were cut into the soil in the late Iron I (Winnett and Reed 1964: 57).

Ein Hanaziv. In 1982 P. Porath of the Israel Department of Antiquities excavated two Late Bronze or Iron Age pit graves, but has not published them in detail (En Hanaziv 1983).

Tell el-Farah (S). Approximately 100 burials including simple graves in the 500, 600, 700 and 800 Cemeteries of Tell el-Farah (S) were dated by W.M.F. Petrie to the period of the 20–22nd Dynasties. In the simple graves, one or two adults, adolescents or children were interred with an assortment of pottery vessels, primarily bowls, plus jewelry (beads, rings, earrings, bracelets), Egyptian amulets and stamps. Over 400 people were interred in single and cist burials in the Tell el-Farah (S) cemeteries between the twelfth and the ninth centuries BCE (Petrie 1930: pls. lxviii-lxxi). T. Dothan identified tombs and graves dating to the end of the Late Bronze and early Iron Age in the 100, 200, 500, 600 and 800 Cemeteries based on the presence of Philistine pottery (T. Dothan 1982: 29-33).

Tel Kishyon. R. Amiran and C. Arnon excavated a thirteenth- to twelfth-century BCE cemetery at the site of Tel Kishyon near Kibbutz Ein Dor in the Jezreel Valley. In Area A, three reasonably well-preserved skeletons plus several skulls and skeletal fragments were recorded. An adult male was interred without grave goods. More than 20 objects, including bowls, plates, lamps and four storejars with juglets, had been provided for a woman. The vessels usually lay near or on top of the skeleton. One small bowl with animal bones in it lay inverted on the chest of an individual. In addition to the pottery forms already mentioned, pilgrim flasks, chalices and a jug were found (Israel Antiquities Authority files, Tel Kishyon; Tel Kishyon 1982).

Megiddo. The Oriental Institute of the University of Chicago excavated five reasonably well preserved and undisturbed rectangular-shaped pit burials cut into the rock

1. For the sake of completeness, this entry has been repeated below under twelfth- and eleventh-century BCE cist graves.

and debris at the foot of Megiddo (17, 61, 62, 71, 237). Each grave held a single adult lying extended on its back, usually provided with a large crater or bowl at its feet and a storejar. While the individual in Tomb 237 lay with its head to the northeast, all others were oriented with their heads to the southwest. Tombs 17 and 62 differed from the others in having been cut with an overhanging ledge. Neither imported wares nor Philistine pottery were present in these graves. The poorest grave, Tomb 61, contained no funerary offerings. The individual in Tomb 62 was buried with bronze and pottery bowls, a large storejar, a crater, a dipper juglet, carnelian and gold beads, two toggle pins including one of silver, gold foil fragments, a gold plaque, a bronze pin and an ivory dish shaped like a fish (Guy 1938: 117, 119, 121, 126, pl. 168). These burials were dated to early Iron I by the excavator and by J. Abercrombie (1979: 306, 309, 311).

Tell es-Saidiyeh. At the site of Tell es-Saidiyeh, a double mound situated immediately south of Wadi Kufrinjeh 1.8 km east of the Jordan River, J. Pritchard of the University of Pennsylvania and J. Tubb of the British Museum excavated a cemetery of simple and cist graves and jar burials dating from the end of the Late Bronze Age and into the Iron Age. The earliest graves were regularly spaced and oriented east–west, with individuals' heads to the west. Later graves were oriented east–west, north–south, and south–north (Tubb 1988: 61). Stone markers stood above the graves of articulated individuals, skulls and select bones of infants, children and adults (Tombs 91, 167, 169, 169B, 173A, 179, 183, 206, 229, 239, 248, 266, 281). Many of the burials were single primary inhumations, but the majority contained only select skeletal remains. The individual lay extended, supine, sometimes with crossed legs and hands crossed over the pelvis. Bodies were clothed or wrapped in Egyptian linen (Tomb 21), and some were encased in bitumen.

The types of goods in the simple graves were similar to those placed in the cist tombs, though of more modest quantity, quality and origin. Whereas many adults were provided with a variety of vessels, personal effects, jewelry and a bronze spearpoint (Tomb 129) or a knife (Tomb 113), many were buried with little more than jewelry (Tombs 213, 217, 225, 250, 276). Children were buried without any goods (Tombs 121, 135, 138), with jewelry or beads (Tombs 51, 104, 111, 112, 125, 131, 186, 236, 245, 247), a scarab (Tombs 65, 111, 237), a ring (Tombs 104, 248), anklets (Tomb 120) or shells (Tombs 104, 120, 136). The pottery assemblage provisionally assigned to the child buried in Tomb 139 is probably misattributed (Pritchard 1980: 26-27). Tombs 27 and 104 were the most elaborate child burials. The child in Tomb 104 was provisioned with three bowls, one of which contained shells, five faience beads, a faience ring, and, just beyond the feet a large upright vessel partially embedded in the ground with a hole in the base, Pritchard's funerary vessel for liquid libations (Pritchard 1980: 17). Tomb 27 contained bronze, carnelian and silver jewelry, a stamp seal and a zoomorphic vessel. As in the cist tombs, Mycenaean IIIB stirrup jars (Tombs 107, 110, 116), Egyptian jars and a bowl (Tombs 105, 109S, 123, 137, 139) and alabaster vessels (Tombs 119, 136) were provided in addition to a range of locally made forms, of which a shallow bowl of coarse ware was most common. When only a single vessel was provided, the pyxis was the most common form (Tombs 9, 173A, 235, 241, 264, 266, 281). There were, however, burials in which the single provided vessel was a jar (Tombs 3, 199), a lamp (Tombs 203, 249A/C), a juglet (Tombs 7, 242), a jug (Tombs 53, 65) or a pilgrim flask (Tomb 197). Pritchard dated the burials to approximately 1200 BCE on the basis of pottery parallels (Pritchard 1980; Tubb 1988).

Tell Taanach. P. Lapp excavated an eleventh century BCE burial of an adolescent female near the cultic structure at Tell Taanach. Her burial appears to have been a ritual interment rather than the customary burial practice. She was robed and adorned, as indicated by two fibulae, a scarab and beads, but was buried without other provisions (Lapp 1964: 27 n. 40).

Cist graves

Akhzib. The earliest Iron Age burials at Akhzib are Iron I cist tombs located on the eastern slope of the tell beneath a Persian pavement outside the city walls. The excavator, M. Prausnitz of the Israel Department of Antiquities, considered these burial structures monuments within a temenos. They were built above ground of very large stones, some with drafted masonry bosses, roofed with large stone plates perhaps forming a gable, and were then covered with sand and sun-dried bricks. 'Gifts' were left outside on top of the structure (Prausnitz, personal communication 1984). The tombs, oriented north–south, measured approximately 1.3 × 0.8 m for a single burial and 1.3 × 1.2 m for a double burial. In one tomb a man and a woman lay side-by-side with their heads to the south. The relative wealth of this grave as well as the honored position of the tomb within the temenos prompted Prausnitz to suggest it was the tomb of a 'Herrscher' of Akhzib. A bronze double-headed axe and a bronze spear lay near the man's head, and two large pilgrim flasks and a copper bowl were deposited around him. The woman's clothing had been secured with a fibula. Scattered within the tomb were pilgrim flasks, a bichrome jug, a sherd of Cypriot White Painted I Ware, a Syrian cylinder seal, an Aegean stamp seal and beads. A clay duck or pig head and a high-footed red jug with seven spouts had been offered after burial on top of the earth covering (Prausnitz 1963: 338; 1982: 31-32; private communication 1984).

Azor. M. Dothan of the University of Haifa and the Israel Department of Antiquities directed excavations at Azor in 1958 and 1960. The Area D cemetery produced primarily simple graves with interspersed mudbrick cist graves (D 75, 76, 77 [?], 80, 84, 85 [?]) and stone cist graves (D5, 7, 8 [?]; within one cist were 18, 21, 22, 28 and 30).

Three Iron I primary inhumations were recovered in the 1960 season, all of which may have been interred in cists. The adult buried in D77 lay in an extended position, head to the west, near the cist burials and at the same elevation, prompting the excavator to suggest that the brick cist had decomposed or disappeared. No associated goods were recorded. The brachycephalic adult male, burial D85, also located in square L10 oriented east–west with his head to the west, lay aside a mass of black mudbrick material—perhaps the remains of a mudbrick cist. The single conclusive example of a simple inhumation occurred in square K10 at roughly the same elevation as D77 and D85. D80, again a supine, brachycephalic male with his head to the west, was accompanied by a large four-handled storejar and bowls of which only fragments were recovered, two fragments bearing the black decoration and bird design (?) of the Philistine repertoire (M. Dothan field notes, 1958: 273, 1975: 146; T. Dothan 1982: 55).

In the three well-preserved examples of cist burials situated side-by-side, D75, 76 and 84, the coffin-shaped cists were built below ground level of unfired bricks laid on their short sides and covered with larger bricks of a similar type. The Philistine wares found in D76 provide a possible twelfth- and first half eleventh-century BCE date for these burials. Cists D75 and 84 each contained a woman, in D84 identified as brachycephalic, but in neither case were objects found with the body. A seventh- to sixth-century BCE storejar similar to the unstratified example bearing the inscription LŠLMY was later attributed to burial D75, prompting the ascription of the inscribed vessel to the same grave. Due to the highly disturbed state of the areas excavated, and to the subsequent attribution of these jars to burial D75, it is plausible that they are unrelated to each other or to this burial. Between the two women, an adult male lay in his cist with a bowl, pilgrim flask, flint scraper, a fragment of a spout, and bowl and jug fragments, providing a date for all three burials (M. Dothan field notes, 1961a: 173; 1961b; 1975: 147; T. Dothan 1982: 55).

In the 1958 season in areas M9 and M10, north of areas J–L, M. Dothan excavated several Iron I stone-lined cist graves. The much disturbed burial D5 was marked by a row of stones, perhaps the remains of a stone cist. Fragments of a large jar lay over the skull, and in the vicinity of the body were recovered four complete or fragmentary Cypro-Phoenician juglets, a wishbone handle, a figurine of a seated goddess with a horned sun atop her head (unparalleled in Israel), bracelet fragments, carnelian beads and a scarab. The scarab depicts three deities processing one behind the other and holding hands. The first deity to the right is Ra, the central deity has been identified with Amun, and the third is Ra again or Sekhmet (M. Dothan field notes, photos 22081, 22232). The elliptically-shaped cist D7, oriented northeast–southwest, contained a skull and bones, early Iron Age sherds, a bronze bowl and a fibula. Nearby vessel fragments, some with red slip and burnish on the inside and outside, and a bronze kohl stick were subsequently ascribed to this burial (M. Dothan field notes, photos 22105, 22107, 22109). A partially-preserved stone enclosure with large regular blocks on one side and smaller blocks on the remaining one and a half sides, all with worked inner faces, overlay some burials (D19, 28 [?], 30 [?]) suggesting an eleventh-century BCE date. D18, 21, 22, 28 and 30 lay within the stone enclosure. D18 consisted of a skull with perhaps some other bones, a one-handled jug and a bead (M. Dothan field notes, photo 22210). All that remained of burial D21 was a crushed skull, bone fragments, a one-handled jug and a lamp fragment (M. Dothan field notes, photos 22209, 22239, 22283). Also within the stone enclosure lay a body, D22, oriented east–west, with an inverted bowl on its chest. A cooking pot rim, two bowl fragments, the first with red-brown slip and burnish on the inside and outside and the second with a red painted band and drippings from the rim, and a Philistine vessel fragment were attributed to this burial. Even though the burial belonging to D28 had been disturbed by the stone enclosure wall, its east–west orientation was still discernible. A large number of objects lying nearby have been ascribed to this interment: a dipper juglet, five black-burnished juglets, a lamp with a rounded bottom, a fragment of a bronze bracelet, a ring fragment and six beads (M. Dothan field notes, photos 22265, 22283). The burial designated D30 consisted of a body, disturbed by the stone enclosure wall, lying at an east–west orientation 0.1 m under D28. With this individual were found the largest number of complete vessels. Grave goods included a dipper juglet, two Cypro-Phoenician Black-on-Red I juglets, a pilgrim flask, a pomegranate-shaped vessel with holes in the two sides of the neck, fragments of a jug and a Philistine bowl, two scarabs, six beads and three cone-shaped stamp seals. One seal is engraved with two horned animals, perhaps deer, standing back to back, the second with a male figure holding a plough stick (?) standing before an animal, and the third with a geometric pattern composed of five dots. An 18th Dynasty scarab is inscribed with the prenomen of Tuthmosis III without a cartouche, Men-en-kheper-Ra, surrounded by the symbolic plants of Lower Egypt. The inscription on the second scarab, translated by Professor Etienne Drioton, reads, 'Amon-Ra loves whoever loves him' (M. Dothan field notes, photos 22213, 22272, 22276, 22277).

Deir el-Balah.[1] The Deir el-Balah cemetery, in use during the late thirteenth and early twelfth centuries BCE, was excavated by T. Dothan of the Hebrew University in Jerusalem. Among the anthropoid coffin burials which Dothan uncovered were simple and cist graves of adults and children (Tombs 100, 107, 108, 110, 112, 115). All burials at Deir el-Balah were oriented east–west. Grave goods included Egyptian and locally made bowls and storejars. A standing storejar with a bowl as a lid and a dipper juglet was a common configuration (Beit-Arieh 1985a; T. Dothan 1972: 65, 68).

Tell el-Farah (S). W.M.F. Petrie excavated 24 stone or mudbrick-lined cists in the 100 and 200 Cemeteries of Tell el-Farah (S). The mudbrick lined cist Tomb 123 contained a single individual. The stone examples held from one to six individuals (104, 107, 133, 134, 207, 210, 220, 223, 230, 232, 234, 236, 238) or massive numbers. In the latter case, Petrie suggested that some of the burials may have been secondary, so he recorded only the number of skulls present (201, 202, 212, 213, 227, 228, 229, 233, 237). Grave goods resembled those provided for simple burials. Bowls predominated among the pottery vessels, with a wide array of non-ceramic items, including metal vessels, jewelry, household items and amusements. Over 400 people were interred in single and cist burials in the Tell el-Farah (S) cemeteries between the twelfth and the ninth centuries BCE (Petrie 1930: pls. lxviii-

1. Cf. the same entry under twelfth- and eleventh-century BCE simple graves.

lxxi). T. Dothan dated tombs and graves to the end of the Late Bronze and early Iron Age in the 100, 200, 500, 600 and 800 Cemeteries based on the presence of Philistine pottery (T. Dothan 1982: 29-33).

Tel Ritma. In the loess at the foot of the western slope of Tel Ritma, located north-northwest of Sde Boqer in the Negev, Z. Meshel excavated a 'few' stone-capped graves. Long, flat stone slabs covered the 0.75 × 2.0 m graves at surface level. Only sherds and bone fragments remained in the disturbed burials. These burials were dated to the eleventh to tenth century BCE by the corresponding Stratum III on the tell which contained Negev Ware and 'Israelite' ware, including red bowls burnished inside and outside (Meshel 1965; 1974: I-II, pl. 7).

Tell es-Saidiyeh. At the site of Tell es-Saidiyeh, a double mound situated immediately south of Wadi Kufrinjeh 1.8 km east of the Jordan River, J. Pritchard of the University of Pennsylvania and J. Tubb of the British Museum excavated a cemetery of simple and cist graves and jar burials dating from late in the Late Bronze Age into the early Iron Age. Fourteen different variations of cists were constructed: fully or partially stone-lined pits, fully or partially mudbrick-lined pits, a rectangular grave with an inner clay kerb, mudbrick- and stone-lined pits, a pit partially lined with stones and sherds, a burial on two mudbrick slabs, mudbrick-lined pits with mudbrick floors, a pit with a mudbrick and stone covering, brick-lined and covered pits, mudbrick-walled tombs, a partially stone-built tomb, brick-built tombs, stone- and mudbrick-built tombs, and mudbrick-walled and roofed tombs. Body treatmenmt was the same as in the simple graves and the goods supplied were similar, but in greater quantity, of finer quality, and often of foreign origin. Food remains in the cists included a scatter of ovicaprid bones overlying the individual in Tomb 34, and the bones of a large animal/cow (?) in Tomb 32. The cist graves exhibited both Egyptian and Aegean features: bitumen (Tombs 101, 159), east–west orientation, an abundance of metal objects (Tombs 24, 32, 34, 41, 46, 159, 191A, 232, 246, 282), and imported goods (Tombs 101, 117, 119) (Pritchard 1980: 10-16, 20-21; Tubb 1988: 1973-80).

Tell Zeror. K. Ohata of the Japanese Society for Near Eastern Research excavated nine mid-eleventh- to mid-tenth-century BCE cist graves at Tell Zeror. The cemetery was located on the southeastern slope of the mound, approximately 200 m west of the top of the northern tell. Built of stone and covered with large stone slabs, the cists measured 2–3.2 × 0.6–1.1 × 0.6–1.3 m on the inside. They were oriented southeast–northwest, and appear—since they contain from one to more than fifteen adults, adolescents, children and infants interred at different times—to have been family tombs. Although the majority of skeletons were fragmentary, the latest burials lay supine with their heads to the northwest. Included among the ceramic offerings were a Cypro-Phoenician juglet (Tomb IV) and flask (Tomb V), and locally made bowls, jugs, juglets, flasks, lamps and a chalice. An unusually large number of metal objects, especially weapons, were also provided: nine daggers, bracelets and rings, all made of iron, plus two javelin heads, a javelin butt, bracelets, rings, earrings and bowls, all of bronze. Additional provisions included stone pendants, glass beads, scarabs, whorls, flints and a 'goddess' figurine of a nude female supporting her breasts with her hands, similar to a Late Bronze Age figurine from the same site (Tomb VI). Outside and between the cist graves were found pithoi, bowls, storejars, juglets, jars, bracelets, rings and daggers (Kochavi 1978: 1224-25; Ohata 1967: 35-41; 1970: 69-72).

Jar Burials

Tell Abu Hawam. M. Dothan of Haifa University and the Israel Department of Antiquities reported Iron I burial jars covered with bowls from a cemetery near Tell Abu Hawam (M. Dothan 1955: 47).

Afula. In the Afula eastern cemetery excavations, directed by M. Dothan of Haifa University and the Israel Department of Antiquites, the mid-twelfth- to mid-eleventh-century BCE pit grave Tomb 1 contained a supine individual with goods arranged near the head, including a jar containing infant bones (M. Dothan 1955: 47).

Amman—Jebel el-Qusur. In 1966 the Jordan Department of Antiquities excavated an Iron Age tomb at Jebel el-Qusur, northeast of Amman, which contained five pottery coffins and six big burial jars of unusual size. The burial jars, with their mouths removed to facilitate inserting the body, were found to contain human remains and small finds similar to those recorded from the eleventh- or tenth-century BCE Sahab Tomb 1 jar burials: bracelets, rings and a dagger (Amman—Jebal el-Qusur 1966; Ibrahim 1972: 33).

Azor. M. Dothan, of Haifa University and the Israel Department of Antiquities, excavated for two seasons in the Azor Cemetery D. In 1958 he opened three squares on a north–south line, squares J10, K10 and L10, and in 1960 he continued north and west, opening an additional two squares, M9 and M10 (M. Dothan 1961c: fig. 1). Seventeen Iron I jar burials, many in a fragmentary state, had been dug into the kurkar in squares J10 and K10, in the vicinity of the mass cist tomb D79 and the mudbrick cist tombs D75, D76 and D84. A jar and urn burial were themselves enclosed in a frame or cist—urn burial D63 in a stone-built frame and D91 in a mud-brick cist. Five of the seventeen interred individuals had been buried in two jars or cooking pots joined at the mouth or the shoulder. One such burial encased an infant and a four-year-old (?). All the other individuals were buried in single vessels. Five jars contained only bone fragments, three jars held bones and skulls, and five jars yielded only skulls. These burials were relatively poorly provisioned. A single scarab, beads and shells supplemented the pottery repertoire, which included a preponderance of bowls and craters with Philistine painted decoration, jars and jugs. Many of the burials had been disturbed by later Arab period interments. Also, burials were dug in one above the other or one beside the other, disturbing the initial burial and rendering it difficult to distinguish between the two interments.

The Iron Age burials recorded in the field notes will now be detailed in numerical order. A mend from side-by-side assemblages D55 and D56 suggests they derived from a single disturbed jar burial. The skull and bones of a four-year-old mesocephalic child lay scattered amidst a Philistine bowl, bowl fragments, a pyxis, a jug, jar fragments, chalice fragments, iron (?) and silver bracelet fragments, beads and a scarab. The 19th–20th Dynasty scarab depicts the kneeling god Hapi, god of the rising Nile, surrounded by three crocodiles, representations of the god Sebek. D57 may be similarly reconstructed as a jar burial. A skull lay among fragments of a large jar, with sherds from cooking pots with triangular, flattened out-turned rims, a carinated bowl, a bowl decorated with a red and black checkerboard pattern, jugs decorated with red and black bands, and a fragment of a bronze pendant. Burial D60 differed from the other examples in consisting of bones and faience beads placed inside two cooking pot rims arranged one on top of the other. An erect, large, handleless jar, D62, held skeletal remains, a pilgrim flask and a bowl. From around the jar were retrieved bowls and jug sherds decorated with red and black bands, the upper part of a jug with a basket handle, a two-handled jar, jar fragments, jug fragments and chalice fragments. Jar burials D64 and D64 A (disturbed by later interments) lay side-by-side. Like nearby D67, the D64 infant (?) skull had been buried in two jars, one found slightly above the other. The upper half of a third jar, D64 A, lay alongside the two jars of D64. Sherds from jars and a Philistine bowl with black decoration remained of the goods originally provided for the deceased. A skull inside a large, rimless jar and a nearby lamp and bowl were designated Burial D66. Burial D67 consisted of a pit dug into the kurkar, into which were placed two jars, joined at the shoulder, with bones inside. In burial D72, a large jar sherd held bones, fragments of a Philistine bowl with a small horizontal handle, a jar and a lamp. In the upper half of the large jar, D78, were found a skull, a Philistine bowl fragment with black decoration, a jar rim, a bone pendant, two faience beads, two shells and a glass body fragment, probably intrusive. Burial D86 consisted of two jars halved lengthwise, facing one another, with skeletal remains, a pyxis and a jar body and handle fragment inside. Pieces of two four-handled biconical jars, bowls, including one with bands and spirals painted in red and black, a red-slipped and burnished pyxis, a chalice fragment and a painted lamp fragment lay in the vicinity. D87 and D84, which lay directly below, may belong to a single interment. Bowl fragments from D87 mended with sherds from D88 and D89 to the east and west respectively, illustrating the highly disturbed nature of the deposit. D84 consisted of a skull with a small bowl, a jug, a pyxis and a Philistine beer jug, but no burial jar. D87 yielded a burial jar with no skeletal remains, jugs, bowls a ring and Philistine craters. D88, a sherd of which mended with D87, yielded a single large jar, kernos fragments, bowls, jars and a pilgrim flask. In D89, fragments of a large jar were found together with the skull and bones of a nine-year-old brachycephalic child and a Late Bronze Age dipper juglet. The excavated portion of burial D91 revealed part of a rectangular cist built of mudbricks encasing an interment in two jars. Inside the large and smaller jar (fitted together mouth-to-mouth) were found skeletal fragments, but in the cist next to the jars lay the skull of a child, perhaps intrusive, a metal bowl, fragments of bowls with and without Philistine decoration, a cooking pot, a lamp, a pilgrim flask, a beer jug, an iron nail and two intrusive bronze coins (M. Dothan field notes).

Tell el-Farah (S). W.M.F. Petrie, working on behalf of the British School of Archaeology in Egypt, excavated two Iron I child jar burials in the 500 Cemetery of Tell el-Farah (S). Burials 513 and 516 each consisted of a pit into which had been placed a single jar with the remains of a child and a few provisions. Both burials included pottery vessels, predominantly bowls, in addition 513 contained a bangle and an amulet, and 516 contained beads, a scarab and a shell (Abercrombie 1979: 255-56; Petrie 1930: pls. 31: 315; 32: 148; 33: 39-40, 64, 69).

Kfar Yehoshua. A. Druks, of the Israel Department of Antiquities, excavated a twelfth- to eleventh-century BCE jar burial in the western Jezreel Valley near Kfar Yehoshua. Two facing storejars, with their necks and rims removed, accommodated the extended body of a forty-year-old man wearing a gold scarab finger ring on his left hand. Mortuary provisions included terracotta and bronze bowls, jars with ovicaprid bones, ox and pig bones, a bronze knife and three large pilgrim flasks. Outside of the burial jar containing the upper half of the body were found a large eight-handled crater, a bowl and a chalice. The excavator also reported burnt earth surrounding and inside the jar containing the head (Druks 1966: 214-16, 220).

Tel Kishyon. R. Amiran and C. Cohen, of the Israel Department of Antiquities, excavated a thirteenth- to twelfth-century BCE cemetery on the southwest slope of Tel Kishyon. In Area A level I, approximately 0.3 m below ground surface, they uncovered the scattered sherds of half a jar containing a skull and skeletal remains, a chalice, small bowls, lamps, a small pilgrim flask and other vessels (Israel Antiquities Authority file, Tel Kishyon: photos 11736–38).

Megiddo. In the Oriental Institute of the University of Chicago excavations at Megiddo, four Iron I infant burials, one of which was in a jar, were found in Tomb 37. This tomb was a cave with evidence of both domestic and funerary use. Three of the infants lay extended on their backs (37B, 37C1). The fourth (37C2) had been inserted into an early Iron Age jar, with its top broken off, set into an irregularly-shaped hole in the floor. The infant buried in the jar was less than one year old and was adorned with four bronze bracelets and numerous beads (Guy 1938: 77, 79).

Tell el-Oremé. An Iron I jar burial, similar to the Kfar Yehoshua example, was excavated by G. Edelstein of the Israel Department of Antiquities at Tell el-Oremé (A. Druks, private communication 1984).

Sahab. Sahab Tomb 1, located in Area C on the western slope of the mound, was a large natural cave with a narrow entrance and a 'chimney-like opening' in the ceiling. In the uppermost level, dating to the eleventh or tenth century BCE, men and women were buried in four pairs of jars and an infant was placed in a smaller jar. The excavator, M. Ibrahim, noted the 'burnt effect of bones'. Bracelets, rings and a dagger accompanied the burials (Ibrahim 1972: 31).

Tell es-Saidiyeh. The University Museum of the University of Pennsylvania excavations at Tell es-Saidiyeh, under the direction of J.B. Pritchard, unearthed four children's storejar burials dated to approximately 1200 BCE. In Tomb 120, a large storejar with its bottom shorn off was set next to a semi-circle of stones. The jar contained the disarticulated remains of at least three small children adorned with cowrie shells and bronze bangles (Pritchard 1978: 23). The child buried in Tomb 126 was buried without provisions, but five bases of Pritchard's Type 53 funerary vessels overlay the burial. These wheel-made jars, with short, wide necks, high shoulders and no handles, had a hole in the center of an unfinished, flat base. Similar vessels are known from Aniba, Deir el-Medineh and Saft in Egypt, and from the Egyptian administrative sites of Tell el-Ajjul, Beth Shan Level VI and Deir Alla Level F. Pritchard proposed that the unfinished base was not meant to be seen but rather buried, and that the hole functioned as a funnel for liquid libations offered to the dead below (Pritchard 1978: 7-8, 24). Both burials 120 and 126 were located in walls near corners or junctures. Tomb 131, the only other burial within a wall, was also a child interment, suggesting that these burials were intended as foundation deposits. In Tomb 121, two halves of storejars, perhaps covered with bowls, held the remains of a single child buried without objects. In Tomb 136, a storejar containing the disarticulated bones of a child had been placed at the feet of the uppermost of two skeletons buried one on top of the other. The goods provided for the child could not be distinguished from those intended for the adults (Pritchard 1978: 26).

In his excavation, J. Tubb of the British Museum encountered three types of jar burials. In the first, predominant type, the mouth of the jar was sealed with a bowl, a stone or the base of another jar. Tomb 63 contained bronze or iron bracelets and anklets, beads and amulets. Tubb also excavated 'double-pithos' burials. The body was encased in two large pithoi joined shoulder-to-shoulder with their necks removed. The junction of the two vessels was sealed with storejar sherds or stones. Grave goods were found inside and outside the jars, similar to those in the Kfar Yehoshua jar burial. Tubb's third type of jar burial was the 'poor version' of the double pithos in which the body was covered with storejar sherds, or, in two cases, the head was set inside a jar with its neck broken off (Tombs 43, 45). Tubb's excavations uncovered infant burials with no gifts (Tombs 20, 29), infants with jewelry (Tombs 40, 63, 156, 209), an infant with a basalt quern and grinder (Tomb 243), and an adult with just jewelry (Tomb 207). Bronze and ceramic bowls, and ceramic pyxides, dipper juglets, jugs and lamps were provided in jar burials (Tubb 1988).

Tell Zeror. At Tell Zeror, K. Ohata of the Japanese Society for Near Eastern Research excavated 66 storejar and 11 pithoi burials from the Late Bronze and Iron Ages. Two storejars were set mouth-to-mouth, or, in some cases, two pieces (ordinarily from storejars) were laid together after the rims and narrow necks were removed. The majority of these burials contained the 'spoiled' bones and teeth of babies or children (Ohata 1970: 71-72). M. Kochavi excavated additional examples (A. Druks, private communication 1984).

Anthropoid, Wooden and Stone Coffin Burials

Beth Shan. The University Museum of the University of Pennsylvania excavations uncovered the remains of nearly 50 anthropoid sarcophagi distributed in tombs throughout the Northern Cemetery in Beth Shan: Tombs 60, 66, 69, 90, 107, 202 A–B, 219 A–B, 221 A–C and 241. The tombs were probably cut in the Early Bronze IV period, and all but seven were altered in reuse (Oren 1973: 101-02).

Most of the anthropoid coffin lid depictions were 'naturalistic', with life-size, molded features, compared to the 'grotesque' lids with larger-than-life, appliquéd features. The naturalistic representations followed Egyptian conventions in size, hairstyle and attempted portraiture. Headdresses consisted of wide bands, occasionally decorated with stylized lotus flowers. Only one face sported an Osiris beard; the remaining examples were beardless, as were the depictions from Tell el-Yahudiyah and Aniba in Egypt (T. Dothan 1982: figs. 17,19, pl. 26). Tombs 66 and 90 yielded five examples of the 'grotesque' type of lid. Three lids depicted individuals wearing helmets or caps, perhaps wound like a turban (Tombs 90, 90C). The fourth headdress was decorated with vertical fluting, and the fifth with a zigzag line. T. Dothan compared the headgear to that worn by the Sea Peoples, particularly the Philistines, as depicted on the reliefs of Ramesses III at Medinet Habu (T. Dothan 1982: 274). E. Oren cited the Medinet Habu reliefs and the lack of Philistine pottery found with the sarcophagi in support of his identification of the depicted individuals with the Denyen (Oren 1973: 138-40). These depictions lacked Egyptian conventions such as the wig and Osiris beard; however, in conception and arrangement with the hands lying on the chest, they remained faithful to the Egyptian prototype. Perhaps the example from Tomb 90C with the zigzag decoration and circles represented a further stylized version of the hanging lotus buds atop the hair, similar to the example in Deir el-Balah Tomb 118.

Most of the tombs were violated in the Roman or Byzantine period, so it was difficult to ascribe the scattered finds to particular burials. However, most were found with a cosmopolitan collection of vessels and objects, including a relatively large quantity of Egyptian items. The most common funerary provisions were saucer lamps with nozzles blackened from use. Other vessels commonly provided included bronze vessels, bowls, pilgrim flasks and stirrup vases dating from the late thirteenth through the early eleventh century BCE. In addition to vessels, the deceased were buried with jewelry, a gold mouthpiece, fiddle-shaped gaming boards, *ushwabtis*, imitation Mycenaean III female figurines and Egyptian scarabs, seals, amulets, lotus representations and pendants of Bes, Ptah and other deities (Oren 1973: 104-31).

Deir el-Balah. T. Dothan of the Hebrew University, Jerusalem, excavated thirteenth- to twelfth-century BCE anthropoid coffin burials at the site of Deir el-Balah. These were the earliest examples of Levantine coffins with delineated heads and shoulders, similar to the examples found in Egypt proper. The ceramic coffins, cylindrical in shape and tapering towards the squared off foot, were placed in pits cut in the kurkar and oriented roughly east–west. Tombs 114, 116 and 118 each contained the remains of two extended adults, at least one of whom was male, and fragmentary remains of one or two additional individuals. The only published example of the dominant 'naturalistic' type of lid depiction was from Tomb 114, with a delineated head and shoulders. The face mask presents a rather glum countenance, and is framed by a typical Egyptian coiffured wig with long, straight, blunt-cut hair tucked behind the ears, an Osiris beard and hands crossed over the chest. The mask had been modelled separately and applied to the lid as a unit (T. Dothan 1973: 131). The coffin lids in Tombs 116 and 118 were two of the five examples from Deir el-Balah exemplifying the 'grotesque' type, lacking delineated shoulders or head. This type, rather than the delineated or naturalistic representation of Tomb 114, also appeared in tombs at Tell el-Farah (S), Lachish and Beth Shan. The 'grotesque' face with appliquéd features on the Tomb 116 coffin covered an adult male, an adolescent, a third individual and the teeth of two adults and one juvenile (T. Dothan 1979: 92, fig. 70).

The contents of Tomb 114 illustrate the types of gifts provided for the deceased, in this case an adult male, a second adult, a young person and a three- or four-year-old. As in Tombs 116 and 118, a large four-handled storejar with a dipper juglet inside, capped by a bowl, stood erect near the head of the coffin. Inside the coffin, bronze vessels and knives, and additional vessels lay alongside the bodies. Jewelry and amulets were worn by the deceased: gold and carnelian beads, stone and bone pendants, earrings, Egyptian amulets frequently of Bes or Ptah-Sokhar, and scarabs, including one with the name of Ramesses II (T. Dothan 1979: 5, 20, 24, figs. 8, 10). Additional vessels lay scattered around the outside of the coffin within the grave: Egyptian, Mycenaean and locally-made jars, goblets (Tombs 114, 116), flasks (Tombs 116, 118) and bowls (Tombs 116, 118). Other funerary provisions found in this cemetery, but not provided in Tomb 114 included a seal, gaming pieces and statues of three Egyptian deities: Horus, Amon and an ithyphallic god (T. Dothan 1979: 44).

Tomb 118 exhibited several distinctive features. A variant arm position and highly debased lotus garland headdress were depicted on the coffin lid, ivories and a bronze mirror were deposited in the coffin, and libation (?) vessels were arranged around it. One storejar (marking the location of the burial) projected above ground level, while a second jar of the same type stood beneath it on the tomb floor. Two Egyptian type v-shaped bowls with perforated bases also lay near the coffin (T. Dothan 1979: 69-70, fig. 122).

Tomb 111 contained a unique stone sarcophagus made of local limestone. Unfortunately the tapered head end of the lid had been broken away and the sarcophagus was devoid of contents, but 'Egyptian type sherds' and scattered bones were retrieved from the vicinity (Beit Arieh 1985a: 48). As with the other coffins from the site, it may date from the end of the Late Bronze Age. In a Middle Bronze II interment from Tell ed-Daba Stratum F, a Canaanite in a contracted position equipped with a Syro-Palestinian battle axe and a bronze dagger had been buried in a limestone coffin. Several additional examples were also reported from the site (van den Brink 1982: 5, 25-26, 37-38).

Tell el-Farah (S). The British School of Archaeology in Egypt conducted excavations at the site of Tell el-Farah (S), Sharuhen. Three of the bench tombs, 935, 552 and 563, contained anthropoid coffin fragments. Tomb 935 (the earliest of the three) had been vandalized, and only fragments of the coffin without the lid remained (Macdonald *et al.* 1932: 25). Tombs 552 and 562, known as the tombs of the Philistine Lords, have been dated to the twelfth and possibly early eleventh century BCE, and to end of the twelfth to the first half of the eleventh century BCE, respectively. The coffin lids were modelled in the grotesque style with faces sporting Osiris beards. Scarabs, Egyptian and Egyptianizing pottery found by W.M.F. Petrie, and the paucity of Philistine vessels identified by T. Dothan, attest to the Egyptian rather than Philistine origin and implementation of this type of burial (T. Dothan 1982: 32; McClellan 1979: 62; Macdonald *et al.* 1932 pl. XIX; Petrie 1930: 8, pl. LXIX).

Lachish. Anthropoid coffins were found by the Wellcome–Colt/ Wellcome–Marston Archaeological Research Expedition in Lachish Cave 570. The cave, measuring approximately 12 m in diameter with plastered floor and walls, was cut into the Middle Bronze Age fosse. One of the coffins was painted with a hieroglyphic inscription and with crude, poorly preserved depictions of the Egyptian deities Isis and Nephthys (T. Dothan 1982: 276; Tufnell 1958: 248). In addition to the coffins, the cave contained human teeth, local pottery (including bowls, dipper juglets, a lamp, a jar, a pilgrim flask, a mini-pithos and a storejar) and jewelry, including an earring, beads, scarabs and two Uzat eyes. O. Tufnell originally dated the tomb to 1225–1175 BCE. T. Dothan lowered the date to the first half of the twelfth century BCE on the basis of the Philistine pottery found at the site. In support of Tufnell's dating, E. Oren noted that the pottery found with the coffin dated to the same period as the collection from the Fosse Temple which was destroyed late in the thirteenth century BCE (Oren 1973: 140).

Tel Midrass. A 'naturalistic' lid fragment was found on the surface of Tel Midrass, el-Midrassa, situated six kilometers east of Beth Shan (Oren 1973: 140).

Sahab. The two Sahab coffins unearthed by M. Ibrahim were the only wooden Iron Age coffins preserved. Sahab Area C Tomb 1, an irregularly-shaped cave with a chimney-like opening in the ceiling, was used initially for primary burials on benches. The cave was used secondarily for coffin burials, and, later for jar burials of men, women and infants. One of the fragile wooden coffins contained an infant, and the second held a 'warrior' with a dagger, a bronze anklet and an iron bracelet (Ibrahim 1972: 32).

Cave, Shaft and Chamber Tombs

Amman—Jebel Nuzha. R.W. Dajani excavated a rock-cut cave, measuring approximately three meters in diameter, at Jebel Nuzha, Amman. Dajani compared the 160 retrieved pottery vessels to the assemblages from Tell Beit Mirsim C, Tell el-Farah (S) 500–600 Cemeteries, Megiddo VIIb–VIa, Dothan Tomb 1, Deir Alla E and Madeba. The pottery was virtually all locally made; there were no Mycenaean, Cypriot or Philistine wares (R. Dajani 1966c: 48-9).

Amman—Umm el-Jimal. M. Piccirillo published a thirteenth- through tenth-century BCE pottery assemblage from a tomb at Umm el-Jimal, near Zerqa in the Amman district. The bowls, lamps, jar and crater probably originated in a cave or bench tomb used for multiple burials (Piccirillo 1976).

Baqah Valley. With a magnetometer, P. McGovern of the University of Pennsylvania Baqah Valley Project discovered an undisturbed twelfth- through first half eleventh-century BCE tomb on Jebel al-Hawayah, in the Baqah Valley in Jordan. The tomb consisted of a forecourt and a chamber measuring 20 square meters. Cave A4 held a minimum of 233 individuals, primarily in secondary bone piles: 92 males (53.8%), 50 females (29.2%) and 29 individuals of undetermined sex (17.0%). Women died between 17 and 25 years of age, and men between 25 and 35. Approximately 18% of the population survived into their forties, and 8% reached 45 years of age or more. Among the sub-adults, 24% died aged 8 to 16 months. The single newborn suggests that neonates were buried elsewhere. Retrieved burial provisions included 70 complete vessels, 57 beads, 21 copper-base and two iron (steel) rings, 5 copper-base toggle pins, 79 marine shells, 3 probable spindle whorls, a drop pendant, a Mitannian Common-Style cylinder seal, a stamp seal, a scarab and a flint sickle blade. This example, together with a seventh-century BCE tomb from Tell Ira, constitute the only reported instances of separating men from women and children at burial. Men, who outnumbered the others by a 2:1 ratio, lay to the north, and women and children to the south (McGovern 1981, not mentioned in McGovern 1986). Twelve crania had been stacked in a row along the western cave wall. In the Late Bronze II burial Cave B3, 200 vessels had been provided for 50 individuals, but in the Iron Age burial cave a meager 78 vessels accompanied more than 220 bodies. In the Iron Age tomb, supplies consisted of bowls, lamps, jugs, juglets, craters, strainer-spouted jars and chalices; basalt mortars; jewelry of carburized iron, bronze, glass, faience, semi-precious stone, bone and shell; plus toggle pins, buttons, one scarab, one stamp seal and one cylinder seal. No weapons or tools, except the possible spindle whorls and a flint sickle blade, were provided. Preliminary faunal analysis identified rodent, bird and reptile remains, but none of the larger animals or fish most common in Late Bronze Age assemblages (McGovern 1981; 1982a: 123; 1982b: 52; 1986: 53-61, 305-14, 315-16).

Beth Shemesh. The Haverford College Expedition, under the direction of E. Grant, excavated burial Cave 11 at Beth Shemesh, Ain Shems. The cave was used from the

Early Bronze Age through the tenth century BCE. Iron Age objects included Philistine bowls and craters, Egyptian amphoriskoi and a pithos, a Black-on-Red I–II sherd and two scarabs of Ramesses III (T. Dothan 1982: 50-51; Grant and Wright 1939: 125-26).

Dothan. Dothan Tomb 1 is unique in plan. J.P. Free of Wheaton College (Wheaton, Illinois) uncovered a shaft with seven steps leading down to a doorway and then into an irregularly-shaped chamber with domed roof, six niches, two crypts and a window (Cooley 1968: 14). Two large storejars, each containing a dipper juglet, were positioned outside the chamber window (Cooley 1968: 91), similar to tombs at Ugarit. Remains of 288 individuals were retrieved from the cave. The vast majority lay jumbled with their gifts along the cave periphery. A few individuals, presumably the latest burials, were laid out extended or contracted on the chamber floor with no fixed orientation. Several of the deceased were provided with mudbrick pillows and mudbrick or stone beds or platforms. Three thousand one hundred and forty-six artifacts including vessels, furnishings, personal possessions and cultic vessels lay along the tomb periphery and around the bodies. The tomb contents date from the fourteenth through the end of the twelfth century BCE. Level I (1200–1100 BCE) attributions include 27 skulls, 48 lamps, 43 pyxides, 37 bowls and numerous jugs (Cooley 1968; Free 1960: 12).

Tell el-Farah (N). In the Tell el-Farah (N) excavations directed by R. de Vaux of the Ecole Biblique et Archéologique Française de Jerusalem, a single tomb of unspecified plan was attributed to Level VII. Several inhumations were accompanied by a miniature flask, a black juglet, a piriform juglet and a one-handled biconical jar. The vessels dated from the eleventh through the ninth century BCE, and perhaps later (Chambon 1984: 67, pl. 58.24-27).

Gezer. R.A.S. Macalister's excavations for the Palestine Exploration Fund uncovered one twelfth- to eleventh-century BCE cave tomb at Gezer/Tell el-Jazari/Tell Abu Shusheh. Cave 8I, initiated in the Late Bronze II period and later reused as a cistern, was unusual in containing a stone-covered pile of human, sheep, goat and cow bones. The small finds—including a Hathor-Astarte plaque, pillar figurines, scarabs, pendants, an eyebead, a rattle, an arrowhead, one quadruped model and iron fragments—belonged to later Iron Age burials (Macalister 1912: 81-82).

Gibeon. The necropolis at Gibeon, al-Jib, was utilized from the Early Bronze Age through the Roman period. A.K. Dajani excavated one Iron I–II burial cave situated on the slope east of the spring, and noted the presence of five other rock-cut tombs in the vicinity, all disturbed in antiquity. The cave, which measured 8.3 × 7.3 m, contained a large quantity of human bone, including male and female skulls, plus 400–500 pots of the Iron I and II periods. The pottery, which appeared to be locally made, except for the spouted-strainer jugs, consisted of 45 percent lamps, followed in decreasing frequency by bowls, dipper juglets and pyxides. Other grave goods included a zoomorphic figurine, jewelry, household articles, eight scarabs and a seal (A. Dajani 1951: 48; 1953: 66, fig. 21).

Haifa. In 1978, Y. Algavish of the Israel Department of Antiquities conducted salvage excavations of a tomb located in the Neve Yosef neighborhood of Haifa. The collapsed roof precluded establishing the plan, so the tomb may have been a bench tomb. Algavish dated the Cypro-Phoenician juglets, bowls, plates and vessels to the eleventh century BCE, but a tenth-century BCE date is more likely. P.L.O. Guy excavated seven tombs from the same period on the road to Neve Sha'anan, but the exact location and the specifics of burial were not published (Haifa—Newe Yosef 1978).

Hebron. Israel Department of Antiquities archaeologists excavated dwelling caves in Hebron dating from the Chalcolithic period and the Early Bronze Age which were reused for burial during the end of Iron I and the beginning of Iron II (Hebron 1966).

Irbed. R.W. Dajani excavated four Iron Age caves at Irbed, a site located 110 km north of Amman near Tell el-Husn. A passage with four rock-hewn steps connected burial caves A and B. Pottery vessels in Tomb B demonstrated that the cave was in use from the end of the thirteenth through the end of the ninth century BCE and again in the Roman period (R. Dajani 1966a: 88-95). Tomb D, dating from 1350–1100 BCE, of unspecified plan or dimensions, contained bowls, Cypriot bilbils, lamps with smoked nozzles, knife blades and a rectangular stone pendant (R. Dajani 1964).

Two additional tombs located in the same vicinity were uncovered during salvage excavations in 1984. Both tombs were robbed, but one contained sherds spanning the Early Bronze Age to Iron II (C.G. Lenzen, Site report at national meetings of the American Schools of Oriental Research, 1984).

Jericho. At Jericho, J. Garstang excavated a single burial, Tomb 11. It was isolated from the others in the necropolis and differed in plan, resembling a pit. Accompanying the later interments, which had been 'partially cremated', were a large number of armlets of bronze and some of iron, a scarab with the name of Tuthmosis III and a scarab depicting Hadad standing on the back of an animal. The tomb is dated to approximately 1200 BCE (Garstang 1932: 37).

Lachish. Caves 559 and 571, dated by O. Tufnell of the Wellcome–Colt/Wellcome–Marston Archaeological Research Expedition to c. 1250–1150 BCE and 1225–1175 BCE respectively, were unfortunately both disturbed. Cave 559 contained the standard assemblage of vessels: bowls, lamps, jugs and dipper juglets, and some imitation Cypriot Base Ring and imitation Mycenaean wares. A spearhead, kohl sticks, beads and scarabs were also provided (Tufnell 1958: 246). Cave 571, a rock-cut circular chamber measuring approximately three meters in diameter, yielded a somewhat richer assemblage than its contemporary, with bowls, lamps, Base Ring ware, Mycenaean imports, a storejar, a miniature pithos, one ring, a Late Bronze Age type plaque of a naked woman with an Hathor coiffure holding her breasts ('Astarte'), a Ptah Sokhar figurine and a debased Taurt or hippopotamus (Tufnell 1958: 250).

Cave 570, a 12 m in diameter cave with plastered walls and a floor, dated by Tufnell to c. 1225–1175 BCE, is described above under anthropoid coffin burial.

Madeba. The Iron Age burial excavated by G.L. Harding was in one of several natural caves located east of the Madeba tell. Harding and B.S.J. Isserlin both dated the tomb to c. 1200–1150 BCE, Harding comparing the ceramic assemblage to Tell Beit Mirsim C, and Isserlin comparing it to Tell Beit Mirsim B1 (Harding 1953: 27; Isserlin 1953: 33). Although skeletal remains were not reported, the quantities of vessels and small finds indicate multiple burials. Recovered from the cave were 56 bowls, 26 lamps, a pilgrim flask, a jug, a jar and a vase. Metal objects included toggle pins, arrowheads, blades, rings and earrings. Ramesside-type scarabs, an Uzat eye, a small crouching ram (?) figurine, oblong stone pendants, beads and cowrie shells were also provided for the deceased (Harding 1953: 28-33).

Mafraq. M. Piccirillo published pottery from the site of Mafraq, located on the Jordanian eastern border at the desert margin, not far from the site of Umm el-Jimal near Zerqa in the Amman district. The number of retrieved vessels and the lack of tomb plan suggest that the vessels came from a cave tomb. Upon comparison with the pots from Irbed Tombs A, B and C, Piccirillo dated the craters, bowls, jars and lamps from the thirteenth through the tenth century BCE (Piccirillo 1976).

Megiddo. At the site of Megiddo, the Oriental Institute of the University of Chicago excavated several twelfth-century BCE burials interred in earlier chambers. Tombs 37, 39 and 76 were reused caves and rock-cut chambers probably dating from the Middle Bronze I period. Tomb 37, used for both funerary and domestic purposes, differed from the others as the burial place of four solitary infants. The infant jar burial 37C2 has been described above under jar burials. The infant designated 37B lay supine, its head (missing) to the south, with a bracelet on its left upper arm. Infant 37C1 lay supine with its head to the east. These four infants were probably interred under the floor of the family dwelling rather than with the older individuals (Guy 1938: 77). Tomb 39, a Middle Bronze I shaft tomb with two irregularly-shaped chambers, yielded scant skeletal evidence, an 'intentionally killed' gold medallion with a Cappadocian symbol, and twelfth-century BCE pottery including a lamp, bowls, pilgrim flasks, chalices, dipper juglets, a crater, storejars and two pyxides (Guy 1938: 119). Tomb 76, a three-chambered rock-cut tomb, was dated by J. Abercrombie to the Early Iron–Middle Iron period. Few objects were found in the tomb: lamps, dipper juglets, pilgrim flasks, chalices, craters, a bronze bracelet, bronze rings, a bone pendant and flints (Abercrombie 1979: 310; Guy 1938: 127).

Tomb 221 consisted of four chambers entered through a stepped shaft. Ceramic mortuary provisions included craters (one with three loop feet), lamps, bowls, pilgrim flasks, two storejars, a chalice and a pyxis. An iron bracelet, two flints and a perforated shell completed the assemblage. Notable features included a large storejar found standing erect at the entrance to Chamber A, and deep pits cut into the floor—interpreted by the excavators as later storage silos, but by Abercrombie as a cistern-like pit comparable to the ones cut in Samaria Tomb 103 (Abercrombie 1979: 311; Guy 1938: 121). Several additional twelfth- to eleventh-century BCE cave interments contribute little to our understanding of Iron Age burial practices, since they were poorly preserved or subsequently disturbed: Tombs 5, 27, 29, 30 and 64 (Guy 1938: 117, 127).

G. Schumacher of the German Society for Oriental Research excavated a single cave tomb from this period. The predominant pottery forms were lentoid flasks and craters. Also found in the cave were bowls, jugs, lamps, a chalice, two whorls, an iron ring and knife, a bangle and a needle (Schumacher 1908: 166-68, photos 241–48).

Tell en-Nasbeh. The expedition directed by W.F. Badè of the Pacific Institute of Religion in Berkeley, California excavated Tomb 32 in the eastern section of the West Cemetery of Tell en-Nasbeh. Tomb 32 was a very large natural cave, measuring 11 × 6 m, perhaps with a rough stone bench at the far end of the cave. Hewn for burial in the Early Bronze Age, this cave was reused in the Early Iron–Middle Iron and Byzantine periods. The majority of finds dated from the mid-twelfth through the mid-eighth century BCE, especially to the tenth and perhaps ninth centuries BCE, and so will be presented below (McCown 1947: 77-82; Wright 1948: 472).

Bench and Arcosolia Tombs

Aitun. A necropolis near the site of Tell Aitun, located four kilometers north-north-east of Tell Beit Mirsim, included tombs from the Late Bronze Age, the Iron Age and the Hellenistic and Roman periods. The hillside opposite the southwest slope of the tell, designated Area C, was utilized for burial primarily in the Iron Age. The earliest excavated Iron Age tomb, C1, dates from the twelfth and perhaps into the tenth century BCE. After clearing the collapsed ceiling, the entrance was found to lead into the long side of a rectangular chamber. This is an unusual feature, which suggested to the excavator, G. Edelstein of the Israel Department of Antiquities, that the tomb had been expanded at a later stage. This small chamber had arcosolia to the right and opposite the entrance, and a passage into a second chamber with two niches (probably for lamps) to the left. The second large rectangular chamber, which measured 4.9 × 1.8 × 3.0 m, was provided with three arcosolia, one on each side, and a round repository approximately 1.1m deep cut in a corner of the chamber floor. The five loculi measured 2.2–1.5 × 1.0–0.8 × 1.2 m. Loculus 1, which had been robbed, yielded bone fragments, lamps, sherds, beads and copper rings. Loculi 2 and 6, also rifled, contained only copper earrings. In undisturbed loculus 4 lay a skeleton surrounded by beads, seven skulls, and ceramic sherds. Skeletal remains of at least 15 people lay on the floor and in the arcosolia. Offerings of the first phase of use had been piled two meters high along one side, but second phase goods remained *in situ*. The lower level burials had been provided with local wares and Philistine pottery, with bracelets, rings, and two conoid stamp seals, one depicting a man riding (?) an animal, and the second decorated with three animals perhaps nursing. An upper-level skeleton lay supine with a copper bracelet on its arm, surrounded by lamps, a flask, a Philistine crater and jar, beads and two bronze socketed arrowheads. The repository was filled with an entire skull at the bottom and a jumble of bones, beads, a scarab, a copper ring and metal bracelet fragments. The vast majority of vessels were of local form and ware: 48 lamps (two with red painted rims and most without signs of use), 37 bowls, 15 storejars, 13 chalices, 3 dipper juglets, one of which was found inside a storejar, 3 pilgrim flasks, 4 globular jars, craters, a pyxis and a strainer (Edelstein, unpublished manuscript). Eight pottery vessels fashioned of a different clay and fired at a higher temperature were determined by petrographic analysis to have been made in Ashdod: five Philistine jugs, a red-slipped pyxis, a red-slipped bottle of Cypriot shape, and a bowl decorated with brown wavy lines on a white slip background. Edelstein distinguished a subgroup of the coastal pottery which was white slipped and occasionally decorated with Philistine motifs. Examples included a jar with a button base, an amphoriskos decorated with red and black lines, two pilgrim flasks including one with an unusual flaring neck, three bowls and seven craters, one of which was decorated with a small bird cramped in the corner of the metope. Three sherds of Cypriot Black Slip I and II were also identified. A scaraboid stamp depicted an animal and two figures, perhaps one leading and one riding the animal. A rectangular stamp was carved with an insect on one side, and a uraeus serpent and feather or hawks on the second side. Small finds included silver and crescent-shaped earrings, copper bracelets, anklets, rings, finger rings, toggle pins incised with geometric decoration, a bracelet and a tweezer of iron, cowrie shells, pendants of hematite, of bone and of red stone, and beads of bone, hematite, faience, amber and red colored stone (T. Dothan 1982: 44; Edelstein unpublished manuscript; Edelstein, Ussishkin, Dothan and Tzaferis 1971: 86-87; Edelstein and Glass 1973; Tel 'Aitun 1968).

Further along the same ridge in which the twelfth-century BCE tomb was discovered, T. Dothan and A. Mazar of the Hebrew University, Jerusalem, excavated two tombs in use from the second half of the eleventh through the ninth century BCE. In one tomb, five steps led into a long, narrow, rectangular corridor with arcosolia on three sides. Narrow channels connected two of the arcosolia with a pit in the floor, which did not function as a repository. Two lamp niches had been carved in the walls and a lamp was found in the vicinity of one of them. The few finds dated to the second half of the eleventh century BCE (Edelstein, Ussishkin, Dothan and Tzaferis 1971: 87). The second tomb, also approached by stairs, consisted of an irregular, elliptically-shaped chamber with five arcosolia and a 1.2 m deep pit in the chamber floor. More than 200 objects lay scattered in the tomb concentrated near the arcosolia, demonstrating to the excavators that the tomb had been disturbed. Among the burial provisions were tenth- and ninth-century BCE pots, a kernos, two bronze belts and numerous other metal objects. Eleventh-century BCE pots at the bottom of the pit provided the *terminus post quem* (Edelstein, Ussishkin, Dothan and Tzaferis 1971: 87-88).

T. Dothan attributed a collection of Mycenaean-influenced cultic vessels and figurines including kernoi, zoomorphic vessels, rhytons and female mourning figurines to the Aitun cemetery (T. Dothan 1969). Excavations demonstrated that the tombs contained primarily local wares, suggesting that the assemblage may have originated from another site.

Akhzib. N. Makhouly and M. Prausnitz (the former in the 1940s and the latter from the late 1950s through the 1980s) have excavated for the Israel Department of Antiquities two necropoli at the coastal site of Akhzib, ez-Zib. The eastern cemetery, er-Ras, is situated on a rocky ridge extending east of the village at a distance of three-quarters of a kilometer. The southern cemetery, el Buq-baq, is located half a kilometer south of Akhzib on a rocky knoll covered with sand. The two cemeteries have been attributed by Prausnitz to the Israelites and Phoenicians respectively, and have been dated from the end of the eleventh through the eighth century BCE. Identical red-slipped and painted 'Sidonian' pottery was found in both cemeteries.

In a typical bench tomb from the eastern cemetery, steps down a shaft as much as three meters deep led into a single rectangular chamber in which the bodies were laid out on the floor or later on benches cut on three sides of the tomb. Makhouly detailed the contents of the disturbed Tomb LVI: two painted holemouth jars, a jug, a lamp, two juglets, an alabaster vase, bronzes, a fibula, two nails, two ring fragments and iron nails (Israel Antiquities Authority British Mandate Period File, ez-Zib). Prausnitz reported red and bichrome ware predominant, some red-slipped and painted 'Sidonian' pottery and rare Cypriot imports. The single, eastern cemetery bench tomb published in detail by Prausnitz, Tomb 4012, held 350 'family' members interred over a 250–300 year period (Prausnitz 1969: 88; 1975b: 27; 1982: 37; private communication 1984).

Four (Prausnitz) or five (Makhouly) different burial types coexisted in the southern 'Phoenician' cemetery, el Buq-baq. Adjacent to simple graves were bench tombs similar to those in the eastern cemetery. The southern cemetery tombs were entered through a much shallower shaft and a carefully chiselled and smoothed square or rectangular opening was cut in the tomb ceiling for a hypothetical superstructure of a platform and table altar. Some of these tombs were particularly well-built of dry-laid masonry. Benches along the three walls were usually rock-cut, although Prausnitz found remains of wooden benches. In addition to the hundreds of inhumation burials, occasional cremated remains were perhaps deposited secondarily in these tombs. Makhouly excavated three such tombs, III, V and XIII, all of which were disturbed, and Prausnitz excavated two reasonably intact examples, Tombs 606 and 979. Tomb 606 consisted of a rectangular entrance with a door leading into a rectangular burial chamber. Ninth- to eighth-century BCE Samaria Ware bowls and platters, Phoenician pottery, bowls, jugs and red-slipped wares were found with extended burials on the floor. Small bowls containing incinerated bones were uncovered near the floor. The approximately 200 bodies in Tomb 606 had been provided with dozens of vessels, but no lamps. Bowls on high-footed stands perhaps functioned as lamps in the southern cemetery. Above the tombs near the hypothetical altars, the most commonly recovered vessels were incense stands, cups, lamps, bowls, plates, jugs and storejars (Israel Antiquities Authority British Mandate Period Files, ez-Zib; Prausnitz 1960: 260; 1969: 87; 1975b: 26-27; personal communication 1984).

Recent excavations have unearthed unusually finely executed gabled-roof chambers constructed of ashlar masonry (E. Mazar, private communication 1988).

Ashdod-Yam. At Ashdod-Yam, located 6 km south of Tell Ashdod and 10 km north-east of Tell Ashkelon, R. Gophna and D. Meron of the Israel Department of Antiquities excavated a single Iron Age tomb dating from the first half of the twelfth century BCE. The tomb resembled Gezer Tombs 9 and 28 in plan. The main chamber, measuring approximately four meters square, had a central pillar hewn from the kurkar to support the roof, and there was a second, smaller chamber. The grave goods and skeletal remains found strewn on the floor indicated that the tomb had been disturbed. Although located on the coast in Philistine territory, there was no Philistine pottery. The bowls, lamps, jars, juglets, amphoriskoi and pilgrim flask were indigenous types. An amethyst scaraboid and two rhomboid carnelian beads completed the assemblage. The five skulls and bones studied by B. Arensburg exhibited 'north African affinities', prompting the excavators to interpret the tomb as a burial for north African mercenaries in the Egyptian army (Gophna and Meron 1970).

Tel Bira. M. Prausnitz of the Israel Department of Antiquities excavated tombs in the slopes opposite Tel Bira, Bir el-Gharbi. The site is located near Kibbutz Yasur in the westernmost foothills of the Galilee mountains, nine kilometers southeast of Acco. Benches around a central depression had been carved from the rock in a long rectangular passage probably cut in the Middle Bronze Age. On the benches lay supine, extended bodies covered with stones and surrounded by funerary provisions including one or two pilgrim flasks, tools and ornaments of the eleventh to tenth century BCE. 'Cult' objects, incense burners, lamps, jugs and 'other' vessels lay in the central depression. These cult objects, unfortunately unspecified, constitute a rare example of cultic objects found in a tomb (Prausnitz 1962; 1975a: 25).

Tell el-Farah (S). The origin of the bench tombs in the Tell el-Farah (S) cemeteries excavated by W.M.F. Petrie of the British School of Archaeology in Egypt has been the subject of controversy. In a refutation of Jane Waldbaum's thesis that two different Aegean groups produced the tombs in the 900 and 500 Cemeteries (Waldbaum 1966), W. Stiebing has plausibly demonstrated the possibility of indigenous development (Stiebing 1970). R. Gonen cited Cypriot examples with a central depression and continuous bench around the periphery of the tomb dating from as early as the Early Cypriot period in support of Stiebing's contention that the bilobate and Philistine tombs represent new types created by combining Cypriot features with local traditions (Gonen 1979: 116-18).

Early tombs from the 900 Cemetery consisted of a stepped dromos leading down into a round or square chamber with a central depression. In Tombs 934, 935 and

960, a buttress protruding from the back wall opposite the entrance divided the chamber into halves. From north to south the tombs were numbered 960, 934, 935, 936, 921, 914, 902, 905 and 920; only 960, 934, 935, 914 and 905 will be detailed. Bodies lay extended on the benches. In at least one case, Tomb 905, larger pots and storejars were stacked in the central well. Pottery, weapons, household articles, alabaster objects and jewelry of gold, silver, precious and semi-precious stones were recovered from these tombs. Each tomb also contained scarabs ranging in date from the early 19th Dynasty to the middle of the 20th Dynasty ending with Ramesses IV. The anthropoid coffin fragments found in Tomb 935 are detailed above under anthropoid coffin burials.

The five 'tombs of the Philistine Lords' in the 500 Cemetery are in part contemporary with, and similar to, the tombs in the 900 Cemetery. The five tombs, 532, 542, 544 (omitted from the discussion), 552 and 562, date from the twelfth through the first half of the eleventh century BCE (see McClellan 1979 for a chronological ordering). The 500 Cemetery tombs have slightly longer dromoi than the 900 Cemetery tombs, and trapezoidal chambers. Tombs 542 and 552 have small subsidiary chambers directly behind the main chamber. Benches and arcosolia above them were hewn into the walls in both chambers. Bodies lay on the benches (Tombs 532, 542), and were arranged in pairs in Tomb 532. Ceramic provisions included primarily locally-made bowls, chalices, lamps and pilgrim flasks, with the addition of a few Philistine vessels and some Egyptian or Egyptianizing pots (Tombs 552, 562). A knife (Tomb 562), daggers (Tombs 542, 552), a spear butt (Tomb 552), jewelry (Tombs 532, 552, 562), bronze bowls (Tombs 532, 562) and scarabs (Tombs 532, 542, 562) had also been provided for the deceased. The anthropoid coffin fragments from Tombs 552 and 562 are detailed above under anthropoid coffin burial (T. Dothan 1982: 29-33; Macdonald *et al.* 1932: 23-26; Petrie 1930: 7-8).

Tell Gezer. R.A.S. Macalister's excavations of Tell Gezer/Tell el-Jazari/Tell Abu Shusheh for the Palestine Exploration Fund uncovered three tombs which were all in use from the late thirteenth through the early tenth century BCE: Tombs 9, 58 and 59. Each of the three tombs had been fashioned with irregularly-shaped benches around the far side of a roughly circular central chamber. Tomb 9 consisted of a shaft with steps leading down into a central chamber with two subsidiary chambers, each provided with a bench or benches along the wall opposite the entrance. Two rock pillars supported the roof in the central chamber. Skeletal remains lay not on the benches but on the floor along with arrowheads, a loomweight, a bowl, a lamp, Mycenaean stirrup jars, Cypriot bilbils and a Philistine crater, pyxis and a stirrup jar decorated with 'a creative individualism quite unlike the usual Philistine ceramics' (T. Dothan 1982: 52 for a phase 1 date). This tomb was reused in the Roman period (Macalister 1912: 308, pl. LXXI).

Tomb 58 was also hewn in Late Bronze II, continued in use until early in the tenth century BCE and was reused in the Hellenistic period. The central chamber, encircled by three roughly cut benches, led into two sunken, small, circular cells each entered by two steps. One cell appears to have functioned as a repository, for most of the objects were found in it. Skeletal remains of young men, older men, mature men, an old person and a woman were scattered throughout the tomb and collected in ceramic vessels. An unusually large number of chalices were buried in this tomb, sometimes with a pilgrim flask, a juglet or bowl, and a lamp. In addition to those forms, jugs, a saucer, Philistine and Mycenaean vessels, finger rings, decorated ivory bars, alabaster saucers, flint knives, an iron band and knife, beads and a figurine were supplied for the deceased. T. Dothan dated the Philistine wares found in the second phase of the tomb's use to her phase 2 (T. Dothan 1982: 52-53; Macalister 1912: 321-25, pls. LXXXXI-LXXXIII).

Gezer Tomb 59 has been variously dated to between the twelfth and the tenth centuries BCE (see Abercrombie 1979: 280). A dromos with four steps sealed by a large closing stone led into a central chamber with five recesses arranged around the periphery. One of the recesses contained the majority of finds and so was considered a repository. Skeletal remains of more than 30 individuals were found in bowls, 5 lamps, and a sherd of a large two-handled jar. Grave goods included 100 vessels, 40 of which were lamps, a diversified collection of Philistine vessels primarily of T. Dothan's phase 2 (T. Dothan 1982: 53) and Cypro-Phoenician Black-on-Red I–II wares. A stylized head of Mycenaean origin, beads of glass paste and carnelian, a decorated ivory comb, small bronze objects, two flint knives, a Bes amulet and animal bones completed the assemblage (Macalister 1912: 329-31, pls. LXXXIV–LXXXV).

S. Loffreda dated Gezer Tombs 28 and 31 to the Iron I period on the basis of his tomb plan typology (Loffreda 1968: 255). Although the contents indicated an Iron II date, as noted by W. Dever (Dever 1976: 442), the tombs may originally have been cut in the Iron I period. These tombs are described with the Gezer tenth- to third quarter eighth-century BCE bench tombs.

Lachish. The Wellcome–Colt/Wellcome–Marston Archaeological Research Expedition excavated Lachish Cave 4002, a circular-shaped chamber with a plastered floor and five loculi. It may have been hewn in the Middle Bronze Age and used only through the end of the Late Bronze Age. An equine mandible was found in the tomb. Of the two layers of bodies, only the upper layer was sufficiently well-preserved to distinguish two extended bodies lying with their heads to the north facing west. The deceased had been provided with a bowl, two lamps, a storejar, a dipper juglet, a cup, Mycenaean sherds, a bronze knife and beads (Tufnell 1953: 239-40).

Megiddo. The two twelfth-century BCE Megiddo bench tombs excavated by the Oriental Institute of the University of Chicago, Tombs 1101–1102 and 1090, were irregularly-shaped chambers. Tomb 1101 recesses C and D were attributed to the twelfth century BCE without dating evidence (Guy 1938: 24). In Tomb 1090, steps led through two irregularly-shaped rock-cut chambers into a third chamber, C, in which eight adult skeletons lay on a 1.2 m high shelf which extended around the circumference of the chamber. Fourteen objects were recorded from this disturbed tomb: a lamp, bowls, chalices, three pilgrim flasks, craters and two storejars (Guy 1938: 126).

Tell en-Nasbeh. The expedition directed by W.F. Badè of the Pacific Institute of Religion, Berkeley, California, discovered Tomb 32 in the eastern section of the West Cemetery of Tell en-Nasbeh. Tomb 32 was a very large natural cave, 11 × 6 m, perhaps with a rough stone bench at the far end of the cave. Hewn for burial in the Early Bronze Age, this cave was reused in the Early Iron–Middle Iron and Byzantine periods. The majority of finds dated from the mid-twelfth through the mid-eighth century BCE, especially to the tenth and perhaps ninth centuries BCE, and so will be presented below under tenth- to eighth-century century BCE cave tombs (McCown 1947: 77-82; Wright 1948: 472).

Sahab. Sahab Tomb C had an unusual plan. The stepped entrance hewn into the rock, the benches at either end of the single broad room measuring 8.2 × 4.5 × 1.8 m and the chimney-like construction near the southeast ceiling corner prompted the excavator, R. Dajani, to presume that the cave originally functioned as a dwelling. Pavements criss-crossing the cave north to south and east to west divided the chamber floor into quadrants A–D. Burials in quadrant C dated to the fourteenth and thirteenth centuries BCE, in D to the thirteenth and twelfth centuries BCE and in B to not earlier than the end of the eighth century BCE. No burial remains were found on the benches. Although goods filled the tomb, the greatest accumulation occurred under the chimney. However, most of these artifacts dated to the late Iron Age and later. Lamps were the most common vessel, accompanied by pilgrim flasks, bowls, jugs, a Mycenaean stirrup jar, a basalt bowl and an anthropomorphic vessel. Other goods included nine metal blades, daggers, knives, arrowheads, toggle pins, anklets, rings, kohl sticks, pendants, seals, stamps, a pottery rattle and an unusual figurine. This figurine, similar to the example from the eighth-century BCE Amman Tomb C, displays hermaphroditic features: a red face with full black mustache and beard and breasts and arms encircling a pregnant belly. Tiers (?) of four spirals arranged at ninety degree angles form the headpiece worn by both figures (R. Dajani 1970; Horn 1971).

The latest burials in Sahab area C Tomb 1 were in jars, the middle level burials were interred in wooden coffins, and at the lowest level in the cave a large number of skeletons, including an infant cradled in a woman's right arm, lay on bedrock benches in the northwest part of the cave. Each individual had been provided with a rock 'pillow' and a lamp. Goods attributed by the excavator, M. Ibrahim, to the earliest level established a twelfth-century BCE date: bowls, jugs, Egyptian alabaster vases, daggers, arrowheads, anklets, rings, needles, nails, a disk of gold, an Egyptian scarab, a small steatite figurine and many beads (Ibrahim 1972: 32).

Cemeteries

Dhahr Mirzbaneh/Ein Samiya. D. Lyon, P. Lapp, Y. Meshorer and Z. Yeivin have excavated graves hewn in the soft chalk in the 3 km long necropolis extending from Dhahr Mirzbaneh to Ein Samiya. W.F. Albright identified tombs dating from the Bronze Age through the Arabic period, but none from the Iron Age have been published (Albright 1923a: 39; Ein Samiyeh 1971: 23; Lapp 1966: 6; Yeivin 1976: 357).

En Hanaziv. N. Tsori in 1951, Y. Porath in 1970 and 1972, and P. Porath in 1982–85 excavated tombs in the extensive En Hanaziv cemetery situated approximately 13 km south of Beth Shan and 2 km north of Tel Rehov. Construction work in 1972 revealed a number of graves the majority of which dated from the Iron Age (Tel Rehob 1972: 11). Some of the shaft graves had one or two chambers originally hewn in the Middle Bronze I period and were reused in the Late Bronze II and Iron I periods. The characteristic tomb of the Late Bronze Age to Persian period consisted of a vertical rectangular shaft with a long narrow burial chamber cut into one of the long walls. The chamber was lower than the shaft floor and the step down into the chamber was blocked with a closing stone. The graves usually contained a single individual with pottery and metal offerings arranged near the head. Iron Age I usage was determined by pottery typical of Megiddo VI and Beth Shan VI (En Hanaziv 1972; P. Porath 1985: 194; Y. Porath 1973: 259).

N. Tsori excavated three Iron I burials in reused Middle Bronze I tombs (9–10,12) and ten burials in tombs cut in Iron I (2, 8, 11, 14–15, 19, 21, 22, 23, 25). The Iron Age examples 2 and 14 consisted of a vertical shaft with a burial niche cut along the bottom either of a side wall (2) or off a corner (14). Tsori described the ceramic bowls, cups, jars and lamps as being of crude ware and execution, similar to vessels from Beth Shan VI and Megiddo VII (Tsori 1975: 11).

Cremation Burials

Akhzib. The earliest open and urn cremation burials at Akhzib may date from the late eleventh century BCE, but most are datable to the tenth and ninth centuries BCE, and so are presented below under tenth- to eighth-century BCE cremation burials (Prausnitz 1969).

Azor. The earliest Iron Age cremation burial in the southern Levant, Azor Area D Grave 63, has been dated to the second half of the eleventh century BCE on the basis of pottery parallels with Tell Qasile X. This unique burial consisted of a two-handled jar capped with a stone standing in the sand surrounded by a square, one meter high stone-built frame. Inside the jar were the calcined bones of humans and animals plus several objects. Among the calcined bones D. Ferembach identified a 40 to 45-year-old brachycephalic male, a 12 to 16-year-old, birds and domestic animals including pig. In addition to the bones, the jar contained a pilgrim flask, a bronze bowl and a gold mouthpiece. E. Oren compared a similar mouthpiece from Beth Shan, probably belonging to a coffin burial, to examples in Mycenaean and Cypriot funerary deposits (Oren 1973: 119). Four one-handled jugs stood next to the burial jar inside the frame. These jugs were red or orange-slipped with ring bases and handles extending from the neck to the body of the vessel. A child's skeleton found extended under the jar may not have been related to the cremation burial. The excavator, M. Dothan, attributed the burial to a 'new ethnic element' (M. Dothan field notes; 1960: 260; 1961c: 173; 1975: 147; T. Dothan 1982: 55, 57).

Jericho. In 1932 and 1933, J. Garstang of the Nielson Expeditions identified 14 early Iron Age I burials at Jericho. The later burials in Tomb 11, a unique pit-like tomb isolated from the others, may have been 'partially cremated'. Burial goods included a large number of armlets of bronze and some of iron, a scarab with the name of Tuthmosis III and a scarab with a depiction of a northern deity astride the back of an animal (Garstang 1932: 37; 1933: 37).

Burials from the Tenth through the Third Quarter of the Eighth Century BCE

Simple Graves

Tell el-Ajjul. W.M.F. Petrie of the British School of Archaeology in Egypt excavated 13 Tell el-Ajjul graves in use during the tenth and ninth centuries BCE: 1010, 1011, 1023, 1029, 1033, 1059, 1067, 1074, 1079, 1083, 1111, 1112 and 1139. The nature of the interment was not specified except for Tomb 1074, which contained a single primary burial, perhaps an adult, in supine position. Among the provisions were a bowl, a Cypro-Phoenician juglet, a faience cup, beads, bangles, scarabs, amulets and a bone lid. The graves demonstrated no conformity in dimensions or orientation. Mortuary supplies included locally-made vessels, primarily bowls, jars and juglets, nine Cypro-Phoenician juglets, a Phoenician urn, a Philistine bowl, a Cypriot oil bottle, two spouted jugs and a single black-burnished juglet. Eight of the graves contained a metal object, either bronze or iron, and four burials yielded six scarabs (Abercrombie 1979: 206-11; Petrie 1932: pls. LVI–LVIII).

Akhzib. In 1941, on behalf of the British Mandatory Government in Palestine Department of Antiquities, N. Makhouly excavated pit graves in Trench C of the el Buq-baq cemetery, located a half kilometer south of Akhzib (Israel Antiquities Authority British Mandate Period File, ez-Zib, photo 26.691). Work resumed at the site with the excavations of M. Prausnitz, also under the auspices of the Department of Antiquities. His excavations uncovered pit and cist graves dating from the tenth and ninth centuries BCE, which he noted were the sole type in the southern cemetery oriented north–south, similar to the burials at Tell Zeror and Khaldé (Prausnitz 1982: 32). Prausnitz also cleared inhumation burials grouped around a central quadrangle with offerings and remains of meals deposited above (Prausnitz 1975b: 27).

Tel Amal. S. Levy and G. Edelstein of the Israel Department of Antiquities conducted salvage excavations at Tel Amal, Nir David, situated northeast of Beth Shan. They uncovered five tombs dug into the earth. Due to problematic stratigraphy, the tombs were attributed to levels III and/or IV, which dated to the tenth and ninth centuries BCE. In four of the tombs the body lay with stones piled around the head and with a small, elongated, handleless jar with a high button base nearby. A wine decanter was also found. Levy and Edelstein compared the button base jars to seventh-century BCE Assyrian examples from Tell Halaf and Nineveh, and to sixth-century BCE vessels found at Tell en-Nasbeh, so the burials should probably be dated to the seventh or sixth century BCE (Levy 1962; Levy and Edelstein 1972: 241).

Azor. A single, simple grave was uncovered by S. Pipano during the course of salvage excavations in the southwestern part of the hill of Azor. Three individuals had been laid in the sand, each with a small juglet under the head (Pipano 1984).

Tel Bira. Nine kilometers southeast of Acco, in the westernmost foothills of the Galilee mountains, M. Prausnitz of the Israel Department of Antiquities excavated a cemetery opposite Tel Bira, Bir el-Gharbi. The cemetery produced burials of the Middle Bronze I and II, Late Bronze, and Iron I and II periods. The Iron II ninth- to eighth-century BCE burials were rock-cut pits measuring approximately 1.8 × 1.5 × 1.2 m, containing an individual, and, rarely, a pair. Offerings were retrieved from niches cut near the graves and from shelves created by widening the rock-cut pit approximately one meter from the surface. A great number of jars, jugs and bowls, some of which contained charred animal bones, had been deposited on the shelves (Prausnitz 1962; 1975b). These graves with rock-cut shelves resemble earlier tenth-century BCE examples from Lachish (Tufnell 1953: 172).

Dhiban. A single grave was identified and the presence of others suspected in an Iron Age necropolis east of Tell Dhiban in Jordan (Reed 1952: 22; Winnett and Reed 1964: 57).

Tell el-Farah (S). W.M.F. Petrie of the British School of Archaeology in Egypt excavated twelfth- to ninth-century BCE simple and cist graves in the 100, 200, 500 and 600 Cemeteries of Tell el-Farah (S) (Petrie 1930: pls. LXVIII–LXXI). They are detailed above under twelfth- and eleventh-century BCE simple and cist graves.

Joya. S. Chapman, who published the pottery from Khaldé, Khirbet Silm and Joya, suggested that cremation and inhumation were practiced together at Joya as they were at Khaldé (Chapman 1972: 57). See the description of the tenth- to eighth-century BCE Khaldé simple graves for details.

Khaldé. The site of Khaldé lies 10 km south of Beirut, situated on two promontories which gradually slope down to the sea. Interment in simple graves cut into the sand was practiced from the tenth through the end of the eighth century BCE. The majority of individuals were covered with stones and provided with pottery vessels including plates with fish skeletons still on them. R. Saidah excavated 178 burials of 120 adults, 37 adolescents and 23 infants. On the basis of a study of the Khaldé skulls, plus one thirteenth-century BCE skull from Byblos and seven skulls from Sidon, W. Shanklin and M. Ghantus concluded that

> for some centuries the people dwelling along the shores of the Mediterranean in Lebanon were a rather homogeneous group all with cranial indices in the doliocephalic and mesocephalic range. Not a single skull was observed in the brachycephalic group representative of the modern mountain dwelling Lebanese (Shanklin and Ghantus 1966).

One hundred and four of the 178 bodies were buried in a north–south orientation, similar to Akhzib and Tell Zeror. In some cases cremated remains in urns were interred together with the inhumations. Inhumation and cremation burial together were probably also practiced at the sites of Khirbet Silm and Joya in the Lebanese foothills near the Litani River south of Khaldé (Chapman 1972: 57).

Six burials have been dated by the excavator to the tenth to ninth century BCE Niveau IV: Tombs 21, 22, 23, 165, 166 and 167. While the burials exhibit distinctive features, without their relative locations it is inopportune to propose an interpretation. The three superimposed burials, 21, 22 and 23, were all adults. The individual in Tomb 21 lay on its left side with its head to the north facing west. An oenochoe and three bowls lay near the head and an amphora stood near the feet. The bodies in Tombs 22 and 23 were each covered with stones from the neck down and sparsely provided for. Burial 22, with its head to the west, lacked any provisions, and 23, with its head to the north facing west, was provided with a single jug positioned near the head (Saidah 1966: 73-74).

The physical relationship of Tombs 165, 166 and 167 to the preceding burials is not clear, but, whereas the preceding three were adult burials, these three were infant and adolescent burials. In Tomb 165, an infant lay in the fetal position on its back with its head to the east facing north, with a small red and black decorated amphora near its head. Tomb 166 contained an adolescent lying on its left side with its head to the west, with a spouted jar, two pilgrim flasks and a one-handled flask, all intentionally broken at the time of burial. The adolescent lying on its right side with its head to the north facing west in Tomb 167 was relatively well provided for. A scarab lay *in situ* on the chest (Saidah 1966: 76, 78, 80), and three bowls, two flasks, one pilgrim flask, a spouted jug and a zoomorphic vase in the shape of a ram, all decorated with red and black, lay in proximity to the body.

Four tombs, 1, 2, 3 and 4, were assigned on the basis of pottery parallels to Niveau III dated from the end of the ninth to the end of the eighth century BCE. Interment practices continued unchanged from the preceding century. The adolescent in Tomb 1, supine with its head to the west, was provided with a bowl at the knees and a mushroom-top jar at the head. A second adolescent, in Tomb 2, lay extended in the sand with its head to the north facing west, resting on a rock pillow (?). This individual was buried with a 19–20th Dynasty type scarab on the chest, and a pilgrim flask, a bowl and an amphoriskos near the head. In Tombs 3 and 4, two individuals positioned on their side and stomach lay head-to-head with large stones over their chest cavities. Pottery vessels, including a red-slipped jug with trefoil mouth, a Samaria Ware B bowl, jugs, a pilgrim flask and small flasks, were positioned around them. An urn containing burned bones lay among the vessels near the back of individual 355 in Tomb 3 (Saidah 1966: 57-63).

Saidah published an additional group of 17 burials, one of which was cremated. Two of the burials were well preserved, but unfortunately not dated. One contained an 'enfant' wearing a necklace with a blue frit scarab and a figure, perhaps Bes or Ptah. In the second burial, an adult of undetermined sex was buried with a scarab at the neck, a bronze fibula on the chest, a bronze bracelet on the upper right arm, and a pilgrim flask and an iron blade at the left side (Saidah 1967: 167).

Lachish. Approximately 32 simple burials dating from the tenth century BCE were excavated at Lachish by the Wellcome–Colt/ Wellcome–Marston Archaeological Research Expedition. Characteristically, a single body with its head to the north, frequently face up, was laid extended in an earth cut grave in the vicinity of the Fosse Temple. In some of the graves, narrow shelves ran along the two long sides of the grave, similar to later examples from Tel Bira (Prausnitz 1962; Tufnell 1953: 172). A bowl, dipper juglet and frequently a jar (rarely lamps or storejars) were placed near the head or feet of the deceased. Some graves lacked provisions (138, 195) and in others the only objects found with the body were personal items such as scarabs, seals, beads, anklets or bracelets. The richest burial, Grave 110, contained two bowls, two dipper juglets, two mini amphoras, one storejar, one plaque, one seal, a bangle, cowrie shells and beads of carnelian, crystal, serpentine and coral (Tufnell 1953: 172). In several of the graves, a storejar stood erect as it had been placed at the time of burial between or near the feet of the deceased (132, 139, 147, 182 at the head). O. Tufnell dated all the following burials to the period between the late tenth and the early ninth century BCE: Pit 102, Graves 110, 132, 137, 138, 139, 147, 154, 159, 160, 167, 169, 182, 189, 191, 192, 193, 194, 195, 196, 197, 198, 222, 229, 231, 236, 239, 519 (Tufnell 1953: 172-74).

The ninth- and eighth-century BCE simple burials from Lachish do not differ from the tenth-century BCE examples. Tufnell ascribed the following burials to the ninth and eighth centuries BCE: Pit 507, Graves 147, 152, 154, 159, 167, 182, 191, 4027, and Tomb 1004 (Tufnell 1953: 172-73, 197-98, 200, 220, 236, 244).

Tell er-Ruqeish. A necropolis located 50 m south of Tell er-Ruqeish was first excavated by J. Ory in 1939. Three different modes of burial were found to be practiced contemporaneously: primary inhumation, open/primary cremation and inurnment. From the ninth to the seventh century BCE, 20 inhumation burials of single adults, usually males in a supine position, were cut into the kurkar throughout the excavated area. The associated pottery has been variously dated by S. Loffreda to the ninth to eighth century BCE (Loffreda 1968: 263), by W. Culican to the ninth century BCE (Culican 1973), by P. Bienkowski to c. 850 BCE (Bienkowski 1982: 84) and most recently by R. Hestrin and M. Dayagi-Mendels to the eighth to seventh century BCE, following the resettlement of Tell er-Ruqeish as part of the Assyrian economic reorganization (Hestrin and Dayagi-Mendels 1983: 56). Very few objects were recovered from these burials, though it must be noted that several graves were uncovered just below the present ground surface. The single individual buried with noteworthy objects had been provided with Cypro-Phoenician bowls, of which only fragments remained, and a jug. One burial differed from the others in containing four skulls and isolated sherds, similar to burials from Ashdod, Azor Area M and Tell el-Farah (S) (M. Dothan 1971: 213; Tell Ruqeish 1974: 4-5).

Khirbet Silm. S. Chapman, who published the pottery from Khaldé, Joya and Khirbet Silm, suggested that cremation and inhumation were practiced together at Khirbet Silm as they were at Khaldé (Chapman 1972: 57). See the description of tenth- to eighth-century BCE Khaldé simple graves for details.

Cist Graves

Akhzib. On behalf of the Israel Department of Antiquities, M. Prausnitz excavated tenth- and ninth-century BCE pit and cist graves in the el Buq-Baq cemetery, located a half kilometer south of Akhzib. Prausnitz noted that these burials were the sole types in the southern cemetery oriented north–south, similar to burials at Tell Zeror and Khaldé (Prausnitz 1982: 32).

Azor. M. Dothan of Haifa University and the Israel Department of Antiquities excavated a stone-lined cist, grave D79, in the Azor Area D cemetery. The cist, which was preserved to two courses, measured 3 × 2 × 1 m. Six supine inhumations with all but one oriented with their heads to the west, were stacked in four levels in the cist. D. Ferembach's osteological analysis identified a brachycephalic male and a mediterranean-type female. The lowest level in the stone cist, Level IV, contained six skulls, scattered long bones and a single articulated skeleton lying extended on its back diagonally across the cist with its head to the northwest. Goods attributed to this lowest level included ten juglets, of which two were black-burnished and five were Cypro-Phoenician, two bowls, agatite and faience beads, a flint knife fragment, bracelet fragments, a silver and a metal earring, and a scarab (M. Dothan Field notes 79/28B). In Level III, a group of four skulls placed near the north wall of the cist was provided with seven juglets including four Black-on-Red juglets or fragments, two jugs, one pyxis, one lamp, beads, an iron knife (?) and a steatite scarab (M. Dothan Field notes 79/28A). Very few finds were ascribed to the four-centimeter-deep Level II. Three individuals, two lying with their heads to the west and a third lying diagonally across the cist with its head to the southeast, were provided with beads and a metal fibula. The latest level, Level I, included a skull, several long bones, and two individuals lying next to each other, with their heads to the west, parallel to the north wall. The Level I couple lay directly above the Level II couple. The Level I individuals were buried with a black juglet, two red juglets, a chalice, three beads, a bronze fragment, a seal and perhaps a scarab (M. Dothan Field notes 79/50; 1960: 260; 1961c: 174; 1975: 147).

Tell el-Farah (S). W.M.F. Petrie of the British School of Archaeology in Egypt excavated twelfth- to ninth-century BCE simple and cist graves in the 100, 200, 500 and 600 Cemeteries of Tell el-Farah (S). Twelfth- and eleventh-century BCE examples have been detailed above. In the 200 Cemetery, 24 cist burials accommodated from one up to more than 126 individuals, and eight cists held only skulls (212, 213, 225, 227, 228, 229, 233, 237).

All of the tenth- to ninth-century BCE 'Solomonic' graves in the Tell el-Farah (S) 100 and 200 Cemeteries, except two children's burials (204-205, 222), were stone-lined and covered with large limestone slabs. Tomb 201, a stone-lined, floored and covered cist, measuring 3.86 × 1.22 × 1.75 m, held 116 adults' and six children's skulls arranged in layers. In the uppermost layer, four bodies lay extended side-by-side, and on their feet rested a second row of bodies. These bodies covered a jumble of skeletal fragments and goods including bowls, chalices, jugs, a storejar, a lamp, horse trappings made of bone, iron weapons, bracelets, two gold fragments of a diadem, a chalice painted with a lotus flower and bud design known from Assyria and Iran (Maxwell-Hyslop 1971: 226), a dagger, more than 20 scarabs, small human figurines and beads in the shape of heads with feathered headdresses (?) (Petrie 1932: 12, pl. XL). Tomb 202, a contemporary of Tomb 201 and similarly constructed, contained fewer bodies but a comparable quantity of pottery vessels (Petrie 1932: 12). The children in Tomb 204-205 lay one on top of the other, each with gold beads. In Tomb 222 the children were adorned with carnelian beads, bronze anklets, toe and finger rings, and earrings of gold, silver and electrum. A small bronze bowl, malachite and haematite pebbles, and quantities of red ochre had been placed near their heads (Petrie 1932: 11).

Khaldé. R. Saidah excavated one late ninth- to late eighth-century BCE cist tomb at Khaldé, Tomb 121. Constructed with sandstone walls and covered with flagstones, the cist measured 2.35 × .95 × 1.3 m on the interior. Inside, Saidah uncovered a single skeleton lying along the west wall with its head to the north, several broken human bones deposited in the northwest corner and three amphoras functioning as burial jars. The relatively fine funerary provisions included two flasks, an oenochoe, six bowls, of which two had red slip inside and over the rim, four dipper juglets, a 22nd Dynasty scarab from the reign of Osorkon IV with a solar bird, an ankh and a scarab flanked by *nb*, and a second scarab depicting a winged sphinx and the tree of life (Saidah 1966: 64-72).

Palmachim. R. Gophna and S. Lipschitz excavated two cist tombs constructed of kurkar slabs at the coastal site of Palmachim, situated six kilometers south of Tell Ashdod. In one tomb they found numerous skeletons, ninth-century BCE pottery and a bronze bowl. The second contemporary tomb was reused in the seventh century BCE (Palmachim 1973).

Tel Qedesh. Two strata of cist graves were exposed while digging a drainage channel in the Jezreel Valley plain 50 m north of Tel Qedesh, Tell Abu Qudeis. The upper level burials dated from the late Roman period, and the lower level cist graves corresponded in date to the tenth- to early ninth-century BCE Strata IV–V on the tell. The cist tombs consisted of a shallow stone-lined pit, in which the body was placed and surrounded by vessels. Mortuary provisions included a cooking pot (a highly unusual item in a simple grave), one-handled jugs, a bowl, a chalice, a Cypro-Phoenician juglet, a metal blade and a zoomorphic vessel (?) in the shape of a horse with a rider (Stern 1968: 193; 1969: 97; Stern and Beit Arieh 1979: 13).

Tel Ritma. Z. Meshel excavated pit tombs cut into the loess and covered with stone slabs on the southern slopes of Tel Ritma. Corresponding levels in the fortress dated to the eleventh and tenth century BCE provide a date for the tombs. These tombs have been detailed above (Meshel 1965; 1974: I, II, pl. 7).

Tell er-Ruqeish. A necropolis located 50 m south of Tell er-Ruqeish was first excavated by J. Ory in 1939. Three different modes of burial were found to be practiced together during the ninth to seventh century BCE: primary inhumation, open/primary cremation and urns bearing cremated remains. North of the summit of the site Ory excavated contemporary stone-built graves (Israel Antiquities Authority British Mandate Period Files, Bir er-Reqeish, photo 035.700).

Tell Zeror. The Tell Zeror eleventh- through early tenth-century BCE family cist graves have been detailed above (Kochavi 1978: 1224-25; Ohata 1967: 35-41).

Jar Burials

Amman—Jebel el-Qusur. The Iron Age tomb at Jebel el-Qusur, northeast of Amman, with eleventh- to tenth-century BCE ceramic coffins and unusually large burial jars has been detailed above under twelfth- and eleventh-century BCE jar burials (Amman—Jabal el-Qusur 1966; Ibrahim 1972: 33).

Amman—Royal Palace. The tenth- to seventh-century BCE tomb located near the Royal Palace in Amman with anthropoid coffins and jar burials is detailed below under anthropoid coffin burials (Yassine 1975: 58).

Azor. The eleventh- to tenth-century BCE Azor Area D jar burials have been detailed above (M. Dothan field notes).

Dhiban. Shaft tomb J5 was the only one of the late tenth- to seventh-century BCE Dhiban tombs to contain jars thought to have been used for burial. A.D. Tushingham recovered fragments of four large storejars with their necks broken off. One jar handle bore a seal impression of the letter *ḥet*. These large storejars may have served as burial receptacles for children, a modest version of the anthropoid coffin of which fragments were also found in the tomb (Tushingham 1954: 24-5; 1972: 91-2). This tomb is described below under anthropoid coffin burial.

Dothan. The excavator of Dothan, J.P. Free of Wheaton College, Wheaton, Illinois, dated six infant jar burials to the period from 900–700 BCE. J. Abercrombie redated the burials to the eighth to seventh century BCE. The six intramural burials consisted of infants placed in jars which were interred in pits. Gifts on the bodies and in the immediate vicinities included lamps, a jar, beads and bangles. The burials are detailed below under eighth- to sixth-century BCE jar burials (Abercrombie 1979: 233-34; Free 1954: 18; 1956: 46, fig. 11; 1959: 26; 1960: 9).

Megiddo. During the Iron II period at Megiddo, small children, perhaps cremated, were accorded intramural jar burial (Schumacher 1908: 18, fig. 14).

Mt Nebo. S. Saller published Iron II (1000–586 BCE) tombs located at the base of Jebel Hussein and the next ridge, north of Mt Nebo near Madeba. In Tomb UCV-84, among the approximately 250 individuals and 650 objects (including ceramic coffin fragments) was found a single large jar containing a burial and a small pot (Saller 1966: 179).

Sahab. The eleventh- or tenth-century BCE Sahab Tomb I, with men, women and an infant buried in jars, has been detailed above under twelfth- and eleventh-century BCE jar burials (Ibrahim 1972: 31).

Anthropoid, Wooden and Stone Coffin Burials

Amman—Jebel el-Qusur. A. Dajani of the Jordan Department of Antiquities reported anthropoid coffins from a tomb on Jebel el-Qusur. The tomb contained five pottery coffins comparable to examples from Sahab A, Beth Shan and Tell el-Farah (S), plus six 'big burial jars of unusual size' and Iron II pottery (Amman—Jabal el-Qusur 1966).

Amman—Royal Palace. In a cistern-shaped tomb located near the royal palace in Amman, K. Yassine excavated five anthropoid burial coffins and more than 30 skeletons either in jars or simply interred around the coffins. The ceramic, cylindrical coffins with flat bases were poorly preserved. Two had modelled or 'naturalistic' faces with an Osiris beard and arms, but the head and shoulders were not delineated. Four handles on each side rendered the coffin portable and the sixteen handles at the back arranged in two rows may have functioned as legs or supports. Two or three individuals lay in each of the coffins. Mortuary provisions included tenth- to seventh-century BCE pottery, bronze bowls and a cylinder seal (Yassine 1975: 57-8).

Dhiban. At the site of Dhiban, A.D. Tushingham excavated eight tombs hewn in the south bank of the wadi, designated Area J. Three late tenth- to seventh-century BCE interconnected rock-cut tombs, J4, 5 and 6, all contained terracotta coffin fragments (Tushingham 1972: 89-96; Winnett and Reed 1964: 58-60, plan 97). Further details are provided below under eighth- to sixth-century BCE anthropoid, wooden and stone coffin burials.

Jerusalem—Old City Walls. Of the three tombs found under the Old City Walls 55 m south of the citadel, one had stone troughs. Cave 1, measuring 2.93 × 3.03 m, consisted of a single room with two entrances. The entrances led into parallel corridors with a bathtub-shaped stone coffin carved from the bedrock between them. A second similar burial-place was cut into the rock along the back wall, perpendicular to the first. Slight ledges on the eastern and western short ends of the central burial-place may have supported a lid. Both burial-places had 'pillows' shaped to support the head and neck. The northern entrance and central burial were built using the earlier Egyptian *'amah* (0.45 m), while the southern corridor and back burial conformed more closely to the longer Egyptian *'amah* (0.52 m). The seeming discrepancy has been explained as an early burial, similar to a tomb in Silwan, to which an additional burial-place for an equally distinguished family member was added at a later time. Since the tomb was devoid of contents, it was dated to the ninth to seventh century BCE on the basis of architectural affinities with the Silwan tombs, and of the primarily eighth-century BCE pottery found outside the entrances to the tombs (Broshi, Barkai and Gibson 1983).

Jerusalem—Silwan. D. Ussishkin distinguished three styles of rock-cut tombs in different regions of the Silwan cemetery: monolithic above-ground tombs, tombs with gabled ceilings and tombs with flat ceilings.

There were seven examples of gabled-ceiling tombs designed to accommodate a single individual or a pair: Tombs 6, 9, 10, 13, 14, 16 and 19. The incomplete Tombs 4, 5, 8 and 32 were probably also gabled-ceiling tombs. These tombs were all relatively small and very similar in architectural features, size and the fine craftsmanship evident in their execution. They were carved along the central portion of the lower cliff with no easy access. D. Ussishkin suggested that the recessed door frame cut around the square opening was a panel for an inscription although none were so used. From the opening a single step led down into a rectangular chamber with a gabled ceiling, the axis of which followed the long axis of the room, and a covered 'trough-niche' cut into one of the side walls. A carved 'window' separated the niche from the main room. At the bottom of the niche below the window sill was the sunken trough or basin with pillows for one or two positioned at one end. The pillows were hollowed out to support the head and neck. In Tombs 10 and 16, with places for two bodies side-by-side, the outermost body lay at a slightly higher elevation (Ussishkin 1986: 229-33, 237-41, 247). In all but one case, the tombs were designed for a single individual or a pair, probably a man and his wife, as recorded in the Tomb 35 inscription, for '. . .]Yahu and his slave-wife'. Ussishkin believed that in all the tombs burial rituals were performed and offerings presented. In the gabled-ceiling tombs the trough-cover formed a shelf on which offerings could be placed for the dead reposing below. Tomb 13 also had a corner shelf for 'offerings, memorial-lights or the like'. In Tomb 16 a cup-like depression carved in the rock between the two pillows was interpreted as a receptacle for holding scents and perfumes (Ussishkin 1986: 89, 102-103, 255).

Ussishkin speculated on the date and occupants of the gabled-ceiling tombs. These gabled-ceiling tombs were unparalleled in Iron Age Israel and Judah except for a small group carved into the east slope of the Kidron Valley between the tombs of Zechariah and Absalom (Ussishkin 1986: 257 n. 5). Examples of tenth- to sixth-century BCE monumental gabled-ceiling tombs from Ararat, Phrygia, Cyprus and Etruscan Italy demonstrate that this style employed at various places in the north-eastern Mediterranean basin was designed to resemble residences and that the ceiling was a skeumorph of a wooden-beam gabled ceiling (Ussishkin 1986: 276). Ussishkin argued that the idea of stone-cut tombs was ultimately of Egyptian origin, but that the idea was disseminated by the Phoenicians. In Judah, the Egyptians themselves, more likely the Phoenicians—or perhaps both—provided the inspiration for the Silwan tombs. For Ussishkin, a Phoenician introduction into the region is supported by the premise that these tombs were the first tombs carved in the Kidron Valley, an area associated with the cult of the Canaanite gods. Nearly one-third of the tombs were never completed, and no inscriptions were carved into the panels. Ussishkin, therefore, proposed that the tombs were carved during the reigns of the pro-Phoenician monarchs Jehoram, Ahaziah and Athaliah (851–836 BCE) for officials who were killed or expelled during the successful overthrow of the government organized by Jehoiadah the priest (Ussishkin 1986: 281-87).

Similar trough-niches but without covers were hewn in the flat-ceiling tombs 20, 27, 42 and 50, in the hybrid Tombs 1 and 15, and possibly in the monolithic Tomb 35. All were cut in the wall with access through a 'window'. The body lay below the level of the window sill so even though it was not covered and the window could not be closed off, the body would not have been visible from the main chamber (Ussishkin 1986: 241-43). No pattern emerged in the distribution of this style of burial-place or in the type of tomb in which it occurred. In Tombs 15 and 24, benches were cut in the tombs in addition to trough-niches (Ussishkin 1986: 93-99, 132-34, 246). Ussishkin proposed an 851–836 BCE date for the gabled-ceiling tombs, and suggested the other tomb types may have been relatively later but that all dated to the first Temple period, before the Babylonian conquest (Ussishkin 1986: 283-84).

In addition to the above examples of troughs which were separated from the main chamber by a window-like opening, Tombs 2 and 43 had a coffin and trough respectively in the chamber proper. Tomb 2, the largest single tomb, was similar in plan to Tomb 3 ('The Tomb of Pharaoh's Daughter') with an entry corridor leading through a vestibule and on into the main square-shaped chamber. Whereas Tomb 3 had a bench against the left-hand wall for the deceased, Tomb 2 had a stone-coffin, without a lid, carved from the rock in the rear of the chamber parallel to the back wall (Ussishkin 1986: 44-46). All that remains of Tomb 43 is a single chamber with a flat roof and a right-angled cornice just below the ceiling, and a burial-place similar to the troughs but cut into the floor near the right-hand wall. In the bottom of the trough was a peculiar installation resembling a miniature trough, which Ussishkin suggested may have held burial-offerings such as a statue. Additional burial-places may have been cut along the left-hand and rear walls as well (Ussishkin 1986: 256).

Mt Nebo. S. Saller published two of the several Iron II (1000–586 BCE) cave tombs located at the base of Jebel Hussein and the next ridge, north of Mt Nebo near Madeba. Among the approximately 250 individuals and 650 objects in Tomb UCV-

84 were found a jar burial and large, flat, ceramic coffin fragments. The coffin sherds were compared to examples from the Adoni-Nur tomb in Amman, Dhiban J3 and Sahab (Saller 1966: 259, 289).

Sahab. On a gently sloping hillside facing the site of Sahab, an anthropoid coffin lay in a 'cistern-like excavation in the rock'. The tomb had been disturbed, but tenth- to ninth-century BCE sherds found near the tomb mouth provided a date. The coffin, which measured approximately 1.8 m long, had a flat bottom and tapered towards the feet. The lid was 'carelessly finished' with molded features and handles serving as ears and a beard (Albright 1932: 295-97).

Bathtub Coffin Burials

Tell el-Farah (N). The excavations of Tell el-Farah (N), directed by R. de Vaux of the Ecole Archéologique Française de Jérusalem, unearthed a bathtub coffin in a central room of a palace, either in Stratum 2 level VIId locus 148, or level VIIe locus 117 immediately above. These levels were dated to the ninth to eighth century BCE and the seventh century BCE respectively. The coffin is probably to be dated to later in the eighth or seventh century BCE, as are all the other examples found in the region, and so will be presented below under eighth- to sixth-century BCE anthropoid, wooden and stone coffin burials (Chambon 1984: 57, pl. 47 figs. 10-12).

Cave, Shaft and Chamber Tombs

Tell Abu Hawam. In 1923, P.L.O. Guy identified a large necropolis extending over an area of more than 200 dunams on the slopes of Mt Carmel, one kilometer north of Tell Abu Hawam. Seven tenth-century BCE tombs (I–VII) were excavated, but III and VI had to be abandoned before completion due to the danger of collapse. These seven tombs exhibited no particular orientation in tomb plan or body placement; however, all had been disturbed. In the 7 × 4 m rectangular cave designated Tomb I, the bodies and their gifts had been laid in two sunken pits each measuring 1 × 2 m. Grave A contained the fragmentary remains of two stone covered, extended inhumation burials oriented with their feet towards the entrance. Small jugs lay near the heads and lamps sat at mid-body. A bowl, four jugs including a Cypro-Phoenician example, two blue glazed beads and sherds were found buried with the bodies. Bone and pottery fragments were all that remained in Grave B. In Tomb II, only partially excavated, Guy found a similar pit containing a single extended burial with its feet towards the entrance accompanied by two bowls, a storejar, a lamp, a jar, a fish-hook and numerous bronze objects including a fibula, an earing, an arrowhead, a finger-ring with blue paste bezel and bangles. Guy suggested that the large and small burial pits in Tomb IV may have accomodated an adult and a contracted adult or a child respectively. In Tomb VII, the disturbed skeletal fragments have been interpreted as a single primary burial covered with a pile of stones. Remains of the burial provisions included fragments of a black Cypriot bilbil and of Cypriot- and Phoenician-looking pottery (Guy 1924: 48-52). The practice of placing bodies in pits in the chamber floor and covering them with stones prevailed in Akhzib and in the one or two Persian period shaft tombs at the nearby site of Atlit. The Atlit sixth-century BCE shaft tombs were found in a Phoenician burial ground with eighth- to seventh-century BCE cremation graves (Johns 1975: 134; Stern 1982: 71-2).

Akhzib. In the eastern cemetery of Akhzib, er-Ras, M. Prausnitz of the Israel Department of Antiquities excavated shaft tombs in use from the eleventh through the end of the eighth century BCE. As in the Tell Abu Hawam and Atlit tombs, bodies were placed in pits in the chamber floor and then covered with stones (Prausnitz 1969: 88, 1982: 37; Stern 1982: 71-2).

Amman—Jebel el-Jedid. A cave tomb cut into the base of Jebel el-Jedid, Amman C, was used for burial from early in the eighth through the seventh century BCE, but then quarried away in Roman times. Numerous tomb contents were retrieved, considering that the tomb had later been decimated. Among the ceramic provisions were eight jugs, six bowls, five dipper juglets, five dishes, four lamps, four oil flasks, three painted flasks, one decanter and one tripod cup. Other finds included an alabaster and a limestone palette, shells from the Mediterranean coast, a bronze fibula, bronze and iron rings and bracelets, and a hermaphrodite deity figurine. This unusual figurine, with no parallels west of the Jordan River, had a bright red face with a black beard and mustache, a headdress of spirals, women's breasts and a pregnant belly. G.L. Harding tentatively identified the deity as Ashtor–Khemosh (Harding 1951: 37-38).

Amman—Umm el-Jimal. The thirteenth- to tenth-century BCE pottery assemblage which probably originated from a cave tomb at Umm el-Jimal, near Zerqa in the Amman district, has been detailed above under twelfth and eleventh century BCE cave, shaft and chamber tombs (Piccirillo 1976).

Bethlehem. S.J. Saller published a collection of 161 complete vessels probably originating from one or more tombs in Bethlehem. Included in the tenth- to seventh-century BCE assemblage were 46 lamps (the photographed examples showed signs of use), 30 with round bottoms, 14 with disc bases, and 2 with flat bases; approximately 46 juglets, of which one was Cypro-Phoenician and 12 were black-burnished; 31 bowls; 31 jugs; 12 jars; 5 cooking pots; and 2 chalices (?) (Saller 1968).

Beth Shemesh. D. Mackenzie of the Haverford Expedition began excavating at Beth Shemesh, Ain Shems, in 1911. One of the tombs from the necropolis northwest of the settlement site dated to the late tenth to ninth century BCE. This tomb may have remained in use into the eighth century BCE, in view of the wealth and selection of tomb goods which are unusual for the tenth and ninth centuries BCE, and of the presence of pillar figurines and models which are more common a century or more later. Tomb 1/11 was a natural grotto located at the foot of a limestone bluff. Two niches were added and 'an artificial funnel opening was pierced through the roof'. There is no mention of skeletal remains, but the size of the cave, the main chamber measuring approximately eight meters in diameter and the side chambers 5 × 4 m and 5 × 5 m, plus the large quantity of objects suggest numerous interments. The majority of the pottery was locally made, and the predominant form was the lamp, of which there were at least 74 examples all with signs of use. Philistine bowls and craters, a kernos (?), a Black-on-Red I–II sherd and an Egyptian pithos and amphoriskoi were also retrieved from the tomb. Egyptian amulets included two scarabs of Ramesses III, an eye of Horus, a Bes, an Isis, a Sekhet, a squatting monkey and a faience rhino. Jewelry and personal items included engraved conical seals, scaraboid beads of faience, paste, stone and ivory, pendant amulets and hundred of beads, primarily of carnelian. Among the more unusual objects were anthropomorphic and zoomorphic figurines and models: a female pillar figurine, a head of a male 'divinity', a complete horse, a horse head with an open tube for a mouth, spouted dove fragments, two model thrones and a rattle (T. Dothan 1982: 50-51; Grant and Wright 1939: 125-26; Mackenzie 1912–13: 52-63 pl. xxiii).

Dhiban. In Dhiban Area J, A.D. Tushingham excavated five tombs of similar plan situated side-by-side along the slope: Tombs J4–8. They consisted of a dromos, with stairs occasionally preserved, leading into a diamond-shaped chamber with shelves or lamp (?) niches cut into one or more of the sides. Tunnels connected Tombs J4–6. In Tombs J6 and J7, shallow, rudimentary pits located at the rear of the chambers may have functioned as repositories. It is also possible that the 'Burnt Bone Deposit'—a circular hole 1.3 m in diameter located 3.5 m east of J4, which was filled with broken and burnt human bones, sherds and bronze fragments—functioned as a repository rather than as a source of fertilizer, as was suggested by the excavators. The tombs' contents date from the late tenth through the seventh century BCE, primarily from the ninth century BCE. All of the tombs contained lamps; of the 230 objects in J6, 139 were lamps. All but J7 had jewelry; J6 and J7 had craters and jugs; J4, J5 and J6 contained coffin sherds probably dating from the eighth to the seventh century BCE; and J5 had storejars with broken necks suggested to have functioned as burial receptacles for children (Tushingham 1954; 1972).

Ez-Zahariyah. A single tomb has been recorded from Ez-Zahariyah, located 22 km south of Hebron on the Hebron–Beer Sheva road. A door on the northwest side opened onto an atrium which led into two burial chambers. Such elaborately cut tombs without benches were unusual. The atrium contained only pottery. Along the walls of chamber A lay human skeletons accompanied by a few pots including lamps with signs of use. In Chamber B, several lamps and other pottery were found with decomposed, disturbed human skeletons near the entrance and along the walls. Published pottery included 21 juglets, 15 bowls, 11 jugs, 10 lamps, 3 storejars, 3 chalices, an amphoriskos, and an 'Astarte figurine' jug modelled like a woman with one arm across her breasts. The assemblage has now been dated from as early as the tenth through the early sixth century BCE. The excavator, D.C. Baramki, dated the pottery to around 1000 BCE (Baramki 1934–35). Noting archaic black burnished juglets, ring burnished bowls and bowls with wheel burnish over the entire vessel,

Albright redated the assemblage to 900–750 BCE, beginning perhaps as early as the tenth century BCE (Albright 1943: 158-59). Comparing the pottery to the Khirbet el-Qôm assemblage, W. Dever opted for an eighth- or seventh-century BCE date (Dever 1970: 149). J. Holladay noted some late seventh- or early sixth-century BCE elements in the assemblage (Holladay 1976: 277).

Tell el-Farah (N). The single Iron Age tomb uncovered by the excavations of R. de Vaux of the Ecole Archéologique Française de Jérusalem at Tell el-Farah (N) was dated by the four vessels in it to the eleventh to ninth century BCE or perhaps later. The tomb has been described above under twelfth- and eleventh-century BCE cave, shaft and chamber tombs (Chambon 1984: 67, pls. 58.24–27).

Gezer. Three tombs excavated by R.A.S. Macalister at Gezer/Tell el-Jazari/Tell Abu Shusheh date from the mid-late tenth century BCE: Tomb 84–85 on the southeast slope of the tell and Tomb 138 on the northwest slope. Tomb 8I, described above, also continued into the ninth or eighth century BCE. The quantity of pottery vessels and small finds in Tomb 84–85 suggest multiple burials. Within the two connected chambers were juglets including red-polished examples, pyxides, an imitation stirrup jar, bilbils, a vessel with a wishbone handle and a three-legged strainer vessel, in addition to jugs, flasks, bowls and lamps. Other goods included bronze fibulae, anklets, a rosette, an axehead and a small green figure of Sekhet (Macalister 1912: 334-35, pls. LXXXVII–LXXXIX). All that remained in Tomb 138 were meager pottery specimens: a small alabaster pot, two jars, a chalice, a bowl and a lamp (Macalister 1912: 350).

Gibeon. The necropolis at Gibeon, al-Jib, was utilized from the Early Bronze Age through the Roman period. A. Dajani excavated an Iron Age burial cave on the slope east of the spring and noted the presence of five other rock-cut tombs in the vicinity, all disturbed in antiquity. The cave, which measured 8.3 × 7.3 m, contained abundant bones of males and females and approximately 500 pots of the Iron I and II periods. The pottery which appeared to be locally made, except for the spouted-strainer jugs, consisted of 45 percent lamps followed in decreasing frequency by bowls, dipper juglets and pyxides. Other grave goods included a zoomorphic figurine, jewelry, household articles, eight scarabs and a seal (A. Dajani 1951: 48; 1953: 66, fig. 21).

Haifa. In 1978 Y. Algavish of the Israel Department of Antiquities conducted salvage excavations of a tomb located in a Haifa neighborhood. A collapsed ceiling precluded determining the tomb plan, so it may have been a cave or a bench tomb. Algavish dated the Cypro-Phoenician wares to the eleventh century BCE, but a tenth-century BCE date is more likely (Haifa—Newe Yosef 1978).

Hebron. Israel Department of Antiquities archaeologists excavated dwelling caves in Hebron from the Chalcolithic period and the Early Bronze Age which were reused for burial during the end of Iron I and the beginning of Iron II (Hebron 1966).

Irbed. R.W. Dajani excavated three disturbed Iron Age tombs at the site of Irbed, located 110 km north of Amman. Tombs A and B were interconnected chambers. Tomb A was utilized from the tenth to the end of the ninth century BCE, while B was in use during the thirteenth, the twelfth and the tenth to ninth centuries BCE, and again in the Roman period. Lamps, bowls, jugs, juglets and a figurine fragment of a nude female torso holding a round object to her chest (bread, tambourine or drum; cf. Hillers 1970; C.L. Meyers 1991) had been provided for the deceased in Tomb A. The Tomb B assemblage included a larger number of the same vessel forms, though bowls were more numerous. Bowls, including carinated and a footed example, a strainer jug on three feet, a Cypro-Phoenician juglet, a toggle pin, a cosmetic palette and a terracotta fragment of a nude, armless, female torso were retrieved from Tomb B (R. Dajani 1966c).

Two additional tombs located in the vicinity of the others were uncovered during salvage excavations in 1984. Both tombs were robbed, but one contained sherds spanning the Early Bronze Age to Iron II (C. G. Lenzen, presentation at the national meetings of the American Schools of Oriental Research 1984).

Jericho. Tomb A85, of indeterminate plan, held 12 skulls, bodies stacked on top of each other and tenth century BCE pottery. Bowls predominated, plus there were jugs, juglets and dipper juglets, but no lamps. A ring and black and red beads were also retrieved from the tomb (Kenyon 1965: 482-83, 489).

S. Loffreda suggested that tombs WH1 and WH2 might have been hewn as early as the late ninth century BCE, based on his rock-cut tomb plan typology (Loffreda 1968: 257); however, the preserved tomb contents dated from the late eighth through the sixth century BCE (Kenyon 1965: 491-513). These tombs are described below under eighth- to sixth-century BCE cave, shaft and chamber tombs.

Jerusalem—City of David. R. Weill excavated four tunnels and caves in the rocky slopes below the City of David which he identified as the burial places of the kings of Judah. From T4, a tunnel cut in an earlier period and reused in the ninth century BCE, Weill reported numerous decapitated skeletons lying next to one another (Weill 1920b: 14; 1920 c: 156). According to K. Kenyon, these tunnels were not burial chambers, but 'cisterns of rather unusual form' (Kenyon 1974: 156).

Jerusalem—Silwan. D. Ussishkin distinguished three styles of rock-cut burials in different regions of the Silwan cemetery: monolithic above-ground tombs, tombs with gabled ceilings and tombs with flat ceilings. The tombs without benches, which could be classified as chamber tombs, have been described above with anthropoid, wooden and stone coffin burials because of the presence of stone-troughs or coffins (Ussishkin 1986).

Lachish. Excavations of the Wellcome–Colt/Wellcome–Marston Archaeological Research Expedition at Lachish demonstrated that very few tombs were initiated in the period from the tenth through the early eighth century BCE: Tombs 219 and 224, and Cave 1002. However, several Middle and Late Bronze Age caves and tombs were structurally altered and reused for dwelling or mortuary purposes in the Iron Age: Tombs 107 (?), 120, 244 (?) and Cave 6011.

Tombs 107 and 120, cut in the Middle and Late Bronze Ages respectively, were used for dwelling or burial around 900 BCE, and for the deposit of bones from approximately 700–600 BCE. Around 900 BCE, the interior of Tomb 120 was divided into three chambers by the addition of stone walls and some cutting away of the rock. In both tombs, human remains were covered with a layer of charred animal bones, primarily pig. Both the human and animal bone had been dropped into Tomb 107 through a hole in the roof (Tufnell 1953: 187). More than 1,500 bodies, with skulls separated, were interred in Tomb 120. Some of the bones appeared burned, as was the case in Cave 1002. It is unclear if any of the human remains date from 900 BCE. From Tomb 120, amulets, pendants, scarabs and Cypriot wares were specified among the tenth to ninth century BCE provisions. Dipper juglets, large bowls, a cooking pot, a female pillar figurine and a rattle were attributed to the seventh century BCE. The full repertoire of burial goods included 33 dipper juglets, 17 bowls, 12 jugs, 8 cooking pots, 5 storejars, 2 lamps, a female pillar figurine with a typically Greek or Cypriot smile, a rattle, scarabs, scaraboids, bronze, iron and silver jewelry, an arrowhead and bone pendants and gavels (Tufnell 1953: 193-96).

Tombs 219 and 224 were cut in the middle to late ninth century BCE. Tomb 219, utilized for approximately one century, was approached through a narrow sloping passage leading into three chambers each entered through a square doorway. Lamps, jars, a juglet, a minipot, a bone pin, beads, a faience playing piece and a stone weight constituted the recovered burial provisions (Tufnell 1953: 210). Tomb 224 was a well-provisioned tomb from the middle to late ninth century BCE. More than 160 pottery vessels, including 50 dipper juglets, 37 bowls, 36 jugs and 33 lamps, an iron knife and armour scales, bronze jewelry, scarabs, scaraboids, faience and bone amulets, a sacred eye and beads were uncovered with eight skulls and intact burials (Tufnell 1953: 215-17).

Two caves were also employed for burial in the tenth and ninth centuries BCE: Caves 1002 and 6011. Irregularly-shaped Cave 1002 in Area 1000 southwest of the settlement yielded 13 undisturbed layers of burials with more than 600 pots and objects dating from c. 810–710 BCE. The tomb was so denuded that only a pit remained. According to the excavators, if it was an original Iron Age construction, 'it may have been similar to Tomb 1 at Ain Shems, where the main room and two subsidiary alcoves were circular, with a ventilation shaft in the roof' (Tufnell 1953: 174). Some of the skulls and pots showed signs of burning, and there were remains of secondary burials 'affected by fire before they were reburied' (Tufnell 1953: 229). The lowest levels, 11–13, contained 228 vessels of which 111 were jugs, plus a model couch, a horse and rider figurine (the earliest of the horse and rider figurines from stratigraphically excavated tombs), scarabs, scaraboids, seals, Egyptian amulets, jewelry and armour. In the middle layers, 6–10, 88 of the 198 vessels were jugs; also recovered were 48 dipper juglets, 28 bowls, 24 lamps, 3 rattles, 2 female pillar figurines, a model chair, scarabs, scaraboids, seals, a number of Egyptian amulets, jewelry, a fibula, an iron knife and a stone hone. The upper layers, 1–5, included 178 vessels with jugs again predominant, two rattles, three female figurines, one with a molded head and one with a 'beak' face, a pillar bird in flight, another anthropomorphic figurine, scarabs, scaraboids and seals of poor workmanship, a few Egyptian amulets of inferior quality, and a moderate amount of metal (Tufnell 1953: 229-36). Storejars with 'royal' stamps were included in the assemblage (*ibid.*, 48). Cave 6011, in Cemetery 6000 north of the settlement, was cut in the Early Bronze Age and reused in the mid-tenth century BCE. Under the collapsed roof, the excavators found two bodies, storejars and a lamp (Tufnell 1953: 247).

Madeba. M. Piccirillo published the pottery from the Madeba B cave tomb in Jordan. The tomb, located south of the tell, had a large shelf formed by the natural bedding planes along the northwest side of the cave. Deteriorated, disarticulated skeletal remains did not permit estimating a body count, and suggested disturbance in antiquity. Published vessels included craters, a three-footed strainer cup, several biconical vessels, some Assyrian-style bowls with raised petal-like decoration on the bottom, two chalices, mushroom-top jars, black juglets, lamps with rounded and slightly stump bases and a Cypro-Phoenician flask and bottle. A broken figurine has been identified as a '(?) fertility goddess with sheep (head missing but one horn still present)'. H. Thompson dated the assemblage from the late eleventh or early tenth through the mid-eighth century BCE, with the bulk of the material from the mid-eighth century BCE (Piccirillo 1975; Thompson 1984: 148, 172).

Mafraq. The thirteenth- to tenth-century BCE cave tomb excavated by M. Piccirillo at Mafraq in Jordan has been described above under twelfth- and eleventh-century BCE cave, shaft and chamber tombs (Piccirillo 1976).

Tel Mevorakh. A chance find near the northwestern foot of Tel Mevorakh revealed a tenth-century BCE shaft tomb containing approximately 70 pottery vessels. Included among the vessels were red-burnished Phoenician and Cypro-Phoenician wares (Stern 1977: 866).

Tell en-Nasbeh. The Pacific Institute of Religion's expedition directed by W.F. Badè located Tomb 32 in the eastern section of the West Cemetery of Tell en-Nasbeh. While there is general agreement as to the mid-twelfth-century BCE date for the earliest Iron Age contents, the period best represented has been dated by J. Wampler to the tenth through the eighth century BCE, and by G.E. Wright to the tenth and perhaps the ninth centuries BCE (Wright 1948: 472). Pottery vessels included 40 black-polished juglets, 12 jars with red and black painted bands, 12 Cypriot bottles, approximately 10 Cypro-Phoenician juglets, craters, chalices, spouted jars, pyxides and a bird vase. Numerous toggle pins, 5 fibulae, 16 button seals, several scarabs including at least 5 with the throne name of Tuthmosis III, 50 bronze bracelets and beads primarily of carnelian had also been provided for the dead. The osteological remains were not published, but the extended period of use of this cave indicates repeated use (McCown 1947: 77-82).

Nazareth. In 1973 F. Vitto excavated a rock-cut tomb in Nazareth. A narrow shaft led into a single chamber with two pits in the floor, one of which was covered with a stone. Bones of numerous individuals, jar fragments, scarabs of the Iron II period, beads, and bronze and iron fragments lay scattered on the chamber floor (Bagatti 1977: 920; Nazareth 1973).

Mt Nebo. Several tombs have been found in the vicinity of Jebel Hussein, located north of Mt Nebo near Madeba. The two fully-published cave tombs UCV-20 and UCV-84, in use from 1000–586 BCE, accommodated inhumations, secondary burials on a shelf, jar burials, anthropoid coffin burials evidenced by coffin fragments and, perhaps, cremation burials.

Tomb UCV-20 consisted of a natural cave with a large chamber measuring 10.35 × 15.50 m and a smaller chamber measuring 4.9 × 3.6 m connected by an arched opening. In the center of the large chamber floor was a big hole with a groove leading into it together with smaller holes scattered around the large hole, reminiscent of the holes and channels in the floor of Samaria Tomb 103 (Crowfoot, Kenyon and Sukenik 1942: 21). Approximately 750 skeletons had been packed into the tomb, in an orderly fashion, and 'cremation strata' were detected all over the cave. Of the approximately 800 pots, 250 were unused lamps with flat and disc bases. Other ceramic provisions included 11 or more complete censers or tripod cups, small bowls, plates, chalices, Cypro-Phoenician, black-burnished and plain juglets, jugs, a pilgrim flask, craters, large and small jars, and cooking pots. In addition to pottery, the tomb yielded a basalt bowl, a cylinder seal, an Eye of Horus, a scarab, beads, pendants, a silver earring, iron rings, 58 bronze rings, fibulae, shells, astragali, a spindle whorl and a disc.

Tomb UCV-84 also consisted of two chambers, both measuring approximately 4 × 5 m with an arched opening between them. Approximately 250 individuals with 650 objects including large flat coffin sherds were found in this tomb. Human bones were uncovered in a large jar, on the northwest shelf covered with large stones, in a hole in the floor, and arranged in layers with lamps. 'Cremation strata' were recorded across one large area in one of the chambers. Burial provisions included approximately 300 lamps, some on stands, more than 60 juglets, many of which were Cypro-Phoenician, censers, cups, bowls, plates, jugs, pilgrim flasks, craters, jars, strainers, an Assyrian bowl with petal design, a jar containing 30 astragali, blue grains apparently cosmetics, an ornamented bone bird (?), stone pendants, beads, a ceramic horse, shells, glass, bronze and iron rings and two female pillar figurines. One figurine held a tambourine, and the second depicted a young woman with crossed arms, her right arm under her left breast (Saller 1966).

Khirbet Rabud. M. Kochavi of Tel Aviv University surveyed Uss-es-Saqrah, the cemetery hill southeast of Khirbet Rabud. Approximately 100 tombs were identified, all natural caves which had been robbed. Seventy-five percent of the tombs dated from the Late Bronze Age, a few from the Early or Middle Bronze Age, and the rest from the Iron Age. Tombs 14 and 20 yielded tenth- to ninth-century BCE bowls and a lamp. Isolated Iron Age tombs were also cut into the tell slopes, especially on the west side (Kochavi 1973; 1974: 19, 26).

Ras et-Tawil. M. Rajbi of the Israel Department of Antiquities excavated a burial cave on the western slope of the mound of Ras et-Tawil, located between Bethlehem and Hebron. Seventy complete vessels and fragments of ninth- to sixth-century BCE jars, jugs, juglets, bowls, chalices and other forms were extracted from the 3 × 5 m cave whose roof had collapsed (Ras et-Tawil 1974).

Samaria. During the course of the excavations directed by J.W. Crowfoot, a group of tombs was found on the north slope of the tell of Samaria. Tomb 103, a roughly retouched cave was the only well-preserved example. The others to the northwest of Tomb 103 had been completely destroyed so all that remained were the pits in the floors and their contents. All the tombs dated from the second half of the eighth century BCE. A contemporary bench tomb was excavated by F. Zayadine on the hillside of Munshara, south of Samaria.

Tomb 103 was an irregularly-shaped cave, measuring 5 × 4.7 m, with the remains of a rock pillar in the center. A second chamber measuring 2.4 × 1.9 × 1.55 m held the skeletons of three adults and one child, all oriented with their heads to the east. Outside the chamber, to the west, a bench-like projection 0.44 m high was cut from the rock. Inside the cave, six holes were cut into the chamber floor. Some had a double-rimmed mouth to carry a cover stone, and two were connected by a narrow channel. The holes opened into bottle-shaped pits varying in depth from 2.2–4.5 m and in lower diameter from 1.8–2.9 m. The pits held ceramic vessels, primarily bowls (I, II, IV, V, VI), bone or bronze spatulae (I, II, III, IV), beads (I, III, IV—eye bead), rattles (II, V, VI), spindle whorls (IV, VI), arrowheads (I, V), fibulae (III, IV) and ovicaprid bones. Pit II also contained a scarab and a faience head of Bes. J. Crowfoot, K. Kenyon and E. Sukenik explained the pits as 'receptacles of offerings connected with the cult of the dead as regularly practiced in ancient Israel in spite of the attacks of the prophets'. E. Sukenik compared this tomb, with its drain and pits, to the fourteenth to thirteenth century BCE Ugarit tombs equipped for feeding the dead (Crowfoot, Crowfoot and Kenyon 1957: 197-98; Crowfoot, Kenyon and Sukenik 1942: 21-22; Sukenik 1940: 59-60).

Shechem. Beginning in 1956, Drew University and McCormick Theological Seminary with the American Schools of Oriental Research resumed excavations of Shechem/Balatah under the direction of G.E. Wright. The survey identified Bronze Age tombs reused in the tenth and ninth centuries BCE at two sites north of the tell. Middle Bronze I tombs at Araq et-Tayih, situated on the lower slopes of Mt Ebal, northwest of the tell (Site 2), were reused in the Middle Bronze IIC, the Late Bronze Age, the tenth and ninth centuries BCE, and the Hellenistic and Byzantine periods (Bull *et al.* 1965: 32-33; Bull and Campbell 1968: 22). A tomb containing Late Bronze II and tenth-century BCE sherds was noted in the flanks of the Wadi Sur (Site 38) north of Shechem (Bull and Campbell 1968: 38).

Bench and Arcosolia Tombs

Aitun. Seven tombs in the cemetery southwest of Tell Aitun were in use between the tenth and the first half of the eighth century BCE, including the eleventh- to ninth-century BCE tomb excavated by T. Dothan and A. Mazar described above. D. Ussishkin excavated four tombs, 1 and 2 which he considered exceptional, and 3 and 4 which he felt typified Aitun burial practices. All four tombs had been robbed; few whole vessels or sherds were retrieved. V. Tzaferis excavated an additional two tombs northeast of the tell, in use during the first half of the eighth century BCE.

A large stone slab blocked the 0.55 × 0.65 m opening into Tomb 1. Four steps led down through an entryway flanked by a front view of lions carved in the rock. The tomb proper consisted of a front chamber with a wide arcosolium or bench on either side, and a back chamber with a bench/arcosolium on each of the three sides and animal heads carved in the four corners. Another unique feature of Tomb 1 was traces of fire, soot and a thin grey deposit in each of the arcosolia. Cooking pots and lamps were blackened with soot, but none of the skeletal remains showed signs of burning, suggesting that the ash resulted from cooking food, burning spices and lighting lamps. In a corner of the rear chamber, a stone slab covered a bone repository measuring 0.40 × 0.80 × 0.60 m. Whereas the other tombs had lamp niches and most of the recovered lamps showed signs of use, Tomb 1 lacked niches, but the carved, flat animal heads may have served as shelves for lamps.

D. Ussishkin suggested that the lions' protruding tongues imitated Neo-Hittite style, and therefore these carvings should be compared to Syro-Hittite lion orthostats which flanked monumental entrances to protect the inhabitants. A. Kempinski noted a gazelle head carved in an Akhzib tomb as the only other occurrence of animal heads carved in Iron Age tombs. This claim was rejected by the excavator of Akhzib, M. Prausnitz (M. Prausnitz, private communication 1984; Ussishkin 1974: 125 n.14). Bowls predominated among the ninth- and especially eighth-century BCE forms. The full range of forms included bowls, a spouted bowl, cooking pots blackened with soot, one-handled jugs including an example with brownish-red slip painted with brown-grey bands, juglets, lamps with rounded and stump bases, all blackened with soot, and a storejar. Two faience scarabs were found in Tomb 1: one depicting Bes, and the second depicting a scorpion whose legs were not joined to its body. Ussishkin interpreted these scarabs as amulets to protect the bearer (the deceased?) against sickness and bad luck, and against scorpion bites, respectively.

In Tomb 2, a dromos with four steps led down to the stone-blocked entrance and two more steps led down to the chamber floor. The rectangular chamber had two large arcosolia on each side, each measuring 2 × 1 × 1 m. Each arcosolia was provided with a lamp niche, and lamps with traces of soot were found in the chamber.

Signs were scratched in the wall of one of the front arcosolia near the lamp niche. A large repository for bones, 1.8 m deep, was carved in the back wall of the chamber.

The plans of Tombs 3 and 4 were similar. In Tomb 3 there were five arcosolia, two to a side and one in the back. A single lamp niche was carved near the ceiling in a pier between two of the arcosolia. Unlike Tombs 1 and 2, there was no repository in this tomb. A parapet 0.05–0.08 m wide and 0.02–0.03 m high ran along the front edge of the arcosolia to keep the deceased from falling off. In Tomb 4, which was the smallest of the four tombs, a shaft and stairs led down into a chamber with three irregularly-shaped arcosolia, two of which were provided with stone pillows and a single lamp niche carved in a side wall. Into the chamber floor had been cut a bone repository, situated partially under one of the arcosolia, and a small cup-like depression 0.12 m in diameter and 0.06 m deep, near the entrance (Ussishkin 1973; 1974).

V. Tzaferis excavated two tombs northeast of the tell, A1 and A2, both dated by the pottery to the first half of the eighth century BCE. Tomb A1 was one of many chambers off a central court, similar to the arrangement at Beth Shemesh, Gezer 9U and Jerusalem—Sultan Suleiman St. 1 (V. Tzaferis, private communication 1984). This natural cave which had been adapted for burial, typified tombs in the northeast sector of the cemetery. Three steps led down into an elliptically-shaped chamber measuring 4.3 × 3.5 m, with two benches or arcosolia cut along the periphery, each with a lamp niche. Nine jugs, eight bowls, five lamps, three terracotta horse figurines, and bones in the arcosolium located opposite the entrance were all that remained in the plundered tomb. In Tomb A2, also a natural cave adapted for burial, a long narrow entryway with a finely carved doorway led into a central court 2.5 m square. The court had chambers on three sides, but only one was excavated. This rectangular chamber had a bench on either side and a large rectangular repository across the rear of the chamber. Fragments of 15 bowls, 8 lamps and 3 jugs lay on the benches, on the floor and in the repository (Tzaferis 1982b).

Akhzib. In the southern, el Buq-baq, and the eastern, er-Ras, cemeteries at Akhzib, M. Prausnitz of the Israel Department of Antiquities excavated rock-cut tombs in which the dead had been laid on wooden and rock-cut benches around the tomb periphery. Prausnitz dated the tombs in both cemeteries from the tenth through the end of the eighth century BCE (Prausnitz 1969: 88; private commnication 1984).

Amman—Jebel Jofeh. All the published Iron II tombs in the Amman vicinity were cave or chamber tombs except for Tomb A, located on the north side of Jebel Jofeh, and an eighth- to fourth-century BCE tomb in the Um Uḏaina area. Tomb A consisted of a single trapezoidal chamber with a low bench along one of the side walls and 'cupboard-like recesses' in each of the far corners. One of the recesses contained a mass of broken animal bones. Knuckle bones were found mixed with pottery throughout the tomb. The only human bone, in fragmentary condition, was found near the entrance. Burial goods included small bowls, chalices, lamps, flasks, tripod cups, jugs, a decanter, a juglet, a used cooking pot, a lantern, a bottle, two bronze earrings, the horse's head of a horse and rider figurine and an inscribed ivory seal. The pottery, which included Ammonite wares decorated with red and black stripes on a white background, was dated by G.L. Harding to the eighth century BCE, and judged of 'rather poor quality' (Harding 1945: 67-73). E. Henschel-Simon redated the pottery to the eighth and seventh centuries BCE, primarily from the end of the seventh century (Harding 1945: 74).

Tell Beit Mirsim. In 1980, after learning of illicit digging activity, E. Braun of the Israel Department of Antiquities conducted salvage excavations of tombs on the southwest slope of Tell Beit Mirsim. The five reported Iron II tombs displayed a variety of architectural features, all found in the Aitun tombs. Tomb 1 consisted of a vertical shaft leading into a square chamber with a supporting pillar. A square entrance led from the first chamber into a second large chamber. Late Bronze I and II vessels including Cypriot wares, Iron II pottery vessels, beads, scarabs and metal fragments were found in the tomb. Tomb 4 was similar to the Aitun tombs: steps led down into a rock-hewn chamber with deep niches on three sides and depressions cut into the floor on either side of the entrance. Many Iron II pots were found in the niches and in the two floor depressions. In Tomb 5, a square shaft with steps descended into a rectangular chamber with a shelf along the short wall opposite the entrance, several shallow depressions in the floor including two near the entrance, and a lamp (?) niche in the far corner near the ceiling. In Tomb 6, shallow niches were hewn in three sides of a natural cave and the finds were similar to those in Tombs 4 and 5 (Braun 1982; private communication 1984).

Beth Shemesh. E. Grant and G.E. Wright, of the Haverford Expedition, dated the empty tombs 15 and 16 at Beth Shemesh to the tenth to sixth century BCE. Steps led down to the floor of a square chamber with a bench ringing the periphery and a round repository pit cut in one of the far corners (Grant 1931: 16, 18, 29). On the basis of his rock-cut tomb typology, S. Loffreda dated these tombs to the seventh to sixth century BCE (Loffreda 1968: 251). Tomb 14, described below, may have been in use from as early as the tenth century BCE (Grant 1931: 10, 15; Stern 1982: 77, 83).

Tel Bira. At the site of Tel Bira, Bir el-Gharbi, near Kibbutz Yasur in the western Galilee, M. Prausnitz of the Israel Department of Antiquities excavated Middle Bronze Age tombs which were structurally altered in the Iron Age and fashioned into bench tombs. Prausnitz dated these tombs to the eleventh to tenth century BCE, as has been noted above. In 1967 and 1970, Israel Department of Antiquities personnel returned to the area to conduct salvage excavations near Kibbutz Yasur, and found a number of caves with stone-built benches. On the benches lay skeletons stacked one on top of the other, lamps and Cypro-Phoenician juglets (Western Galilee 1967; Yasur 1970).

Dhiban. The Iron Age necropolis at Dhiban, designated Area J, was situated east of the tell. A.D. Tushingham directed the excavations of eight tenth-century BCE tombs: J1 and J3 were bench tombs and J4–J8 were cave tombs. Both J1 and J3 were disturbed. Tomb J1 continued in use into the seventh century BCE. This tomb, which measured 5 × 3 m, had a large pit between the rock-cut bench and the rear wall, similar to Aitun Tomb A2 and Gezer Tomb 142. Tomb J3 was of similar plan, and contained a variety of objects including 44 lamps of poor quality, all with signs of use, a bowl, a plate, beads, rings, pins, a scarab and a clay wheel from a toycart or chariot. The excavators collected the teeth of at least 45 adults, approximately one third of whom were less than 21 years old; one 14-year-old; three 12-year-olds; one child less than 10 years old; two 5-year-olds; and at least eight children five years old or younger. An anthropoid clay coffin was apparently utilized for the latest burial in the seventh century BCE. The 'Burnt Bone Deposit', detailed above under tenth- to eighth-century BCE cave, shaft and chamber tombs, may have functioned as a repository (Tushingham 1972: 104; Winnett and Reed 1964).

Gezer. Five of the bench tombs excavated by R.A.S. Macalister at Gezer continued in use from the twelfth down into the tenth century BCE: 9U, 28, 31, 58U and 59 (Macalister 1912: 308, 312, 314-15, 321-31). S. Loffreda dated Tombs 28 and 31 to the Iron I period on the basis of his tomb plan typology, even though the recovered contents dated from Iron II (Dever 1976: 442; Loffreda 1968: 255). While the tombs may have been cut in Iron I, their attested use was in Iron II, and so they are described here. Tomb 28 consisted of a single roughly trapezoidal chamber measuring approximately 6 × 7.5 m at its greatest extent. Five steps led from the entrance down to the chamber floor, where a bench approximately 0.30 m high ran around most of the periphery of the tomb and an additional portion abutted the central pillar (Macalister 1912: 312). Two roughly circular chambers measuring 6.5 × 6.5 m and 3.0 × 3.5 m comprised Tomb 31. In the larger chamber, a bench divided into three sections and a slightly hollowed sunken bench ran along the two sides. The floor was pitted with three depressions each containing bones (Macalister 1912: 314).

Tombs 142 and 96 date from the early tenth and late tenth century BCE respectively. Tomb 142 was similar in plan to Aitun Tomb A2 and Dhiban J3, with steps leading down to the floor of a rectangular cave with a continuous bench around all four sides and a pit or repository between the bench and the rear wall. A variety of goods had been provided for the deceased: nine lamps, a one-handled storejar, a small amphoriskos with a thick neck decorated with red and black bands, an incense stand, a bone pendant, and a fibula (Macalister 1912: 353-54, pl. CIII). Tomb 96 was an irregularly-shaped cave with benches along the sides and two chambers extending out of the back wall which may have functioned as repositories. More than 100 individuals were buried with a commensurate number of objects. Included in the assemblage were chalices, jars, flasks, bowls, lamps, a spouted jar, an iron ring and blades, bronze rings, bracelets and pins, more than 70 beads, 9 steatite scarabs and a stamp seal (Macalister 1912: 336-37, pl. XC).

Haifa. In 1978 Y. Algavish of the Israel Department of Antiquities conducted salvage excavations of a tomb located in a Haifa neighborhood. A collapsed ceiling precluded determining the tomb plan, so it may have been a cave or a bench tomb. Algavish dated the Cypro-Phoenician wares to the eleventh century BCE, but a tenth-century BCE date is more likely (Haifa—Newe Yosef 1978).

Halif. Under the direction of J.D. Seger, the Lahav Research Project excavated five tombs dating from the middle of the tenth through the middle of the eighth century BCE. Of the three tombs situated in a hillside facing the mound, two had been robbed, but the third was intact. Each of these three tombs had benches on three sides and deep barrel-shaped repositories hewn in the back corners. In the undisturbed Tomb 3, decomposed bones lay on the chamber floor and on the benches along with more than 200 complete vessels. The only detailed finds were the unusual objects including two iron blades with bone handles, several iron and bronze bracelets, a silver earring and an unspecified zoomorphic figurine (Seger 1972). The excavators suggested that Tomb 4 was never completed. A forecourt and corridor with four steps led into the middle of the long side of a rectangular chamber, measuring 1.3 × 4.1 × 2.2 m, with benches at both ends and a round repository at the far end of each bench. While the pottery—together with a disarticulated skeleton and bones on the bench, the floor and in the repository—may date from the Iron Age, it appears that the two sheep or goat skulls in the northern repository, the skull of a six-year-old and the three adults lying on the floor may be modern intrusions (O. Borowski, unpublished manuscript).

Tomb 6, located on a hill southwest of the tell, was unfortunately also robbed in antiquity. It is a fine example of a bench tomb, well-cut, with many features that appear in eighth–seventh century BCE bench tombs. A forecourt and one step down led into the short end of a rectangular chamber measuring 5.5 × 2.2 × 2.0 m, with benches on three sides and a square repository in each of the far corners. Each bench had a parapet along the exposed side, and, at one end, a stone pillow with a small circular depression near the parapetted edge. A lamp niche was carved into the chamber wall near the head of the deceased. Ceramic vessels included three lamps, three juglets including a black juglet, two jugs, two jars, one with a dipper juglet inside, a pilgrim flask, a large platter and a plate with a pomegranate in the center (Seger *et al.* 1978).

In 1965, A. Biran and R. Gophna excavated a tomb on the southwest slope where the Lahav Project later dug the tombs described above. An *in situ* blocking stone was moved to reveal a stepped entrance shaft leading down into a chamber measuring 3.0 × 2.5 m. The chamber was provided with a bench 0.5 m high and 1.6 m wide along the rear wall, and a pit 0.7 m deep separated from the bench by a stone wall. A bronze lamp still sat in a niche in the repository, and a second niche may also have held a lamp. More than 350 tenth- to sixth-century BCE vessels were recovered from the tomb. The repository held ceramic vessels from the tenth to ninth century BCE: more than 60 juglets, 15 lamps, bowls, jugs and a chalice, some Cypro-Phoenician juglets, but primarily pots of the local red-burnished tradition. Also retrieved from the repository were 34 bronze anklets, 2 scaraboid seals, 5 cat amulets, and the bronze lamp still in the niche. The finds from the chamber floor and the bench dated from the ninth through the sixth century BCE. Bowls, lamps, jugs, juglets, an ivory box, a 'Phoenician-style' seal of a two-winged figure facing right holding a flower and a bronze anklet were found on the bench. More of these types including 25 lamps, a two-handled rilled-rim cooking pot, two double-pronged iron pitchforks and a limestone 'roof-roller' lay on the chamber floor (Biran and Gophna 1965; 1970).

Tel Ira. A. Baron and I. Beit-Arieh surveyed and excavated tombs in a necropolis on the east slope of Tel Ira. This is the only identified cemetery in the Negev, and the southernmost occurrence of the bench tomb. Tomb 15 was the only tomb conclusively dated to the tenth to ninth century BCE.

Tomb 15 was a three-chambered tomb. Three steps led down into vaulted chambers to the right of and opposite the entrance into the central chamber. There were two benches in each chamber equipped with pillows and parapets. Twenty-three individuals were recovered from Chamber I, 12 of them lying on the benches. On the southern bench,

> [t]he articulated skeleton of an adult female was found, extended, with slightly flexed legs, along with that of a juvenile, seven to eight years old, with their heads near the entrance of the tomb, rather than on the pillow at the farther end. The phalanges of the adult's right hand were curved across the ribs of the juvenile, with the bones of her arm bent and elevated, as if she has been holding the child in her arms during the interment.

On the north bench lay three layers of bodies. On the bottom was a female approximately 60 years old with spinal arthritis. Above her had been placed five adults, three with the heads on the pillow and two laying in the opposite direction. Five juveniles lay oriented crosswise on top of the adults. 'Portions of three partially articulated skeletons, one in a semi-upright position, were recovered from the area east of the bench.' The chamber had obviously been plundered, for only eighth to seventh-century BCE sherds and modern debris were found among the skeletal remains. In Chamber II, benches extended along the southern and western walls, and a lamp niche and 'incompletely cut bone repository' were hewn into the east wall opposite the entrance. Fragmentary remains of two individuals with their heads to the east, some charred bone, a red jug and a lamp lay on the south bench. On one of the individuals, a juvenile, the excavators identified 'blackish remnants of decomposed fabric mingled with the bone and adhering to the skull, suggesting that the body was wrapped in a shroud'. Bone and iron fragments lay on the second bench. Chamber III appeared undisturbed. Three steps led down into a chamber with benches along the side walls, with a pillow on one of the benches, a shelf along part of the back wall and a lamp niche cut into the wall above one of the benches. A minimum of eight individuals were counted from a bone pile on the floor. On top of the pile lay three articulated skeletons, two of which were identified as a female and a sub-adult. An additional person lay extended on the bench. The excavator suggested that flecks of charcoal and charred bone found in the bone pile, similar to the charred bone in

Chamber II, 'may have resulted from accidental combustion caused by contact of the flames from lamps with tomb gases'. Tenth- to ninth-century BCE pottery forms were found on the floor, a bench and the back shelf. A black-burnished juglet, fragments of a three-handled storejar with a spout and the base of a spiral-burnished bowl with a ring base demonstrated the tomb remained in use through the eighth to seventh century BCE (Baron, unpublished manuscript, 1987).

Irbed. R. Dajani excavated Irbed Tomb C, a bench tomb in use between the early tenth and the late ninth century BCE. This oval-shaped cave measured 5 × 4 × 1.7 m with a 0.60 m high bench along the back wall. On the bench lay an individual with ceramic vessels positioned near its head (R. Dajani 1966a: 88, 97, pl. XXXVI).

Jerusalem—Old City Walls. In 1967, M. Broshi, G. Barkai and S. Gibson surveyed three tombs under the western Old City walls, 55 m south of the citadel, between and under two Turkish towers. Caves 1 and 2, both single chamber tombs, were empty, and 3, unpublished, was under a Turkish tower. Cave 1 was provided with two stone troughs or coffins, and so has been described above under tenth- to eighth-century BCE anthropoid, wooden and stone coffin burials. Cave 2 was entered through a finely worked facade with two borders and an inverted 'V' engraved over the door lintel. Broshi, Barkai and Gibson considered the facade to be Phoenician inspired, reminiscent of the facade on Salamis Tomb 85–85A, the facade of Solomon's Temple, the Tell Tainat temple and depictions on Phoenician burial stelae. Inside, a step the width of the chamber descended to a room on both sides of which was a bench equipped with a headrest and parapet. Alongside each bench, a niche with a headrest and parapet was hewn into the wall to accommodate a second individual. Stone plates closed off the recessed niches. All four headrests, on the two benches and in the two niches, were positioned away from the door. Cut into the back wall was a deep loculus or repository with a gabled roof, similar to repositories in Silwan tombs. Broshi, Barkai and Gibson dated the tombs to the ninth to seventh century BCE on the basis of architectural parallels with the Silwan tombs and eighth-century BCE lamps and bowls with wheel burnish found around the tomb entrances (Broshi, Barkai and Gibson 1983: 25).

Jerusalem—Silwan. D. Ussishkin distinguished three types of burials carved into the Silwan cliffs: tombs with gabled ceilings (described with anthropoid, wooden and stone coffin burials), tombs with flat ceilings and monolithic above-ground tombs (described below). The flat-ceiling tombs, with bench-niches, benches or a bench-trough combination, were hewn at the far northern and southern ends of the lower cliff and along the length of the upper cliff: Tombs 12, 15, 20 (?), 21–23, 24, 37 and 38 (Ussishkin 1986: 244-46). The flat-ceiling tombs were more numerous than the gabled-ceiling tombs, and they accommodated more individuals than the latter. The flat-ceiling tomb was the type employed throughout Judah. Ussishkin suggested these were family tombs; however, lacking repositories, they could only have accommodated a limited number of family members (Ussishkin 1986: 284, 285

n. 27). The placement of Tombs 32 and 33 and of Tombs 8–10 relative to Tombs 11 and 12 demonstrates that the flat-ceiling tombs were relatively later in date than the gabled-ceiling tombs (Ussishkin 1986: 247-48). According to Ussishkin, all were initially cut in the Iron II period (pp. 283-84).

In Tombs 21–23, benches were carved along the two side walls in the front or rear chamber (Ussishkin 1986: 120, 124, 127-30). Benches were cut around three sides of the relatively small Tomb 12 (p. 86) and around the back room of Tomb 38 (pp. 189-90). Tomb 38, like Tombs 13 and 27, had a small shelf conjectured to have held offerings or memorial-lights (p. 255). A single bench was provided in Tomb 37 (p. 186), and in Tomb 3, 'The Tomb of Pharaoh's Daughter' (pp. 59-60). A unique installation was carved into the Tomb 3 bench. Two channels ran parallel to the edge of the bench, and nearby was carved out a cup-like depression 0.11 m in diameter and 0.05 m deep. Ussishkin suggested that these cuttings, like the example in Tomb 16, dated from the Iron Age and served to hold liquid perfumes or scents (Ussishkin 1986: 59-60, 255). Bench-niches or arcosolia were hewn in Tomb 24 and perhaps in Tombs 20 and 35. In Tombs 15 and 24, benches were cut next to and parallel to trough-niches. Tomb 15 had benches along the two side walls and the wall through which the doorway was cut. Trough-niches were cut beside the benches into the side walls as well as into the back wall (Ussishkin 1986: 93-99). In Tomb 24 benches lined the side and rear walls, and a trough-niche was cut into the left-hand wall beside the bench (pp. 133-34).

Lachish. The Wellcome–Colt/Wellcome–Marston Expedition excavated four cave tombs from the north side of the mound of Lachish, which were probably first utilized in the Middle Bronze Age and reused between the tenth and the sixth century BCE: Caves 4002, 4005, 4010 and 4019. Cave 4002 consisted of a circular chamber with a plastered floor and five loculi. Two extended bodies lay with their heads to the north facing west in the upper burial. Two lamps, a bowl, a storejar, a dipper juglet, a cup, Mycenaean sherds, an iron knife and beads served to date this tomb from 2000–900 BCE (Tufnell 1953: 239-40). A shaft and steps led into Cave 4005, a rectangular chamber with three loculi or benches circumventing the chamber. More than 50 Iron Age burials, including earlier interments pushed aside before decomposition, were found with bangles and very few vessels dating primarily from the end of the tenth century BCE (Tufnell 1953: 240). Tomb 4010, which was part of a series of interconnected tombs, consisted of an irregularly-shaped chamber with a rock partition opposite the entrance and a 0.50 m high bench on each side. All that remained in the violated tomb was evidence of more than five individuals, bowls and dipper juglets (Tufnell 1953: 242). Iron Age sherds were all that remained in Tomb 4019, a plastered circular chamber with four loculi, located in a nearby mortuary complex (Tufnell 1953: 243).

Tomb 218 was also a Middle Bronze Age burial altered for reuse around 900 BCE. Just inside the door, between the rough stone-built benches running along both sides of the entryway, lay a jumble of human bones, skulls and three dozen pots. A large number of Egyptian objects were retrieved from the tomb: five scarabs and scaraboids, a sphinx amulet with a negroid head, faience amulets of Bast, Sekhmet (?), Horus the child, Isis and Horus enthroned, Menyt and animals—a couchant lion, a sphinx, a Barbary ape, a baboon, a ram, a falcon and a sow. Broken skulls, animal bones and eight bracelets lay in Room A. The repository yielded numerous pottery vessels: 44 dipper juglets, 30 bowls, 18 jugs, 5 lamps and a zoomorphic quadruped vase. Mini-amphoras and a cooking pot completed the ceramic repertoire in the tomb. Gold, silver, bronze and bone jewelry, iron lanceheads and arrowheads, beads, shells, and Middle and Late Bronze Age sherds were also retrieved from the repository (Tufnell 1953: 203-209, fig. 25).

Tomb 218 was connected to Tomb 122 by two small holes in the wall, which in turn was connected by a shaft in the floor to Tomb 230. Tomb 230 contained nine mid-ninth-century BCE pots of the types found in the other tombs of the period, but no skeletal fragments (Tufnell 1953: 218). Seven steps led down into the three chambers of Tomb 223. A rough bench or 'mastaba' extended across half of the far wall in the first chamber. The second and third chambers in the rear had been partitioned off with a stone wall. The lower half of an articulated skeleton and burial provisions similar to those in Tomb 218, though in smaller quantities, were found in the rear rooms: 12 bowls, 10 dipper juglets, 8 storejars, 5 lamps, 4 jugs and a chalice. A bird-shaped vessel, a faience amulet of Sekhet, silver, bronze and iron personal ornaments and beads completed the assemblage (Tufnell 1953: 211-14, fig. 27).

Three tombs were hewn during the tenth to ninth century BCE: Tomb 521 in the cemetery south of the mound, Tomb 116 west of the mound and Tomb 6006 north of the mound. In Tomb 521, a shaft led down into a rectangular chamber with a one-meter-wide stone-built bench along a side wall and a narrow ledge at the back. On the bench lay two undisturbed bodies, one on top of the other, with their heads to the west. The uppermost individual was an adult male. Small vessels had been set around their heads, and two storejars lay nearby on the floor. Next to the ledge at the rear of the tomb lay two more articulated bodies. Burial provisions found in the tomb, dating to approximately 1000 BCE, included five bowls, four storejars, four lamps, three dipper juglets, two jugs, a spouted jar, a bowl on three loop feet, iron knives, an iron trident/pitchfork, scarabs and a gaming board (Tufnell 1953: 222-24). Dated by O. Tufnell to 875 BCE, Tomb 116 consisted of a square entrance cut into a 3 m square chamber with benches on three sides. The burials found on the benches had been provided with 17 dipper juglets, 12 jugs, 9 bowls, 6 lamps, 2 chalices, 2 storejars, a scarab, scaraboids, seals, amulets of Bes and Sekhmet, jewelry and an iron knife. This tomb was reused in the seventh century BCE (Tufnell 1953: 190-92). Also dated to c. 875 BCE, Tomb 6006 was of highly irregular shape and plan. A dromos and five steps led into the chamber which had 0.25 m high benches along the walls to the right of and opposite the entrance. A lamp in the niche had been cut into the wall above the bench to the right of the entrance. On the bench opposite the entrance, a female lay extended, with her head to the north, provided with four flasks close to her head and a scarab near her left hand. The disturbed remains of a male were found with an iron knife. A storejar, bowls and a chalice sat on the bench and five dipper juglets lay scattered in the tomb (Tufnell 1953: 247).

Madeba. The late eleventh- beginning tenth- to mid-eighth-century BCE Madeba B cave tomb, with a large shelf formed by the natural bedding planes, is described under tenth- to eighth-century BCE cave, shaft and chamber tombs (Piccirillo 1975; Thompson 1984).

Tell en-Nasbeh. Under the direction of W.F. Badè, three tombs spanning the tenth to eighth centuries BCE were excavated at Tell en-Nasbeh: Tombs 3, 5 and 54. Tomb 54, the earliest tomb, was a roughly oval cave in the northeast cemetery, measuring 7 × 8 m. The tomb had a two-meter-wide bench along the back wall and a cell approximately three meters in diameter cut into the back wall. Mandibles of 54 individuals were found with tenth-century BCE pottery, especially juglets including some black-polished examples, iron rings and arrowheads, objects of bronze, two crude stamp seals and a cylinder seal (McCown 1947: 82). Tomb 5, dated by Badè to c. 1000 BCE, and by G.E. Wright to the tenth to ninth century BCE, is reminiscent of Aitun Tomb 1 and Halif T-6. It is characterized by a square entry and steps down into the short side of a rectangular chamber with rock-cut benches on three sides. In the Tell en-Nasbeh example, an additional chamber 2.25 m square had been hewn in the back, entered from bench level with a step down. The tomb contained a few fragmentary skeletal remains, 62 lamps, all with round bottoms and practically all with signs of use, 52 black-burnished juglets, 50 bowls, jars, chalice fragments, a strainer cup suggested to have been used as an incense burner, a flask with wax in it—perhaps the remains of honey, a swan-shaped vessel decorated with red and black bands, and two scarabs on which Dr M. Pieper of the Egyptian Division of the State Museum of Berlin identified a fish, a lion and a scorpion (Badè 1931: 19-32). Tomb 3, dated by Badè to the ninth century BCE and by Albright to the eighth century BCE, was the most elaborate of this series of tombs. A forecourt measuring 2.25 × 1.3 m, with a niche containing fragments of infant bones and an adult femur (later burials?), led into a chamber measuring approximately 4 × 3 m, with benches on three sides, a repository in the far left-hand corner and an alcove in the far right-hand corner. An unusual feature of this tomb was the placement of three lamp niches; one saucer-shaped, smoked socket was carved out above the alcove, and two were hewn in the far corners of the central pit at the level of the benches. The tomb contained only a few bones, 15 lamps, 10 with rounded bottoms and 5 with disc bases, 8 bowls, 4 black juglets and 4 decanters (Badè 1931: 8-18).

Tomb 14, consisting of two roughly-cut chambers, each with a central pit and benches around all four sides, was in use from Iron II through the Roman period. Badè identified Early and Middle Iron Age sherds, probably to be dated from the tenth through the eighth centuries BCE, as in the other tombs (Badè 1931: 104).

Ramot. V. Tzaferis of the Israel Department of Antiquities excavated a natural cave adapted for burial in Ramot, northwest of Jerusalem. A wall with an opening in its lower part divided the rectangular chamber measuring 5.5 × 3.0 m into a forecourt and a sunken, back burial chamber. Seven bodies lay on the low benches encircling the rear section of the cave. A juglet and two lamps from the ninth to seventh centuries BCE dated the burials (Ramot 1971; Tzaferis 1982a).

Sahab. Sahab Tomb C, excavated by R. Dajani, appeared to be constructed or adapted for domestic occupation with stairs down through a doorway, benches and a chimney. A crisscross pavement divided the tomb floor into quadrants. The earliest remains dated from the fourteenth century BCE, so the tomb has been described above under twelfth- and eleventh-century BCE bench and arcosolia tombs. Early Iron II remains were found in quadrant B under the 'chimney' (R. Dajani 1970).

Samaria. A second half ninth-century BCE bench tomb cut into a hillside south of the mound of Samaria was excavated by F. Zayadine of the Jordan Department of Antiquities. Beneath a collapsed roof, steps led down into a trapezoidal central chamber measuring 3.5 × 2.5 × 4.0 m with a bench against the far wall. Beyond the bench was a second smaller chamber with a 0.40 m wide and 0.10 m high bench along the wall to the right of the entrance. A third small chamber filled with skeletal fragments and 'intentionally' broken jars led off from the far left-hand corner of the second chamber. Jumbles of bones and pottery lay at both sides of the entrance, and a 13 to 14-year-old reposed, supine, on the bench in the chamber (perhaps a later burial). In addition to dipper juglets, lamps, bowls and jars, Zayadine found amphoriskoi and chalices decorated with red and black bands, metal objects, two ivory objects, a bone seal, a scarab depicting two persons praying before a tree of life and 150 pig astragals. Astragals are usually considered children's playthings; however, the fact that these belonged to pigs prompted Zayadine to suggest possible cultic connections (Zayadine 1968).

Additional Iron II tombs have been identified by the Israel Department of Antiquities in the Samaria vicinity (Samaria 1967).

Tubas. In 1971, the Israel Department of Antiquities conducted a salvage excavation of a loculus tomb at the site of Tubas, north of Tell el-Farah (N). Pottery dated the tomb use from the end of the ninth through the beginning of the eighth century BCE, with reuse in the Byzantine period. A square shaft and steps led down into a rectangular chamber measuring 2 × 2 × 4 m with two loculi in each of the side walls and one loculus in the far wall. These loculi began 0.75 m above the chamber floor and measured approximately 1.5 m across and 1.75 m deep. The recessed frame around the loculi may date from the Iron Age, but the reddish-brown stripe painted in the frame and the cross painted on the back wall date to the Byzantine period. Twenty-two pots including five lamps with flanged rims, five plates, three dipper juglets, three pitchers, a bowl with a red band painted on the outside rim, a one-handled jar with a ring base, a cooking pot with an everted triangular rim and a bracelet fragment were retrieved from the tomb (Israel Antiquities Authority files, Tubas, photos 03315–03327).

Khirbet Za'aq. D. Alon of the Israel Department of Antiquities conducted salvage excavations of Bronze and Iron Age tombs at Khirbet Za'aq, located 3.6 km west-southwest of Tell Halif. The typical Iron Age tomb consisted of an elliptically-shaped vertical shaft which led to a square entrance then down some stairs into a burial chamber with two hewn burial-places. Sometimes two additional places were provided in a second chamber. The majority of tombs were used between the eighth and sixth centuries BCE, but local and imported pottery in the lowest levels dated Tomb 18 to the tenth to ninth century BCE. It was subsequently reused in the seventh to sixth century BCE (Khirbet Za'aq 1976).

Above-Ground Monolithic Tombs

Jerusalem—Silwan. D. Ussishkin identified four above-ground monolithic tombs carved from bedrock in the Silwan cemetery, all four hewn in the northern extent of the cemetery: Tomb 3 in the lower cliff, Tombs 34 and 35 in the upper cliff and Tomb 28 isolated in an upper cliff to the north. On the basis of the preserved, accessible examples, the rock was cut away on at least three sides to form a cube-shaped tomb with a superstructure and an internal square burial chamber. Three of the four tombs bore burial inscriptions carved in the facade near the doorway.

For Tomb 3, known as 'The Tomb of Pharaoh's Daughter', the rock was cut away on four sides to form a cube-shaped tomb. The Egyptian cornice cut across the facade was noted as early as the mid-1700s, but N. Avigad was the first to detect evidence of the pyramid-shaped superstructure which had been quarried away (Avigad 1947: 112-15). The tomb had a highly unusual internal plan, similar only to Tomb 2. A short corridor led into a rectangular vestibule and continued on into a square burial chamber with a gabled ceiling. Apparently a bench ran along the left hand wall, and was carved with two channels parallel to the edge of the bench and a cup-like depression to hold perfumes and scents beside the head of the deceased. A burial inscription carved in the upper part of the panel surrounding the entry was nearly destroyed when the doorway was later heightened. Only the final two letters of the inscription remained 'd/q/r' and 'r' (Ussishkin 1986: 47-63, 217, 255).

Tomb 28, presently owned by the Russian Orthodox Church, was probably an above-ground monolithic tomb like the nearby Tomb of Absalom. At a later period *kokim* were added to the original square burial chamber, and the superstructure was quarried away. The panel lacked traces of an inscription (Ussishkin 1986: 143-49).

Ussishkin's limited excavations were sufficient to prove that the side-by-side Tombs 34 and 35 were also above-ground monolithic tombs. Both are now incorporated into residences. Tomb 34 serves as a household cistern and Tomb 35 functions as a storage area and animal pen. Tomb 34 is known for its inscription first published by A. Reifenberg in the late 1940s. The facade was fashioned with one step up to a large recess and opening, and with a projecting margin running the length of the facade near the top. The inscription was carved, not in the recessed panel assumed by Ussishkin to have been cut specifically for inscriptions in the gabled-ceiling tombs, but above the panel, centered over the doorway. The inscription reads, '[This is the] burial of. z. . . whoever op[ens] (this tomb). . . ' (Reifenberg 1948; Ussishkin 1986: 165-72, 217-20). Ussishkin's excavations in front of Tomb 35, 'The Tomb of the Royal Steward', revealed a peculiar installation projecting out from the facade.

The raised platform, with a shelf along one side and a cup-like depression on top, perhaps added later, was interpreted as an offering table, allowing for offerings at all times, not just when the tomb was opened. This was the only outside installation identified in the Silwan cemetery (Ussishkin 1986: 255). Ussishkin suggested that the tomb originally consisted of two side-by-side rooms, with flat ceilings and right-angled cornices just below the ceiling. In the second room, a trough-niche without a cover or a bench-niche, provided with a pillow, was hewn to accommodate a single individual. 'Seemingly', a trough-niche without a cover or a bench-niche for two was carved into the back wall of the first chamber, as expected to conform with the inscriptions carved in the doorway panels. Two inscriptions, the work of different individuals at roughly the same time, were carved in panels in the facade. The long inscription was preserved above the doorway, and the second, shorter inscription is to be found to the right of the doorway. The longer inscription reads, 'This is [the tomb of. . .]Yahu, who is over the house. There is no silver and no gold. only his bones and the bones of his slave-wife with him. Cursed be the person. who opens this'. Tombs 10, 16 and 42 all had burial-places carved for a pair, and in Tombs 10 and 16 the outermost place was slightly elevated. In light of this inscription, pair burials are thought to have accommodated a man and his wife, with the elevated place for the individual of higher status (Ussishkin 1986: 221-23). Ussishkin proposed a new reading for the shorter inscription. He reconstructed, 'the (burial) chamber beside the burial-chamber carved from the rock', with *ṣryḥ* meaning 'chamber or burial carved from the rock', as attested in First and Second Temple period Hebrew and in Nabatean (Ussishkin 1986: 223-26).

Above-ground monolithic tombs carved from the bedrock are unique in Iron Age Israel, being unparalleled in Jerusalem as well as throughout the country. Their uniqueness suggests that they were carved for Judahite officials. Ussishkin proposed they were ultimately of Egyptian inspiration, but the impetus may have come directly from Egypt, or through the Phoenicians, or both (Ussishkin 1986: 277). Tenth- to sixth-century BCE parallels in Israel and elsewhere are cited in support of an Iron II date for all the Silwan tombs. The monolithic tombs have been more precisely dated on the basis of the content and paleography of the inscriptions. The title *'ᵃšer 'al habbayit* from Tomb 35 was used during the period of the Judahite monarchy, but discontinued with the Babylonian exile. Paleographic considerations led Ussishkin to date the inscriptions to the end of the eighth century BCE (Ussishkin 1986: 283), following N. Avigad's date of approximately 700 BCE (Avigad 1953: 150; 1955: 166). J. Abercrombie noted that the longer inscription in Tomb 35 reflected seventh- to sixth-century BCE burial practices, in the absence of precious metal supplied in the tomb, the curse formula and the paired burial (Abercrombie 1984).

Cremation Burials

Tell el-Ajjul. W.M.F. Petrie of the British School of Archaeology in Egypt excavated fourteen tenth- to early ninth-century BCE cremation burials in the Tell el-Ajjul Cemeteries A and J: 1022, 1024, 1038, 1093, 1102, 1106, 1120, 1126, 1134, 1135-36, 1151, 1153 and 1160. Only two of the burials were interred in vessels,

1022 and 1024; the remainder were open cremations. Most of the objects recovered from the burials were locally-made pots; however, two coastal Syrian urns, two Cypro-Phoenician juglets, two Cypriot oil bottles, one arrowhead and two scarabs were also provided (Petrie 1932: pls. LVI–LVIII). D. Harden and F. James later dated these and the Tell el-Farah (S) cremation burials to the eighth or seventh century BCE (Bienkowski 1982: 84).

Akhzib. The earliest open and urn cremation burials at Akhzib may date from the late eleventh century BCE, but most are datable to the tenth and ninth centuries BCE Excavating at Akhzib in 1941, N. Makhouly uncovered a burial jar with a lid in Trench A of the southern cemetery, el Buq-baq (Israel Antiquities Authority British Mandate Period Files, ez-Zib, photos 26.700, 26.701). Makhouly also recorded urns in Tombs XIX and XXIV in the eastern cemetery, er-Ras (*ibid.*, photos 30.142, 30.158). In later excavations, M. Prausnitz of the Israel Department of Antiquities discovered cremated remains solely in the southern cemetery, el Buq-baq, in urns and bowls deposited in tombs or interred in the sand. The earliest cremations were those interred in the bench tombs dating from the end of the eleventh through the end of the eighth century BCE, the tombs with a cut in the roof above which Prausnitz reconstructed an offering table. More than 200 individuals were interred in each tomb, the majority present in the jumble and piles of bones on the benches and on the floor. Within these tombs, most of the cremated individuals were interred in urns, but a few were simply deposited (Prausnitz 1969: 87; private communication 1984, *contra* Prausnitz 1982: 34).

The cremation practices introduced in the eleventh or tenth century BCE continued through the Iron Age at Akhzib. In the eighth century BCE, urns or bowls capped with bowls or saucers containing cremated remains were secondarily placed in tombs such as 606 and 979. In addition to charred skeletal fragments, the urns contained 26th Dynasty scarabs, rings, armlets, earrings and red-slipped and Samaria wares (Prausnitz 1960: 260; 1982: 36; private communication 1984). Among the large rock-cut tombs, cremated remains were interred in round or oval pits in the sand, rarely in a stone frame similar to the eleventh-century BCE burial at Azor. Some of the burials were marked by stelae dated from the eighth through the first quarter of the sixth century BCE (Prausnitz 1975a: 27; 1982: 36; private communication 1984). Other cremations were buried under a '*bāmâ* or '*maṣṣēbâ*,' such as Tomb 645 (detailed below under eighth- to sixth-century BCE simple burials) (Prausnitz 1969: 86; 1970: 377; 1982: 32).

Atlit. In the southeastern part of the mound of Atlit just under a mediaeval period floor, C.N. Johns of the British Mandatory Government in Palestine Department of Antiquities found ninth- to seventh-century BCE cremation burials in a filling containing Iron I sherds (Johns 1933: 151). All other Iron Age cremation burials at the site date from the end of the eighth century BCE.

Tell el-Farah (S). At Tell el-Farah (S), W.M.F. Petrie of the British School of Archaeology in Egypt identified at least 29 urn cremation burials in the 200 Cemetery: 215–19, 223, 233 and 250–72. The urns were interred around and in the large, stone-lined cist Tomb 233. The urns, with an inverted bowl functioning as a lid, were found to contain the charred bones of children and adults with two or three small pots including a local imitation of a Cypriot pot (Petrie Type 83). The Tomb 233 individuals had been provided with iron and perhaps copper bangles, and a silver aegis of Bast. Iron arrowheads were supplied in Tomb 262 (Petrie 1930: pl. LXVIII; 1932: 12-13). Comparing the Black-on-Red juglets and the single Philistine pot found with the Tell el-Farah (S) cremation burials to the assemblage from Tell er-Ruqeish, W. Culican concluded that the Tell el-Farah (S) cremation graves should be dated to 1000/950–800 BCE, postdating most burials in the 200 Cemetery, but perhaps contemporary with the large, collective cist tombs (Culican 1973: 95). D. Harden and F. James dated both these and the Tell el-Ajjul cremations to the eighth or seventh century BCE (Bienkowski 1982: 84).

Joya. S. Chapman, who published the pottery from Khaldé, Khirbet Silm and Joya, suggested that cremation and inhumation were practiced together at Joya as they were at Khaldé (Chapman 1972: 57). See the description of the tenth- to eighth-century BCE Khaldé simple graves for details.

Khaldé. At the coastal site of Khaldé, located 10 km south of Beirut, R. Saidah excavated 422 burials including urns with cremated human remains, and inhumations and cremations buried together in simple pit graves and in cists. Cist Tomb 121 held a complete skeleton, several broken human bones and three large amphoras. The three amphoras were similarly decorated with red and black bands. One amphora, apparently devoid of contents, stood near the eastern cist wall. The second amphora, propped up in the northeastern corner of the cist, held non-burned human bones and two skulls. Positioned next to the skeleton's shoulder was a third amphora capped with an inverted bowl containing a large number of burned bones including some of which were identifiably human. Ceramic offerings in the tomb included five bowls, two flasks and an oenochoé, all red-slipped or decorated with red and black bands, and four dipper juglets. Two scarabs were supplied, the first inscribed with a solar bird, an *ankh* and a scarab flanked by *nb* from the reign of Osorkon IV, and the second with a sphinx and the tree of life. Both Tomb 3 and Tomb 121 dated from the end of the ninth to the end of the eighth century BCE (Saidah 1966: 60, 64; 1969: 130). An open (?) cremation burial was unearthed but not detailed (Saidah 1967: 167).

Lachish. Lachish Tomb 120, excavated by the Wellcome–Colt/Wellcome–Marston Archaeological Research Expedition, contained bones of more than 1,500 individuals including some burnt bone, covered with a layer of charred animal bones, primarily pig (Tufnell 1953: 193). Included in the ninth- through latter eighth-century BCE contents of Cave 1002 were some secondary burials 'affected by fire before they were reburied' (Tufnell 1953: 229). These tombs are detailed above under tenth- to eighth-century BCE cave tombs.

Megiddo. During excavations of Megiddo directed by G. Schumacher of the German Society for Oriental Research in the early 1900s, five urns containing cremated infant remains were unearthed in a temple precinct (Schumacher 1908: 121-22, photos 181–82, pl. 38A). J. Abercrombie noted that the pithoi with horizontal handles and the spouted jug were similar to Tell el-Farah (S) and Tell er-Ruqeish cremation burial vessels (Abercrombie 1979: 304-305).

Mt Nebo. Several tombs have been found in the vicinity of Jebel Hussein, located north of Mt Nebo near Madeba. The two fully-published tombs UCV-20 and UCV-84, in use from 1000–586 BCE, were cave tombs with secondary burials on benches, jar burials, evidence of anthropoid coffin burial and signs of cremation. Both tombs held massive numbers of individuals, approximately 250 in UCV-84 and 750 in UCV-20, together with hundreds of burial goods, including pottery, jewelry, shells, tools and figurines. Both caves contained 'cremation strata'. In Tomb UCV-20, the larger of the two, cremation strata were recorded throughout the cave, while in UCV-84 cremation strata were detected only in one extensive area in chamber 2. Cypro-Phoenician juglets were found in both tombs but there were no other typically Phoenician vessels (Saller 1966).

Qasmieh. At the site of Qasmieh, on the Lebanese coast between Tyre and Sidon, cremated remains were interred in urns. The urns are similar to Akhzib and Tell el-Farah (S) vessels which have been dated from the middle of the tenth to the end of the eighth century BCE (Chapman 1972: 57, 148).

Tell er-Ruqeish. In 1939, J. Ory working on behalf of the British Mandatory Government in Palestine Department of Antiquities, excavated 24 jar and urn burials at the site of Tell er-Ruqeish, located a kilometer south of Deir el-Balah. Most of the vessels contained cremated human remains and Black-on-Red juglets or burnished ware juglets. Two scarabs and beads of carnelian and blue glazed paste were also recovered from two of the jars (Ory 1944: 205).

A. Biran and O. Haas found isolated cremation burials in the sandy hill. Preserved in the sand were urns plus ash lenses resulting from burning bodies with their gifts. The most common pottery vessels were bowls, jars and Cypro-Phoenician style juglets, the majority of which were red-slipped and burnished. Stelae were found near some of the burials, as at Khaldé, but only two were found *in situ*. One stele measured 0.28 m long × 0.22 m wide and a second measured 0.60 × 0.30 × 0.09 m. As at Khaldé, the stelae were associated with urns, open cremations and inhumations. At Tell er-Ruqeish one stele stood near an ash layer with a burned skeleton, and nearby were burned animal bones and a primary inhumation of a disarticulated body with three eighth-century BCE scarabs in hand. Not far from the stele were skulls, and at a greater distance was an urn. The second stele stood over the skull of a disarticulated skeleton, two more bodies and a burial jar (Biran 1974; Tell Ruqeish 1974). These jar, urn and open cremation burials have been dated from Iron II into the Persian period (Biran 1974).

E. Oren uncovered additional cremation burials near the southern wall of his excavation area Y-5 (Oren *et al.* 1986: 89).

In 1940, at the bequest of C.N. Johns, Dr W.J.E. Philips, the senior medical officer of the Jerusalem district, analyzed the skeletal fragments from the urns. He found the urns to contain human adults (R. 5, 6, 7, 10, 11, 19, 23, R. B. 2, 3), a youth (R. 15), a small human (R. 9), a small child and an adult (R. 12), some human and other bones from a separate box (R. 17), and human bones and eggshell (R. 20) (Israel Antiquities Authority British Mandate Period File, Bir el-Reqeish). P. Smith and J. Zias analyzed bones from urns excavated in the 1970s by Biran and Haas. Their analysis showed that the only pattern in bone selection was the inclusion of the skull, and that the bones had been inserted into the jar in no particular order, except that skulls were usually found in the upper part of the vessel. The contents of six urns were identified as four 40-year-old men, one 30-year-old individual of indeterminate sex, and an 18 to 25-year-old female. Three of these people suffered from rheumatism (Tell Ruqeish 1974: 6).

Khirbet Silm. S. Chapman, who published the pottery from Khaldé, Khirbet Silm and Joya, suggested that cremation and inhumation were practiced together at Khirbet Silm as they were at Khaldé (Chapman 1972: 57). See the description of the tenth- to eighth-century BCE Khaldé simple graves for details.

Tambourit. In the village of Tambourit, located 6 km southeast of Sidon, a bulldozer revealed a circular cavity in the chalk. In a recess in the cave, 11 vessels were spared, including 3 bowls, 4 amphoras and 3 jugs, all decorated with red and black concentric bands, and an imported Greek pyxis. Three of the amphoras contained calcined human bones. One of these vessels, number 6, was inscribed with three Phoenician letters on the shoulder, *'qm*, interpreted as a reference to the nearby village of 'Aqmata, which may preserve the ancient name (Bordreuil 1977). The pyxis was suggested to have originated in the Argolid, and was dated to the third quarter of the ninth century BCE (Courbin 1977). Of the remaining 11 vessels, the excavator R. Saidah considered five to be cremation urns holding members of two or possibly three generations of the same family, and he therefore dated the tomb from 850/25–800/775 BCE (Saidah 1977).

Burials from the Last Quarter of the Eighth through the First Quarter of the Sixth Century BCE

Simple Graves

Akhzib. M. Prausnitz of the Israel Department of Antiquities excavated inhumation burials in two different eighth- to seventh-century BCE contexts in the el Buq-baq or southern cemetery at Akhzib. In burial 645, cremated and inhumed remains were interred together. Prausnitz distinguished four phases of use. At the bottom lay a skeleton and a crater-amphora containing cremated remains. A jug and 'Sidonian' red-slipped pitchers and decanters were attributed to these lower burials and to a third body lying above. Above the inhumation and cremation burials lay the skeleton of a male on his back with legs flexed and head in the mouth of a crater-amphora. Half a meter higher was a stele with bowls and platters near its base. Letters and signs engraved on the stele have been interpreted by F.M. Cross as a dedication to Tannit on behalf of the dead. Prausnitz dated the majority of the stelae from the site to the eighth century BCE, but some he dated to the seventh and first quarter of the sixth century BCE. Finally, near the surface were fragments of large eighth-century BCE storejars interpreted as remains of offerings or meals (Prausnitz 1969: 85-87; 1970: 375-76; 1975b: 27).

Simple graves with accompanying offering pits, dating from the first half of the seventh century BCE, were identified as the latest burials in the southern cemetery. The deceased was placed extended on his or her back in a pit measuring 1.6 m long and up to 0.8 m wide, with gifts such as a bowl, a lamp and a jug (Prausnitz 1982: photo E4/16). The offering pits contained a standing stone, an incense stand, a shallow bowl and (occasionally) a seated pregnant female figurine (other examples of which date from the sixth century BCE) (Prausnitz 1982: 35).

Tel Amal. S. Levy and G. Edelstein of the Israel Department of Antiquities conducted salvage excavations at Tel Amal, Nir David, situated northeast of Beth Shan. They uncovered five tombs dug into the earth. Due to problematic stratigraphy, the tombs were attributed to locus 20 levels III and/or IV, which were dated to the tenth and ninth centuries BCE. In four of the tombs, the body lay with stones piled around the head and a small, elongated, handleless jar with a high button base nearby. A wine decanter was also found. Levy and Edelstein compared the button base jars to seventh-century BCE Assyrian examples from Tell Halaf and Nineveh and sixth-century BCE vessels found at Tell en-Nasbeh, so the burials should probably be dated to the seventh or sixth century BCE (Levy 1962; Levy and Edelstein 1972: 241).

Amman—Royal Palace. More than 30 skeletons were simply interred or placed in jars around anthropoid coffin burials in a tenth- to seventh-century BCE cistern-shaped tomb located near the royal palace in Amman (Yassine 1975: 58). This tomb has been detailed above under tenth- to eighth-century BCE anthropoid, wooden and stone coffin burials.

Ashdod. At the coastal site of Ashdod, M. Dothan of Haifa University and the Israel Department of Antiquities excavated animal burials and graves with multiple and massive numbers of humans. The human graves were situated in the industrial quarter of the city, Area D, and the largest examples were dug into open courtyards of buildings located in the potters' quarter. M. Dothan attributed loci 1050 and 1066 possibly to Stratum 3 (VIII); loci 1113, 1114, 1115, 1121 and 1129 to Stratum 3b, ending with the destruction by Sargon in 712 BCE; and loci 1005 and 1006 to

Stratum 3b–a, ending with the destruction by Pharaoh Psamtik. N. Haas, who studied the skeletal remains, distinguished four types of burial: primary burials (loci 1005, 1050, 1051, 1052 [?], 1060[?], 1066, 1121 [?], 1129), secondary burials in common graves (loci 1006, 1114), interments of decapitated bodies or skulls, all in Building 3 (loci 1052 [?], 1113, 1115, 1121 [?]), and refuse dumps with just animal bones (loci 1011, 1055, 1158).

Loci 1005, 1050, 1060 and 1129 contained eight or less individuals. Situated inside the building area, locus 1005 consisted of a small grave with two adult males, probably primary inhumations, and six other individuals represented by skeletal fragments, perhaps the remains of earlier burials. Accompanying ovicaprid and cattle skeletal fragments were interpreted as funerary offerings (Haas 1971: 212). Locus 1050 contained two nearly complete adult males, three additional humans which J. Abercrombie identified as adult females (Abercrombie 1979: 214), and two bowls. The burial of two adults and two children comprised locus 1060. In locus 1129 a 60 to 65-year-old female, a nearly complete 18 to 20-year-old male, a 12 to 14-year-old, and a 4 to 5-year-old were buried with a bowl, a crater, a juglet, a handleless hole-mouth jar, a loom weight and a clay footbath (M. Dothan 1971: figs. 39–49; Haas 1971: 213).

Locus 1113 was atypical with fragmentary remains of 2,434 individuals (Haas 1971: 213). In both locus 1113 beneath the courtyard (?) in Building 2 and locus 1121 beneath the courtyard in Building 3, layers of bones and offerings were covered with dirt, then a second layer of bones and offerings was laid down, and this in turn was covered with dirt and then plastered over. The ceramic vessels in the grave were identical to those found in the structures, and they occurred in the same relative proportions. Many of the bowls, craters, jugs, juglets and storejars found in all the burials were red-slipped and painted with black bands. Very few burial provisions accompanied the massive number of individuals in locus 1113: 14 bowls, 4 craters, 4 juglets, 3 storejars, 3 stands, kernoi, a scaraboid and a burnishing tool (?) (M. Dothan 1971: figs. 39–49). Locus 1121 beneath the courtyard in Building 3 was similar in plan and execution to locus 1113, but with the remains of only 21 individuals, bowls and a juglet (M. Dothan 1971: 94, figs. 39–49; Haas 1971: 213). Locus 1114, beneath the courtyard in Building 1, contained the remains of 376 individuals, faunal remains, 24 jugs and juglets, 15 bowls including a 'Persian type' bowl with a hole in the center of the base, 13 storejars, 4 craters, 3 cooking pots, 2 partial incense stands, 2 kernoi, a chalice foot, loom weights, a faience vessel in the shape of a skull (?), a wheel, and bone and metal jewelry (Abercrombie 1979: 215-16; M. Dothan 1971: 101-103, figs. 39–49; Haas 1971: 213). In locus 1006, the fragmentary remains of 45 individuals without provisions were interred near a wall (Haas 1971: 212).

Loci 1066, 1115 and 1151 contained skulls or post-cranial skeletons. In locus 1066, the skulls and post-cranial skeletons of two men and one woman were buried with six cats, six foreparts of the upper jaws of donkeys and a jug. Ten well-preserved human skulls, perhaps with signs of decapitation, were stacked in a narrow pit one above another, forming locus 1115. Provisions included bowls, a crater, a cooking pot, a jug, storejars, a lamp, a chalice, a jar stand, a scaraboid, a wheel and two quadruped kernoi (Abercrombie 1979: 216; M. Dothan 1971: 103, figs. 39–49; Haas 1971: 212). In locus 1151, seven nearly complete post-cranial skeletons were buried in parallel rows with a lamp and a crater. The only other lamp was in locus 1115 (M. Dothan 1971: figs. 39–49; Haas 1971: 212).

Atlit. On a rocky ridge beyond the east end of the mound of Atlit, C.N. Johns of the British Mandatory Government in Palestine Department of Antiquities excavated a cemetery with one inhumation burial, open cremation burials and an urn containing calcined bones (Johns 1933: fig. 1). Virtually all the excavated burials were of children burned on a wooden pyre and then covered with dirt (Johns 1936–37: 124-25). The single inhumation burial, designated 'ii' and dated to the sixth century BCE, was of a child lying with its head to the east, provided with two anklets, two bracelets, a ring, a glass ornament and an eyebead (Johns 1936–37: 140-41).

Bethlehem. J. Tubb published an assemblage acquired in the 1880s, which was said to have originated in a grave located 'close to Rachel's Tomb, on the way to Bethlehem'. The collection included a female pillar figurine with painted hair, two bronze bangles, five juglets including one black juglet, a jug, a bowl and a pottery alabastron (Barnett 1966: 32 fig. 17a; Tubb 1980). This collection is more likely to have originated from a cave or bench tomb.

Dothan. At the site of Dothan, excavations directed by J.P. Free of Wheaton college, Wheaton, Illinois, uncovered three intramural simple burials. Intramural inhumations have been recovered in this period only from Ashdod and Dothan. In a plastered court of a level 1-A[a] eighth- to seventh-century BCE building sat a bathtub coffin, and a few meters south of it an individual had been inhumed. The individual, lying head to the south, had its hands cut off and placed under the thighs. On one finger was a ring set with a 'jade-like green stone' and a complete Assyrian palace ware bowl lay nearby. Free suggested that the burial may date from the late eighth century BCE, between the Assyrian destruction and rebuilding of Dothan (Free 1959: 26). In an Iron II level dated 900–600 BCE, near infant jar burials lay a man with his fists clenched, his head twisted into an unnatural position and his back broken in two places, perhaps a victim of the Assyrian invasion. Among sub-Area A-105 remains dating from 900–700 BCE, fragmentary human skeletal remains were uncovered with an Assyrian palace ware bowl (Free 1954: 18).

Jerusalem—Mamilla. Two eighth- to seventh-century BCE pottery assemblages, believed to have originated from graves or tombs, were collected by the British Mandatory Government in Palestine Department of Antiquities in the lower region of Mamilla Road, on the slope at the head of the Hinnom Valley in Jerusalem. Tomb 1, found in 1935, contained pots 38.1952–38.1968, and Tomb 2, excavated in 1927, yielded pots 52.97–52.99, now all in the Rockefeller Museum collection. R. Amiran assumed that the assemblages originated in rock-cut bench tombs. She found neither bones nor evidence of rock-cutting, prompting G. Barkay to suggest that the assemblages had originated in simple graves which were more likely to have been obliterated (G. Barkay, private communication 1984). The assemblages included a headless female pillar figurine, one-handled jugs, four dipper juglets, storejar fragments, two southern type decanters and a bottle. Amiran dated the assemblage to the eighth to seventh century BCE, citing close parallels with the Beth Shemesh Tombs 2–8 assemblages (Amiran 1956).

Joya. S. Chapman, who published the pottery from Khaldé, Khirbet Silm and Joya, suggested that cremation and inhumation were practiced together at Joya as they were at Khaldé (Chapman 1972: 57). See the description of the tenth- to eighth-century BCE Khaldé simple graves for details.

Khaldé. The Khaldé simple and cist graves dating from the end of the ninth to the end of the eighth century BCE have been detailed above (Chapman 1972; Saidah 1966; 1967).

Lachish. The simple graves dated by O. Tufnell of the Wellcome–Colt/Wellcome–Marston Archaeological Research Expedition to the period 900–700 BCE have been detailed above under tenth- to eighth-century BCE simple graves: Graves 139, 195, 197, 222, 231, 236, 239, 519 and 4027.

The majority of Iron Age graves were in the 100 and 200 Cemeteries. S. Loffreda noted that most pre-exilic simple interments were oriented north–south, while Persian period interments lay east–west (Loffreda 1968: 260). Both Graves 4007 and 4027 in the 4000 Cemetery, dated by Tufnell to c. 750–550 BCE and 900–700 BCE respectively, were oriented east–west. Both were isolated single inhumations in a cemetery of cave and bench tombs, and they both contained functional items. The individual in Grave 4007 was provided with a pilgrim flask and four arrowheads. In Grave 4027, the individual lay with arms crossed on the chest, the only recorded example from Lachish of this body position, accompanied by two dipper juglets, pins and a flint sickle blade (Tufnell 1953: 242, 244).

Tell el-Mazar. K. Yassine excavated Cemetery A, 220 m north-northwest of Tell el-Mazar. Yassine dated the 84 simple, cist, jar and larnax burials to the Iron IIc–Persian period, but J. Sauer proposed a Babylonian–Persian period date, on the basis of the pottery and selected finds (Sauer 1979: 72). The vast majority of graves were simple burials in which men were laid extended on their backs (29 burials) and women were placed in a crouching position (32 burials). The bodies, dressed or wrapped in cloth or matting, were oriented east–west, 79 percent with their heads to the east (Yassine 1983: 30-33; 1984: 3-6).

Megiddo. The Oriental Institute of the University of Chicago's excavations of the east slope of Megiddo uncovered a single primary inhumation among the large rock-cut tombs. Tomb 236 contained an adult female lying extended on her back, with her head to the south-southwest, without provisions. Similar graves on the tell were dated to c. 600 BCE (Guy 1938: 133 n. 39).

Tell er-Ruqeish. Approximately 20 primary inhumations were uncovered at Tell er-Ruqeish (Israel Antiquities Authority Mandate Period Files, Bir er-Reqeish, photo 035.700). The associated pottery has been variously dated by S. Loffreda to the ninth–eighth century BCE (Loffreda 1968: 263), by W. Culican to the ninth century BCE (Culican 1973), by P. Bienkowski to c. 850 BCE (Bienkowski 1982: 84) and most recently by R. Hestrin and M. Dayagi-Mendels to the eighth to seventh century BCE, following the resettlement of Tell er-Ruqeish as part of the Assyrian economic reorganization (Hestrin and Dayagi-Mendels 1983: 56). The burials have been described above.

Khirbet Silm. S. Chapman, who published the pottery from Khaldé, Khirbet Silm and Joya, suggested that cremation and inhumation were practiced together at Khirbet Silm as they were at Khaldé (Chapman 1972: 57). See the description of the tenth- to eighth-century BCE Khaldé simple graves for details.

Cist Graves

Khaldé. The late ninth- to late eighth-century BCE Khaldé cist grave, Tomb 121, has been detailed above (Chapman 1972; Saidah 1966; 1967).

Tell el-Mazar. K. Yassine excavated Cemetery A, 220 m north-northwest of Tell el-Mazar. Yassine dated the 84 simple, cist, jar and larnax burials to the Iron IIc–Persian period, but J. Sauer suggested a Babylonian–Persian period date on the basis of the pottery and selected finds (Sauer 1979: 72). Three brick-lined cists, Graves 17, 43 and 83, were constructed with a single row of bricks and the body was covered with brick or mud clay, perhaps a collapsed superstructure. Grave 43 was one of the three examples of secondary burial of long bones and a skull; the 'bones were placed in bundles with the skull semi-attached to them'. Yassine also excavated six graves constructed with stones along one side: Graves 12, 13, 26, 49, 65 and 66 (Yassine 1984: 6-7).

Palmachim. R. Gophna and S. Lipschitz excavated two cist tombs constructed of kurkar slabs at the coastal site of Palmachim. Both tombs were dated to the ninth century BCE, but one was reused in the seventh century BCE (Palmachim 1973: 19).

Tel Qedesh. Fifty meters north of Tel Qedesh, Tell Abu Qudeis, two strata of tombs were exposed while digging a drainage channel. The pottery and figurine in the Iron Age tombs were initially compared to assemblages from the tell Stratum IV providing an eighth century BCE date (Stern 1968: 193), but have subsequently been compared to Strata VI–V producing a tenth- to early ninth-century BCE date (Stern 1969: 97;

Stern and Beit Arieh 1979: 13). These cists have been detailed above under tenth- to eighth-century BCE cist graves.

Tell er-Ruqeish. The ninth- to seventh-century BCE cist graves at Tell er-Ruqeish, excavated by J. Ory, have been mentioned above under tenth- to eighth-century BCE cist graves (Israel Antiquities Authority British Mandate Period Files, Bir er-Reqeish, photo 035.700).

Jar Burials

Amman—Royal Palace. K. Yassine excavated more than 30 skeletons buried in jars or simply interred around anthropoid coffins in a tenth- to seventh-century BCE cistern-shaped tomb located near the royal palace in Amman (Yassine 1975: 58). The tomb is detailed under tenth- to eighth-century BCE anthropoid, wooden and stone coffin burials.

Beth Shemesh. D. Mackenzie of the Palestine Exploration Fund excavated nine eighth- to seventh-century BCE bench tombs cut into the rock on the north-northwest side of the mound of Beth Shemesh, Ain Shems. Tombs 5–9 shared a common courtyard. Standing just inside the entrance to Tomb 8 Mackenzie noted a large jar with bones in the bottom of the jar and in the bowl which served as a lid. Mackenzie further commented that '[s]uch bones. . . were commonly found in the vases. Sometimes they were of very small children' (Mackenzie 1912–13: 89). Tomb 8 is detailed below under bench and arcosolia tombs.

Dhiban. In the late tenth- to seventh-century BCE Dhiban tomb J5, fragments of four large storejars were thought to have been used for burial. The jars are detailed above under jar burials, and the tomb is detailed above under tenth- to eighth-century BCE cave, shaft and chamber tombs (Tushingham 1954: 24-25; 1972: 91-92).

Dothan. The excavations at Dothan directed by J.P. Free of Wheaton College, Wheaton, Illinois, unearthed six intramural infant jar burials. One burial was associated with Iron II lamps and other Iron II materials (Free 1954: 18). Towards the western edge of the mound, 400 feet from the previously mentioned burial, three more infant jar burials were discovered in level 1-A[a]. Eighth-century BCE jars had been cracked into at least two pieces to hold and cover the infants (Free 1959: 26). Two infant jar burials in level 2 sub-areas L26 and L27 were attributed to the level I Assyrians. In the first burial an infant with nine beads and an iron bracelet had been inserted into a collared-rim storejar, and in the second, the infant still wore a small iron bracelet on its arm (Free 1960: 9).

Tell el-Mazar. Among the 84 sixth- to fifth-century BCE burials excavated in the Tell el-Mazar cemetery, K. Yassine found only one jar burial. Grave 47 consisted of the bones of a one- to two-year-old child buried in a 'shallow, broken jar' (Yassine 1983: 31; 1984: 7).

Mt Nebo. The Iron II jar burial found in the Mt Nebo cave tomb UCV-84 has been detailed above under tenth- to eighth-century BCE jar burials (Saller 1966: 179).

Anthropoid, Wooden and Stone Coffin Burials

Amman—Royal Palace. K. Yassine excavated five anthropoid coffins in a tenth- to seventh-century BCE cave tomb located near the royal palace in Amman. The coffins have been described above under tenth- to eighth-century BCE anthropoid, wooden and stone coffin burials (Yassine 1975: 57-58).

Dhiban. At the site of Dhiban, A.D. Tushingham excavated eight tombs hewn in the south bank of the wadi, designated Area J. A complete ceramic coffin was preserved in the latest burial, tomb J3, dated to c. 600 BCE. It measured 2.0 m long and 0.40 m at its greatest width. On the lid, which was of one piece, a small glum face was modelled over the place where the head lay in the coffin below. No arms were depicted. Protrusions on either side of the head created the impression of ears, and may have served as handles. This was a much simplified version of the anthropoid coffins introduced into the region by the Egyptians late in the thirteenth century BCE. It could not be determined which goods belonged with the coffin burial, and none were found inside (Tushingham 1972: 86; Winnett and Reed 1964: 58-60, plan 97).

Gibeon. Among the 14 bench tombs at Gibeon published by H. Eshel of the Afula Field School, Tombs 3, 13 and 14 were hewn with a single stone coffin/trough equipped with a sunken headrest and a ledge to support a lid. In Tombs 3 and 13, the coffin was to the right as one entered, and in Tomb 14 it was along the wall opposite the entrance. Eshel suggested that the lid served as a bench 'creating a sort of bunkbed affect', accommodating an additional individual. Tombs 13 and 14, unlike Tomb 3, also had benches along the two other walls (Eshel 1987: 5, 11, 13, 15). All of the Gibeon bench tombs are detailed below.

Jerusalem—Old City Walls. The ninth- to seventh-century BCE tomb presently located under the western Old City walls with stone troughs/coffins has been detailed above under tenth- to eighth-century BCE anthropoid, wooden and stone coffin burials (Broshi, Barkai and Gibson 1983).

Jerusalem—St Etienne. St Etienne Cave 1 with rock-cut coffins is detailed below under bench and arcosolia tombs. Of the seven reconstructed burial chambers in the tomb complex, one was carved with three coffins, whereas the other chambers had three benches (Barkay and Kloner 1976; Barkay, Mazar and Kloner 1975).

Jerusalem—Silwan. The ninth- to seventh-century BCE Silwan gabled-ceiling tombs with stone-cut troughs/coffins have been detailed above under tenth- to eigth-century BCE bench and arcosolia tombs (Ussishkin 1986).

Mt Nebo. The ceramic coffin fragments found in the Iron II (1000–586 BCE) cave tomb UCV-84, situated north of Mt Nebo near Madeba, have been detailed above under tenth- to eighth-century BCE cave tombs (Saller 1966: 259, 289).

Bathtub Coffin Burials

Tell Abu Hawam. R.W. Hamilton, director of the British Mandatory Government in Palestine Department of Antiquities, unearthed a bathtub coffin in Tell Abu Hawam Stratum III. The coffin, which was rectangular with a square bottom and two loop handles on each long side, was found broken but *in situ* in the corner of Room 23Y (Hamilton 1935: 24, pl. XXXVI.100). Hamilton dated Stratum III to c. 1000–925 BCE, but on the basis of recent excavations at Tell Abu Hawam and pottery parallels from Tell el-Farah (N), where similar coffins were found, Stratum III has been redated to 950–650 BCE. The coffin is probably to be dated to the second half of the eighth century BCE or later, in accordance with the other bathtub coffins in the region.

Amman—Adoni-Nur. Three pottery coffins were attributed to the tomb of Adoni-Nur in Amman. Half-way up the southern slope of the citadel, G.L. Harding found a tomb robbed and burned in antiquity with an impressive array of goods on a rock ledge in front of the cave opening, presumably discarded from the tomb. The assemblage included 11 seals, one of which belonged to Adoni-Nur, servant of Ammi Nadav. Ammi Nadav was mentioned in lists of Ashurbanipal providing a mid-seventh-century BCE date for the tomb. Metal jewelry, fibulae, an arrowhead, several pottery vessels and three bathtub coffins were also retrieved from the rock ledge. Among the ceramics were an 'Assyrian dinner service', a Phoenician urn, saucer-lamps, decanters, trefoil-mouth jugs similar to Cisjordanian examples and the typical Transjordanian tripod cup. The single coffin described in detail measured 1.45 × .61–0.58 × 0.52 m, with one round end and one square end, each with two heavy handles. Harding noted that similar Assyrian coffins dated from the time of Nebuchadrezzar and earlier (Harding 1953).

Dothan. The Dothan excavations directed by J.P. Free of Wheaton College, Wheaton, Illinois, unearthed a bathtub coffin in a level 1-A^b eighth- to seventh-century BCE building. The one-meter-long coffin was found in a plastered courtyard of an Assyrian-style building with rooms on three sides. In addition to two skulls, jumbled bones and pots, the coffin contained part of an Assyrian palace-ware bowl dated to the late eighth or early seventh century BCE (Free 1959: 24-25).

Tell el-Farah (N). R. de Vaux of the Ecole Archéologique Française de Jérusalem directed the excavations of Tell el-Farah (N) where three bathtub coffins were found in the central room of a Stratum 2 palace. The coffins were attributed to level VIId locus 148, or to level VIIe locus 117, which was situated directly above. These coffins, which measured approximately one meter long, had one square end with two vertical handles and one round end with a single vertical handle. Rope decoration encircled the vessel below the handles, similar to the coffin found at Tell el-Mazar. A. Chambon noted the similarity of the Tell el-Farah (N) coffins to examples from Ashur and Zinjirli, in contrast to the coffin from Tell Abu Hawam (Chambon 1984: 57 n. 55, pl. 47 fig. 10–12).

Jerusalem—Ketef Hinnom. A bathtub coffin with one round end and one straight end was found in the St Andrew's Church/Ketef Hinnom Tomb 25 repository. The excavator, G. Barkay of Tel Aviv University, dated the tomb's use from late in the seventh century BCE, and the bathtub coffin to the Babylonian Period (G. Barkay, private communication 1984).

Manahat. M.Ch. Clermont-Ganneau reported a bathtub coffin from Manahat (Barkay 1984: 104-105).

Tell el-Mazar. At the site of Tell el-Mazar, located 3 km north-northwest of Deir 'Alla and 3 km east of the Jordan River, K. Yassine excavated 84 graves dating from the Iron IIc to the Persian period. Grave 23 consisted of what Yassine called a larnax, a ceramic coffin measuring 0.98 × 0.48 × 0.55 m, with one square end, one round end, three handles and rope decoration below the rim, similar to the example from Tell el-Farah (N). The coffin contained long bones and a skull (Yassine 1984: 7). J. Sauer argued for a Babylonian to Persian period date for the cemetery, on the basis of the pottery and selected finds (Sauer 1979).

Megiddo. Excavations at Megiddo, directed by G. Schumacher of the German Society for Oriental Research, unearthed a bathtub coffin containing human bones in a Strata III–II context (Schumacher 1908: 145, photo 216). J. Abercrombie dated the burial to the eighth to seventh century BCE on the basis of comparable coffins found at Amman, Dothan, Dhiban (probably an anthropoid coffin) and Mt Nebo (Abercrombie 1979: 305).

Tell el-Qitaf. A ceramic bathtub coffin and accompanying stone bowl were found at the site of Tell el-Qitaf, located near Kfar Ruppin, 5 km southeast of Beth Shan (Amiran 1957–58: 116).

Khirbet el-Qôm. G. Barkay of Tel Aviv University noted a bathtub coffin from Khirbet el-Qôm, now in the Hebrew Union College in Jerusalem's collection (Barkay, private communication 1984; 1984: 105).

Cave, Shaft and Chamber Tombs

Amman—Adoni-Nur. The Adoni-Nur tomb, located half-way up the southern slope of the Amman citadel, was named for a seal found outside the tomb belonging to Adoni-Nur servant of Ammi Nadav. Although the tomb was robbed and burned in antiquity, an impressive array of goods were uncovered on a rock ledge in front of the cave opening, presumably discarded from the tomb. The assemblage included 11 seals, silver, bronze and iron objects, several Assyrian pottery types including a 'dinner service', a Phoenician two-handled vessel (similar to an urn), saucer lamps, decanters, trefoil-mouth jugs similar to Cisjordanian examples, a pottery lantern and a typical Transjordanian tripod cup. Fragments of three bathtub coffins, one restorable, were also found among the retrieved goods. Eighth century BCE seals, the bathtub coffins, pottery and the fibulae provided a late eighth- to seventh-century BCE date (Harding 1953: 48-69).

Amman—Jebel el-Jedid. Three eighth- to seventh-century BCE cave tombs have been reported from the Amman vicinity: tombs A, C and D. Tomb A has been dated by E. Henschel-Simon to the eighth and seventh centuries BCE or to the end of the seventh century BCE (Harding 1945: 73-74). Tomb C, which may date from early in the eighth century BCE, has been detailed above. Tomb D on the north slopes of the citadel hill contained four jugs, two flasks, one juglet and a vase (Harding 1951).

Amman—Jebel Jofeh esh-Sharqi. F. Ma'ayeh published the initial announcement of a rock-cut tomb in the foothills of Jebel el-Jofeh esh-Sharqi, and R. Dajani later published it in detail. The tomb contained more than 150 ceramic objects, including one-handled jugs, bottles painted with red and black bands ('Ammonite Ware'), dipper juglets, decanters, round bottom lamps, bowls, chalices, tripod cups, oil flasks and miniature cooking pots and flasks. Other items included bronze bracelets, finger rings, a nail, a mirror, beads, a pottery head of a veiled 'Astarte' and a square clay shrine complete with architectural details. Dajani dated the assemblage to late Iron II, from 650–600 BCE (R. Dajani 1966b; Ma'ayeh 1960).

Bethlehem. S. Loffreda noted an Iron II tomb from Bethlehem, a 'squarish cave with no benches' (Loffreda 1968: 249). Cave tombs were also identified in excavations under the Basilica of the Nativity; 15 tombs cut into the rock, built of rocks and frequently reused, were located under the pavement. The earliest pottery dated from the seventh century BCE: platters, a 'vase' without a rim and a storejar handle imprinted with a bird and *lammelek mam[shat]* (Bagatti 1965: 270-71).

A tenth- to seventh-century BCE pottery collection, presumed to have originated from a cave tomb in Bethlehem, has been presented above under tenth- to eighth-century BCE cave, shaft and chamber tombs (Saller 1968). J. Tubb published an assemblage acquired in the 1880s and said to have originated in a grave located 'close to Rachel's Tomb, on the way to Bethlehem'. The collection included a female pillar figurine with painted hair, two bronze bangles, five juglets including one black juglet, a jug, a bowl and a pottery alabastron (Barnett 1966: 32, fig. 17a; Tubb 1980). This collection is more likely to have originated in a cave (or bench) tomb.

A lamp in the Pontifical Biblical Institute in Jerusalem's collection was from a tomb in Wadi et-Tin near Bethlehem (W. Fulco, private communication 1984).

Dhiban. The five tenth- to seventh-century BCE chamber tombs from Dhiban Area J, Tombs J4–J8, have been detailed above under tenth- to eighth-century BCE cave, shaft and chamber tombs (Tushingham 1954; 1972).

Dura. A female pillar figurine in the Pontifical Biblical Institute in Jerusalem's collection was reputedly found in a tomb at Dora (Dura, south of Hebron?) (W. Fulco, private communication 1984). Based on the distribution of the various tomb types and the types of tombs in which the other female pillar figurines were found, this tomb was probably a cave tomb or perhaps a bench tomb.

Ein Gedi. Nearly all the vessels in the Clark collection from Ein Gedi were complete, suggesting that the assemblage originated in a tomb. Included in the collection were seventh-century BCE bowls, cooking pots, juglets, jugs, decanters, lamps, a jar, a pilgrim flask, an amphoriskos, a pyxis, a miniature jar and three bronze bracelets (Mazar, Dothan and Dunayevsky 1966: 53-57).

Ein Sarin. A cave tomb was excavated by S.A.S. Husseini of the British Mandatory Government in Palestine Department of Antiquities at Ein Sarin, on the east slope of Mt Gerizim. The late seventh- to sixth-century BCE objects found in the cave included five juglets with long necks, two with handles from the shoulder to the middle of the neck and two with handles to the rim, one with a button base and the rest with small disc bases; a 'stand' fragment; a large bowl entirely red-slipped; a lamp with a rounded base, a splayed rim and signs of use; an ovoid one-handled jar with a pinched lip; a two-handled jug with a painted base; and three bronze bracelets (Israel Antiquities Authority British Mandate Period Files, Ein Sarin, PAM 38,1024–38,1034).

Ez-Zahariyah. The Ez-Zahariyah rock-cut chamber tomb, variously dated from the tenth through the sixth century BCE, has been detailed above under eighth- to sixth-century cave, shaft and chamber tombs (Albright 1943: 158-59; Baramki 1934-35; Holladay 1976: 277).

Gibeon. The cave tomb from Gibeon with pottery spanning the Iron I and II periods has been detailed above under tenth- to eighth-century BCE cave, shaft and chamber tombs (A. Dajani 1951: 48; 1953: 66, fig. 21).

Jericho. Based on his rock-cut tomb plan typology, S. Loffreda suggested Jericho tombs WH1 and WH2 may have been cut as early as the late ninth century BCE (Loffreda 1968: 257), although the recovered burial provisions dated from the late eighth through the sixth century BCE. Tomb WH1, a roughly rectangular chamber with stepped dromos entrance and curved roof, was situated 700 m west of the tell. K. Kenyon's excavations uncovered a single intact burial and 146 skulls, the majority of which were piled against the left-hand wall towards the rear of the chamber, with some scattered across the tomb floor and a group of four just inside the entrance. The WH1 assemblage included predominantly bowls, plus dipper juglets, lamps, cooking pots, a chalice, a jug, an amphoriskos and a pilgrim flask, all dated from the last quarter of the eighth, through the seventh and perhaps into the sixth century BCE. Beads, rings, earrings, bracelets, a fibulae, a scaraboid, a clay dog, a sacred eye, a Bes (?) pendant and shells were also present (Kenyon 1965: 491-513). Tomb WH2, located south of WH1, was of indeterminate plan. As in WH1, the bodies had been decapitated and the skulls placed along the left-hand wall. Tomb WH2 held 17 bodies, one of which may have been intact. Kenyon dated the three jugs, two lamps, two bowls, dipper juglet, pilgrim flask and bronze bracelets and rings to the end of the eighth century BCE (Kenyon 1965: 513).

Jerusalem—City of David. There is controversy as to whether the tunnels in the City of David excavated by R. Weill were originally tombs. Weill found bodies in T4, and seventh- or early sixth-century BCE pottery in tunnels T4 and T8, and in the natural cave L-K (Weill 1920: 159). Tunnels for burial were unparalleled in Iron Age Israel and Judah, prompting K. Kenyon to identify them as 'cisterns of rather unusual form' (Kenyon 1974: 156).

Jerusalem—Tyropoeon Valley. On the western slopes of the Tyropoeon Valley, west of the Western Wall of the Temple Mount, B. Mazar of the Hebrew University in Jerusalem identified several looted and reused rock-cut tombs. Mazar described

> a square shaft hewn in the rock from which an entrance leads into a large plastered burial chamber. In the ceiling of this chamber is an opening, a sort of square chimney; this was the nepeš, which was blocked above with masonry to form a tomb monument. Above the entrance to one of the tombs was a niche apparently intended for a plaque denoting the name of the tomb-owners (Mazar and Ben-Dov n.d.: 59).

The cultic structure above the tomb was reconstructed in analogy to the conjectured altars on the eighth- to seventh-century BCE Akhzib tombs. One Jerusalem tomb contained 250 eighth- to seventh-century BCE ceramic vessels, including one incised with 'Isaiah' and two with other private names (B. Mazar 1976: 40; Mazar and Ben-Dov n.d.: 58). B. Mazar and M. Ben-Dov suggested that the tomb full of pots had been emptied of bones and used as a repository for vessels from other tombs (Mazar and Ben-Dov n.d.: 6 [Hebrew section]). The tombs were later adapted for use as cisterns and ritual baths so no tomb preserves the conjectured tomb plan.

Tell Judeidah. Working in the 1890s, F.J. Bliss and R.A.S. Macalister found three eighth- to seventh-century BCE rock-cut tombs at Tell Judeidah, Tel Goded. Two of the tombs were shaft tombs, and one was a bench tomb. The shaft tombs were small with cylindrical shafts over 2 m deep leading through a doorway into an irregularly-shaped chamber measuring approximately 1.8–2.0 × 1.5 m (Bliss and Macalister 1902: 199). In his Shephelah survey, Y. Dagan identified additional eighth- to sixth-century BCE burial caves east of the tell (Dagan 1982: 42).

Lachish. Lachish tombs 107, 120, 218 and 223 were all cut in the Middle or Late Bronze Age, and reused for dwelling or mortuary purposes around 900 BCE and for burial during the seventh century BCE.

Both Tombs 107 and 120 contained animal bones, primarily pig, overlying the human bones. In Tomb 107, during the seventh-century BCE charred animal bones had 'been thrown in through the hole in the roof' on top of two phases of human burials. Burial provisions included beads, rings, anklets, bone pendants, scarabs, scaraboids, a rattle and amulets of Sekhmet, the lotus pillar, Harpocrates, the cat, Bes, Uzat, Isis and Bast (Tufnell 1953: 187-88). Tomb 120 was unusual in containing a layer of human bones representing more than 1,500 individuals with their skulls separated (or they may have simply rolled to the lower end of the cave) covered by a layer of charred animal bones, primarily pig. D.L. Risdon examined the human skeletal remains and identified crania of 360 adult men, 274 adult women, and 61 immature individuals. In view of the individuals represented, and of the fact that some bones and skulls were calcined and burnt, the excavator J. Starkey was led to conclude that these individuals were victims of an Asssyrian attack. Noting the similarities between the crania from the Lachish cave and contemporary Egyptians, Risdon suggested that the 'population of Lachish was probably derived principally from Upper Egypt' (Ussishkin 1982: 56-57). In Tomb 120, dipper juglets, large bowls, a cooking pot, a rattle and a female pillar figurine date the burial to the seventh or sixth century BCE . The other tomb contents have been listed above under tenth- to eighth-century BCE cave, shaft and chamber tombs (Tufnell 1953: 193-96).

Tombs 218 and 223, detailed above, may have had pit repositories added in the seventh century BCE (Tufnell 1953: 177, 203-209, 211-14).

Cave Tomb 1002, with 13 undisturbed layers of burials and more than 600 pots and objects dating from c. 810–710 BCE, has been detailed above under tenth- to eighth-century BCE cave, shaft and chamber tombs (Tufnell 1953: 174, 229-36).

Mt Nebo. The Mt Nebo Iron II cave tombs UCV-20 and UCV-84 have been detailed above under tenth- to eighth-century BCE cave, shaft and chamber tombs (Saller 1966).

Ras et-Tawil. The ninth- to sixth-century BCE Ras et-Tawil cave tomb has been presented above under tenth- to eighth-century BCE cave, shaft and chamber tombs (Ras et-Tawil 1974).

Samaria. Cave Tomb 103, with pits and a channel carved in the chamber floor, in use during the second half of the eighth century BCE, has been detailed above under tenth- to eighth-century BCE cave, shaft and chamber tombs (Crowfoot, Crowfoot and Kenyon 1957: 197-98; Crowfoot, Kenyon and Sukenik 1942: 21-22).

Tekoa. J. Davis published a most peculiar tomb cut into the soft limestone and nari of Tekoa, six miles south of Bethlehem. Surveys located a number of larger, collapsed tombs in the vicinity, the soft limestone proving unable to bear the stress. A vertical facing cut in the nari led into the main chamber measuring 7.70 × 2.85 m, from which radiated eight recesses each with a repository pit or well. Niches were cut in the back of the main chamber and in several of the recesses. The single undisturbed repository, in recess 1, contained one human skeleton, jugs, juglets, shallow bowls, black juglets, lamps, two iron pieces, one piece of carved bone and two Herodian lamps. The only other noteworthy object from the tomb was a small model chair or couch. Davis dated the tomb use from mid-Iron II through the sixth century BCE with reuse in the Herodian period (Davis 1974).

L. Herr published an assemblage reputedly from Tekoa purchased by G.E. Wright in 1958 from an antiquities dealer. The eighth- to seventh-century BCE collection included 10 black juglets, 8 dipper juglets, 6 lamps, 3 bowls, 3 southern decanters, 2 cooking pots, 1 spouted juglet and 1 brown juglet. Additional objects from the original collection which have since been misplaced include 5 burnished bowls, 2 black juglets and 4 small juglets (Herr 1986).

Bench and Arcosolia Tombs

Abu Ghosh. At least five bench tombs have been identified at Abu Ghosh/Qaryat el-'Inub/Kiriath-Jearim. F. Abel published a tomb with four steps down into a chamber measuring 5 × 3 m, with a bench encircling the chamber and a bone repository in the far left-hand corner. In his 1921 publication, Abel dated the contents from 1200–600 BCE; however, they can now be dated to the eighth or seventh to sixth century BCE. Recovered provisions included a one-handled cooking pot, decanters, lamps with signs of use, bowls, juglets, a large storejar and a female pillar figurine (Abel 1921). In 1925 F. Cooke noted, among the many tombs near Deir el-Azhar in Abu Ghosh, three bench tombs with repositories, which he dated to the early Iron Age. Adjoining tombs A and B measured 3.5 × 2.8 and 3.0 × 3.0 m respectively, with benches roughly 0.8 m wide around three sides, and a repository pit cut into the far right-hand corner of the tomb (Cooke 1925: 115 n. 52). S. Loffreda dated the Abu Ghosh tombs to the seventh to sixth century BCE, based on his rock-cut tomb typology (Loffreda 1968: 247-48).

S. Husseini of the British Mandatory Government in Palestine Department of Antiquities excavated and recorded a fifth bench tomb in 1944. A roughly-cut rectangular shaft with two rock-cut steps led down to a roughly-cut opening blocked by a boulder. The chamber, measuring approximately 4 m square, with benches on three sides and apparently no repository, contained scattered, poorly-preserved skeletal remains and fragmentary pottery (Israel Antiquities Authority British Mandate Period Files, Abu Ghosh, photos 31.544–47, 31.549, 31.556–58, plan A, B). Husseini distinguished two phases of burial. In the lower layer, scattered, poorly-preserved skeletal remains were accompanied by 7 bowls, 5 juglets, 3 saucer lamps, 3 pitchers, 2 pots, a jug, a bottle, a bracelet, 12 earrings, 3 rings, 9 beads, a bronze fibula, an iron knife handle, 4 arrowheads and a black stone spindle (Israel Antiquities Authority British Mandate Period Files, Abu Ghosh, photos 31.614–16, 31.618, plan C). Thirteen bowls, 12 jugs, 5 juglets, 5 jars, 3 saucer lamps, 3 small bottles, 3 decanters, a trefoil-mouth jug, 2 bronze pins, an eye bead, 4 bronze rings, a bronze bracelet, a bronze earring, an iron anklet, 4 bronze spatulae and an arrowhead were attributed to the upper layer. From the combined pottery assemblage, two bowls were red-burnished inside and over the rim, and one bowl was fashioned from well-levigated clay, similar to Samaria fine ware. There was a single black-burnished juglet. Of the 12 lamps, 7 had stump bases, one a flat base, and all showed signs of use. A two-handled rilled-rim cooking pot was decorated with two parallel lines around the shoulder through the handles. There were two southern type decanters with no groove in the rim. Among the one-handled jars, two large jars were red-slipped and one small jar with a flat bottom was red-slipped and burnished. Also in the assemblage were a 'double jug', two small jars attached at the rim and at their widest point spanned by a basket handle, and a crater with four handles and a spout pierced with an extremely small hole (British Mandatory Government in Palestine Department of Antiquities pottery registry numbers 47.4776–47.4839).

Akhzib. In the southern and eastern Akhzib cemeteries, el Buq-baq and er-Ras, the dead were laid on wooden or rock-cut benches in tenth- through late eighth-century BCE tombs (Prausnitz 1969: 88; private communication 1984).

Amman—Jebel Jofeh. Amman bench tomb A, located on the north side of Jebel Jofeh, was in use from approximately 800–600 BCE, with the majority of goods dating from the end of the seventh century BCE. This tomb has been described above under tenth- to eighth-century BCE bench and arcosolia tombs (Harding 1945: 67-73).

Amman—Um Uḏaina

In the Um Uḏaina area of Amman, A. Hadidi of the Jordan Department of Antiquities undertook the salvage excavation of a bulldozed cave tomb. The rectangular chamber measuring 8.5 × 5.5 m, had a domed ceiling and a bench 0.55 m high chiselled from the rock around most of the periphery. Skeletal fragments, bronze and silver jewelry, storejars, plates and lamps lay scattered on the bench. Hellenistic amphorae, three lekythoi and a lamp lay in the northwest corner. Two graves had been built of field stones on the bench in the southwest corner. The skeleton in each grave was oriented east–west, with its head to the east. Bronze earrings and pots were found with these skeletons. A 'narrow water conduit' carved in the chamber corner near the graves suggested to the excavator that the cave originally functioned as a water reservoir. Within the chamber penetrated by the bulldozer, the remains of more than 15 skeletons were found along with rich finds, including a bronze caryatid censer, an Ammonite inscribed seal, core-formed glass bottles, alabaster bottles, bronze bowls, bronze and silver artifacts, iron swords, daggers, arrowheads, lamps and other ceramic vessels. The full assemblage was tentatively dated from the eighth through the fourth century BCE. Eighth- to seventh-century BCE pottery forms included cups, tripod cups, bottles, a four-legged limestone incense burner, lamps and cylindrical jars with two handles and pointed bases. Based on the large number of individuals present, the seal and the rich finds, Hadidi suggested that this tomb belonged to an Ammonite ruling family, as did the Adoni-Nur tomb in Amman (Hadidi 1987).

Khirbet Beit Lei. The two published bench tombs from the eastern slope of the hill of Khirbet Beit Lei, located 8 km east of Lachish, have been variously dated to the seventh and sixth centuries BCE, on the basis of pottery found outside the tombs and filtered in with dirt, and on the basis of the content and paleography of the inscriptions on the tomb walls. Tomb 1, hewn in soft limestone, consisted of a carved entryway (?), a 2 × 3 m antechamber and two burial chambers, each with three benches. An undisturbed, extended burial lay on each of the six benches. On the three benches in the southern chamber lay an old individual, a middle-aged woman wearing a bronze earring, and a 16 to 18-year old, probably a male, with a bronze ring on a finger of his right hand. In the western chamber lay a 20 to 21-year-old woman with an 11 to 13-year-old-child, a middle-aged woman with a 5 to 6-year-old child, and a 16 to 18-year-old (Haas 1963: 93-95). No pottery was found in the tomb, except for Persian period sherds which had filtered in with dirt. Graffiti on the antechamber walls included human figures, ships, circles, lines, crosses and inscriptions in Old Hebrew script. J. Naveh first reconstructed and translated the longer inscription, '[Yahweh] is the God of the whole earth; the mountains of Judah belong to Him, to the God of Jerusalem' (Naveh 1963b: 81; cf. Cross 1970: 301 for an alternative reading). The second long inscription has been translated as 'The (Mt of) Moriah Thou hast favored, the dwelling of Yah, Yahweh' (Naveh 1963b: 86), or, 'Absolve (us) O Merciful God! Absolve (us) O Yahweh!' (Cross 1970: 302). On the basis of the tomb type and the content and paleography of the inscriptions, Naveh concluded that these were seventh-century BCE tombs opened during the reign of Hezekiah and belonging to a family of Levitical singers. The inscriptions would have been rendered by visiting Levites, as most of the population is presumed to have been illiterate (Naveh 1963a: 254; 1963b: 90). F.M. Cross described the script as 'characteristic vulgar semi-formal hand closely akin to the script of the Gibeon jar handles of the sixth cent BC and not far separated from the archetype of the Palaeo-Hebrew scripts of the 4th to the 2nd cent BC'. (Cross 1970: 302-303). Cross argued these were not funerary inscriptions, for they nowhere referred to the dead; rather, they were inscriptions and drawings done by 'chance visitors, refugees or travelers who took shelter in the cave' in 587 BCE (Cross 1970: 304). Naveh concurred with Cross's paleographic argument and accepted a sixth-century BCE date (Naveh 1968: 74 n. 38). Other opinions include A. Lemaire's date of the end of the eighth century BCE or around 700 BCE (Lemaire 1976: 563) and J.C.L. Gibson's post-exilic date (Gibson 1971: 57-58).

A second burial cave without benches contained the remains of less robust individuals, perhaps a different population from that represented in the first tomb (Haas 1963: 96). Only Persian period sherds were found in the tomb, so it has been dated to the Persian period or considered a contemporary of the first tomb (Naveh 1963b: 75 n. 4).

Tell Beit Mirsim. The Iron II bench tombs cut into the southwest slope of Tell Beit Mirsim have been detailed above under tenth- to eighth-century BCE bench and arcosolia tombs (Braun 1982, private communication 1984).

Beth Shemesh. The Haverford Expedition excavated several late eighth- to sixth-century BCE bench tombs at Beth Shemesh: Tombs 2–9 and 14/114. The tombs, cut in the slope of the rock, were entered down steps through a recessed facade with a square cut door and blocking stone. The rectangular chamber had benches or 'divans' on three sides, and often a pit or repository, usually at the rear. Tombs 5–8 were all entered through a common courtyard, similar to the Jerusalem St Andrew's Church/Ketef Hinnom Tomb 20 and Suleiman St. Cave 1. Tomb 9 was entered through Tomb 5. Several of the tombs had been disturbed, but objects and bones were uncovered on the benches, in the repositories and on the floor. The most commonly found objects included lamps, bowls, jugs, juglets, decanters, fibulae and beads. Each tomb displayed distinctive features. Tomb 2 had an 'air shaft' cut into the rear wall, and among the provisions were a bowl containing sheep bones covered by an inverted bowl, a jar with its stopper in place, a bull (?) figurine and large storejars set in the wall next to the repository (Mackenzie 1912–13: 65-69). Tomb 3 produced a trefoil arrowhead and a 'Phoenician' glass bead (p. 70). Black-burnished juglets and eye beads were found in the Tomb 4 repository (p. 72-73). Unusual finds from Tomb 5 included a two-handled rilled-rim cooking pot, a pair of male and female beak-face pillar figurines dubbed 'the divine pair', an iron arrowhead, scarabs, eyes of Horus and tiny pendant figurines (pp. 74-77). In Tomb 7, storejars stood at the foot and head of one of the benches and at the repository entrance. An unusual spouted jar called a 'libation vase' was modelled with a man's bearded face and arms grasping the spout (pp. 80-83). A large storejar stood just inside the entrance to Tomb 8, with bones in the bowl/lid and in the bottom of the jar. 'Such bones. . . were commonly found in the vases. Sometimes they were of very small children. . . It was a common thing to find remains of the skull in a bowl.' The repository yielded a bronze disc with holes to be sewn onto clothing, a scaraboid engraved with Hebrew letters, a horse and beak-face rider figurine and a beak-face figurine similar to the 'divine pair' figurines in Tomb 5 (Mackenzie 1912–13: 83-89). J. Holladay identified seventh- to sixth-century BCE pottery forms in the repositories of Tombs 2 and 4–8 and in Tomb 14 (Holladay 1976: 262-63). Tomb 14/114, similar in plan to the other bench tombs, contained tenth (?) to sixth-century BCE lentoid flasks, two bronze bowls, beads, cowrie shells, bronze arrowheads, iron blades and metal fragments (Grant 1931: 10, 15; Stern 1982: 77, 83).

Dhiban. The tenth- to seventh-century BCE Dhiban bench tombs J1 and J3 have been detailed above under tenth- to eighth-century BCE bench and arcosolia tombs (Tushingham 1972: 104; Winnett and Reed 1964).

Dura. A female pillar figurine in the Pontifical Biblical Institute in Jerusalem's collection was reputedly found in a tomb at Dora (Dura, south of Hebron?) (W. Fulco, private communication 1984). Based on the distribution of the various tomb types and the types of tombs in which the other female pillar figurines were found, this tomb was probably a cave tomb or perhaps a bench tomb.

Ein Gedi. Nearly all the vessels in the Clark collection from Ein Gedi were complete, suggesting that the assemblage originated in a tomb. Included in the collection were seventh-century BCE bowls, cooking pots, juglets, jugs, decanters, lamps, a jar, a pilgrim flask, an amphoriskos, a pyxis, a miniature jar and three bronze bracelets (Mazar, Dothan and Dunayevsky 1966: 53-57).

Ein Aruv. At the site of Ein Aruv, located 12 km north-northeast of Hebron, Y. Tzafrir of the Israel Department of Antiquities excavated a square, rock-cut bench tomb. The remains of four individuals and more than 80 seventh-century BCE pots, primarily jars and lamps, lay on the benches and on the floor (Ein Aruv 1968).

Gibeah. R.A.S. Macalister mentioned that tombs were found at the southern foot of Tell el-Ful, identified with biblical Gibeah. Macalister dated a privately-owned pottery collection reputedly from these tombs to 900–500 BCE (Macalister 1915). L. Sinclair redated the assemblage to the late sixth- to fifth-century BCE, contemporary with Stratum IV-A on the mound (Sinclair 1976: 446).

Gibeon. H. Eshel of the Afula Field School surveyed and published 14 bench tombs first noted by C. Conder and H. Kitchener from the east slope of Gibeon, al-Jib. Eshel identified a standard tomb plan: a 1 × 1 cubit door opened into a single 5 × 5 cubit chamber with 1 × 4 cubit benches around the chamber periphery (Tombs 5, 6, 9 and 12). The tombs exhibited distinctive features. Tomb 1 had two triangular lamp niches cut in the rear wall and a very large repository. Tombs 3, 13 and 14 had stone coffins described above under eighth- to sixth-century BCE anthropoid, wooden and stone coffin burials. Eshel suggested that the lids served as benches, 'creating a bunkbed affect', to accommodate an additional individual. Tombs 13 and 14, unlike tomb 3, also had benches along the other two walls. In tombs 4 and 8 the three benches were each provided with a headrest and parapet similar to tombs in Jerusalem (tombs under the western Old City walls, Ben Hinnom Valley tombs 23 and 28, Silwan, St Andrews Church 25, St Etienne, Suleiman St. 2), Khirbet el-Qôm and Zuba. In tombs 2 and 7 there were only two benches, flanking the central passageway, with a repository in the back, similar to tombs at Lachish, Motza, Jerusalem and Beth Shemesh. Tombs 1, 2 and 4–8 may have had repositories. All were of unusual shape or placement, and may be attributed to later tomb use or quarrying activity (Eshel 1987). Eshel accepted Loffreda's seventh-sixth-century BCE date, adding that 'they [the tombs] may have remained in use after the Babylonian conquest and destruction of Jerusalem in 586 BCE . . . [if so] it would corroborate the evidence that the Land of Benjamin increased in importance after the fall of the kingdom of Judah' (Eshel 1987: 16 n. 28).

At the time of Conder and Kitchener's survey in the 1880s, the tombs were located between a sacred spring and a rock-cut chamber carved with six small niches. In the niches Conder and Kitchener found sardine boxes filled with figs and pomegranate blossoms offered to a local divinity. Nearby was a paved platform used for prayer (Conder and Kitchener 1883: 95-96).

Halif. The tenth- to sixth-century BCE bench tomb on the southwest slope of Tel Halif excavated by A. Biran and R. Gophna has been detailed above under tenth- to eighth-century BCE bench and arcosolia tombs (Biran and Gophna 1965; 1970).

Tel Ira. Twenty five tombs were surveyed from the cemetery on the east slope of Tel Ira, 150 m from the city gate. Unfortunately, all were rifled. This is the only identified cemetery in the Negev and the southernmost occurrence of the bench tomb. All the tombs were bench tombs with one to three chambers and one to three benches in each room. Most tombs had a long dromos leading to a door which had been blocked with a rolling stone, and a single step descending to the chamber floor. Stone pillows, parapets and repositories were present in select tombs. The eight partially robbed tombs which were excavated yielded tenth- to ninth-century BCE pottery forms and eighth- to seventh-century BCE storejars, flasks, bowls, juglets, lamps and jewelry including bronze bracelets, silver rings and beads. I. Beit-Arieh published the plan of one tomb which differs from those documented by A. Baron. Baron's plans illustrate rectangular chambers with right-angled corners. Tomb 16 published by Beit-Arieh had a long dromos leading into a roughly circular chamber with a bench extending along three-quarters of the periphery and a circular repository cut into the wall opposite the entrance (Beit-Arieh 1985b: 22).

Baron documented four of the excavated tombs: 5, 14, 15 and 16. Tomb 15 has been detailed above under tenth- to eighth-century BCE bench and arcosolia tombs. In Tombs 14 and 15 only the front chamber was excavated. The soft limestone had collapsed, destroying evidence of the entry and rendering excavation of the inner chambers difficult and dangerous. Both Tombs 5 and 14 had a pedestal or step near the entrance, which may have been the base of a column needed to support the roof.

Tomb 5 consisted of two rectangular chambers, one behind the other. In the front chamber benches ran along the two long side walls. An articulated skeleton and scattered storejar (?) sherds lay on the bench with a pillow to the right of the entrance. Three steps descended to the back, vaulted chamber. Only bowl and lamp sherds lay on the single bench located on the right-hand side of the chamber. Five complete skulls and numerous long bones lay in a pile on the floor with bowls, some with folded rims burnished on the interior and over the rim, jug fragments including black-burnished sherds, a basalt mortar, a knife and a bead. Based on Lachish tomb deposits, Baron dated Tomb 5 to the early seventh century BCE.

In Tomb 14, fragmentary skeletal remains lay on the single, parapetted bench cut to the left of the entrance. Remains of at least seven more individuals were recovered from the chamber: a flexed burial just inside the entrance to the right, a child approximately two years old, a pregnant woman carrying a well developed fetus and three skulls. Hellenistic sherds overlay eighth- to seventh-century BCE craters, bowls, juglets including black-burnished examples, lamps and a bracelet (Baron 1987).

Jerusalem—Ben Hinnom Valley/Wadi er-Rabibi. More than a dozen Iron II tombs have been noted along the southern cliff of the Ben Hinnom Valley in the Karaite cemetery opposite Mt Zion, towards the Aceldama ('Field of Blood') area near St Onophrius' Monastery (Kloner 1982–83: 38). R.A.S. Macalister published two of the tombs in detail. Tomb 23 was similar to the nearby seventh- or sixth-century BCE Ketef Hinnom (St Andrew's Church) tombs, aside from the Greek inscription over the door. From the rock-cut entry, two steps descended to a central chamber with additional chambers to the right and left of the entrance. Each of the side chambers had slightly elevated platforms with headrests carved to accommodate two bodies. One of the chambers also had a niche hewn in a side wall (Macalister 1900: 225, 248). Tomb 28 looked more like a standard bench tomb with arcosolia added. The single chamber had a bench running along the walls to the right of and opposite the entrance. Cut into the side and back walls at the level of the bench were arcosolia provided with headrests and parapets. A Greek inscription on the face of the bench attests to reuse (Macalister 1901: 145-46).

Jerusalem—Church of the Holy Sepulchre. In 1885 C. Schick published a bench tomb cut into the rock under the Coptic cloister of the Church of the Holy Sepulchre. The tomb consisted of two chambers one behind the other. Benches lined the two side walls in the front chamber and the side and back walls in the rear chamber (Schick 1885). G. Barkay found eighth-century BCE pottery in the vicinity (Barkay, private communication 1984).

Jerusalem—Franciscan Monastery. In 1881 C.R. Conder discovered bench tombs located on the grounds of the Franciscan Monastery in Jerusalem. The chambers had benches along three walls, and a square hole in each far corner opposite the entrance opened into a bone repository (Barkai, Mazar and Kloner 1975: 76).

Jerusalem—Garden Tomb. The Garden Tomb, cut into a vertical escarpment of Turonian limestone 2 m from the St Etienne Iron II tombs, was identified as the tomb of Jesus by General Gordon in the 1880s. G. Barkay has argued that the flat ceiling and side-by-side arrangement of the two chambers indicates an Iron Age construction. Hypothetical benches at the back of the first chamber and around three sides of the second chamber would have been carved out to form sarcophagi in the Byzantine period. All of the objects attributed to the tomb date from the eighth to seventh century BCE. The Garden Tomb Association owns three complete thick-based oil lamps, and the rim and handle of a burnished, deep bowl. In 1904 K. Beckholt, the Danish consul in Jerusalem and warden of the Garden Tomb, conducted a small-scale excavation in the yard. J. Hanauer later published the objects including a terracotta quadruped and a bed/couch (Barkay 1986a; Barkay and Kloner 1976).

Jerusalem—Ketef Hinnom/St Andrew's Church. G. Barkay cleared nine bench tombs hewn in hard chalk on the grounds of St Andrew's Church and the Scottish Hospice in the slopes above the Ben Hinnom Valley. All were disturbed and their roofs collapsed. With the exception of Tomb 20, all were single, roughly square, chamber tombs with one step down and benches on three sides. Adjacent Tombs 13 and 25 were carved with stone pillows and headrests: four head-to-foot in Tomb 13 and six side-by-side in Tomb 25. Six tombs were provided with repositories found to contain pottery and skeletal remains of adults, children and infants. The Tomb 25 repository yielded the most spectacular goods: more than 1000 objects, including 263 whole pots and fragments dating from the seventh through the fifth centuries BCE and the end of the first century BCE. Mortuary provisions included a bathtub coffin, Scythian-Iranian arrowheads of which 45 were iron and two were bronze, bronze axeheads, needles and fibulae, an iron blade, objects of bone, glass bottles, eye beads, rings, earrings, silver seals, a sixth-century BCE coin from Kos, and two small silver amulets engraved with Hebrew prayers, on one of which the name YHWH appears.

Tomb 20 differed from the others in plan, dimensions and decorative details. Four chambers opened off a central court, similar to the arrangement in Jerusalem's Suleiman St. Cave 1 and Beth Shemesh Tombs 5–8. Whereas all other tombs at St Andrew's were hewn using the long Egyptian amah (0.525 m), Tomb 20 was hewn using the short Egyptian amah(0.45 m). The Tomb 20 entry room was carved with a right angle cornice near the ceiling, similar to Silwan and St Etienne tombs (Barkay 1983; 1984; private communication 1984; 1986b).

Jerusalem—Knesset Garden. Bench tombs have been found in the Knesset Garden (Barkay, private communication 1984).

Jerusalem—Mamilla. Two eighth- to seventh-century BCE pottery assemblages believed to have originated from graves or tombs were collected by the British Mandatory Government in Palestine Department of Antiquities in the lower region of Mamilla Road, on the slope at the head of the Hinnom Valley in Jerusalem. Tomb 1, found in 1935, contained pots 38.1952–38.1968 and Tomb 2 (excavated in 1927) yielded pots 52.97–52.99, now all in the Rockefeller Museum collection. R. Amiran assumed the assemblages originated in rock-cut bench tombs. She found neither bones nor evidence of rock-cutting, prompting G. Barkay to suggest that the assemblages originated in simple graves which were more likely to have been obliterated (Barkay, private communication 1984). The assemblages included a headless female pillar figurine, one-handled jugs, four dipper juglets, storejar fragments, two southern type decanters and a bottle. Amiran dated the assemblage to the eighth to seventh century BCE, citing close parallels with the Beth Shemesh Tombs 2–8 assemblages (Amiran 1956).

In 1989 R. Reich of the Israel Department of Antiquities excavated three tombs near Ha'emeq Street, approximately 100 m southwest of the Jerusalem Old City Walls. Two of the tombs, 5 and 7, published in preliminary form, were roughly hewn in the seventh century BCE and used into the sixth anf fifth centuries BCE respectively. The rock ceiling of Tomb 5 had collapsed, but Tomb 7 was found intact. Both tombs had small square openings (c. 0.7 × 0.7 m) sealed by square blocking stones, and were of similar plan. The rectangular chambers had rock-cut shelves along two (Tomb 7) or three (Tomb 5) sides of a sunken, central rectangular pit. Several steps descended from the entrance into the pit, and a rock-cut repository was cut into the northeast corner of each tomb. Bones and an abundance of artifacts were retrieved from each tomb. Tomb 7 produced a uniform repertoire of seventh- to early sixth-century BCE pottery and a Hebrew seal bearing the name ḤNN. Tomb 5 pottery dated from the seventh century BCE through the Hasmonean period. In Tomb 5, a narrow tunnel runs from the central pit into the upper level of the repository. According to Reich, such a tunnel is a 'familiar component of Iron Age tombs in Jerusalem'. Reich interprets the small terracottta horse and rider figurine found in the tunnel opening as a symbolic guardian of the remains interred in the repository (Reich 1990).

Jerusalem—Mt Herzl. Bench tombs were cut into Mt Herzl (G. Barkay, private communication 1984).

Jerusalem—Mt Scopus. G. Mazor and H. Stark of the Israel Department of Antiquities conducted a salvage excavation of a bench tomb found while widening a road on the northern slope of Mt Scopus. An outer court measuring 3 × 1.5 × 1.9 m opened into a single chamber. Benches or arcosolia were cut from the two side walls and the wall opposite the entrance. Fragments of a small, stone sarcophagus and its flat lid were found in the outer court (Mazor 1983).

Jerusalem—Mt Zion. D. Davis and A. Kloner of the Israel Department of Antiquities excavated an undisturbed bench tomb cut into the rock of the western slope of Mt Zion, under the southwest corner of the present day Old City wall. The original rolling stone still blocked the entrance (Kloner 1982–83: 37). The tomb consisted of two chambers situated side-by-side. A single step descended into the first chamber, measuring 3.10 × 2.50 m, with benches along the walls to the right of and opposite the entrance. From the plan and description, it appears as though five individuals lay on the benches in the first chamber. On the bench beside the entrance lay one individual with a second partially articulated individual at its side, but positioned head (missing in both cases, perhaps fallen to the floor) to foot. Remains of three more individuals were found on the bench opposite the entrance. Positioned near where the heads should have been were lamps, and near the feet were jars or jugs. A jumble of bones, primarily skulls, pots and jewelry were found on the floor near the entrance and along the bases of the benches. The second chamber had benches along three sides and a *kok* or repository cut in the near right-hand corner containing a few bones. This chamber contained some bones, many juglets, three bronze arrowheads, a quartz crater and a scaraboid-shaped, inscribed bone seal decorated with a fish. The seal belonging to the woman *ḥmy'hl bt mnḥm*, Ḥamyohel daughter of Menaḥem, has been dated to the second half of the eighth or seventh century BCE (Hestrin and Dayagi-Mendels 1979: 51). B. Arensburg and R. Yak studied the skeletal evidence and determined that the tomb contained remains of 43 individuals: 26 adults (13 male, 5 female and 8 of indeterminate sex) and 17 juveniles and infants, all of common Mediterranean stock (Arensburg and Yak 1985). According to Davis and Kloner, 30% of those represented had died by age six, and children suffered from malnutrition. Arensburg and Yak mentioned that the long bones were separated from the skulls into two piles, but this was not drawn in Davis and Kloner's published plan. Davis and Kloner claimed that 'at least some of the buried belonged to the same family', which would be the only archaeological evidence for family tombs, but there was no mention of family relations in Arensburg and Yak's study (Arensburg and Yak 1985; Davis and Kloner 1978; Derekh Ḥebron 1975).

Jerusalem—Old City walls. The ninth- to seventh-century BCE bench tomb found by M. Broshi, G. Barkai and S. Gibson under the western Old City wall 55 m south of the citadel has been detailed above under tenth- to eighth-century BCE bench and arcosolia tombs (Broshi, Barkai and Gibson 1983).

Jerusalem—St Etienne. The finer of the two bench tombs on the grounds of the St Etienne monastery and the Ecole Biblique et Archéologique Française was initially published in the 1880s and 1890s by resident Pères M. le Bon Ludovic and M.-J. Lagrange. This tomb and an additional nearby tomb have since been studied and published in detail by G. Barkay, A. Mazar and A. Kloner.

Cave 1 has been reconstructed to include an entrance chamber or courtyard and an antechamber from which radiated out two burial chambers to the north, two to the east with a second chamber behind one of these chambers and two to the south, one apparently destroyed by later quarrying. Inside the antechamber doorway was a step with two three-quarter circle sockets for hinges of double doors. Shallow, sunken, rectangular panels, probably copies of wooden panels, and double cornices near the ceiling adorned the antechamber walls. The single object found was a Greco-Roman (?) coffin, approximately half a meter long, with bird and other animal bones inside. Some of the doorways leading into the burial chambers were decorated with carved, recessed frames. Three of the burial chambers were on the same plan; benches (with parapets) lined the side and back walls with one or two steps leading up to the bench opposite the entrance. Horseshoe or Hathor wig-shaped headrests were carved into the end of the side benches near the doorway and at each end of the back bench. Under the right-hand bench a square or rectangular hole opened into an irregularly-shaped repository. The eastern chamber with a second chamber behind it had only two benches along the side walls, and it was decorated with sunken panels and a double cornice near the raised ceiling. A flight of steps led up to the back chamber which was adorned with a double cornice. In place of the benches were three rock-hewn sarcophagi or coffins with ledges to support stone covering slabs. There was no repository in the back chamber (Barkay and Kloner 1976: 56; 1986: 26-35; Barkay, Mazar and Kloner 1975: 72-73).

The reconstructed Cave 2 consisted of a very large antechamber and seven burial chambers: three to the west, two to the north and two to the east. An additional large chamber in the eastern corner had no benches, but was decorated with right-angle cornices near the ceiling. As in Cave 1, the burial chambers had benches on three sides with parapets and Hathor wig-/horsehsoe-shaped headrests, two steps up to the bench opposite the entrance and a repository in most chambers (Barkay and Kloner 1976: 56; 1986: 35-37; Barkay, Mazar and Kloner 1975: 73; Lagrange 1894: 110-15).

Jerusalem—Shimon Hazadik Street. The Israel Department of Antiquities reported a rock-cut bench tomb from Shimon Hazadik Street which contained only later sherds but resembled a seventh- to sixth-century BCE or later bench tomb. The tomb consisted of a single chamber. Two steps led down to a one meter square pit in the middle of the room with parapetted benches around it. A bone repository was cut under one of the benches (Jerusalem—Shimon Hazadik Street 1977).

Jerusalem—Silwan. The tenth- to sixth-century BCE bench tombs in the Silwan cemetery have been detailed above under tenth- to eighth-century BCE bench and arcosolia tombs (Ussishkin 1986).

Jerusalem—Sultan Suleiman Street. A 1938 British Mandatory Government in Palestine Department of Antiquities report mentioned that while cutting 'a deep trench parallel to the north wall of the city from Damascus Gate to the Burj Laqlaq (the Stork's Tower in the northeast corner of the city wall)... some Iron Age II tombs were found in the rock near the government offices' (Jerusalem 1938). A. Mazar published the excavation reports from the Israel Antiquities Authority files.

Cave 1 consisted of four burial chambers and a chamber identified as a repository, all of which were entered from a central court. Each burial chamber had a central depression surrounded by benches on three sides. The fifth room lacked benches and was lower than the others, and so has been identified as a repository. An additional 'repository pit' was cut into the floor of the court near the entrance to one of the burial chambers. This plan of an irregularly-shaped central room, with assymetrically arranged burial chambers radiating out, was also followed in Beth Shemesh Tombs 5–8 and Khirbet Beit Lei 1. Mazar suggested that these were family tombs which had been enlarged as needed. An eighth- to seventh-century BCE date was established from a photograph of eleven *in situ* vessels: six lamps, two juglets, a southern decanter, a dipper juglet and a jug.

Cave No. 2 was cut according to a different plan with two rectangular chambers aligned one behind the other. An arched lintel opened into the front chamber equipped with parapetted benches along the two sides and a repository pit. The back chamber had parapetted benches around three sides, each with a horseshoe-shaped headrest similar to the headrests in the St Etienne and Silwan tombs. The few finds dated from the eighth to seventh century BCE: bowl fragments, jars, jugs, a holemouth jar, a saucer lamp with a round base and an alabaster bottle (A. Mazar 1976).

Jerusalem—Talpiot. E.L. Sukenik published a tomb from the vicinity of Talpiot which G. Barkay has identified as an Iron Age bench tomb reused in the Roman period. Ignoring the *kokim* presumed to have been added later, a stone blocked the entrance to a nearly square burial chamber with one step down to the chamber floor, benches on three sides and a repository cut under a bench in the near right-hand corner (Barkay, private communication 1984; Sukenik 1947: 351-54 fig. 2).

Jerusalem—Via Dolorosa. M.C. Clermont-Ganneau located a bench tomb complex near the Ecce Homo Arch on the present day Via Dolorosa in his exploration of Jerusalem in the 1860s. The burial consisted of three nearly square chambers all with benches, and one of the chambers had a flat roof. Clermont-Ganneau conjectured that these chambers were originally Iron Age bench tombs now connected by tunnels to two houses (Clermont-Ganneau 1869: 52-58).

Jerusalem—White Sisters. A bench tomb with two side-by-side burial chambers was found on the grounds of the convent of the White Sisters located on Nablus Road near St Etienne and the Garden Tomb. The tomb is unpublished, but details such as benches and right-angled cornices where the walls meet the ceiling have been cited to demonstrate that this tomb is of Iron II date (Barkay 1986a: 52-53).

Tell Judeidah. To the east of Tell Judeidah, Tel Goded, F.J. Bliss and R.A.S. Macalister located an Iron Age bench tomb. This impressive tomb consisted of an entrance vestibule or central hall with three high doors on each side leading into nearly identical chambers with benches on three sides (Bliss and Macalister 1902: 199; Dagan 1982: 44; Kloner, private communication 1984).

Kefira. Seven tombs were cut in a row into the north side of Tell Kefira. All had been disturbed, but Iron II and Hellenistic vessels and sherds were found in the repository pit of T.3. S. Loffreda considered T.7 contemporary with T.3 on the basis of its plan. The tombs were single chamber tombs with benches around three sides (Bagatti 1947: 201-16, pls. LXVIII.1–6; Loffreda 1968: 259, 266, fig. 2; Vriezen 1975: 140-41).

Khirbet Kufin. At Khirbet Kufin, R.H. Smith noted the presence of several rock-cut tombs of similar appearance carved along a terrace. In Tomb 4, a large portal with a rounded top led into a rectangular vestibule. Opposite the entry a small doorway opened into a single chamber with one step down and benches around three sides. Most tomb contents dated from the Herodian period and later, but seventh-century BCE decanter sherds were also found. Smith compared this tomb to the second half of the seventh-century BCE Meqabelein tomb (R. Smith 1962: 30-32, 43 n. 71). J. Sauer has proposed lowering the date of the Meqabelein tomb to the 'Iron IIC Persian horizon in Jordan' following 605 BCE (Sauer 1979: 72).

Lachish. Lachish Caves 4005, 4010 and 4019, Middle Bronze Age burials altered and reused in Iron II, have been described above under tenth- to eighth-century BCE bench and arcosolia tombs. Bench Tomb 116, hewn approximately 875 BCE and reused from 700–600 BCE, has also been detailed above.

The Wellcome–Colt/Wellcome–Marston Expedition located five additional seventh- to sixth-century BCE tombs in the 100 Cemetery: Tombs 103, 105, 106, 109 and 114. Tomb 103 was a triple-chambered complex similar in plan to Tombs 105 and 106, used for burial from 700–600 BCE and later reused as a domestic unit (Tufnell 1953: 179). Tomb 105 was also triple-chambered and used from 700–600 BCE (*ibid.*). Tomb 106 contained burial provisions dated from 670–580 BCE and evidence of Byzantine reuse. The unusual plan included an outer court open to the sky. Two steps led down to Chamber A with a bench along the left-hand side. Behind Chamber A was Chamber C with benches along three sides and a well, probably a repository, in the rear. From the entrance of Chamber A in the middle of the right-hand wall was the entrance into Chamber B, identical in plan to Chamber C. At least 25 individuals were buried in the tomb. Among the ceramic vessels lamps predominated, with 163 lamps, 139 juglets, 73 jugs, 71 bowls, 14 cooking pots, 3 mini-pithoi, 1 pilgrim flask and 1 storejar. Additional objects included scarabs, scaraboids, bronze and silver earrings, fibulae, eye beads, an amulet of Sow and a head of Mut. The tomb also contained an unusually large number of models and figurines, most of which were found in Chamber C: rattles, a throne, a dog (?), two female pillar figurines with molded heads and two 'beak-face' female pillar figurines (Tufnell 1953: 179-84). O. Tufnell dated Tombs 109 and 114 to 600–550 BCE; E. Stern proposed a seventh- to sixth-century BCE date (Stern 1982: 78). Tomb 109, subsequently quarried away, appeared to have had benches along the two sides of a square chamber and a pit repository in the near right-hand corner. Although the tomb had been disturbed, it still contained bowls, lamps, jugs and dipper juglets (Tufnell 1953: 189). The plan of Tomb 114 was incomplete and the contents disturbed. The two rooms with benches along the walls and a repository in the east wall of the inner room yielded ceramic vessels including three lamps, three jugs, three dipper juglets and two bowls (Tufnell 1953: 190).

Manahat. O. Negbi identified at least 11 cave openings in the southeast slope of the hill on which the Holyland Hotel is located. In the single detailed tomb, from a square opening two steps led down into a rectangular chamber measuring 3.3 × 6.6 m. A small, roughly square pit in the center of the floor contained bones, a terracotta rattle and Iron II pots including black juglets, decanters and lamps (Negbi 1964).

Meqabelein. The Meqabelein bench tomb has been variously dated by the excavator G.L. Harding to the second half of the seventh century BCE, by E. Stern to the middle of the sixth century BCE (Stern 1982: 79-80), and by J. Sauer to the 'Iron IIC Persian horizon in Jordan' following 605 BCE (Sauer 1979: 72). The detailed tomb was one of many Iron Age–Persian and Roman period tombs noted in the area. A shaft cut away by later quarrying led down into a 3 m square chamber with benches around three sides and 'a shallow gangway in the center'. The tomb contained a rich assemblage of goods. Bowls predominated among the Assyrian and local pottery forms, accompanied by jars, bottles, a decanter, a storejar, a juglet, a tripod cup and a lamp. Objects of bronze, silver and iron included a mirror, fibulae, kohl sticks, bracelets, rings, earrings, an arrowhead and knives. In addition there was a black and white opaque glass kohl pot, beads including eye beads, an eight-sided chalcedony seal mounted on a fibula identical to a seal found in the Amman Adoni-Nur tomb, a second seal and two model horse and rider figurines with riders sporting pointed caps (Harding 1950).

Motza/Mevasseret Yerushalayim. O. Negbi surveyed and published 11 burial caves cut into the hillside bordering the road leading from Motza to Mevasseret Yerushalayim. Tombs I and VII were cleared and the remaining tombs were surveyed. In Tomb I, a square entrance in a recessed facade opened onto three steps leading down into a rectangular chamber with wide benches on three sides and a repository in the far right-hand corner. Seven of the tombs were of similar plan, differing only in the absence or placement of the repository. Tomb VII had two chambers, one behind the other. Two steps led down into the front, small room with benches on two sides. A regular-sized doorway led into the second chamber with benches on three sides and a repository in the corner. Both tombs had been disturbed but the remaining finds were similar: bowls, lamps, plates, a cooking pot, a decanter, a jar and a juglet. A steatite stamp seal carved with a quadruped was found in Tomb I. Negbi dated the tomb use to the seventh to early sixth century BCE (Negbi 1963; 1970)

Naḥshonim. Z. Yeivin and M. Herskowitz of the Israel Department of Antiquities excavated a burial cave located at Kibbutz Naḥshonim, near Tel Aviv. A low stone wall was added to an enlarged natural cave to create a roughly square room. Steps blocked by a closing stone led down into this room, and 'shelves' lined two of the walls. Iron Age and Persian period sherds were found in the room, and a nearly complete skeleton, skulls and Iron Age sherds were found on the other side of the wall, presumed to have been moved there in the Persian period (Naḥshonim 1961).

Khirbet el-Qôm. Four bench tombs have been noted from the slopes of Khirbet el-Qôm, two of which have been published with only one containing datable pottery (Khirbet el-Kôm 1968).

Tomb I was approached through an oval shaft down two steps into the short end of a large, rectangular central chamber. Three burial chambers, each with benches and bones on the benches, extended off the central chamber: Chambers 1 and 2 to the right of the entrance and Chamber 3 opposite the entrance. In Chambers 1 and 3, each bench was molded with recesses to hold the body, head and feet (unique if so—more likely headrests at each end of the bench as at Zuba), and a repository was cut under the bench opposite the doorway. A plain bench ran around the three sides of

Chamber 2. Two inscriptions and several graffiti including a sunburst, crisscross and several letters were cut into and painted on the tomb walls. The inscriptions in Tomb I identified the occupants as siblings, 'Belonging to Ophai, the son of Netanyahu (is) this tomb-chamber' and 'Belonging to Ophah, the daughter [or Uzzah the son] of Netanyahu'. Both inscriptions are dated on paleographic grounds to the late eighth century BCE (Dever 1970: 140-42, 156; 1978: 976).

Tomb II was 'butterfly-shaped' with a rectangular central chamber and two chambers each 'a shelf-like niche about waist-high' extending off each long side of the central chamber. Two semi-circular lamp niches, with no signs of use, were cut into a Chamber 2 wall. A circular repository was hewn into the floor in the far left-hand corner of the central chamber. According to the villagers, pots lay on the tomb floor and in the repository but, at the time of excavation only eighth- to seventh-century BCE sherds and bones were retrieved. This tomb also bore an inscription and graffiti including a carefully carved hand, like the 'hand of Fatima', presumed to ward off evil (Dever 1970: 146-88; 1978). The Tomb II inscription has been variously read and dated. W. Dever, who originally published the tomb, reconstructed an eighth-century BCE inscription reading 'Belonging to Uriyahu. Be careful of his inscription! Blessed be Uriyahu by Yahweh. And cursed shall be the hand of whoever (defaces it!) (Written by) Oniyahu' (Dever 1978: 976). J. Naveh and others following him have read Asherah into the inscription. Naveh proposed, 'Uriyahyu the governor wrote it. May Uriyahu be blessed by Yahweh. my guardian and by his Asherah. Save him (save) Uriyahu' (Naveh 1979: 28-30 n. 10). Z. Zevit read, 'Uryahu, the prosperous, his inscription. I blessed Uryahu to YHWH, And from his enemies, O Asherata, save him...' (Zevit 1984: 43). K. Spronk suggested 'Uriyahu, the singer wrote this: Blessed be Uriyahu by YHWH. and from the distress as much as comes to him over there may He deliver him, Uriyahu, because of his service' (Spronk 1986: 307-10). J. Hadley ventured 'Uriyahu the rich wrote it. Blessed be Uriyahu by Yahweh. For his enemies by his (YHWH's) asherah he (YHWH) has saved him...by Oniyahu...and by his asherah...his a[she]rah' (Hadley 1987: 51). None of the translators suggest that the inscriptions were secondarily added to the tombs, as was the case in the Khirbet Beit Lei tombs. Objects found in the tombs included two inscribed pots, inscribed weights, beads, faience amulets of Bes and the eye of Horus, a female pillar figurine, zoomorphic vessels, horse and rider figurines, clay rattles, bronze bowls, arrowheads, knives, bangles, cosmetic palettes, and various ivory, bone and stone implements, all dated to the eighth to seventh century BCE (Dever 1970: 187-88).

Ramot. The ninth- to seventh-century BCE Ramot burial cave adapted into a bench tomb has been presented above under tenth- to eighth-century BCE bench and arcosolia tombs (Ramot 1971; Tzaferis 1982a: 11).

Tell el-Rechidiyeh. T. Macridy excavated three undisturbed burial caves at the foot of Tell el-Rechidiyeh, located on the coast south of Tyre. Cave A was hewn from the rock with an arched roof, and stone-built (?) benches were added along three sides.

Bodies lying on the benches were provided with jars, craters, pilgrim flasks, bowls, bilbils, a trefoil-spouted jar, three scarabs, a stone pendant, a bone stylette and a clay 'foot'. In Cave B, the benches had fallen apart, and no skeletal remains were mentioned. Goods included jars, an oenochoe, a javelin point, eight knuckle bones, a bronze ring and a scarab. Cave C, with benches on both sides of the entrance, contained three jars, two with ashes and one with burnt human bone. Macridy mentioned 'a preponderance of weapons among the goods'. The pottery, including a mushroom-top jar and a sausage-shaped storejar, was dated by S. Chapman to late Iron Age (Chapman: 1972: 174; Macridy 1904).

Sahab. Sahab Tomb B, excavated by G.L. Harding, was one of many cave tombs located on a low tell on the northwest edge of the village of Sahab. Ten steps led down into a large, rock-cut cavern, measuring approximately 7.5 m square, with a rock-cut bench on one side and a 'chimney-like construction' just the other side of the stairs. The tomb was undisturbed and contained fragmentary and incomplete skeletons including seven skulls and a rich assemblage of eighth- to seventh-century BCE goods. Among the 161 pottery vessels bowls predominated, followed by lamps (several with traces of burning) and jugs, together with pointed bottles, tripod cups, dipper juglets, flasks, a decanter, mugs and a cooking pot. Bronze, iron and silver objects included rings, earrings, anklets, fibulae, arrowheads and a knife handle. A crystal bead, a kohl palette, a limestone cosmetic palette, a fragment of a horse figurine, a ceramic animal head and zoomorphic vessels completed the assemblage (Harding 1947).

Si'ir. In the eastern Hebron hills near Si'ir, the Israel Department of Antiquities excavated two adjacent bench tombs measuring 4 × 3 m and 3 × 3 m. Iron II sherds were found in the tombs (Si'ir 1978).

Khirbet Za'aq. The earliest Khirbet Za'aq bench tomb from the tenth century BCE has been presented above. Tomb 6 with 'burial places' on two sides of the chamber contained eighth- to sixth-century BCE bowls including a Samaria ware bowl, jugs, black dipper juglets, jars and lamps. Tomb 19 use dated from the eighth to the seventh century BCE, and Tomb 18 was reused in the seventh to sixth century BCE. Ten additional tombs have been identified in the vicinity (Khirbet Za'aq 1976).

Zuba. A. Kloner of the Israel Department of Antiquities excavated a bench tomb cut south of Tell Zuba, Zova, located approximately 11 km west of Jerusalem. Other tomb entrances were visible in the cliff face. The entrance opened into a short side of a rectangular chamber, measuring 4.5 × 3.0 m, with benches (parapets indicated on the plan?) on three sides. 'Stone pillows' (drawn as headrests) were provided at each end of the 3.5 m long benches, as in Khirbet el-Qôm Tomb 1. A repository was cut under the bench opposite the entrance. A second chamber jutting off at an odd angle was apparently added later. The second chamber, measuring 3 × 2.2 m, had benches on three sides (parapets indicated on the plan?), a bench-level niche in one of the far corners and a repository in the other far corner. Tomb contents, dating from the late eighth to seventh century BCE, included three lamps, a bowl, a juglet, bronze jewelry, beads and ring fragments (Kloner 1982–83; private communication 1984).

Above-Ground Monolithic Tombs

Jerusalem—Silwan. The four tenth- to sixth-century BCE monolithic tombs in the Silwan cemetery have been detailed above (Ussishkin 1986).

Cremation Burials

Tell el-Ajjul. The cremation burials unearthed by W.M.F. Petrie of the British School of Archaeology in Egypt at Tell el-Ajjul have been dated to the Iron Age by Petrie (Petrie 1932: pls. LVI–LVIII), to the tenth to early ninth centuries BCE by W.F. Albright (see Abercrombie 1979: 206, 208-11) and to the eighth or seventh century BCE by D. Harden and F. James (Bienkowski 1982: 84). The burials have been described above under tenth- to eighth-century BCE cremation burials.

Akhzib. In 1941, N. Makhouly of the British Mandatory Government in Palestine Department of Antiquities found urns in the eastern er-Ras cemetery Tombs XIX and XXIV (Israel Antiquities Authority Mandate Period Files, ez-Zib, photo 30.142). In later excavations, M. Prausnitz of the Israel Department of Antiquities discovered cremated remains solely in the southern cemetery, el Buq-baq, in urns and bowls deposited in tombs or interred in the sand. The burials have been detailed above under tenth- to eighth-century BCE cremation burials.

Atlit. C.N. Johns of the British Mandatory Government in Palestine Department of Antiquities excavated a cemetery on a rocky ridge beyond the southeast end of the mound of Atlit. Of the 18 burials excavated, all were open cremations except for one inhumation (*ii*) and one urn burial (*xvii*c). The bodies of primarily children but also adults, adolescents and infants were burned on small pyres of branches. The cremated remains evidenced no uniformity in direction or in body position. Burials *i* and *vi* contained adults. In *vi*, the calcined adult skull fragments were covered by sherds. The adult designated *i* had been provided with two jars, two juglets, a cooking pot and a lamp. Children tended to be buried without objects (*iii*, *xi*c, *xiii*a, *xv*), with only jewelry (*ii*, *xi*a), or with few vessels (*iv*a, *x*, *xi*b) (Johns 1936–37: 139-52). Johns proposed an eighth- to seventh-century BCE date for these burials, based on the presence of red-slipped and burnished pottery, Cypro-Phoenician juglets, mushroom top jars and urns in dated contexts at Phoenician sites in Cyprus and further west (Johns 1936–37: 121, 134).

In the hills east of Atlit, the Israel Survey identified a fifth- to fourth-century BCE cemetery of shaft tombs, and, north of it, a Phoenician burial ground with graves dating primarily from the Iron Age. The majority of graves contained eighth- to seventh-century BCE cremated remains (Stern 1982: 71-72).

Tell el-Farah (S). The urn burials excavated by W.M.F. Petrie at Tell el-Farah (S), dated to the tenth to ninth century BCE by W. Culican and to the eighth or seventh century BCE by D. Harden and F. James (Bienkowski 1982: 84), have been described above under tenth- to eighth-century BCE cremation burials (Culican 1973: 95; Petrie 1930: pl. LXVIII; 1932: 12-13).

Joya. S. Chapman, who published the pottery from Khaldé, Khirbet Silm and Joya, suggested that cremation and inhumation were practiced together at Joya as they were at Khaldé (Chapman 1972: 57). See the description of the tenth- to eighth-century BCE Khaldé simple graves for details.

Khaldé. The late ninth- to late eighth-century BCE urn burials in Khaldé Tombs 3 and 121, excavated by R. Saidah, have been described above under tenth- to eighth-century BCE cremation burials (Saidah 1966: 60, 64).

Megiddo. The five Megiddo urns containing cremated infant remains are detailed above under tenth- to eighth-century BCE cremation burials (Abercrombie 1979: 304-305; Schumacher 1908: 121-22, photos 181–82, pl. 38A)

Mt Nebo. The two Iron II Nebo cave tombs UCV-20 and UCV-84 with 'cremation strata' have been detailed above under tenth- to eighth-century BCE cremation burials (Saller 1966).

Qasmieh. At the site of Qasmieh, on the Lebanese coast between Tyre and Sidon, cremated remains were interred in urns. The urns are similar to Akhzib and Tell el-Farah (S) vessels, which have been dated from the middle of the tenth to the end of the eighth century BCE (Chapman 1972: 57, 148).

Tell el-Rechidiyeh. On the coast south of Tyre at the foot of Tell el-Rechidiyeh, in the early 1900s, T. Macridy excavated three undisturbed late Iron Age bench tombs. Cave C yielded three jars, two containing ashes and one containing burnt human bone (Chapman 1972: 174; Macridy 1904: 568). The tomb is detailed above under eighth- to sixth-century BCE bench and arcosolia tombs.

Tell er-Ruqeish. The Iron II to Persian period open cremation and urn burials excavated at Tell er-Ruqeish by J. Ory, A. Biran and E. Oren have been detailed above (Biran 1974; Oren *et al.* 1986: 89; Ory 1944: 205; Tell Ruqeish 1974).

Khirbet Silm. S. Chapman, who published the pottery from Khaldé, Khirbet Silm and Joya, suggested that cremation and inhumation were practiced together at Khirbet Silm as they were at Khaldé (Chapman 1972: 57). See the description of the tenth- to eighth-century BCE Khaldé simple graves for details.

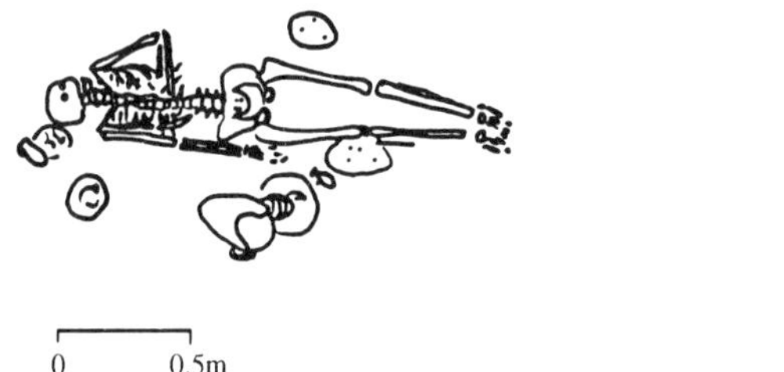

Fig. 1. Simple burial, Tell es-Saidiyeh Tomb 142 (Pritchard 1980: 27)

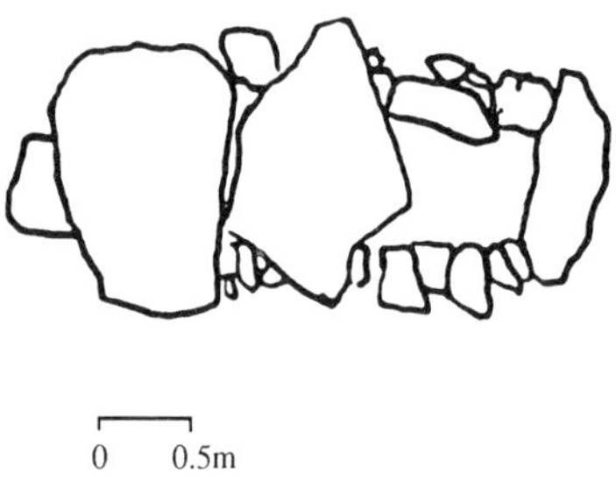

Fig. 2. Cist burial, Tell Zeror V (Ohata 1967: pl. VIII)

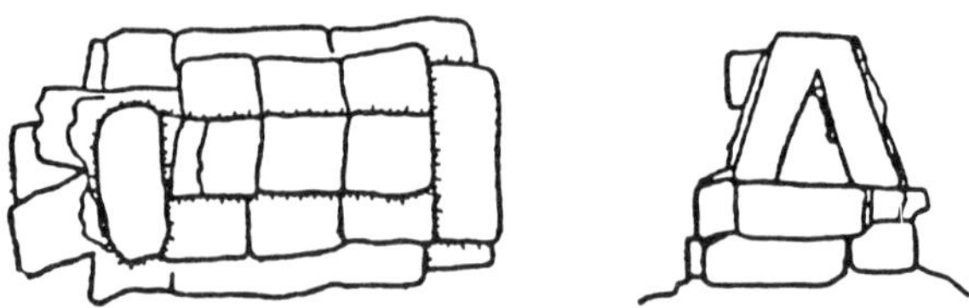

Fig. 3. Mudbrick vaulted cist tomb, Tell el-Maskhuta L12.12508 (Redmount 1989: fig. 152)

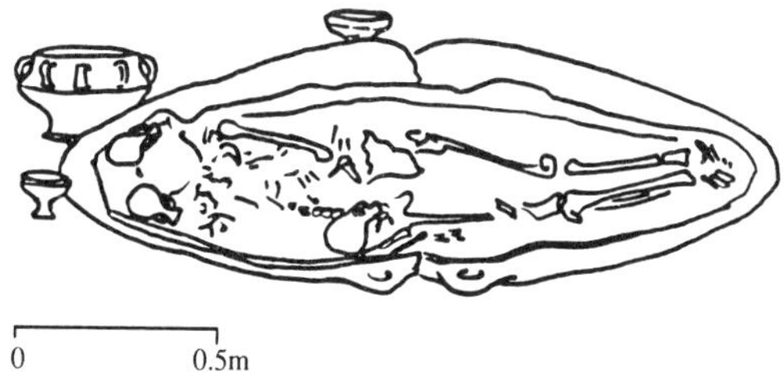

Fig. 4. Jar burial, Kfar Yehoshua (Druks 1966: fig. 1)

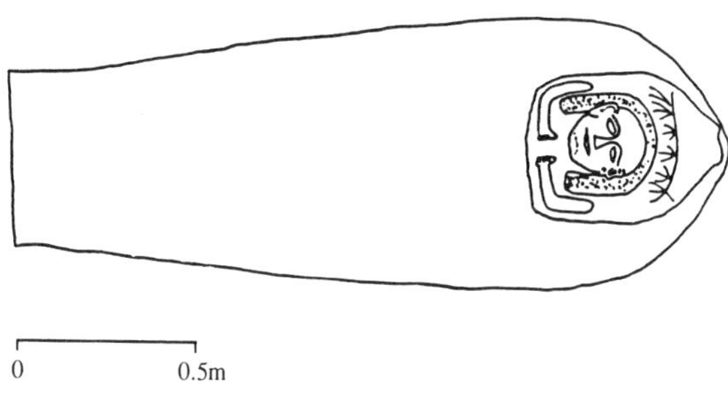

Fig. 5. Anthropoid coffin burial, Deir el-Balah Tomb 118 (T. Dothan 1979: fig. 122)

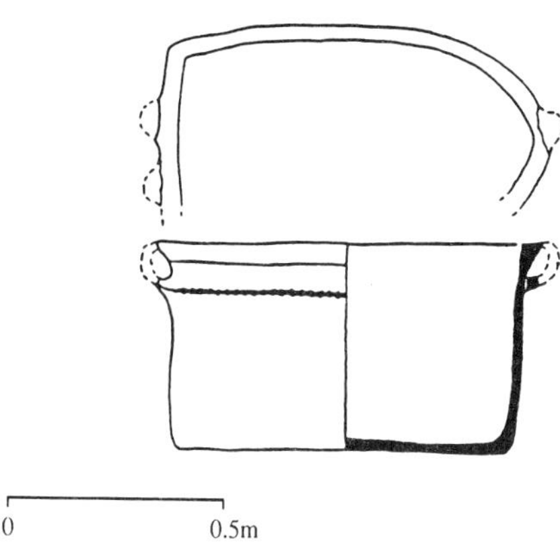

Fig. 6. Bathtub coffin burial, Tell el-Farah (N) (Chambon 1984: pl. 47.10)

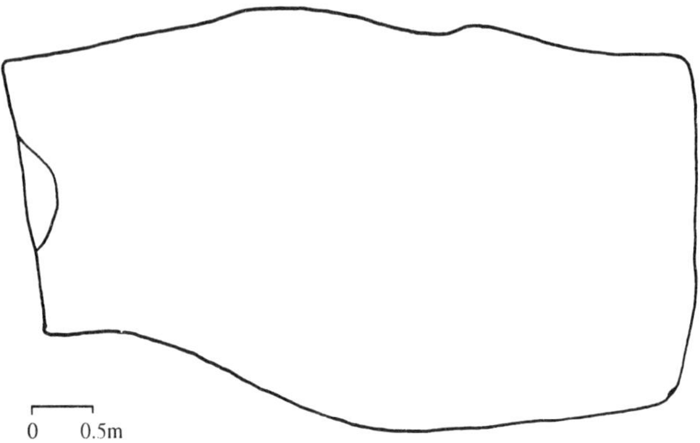

Fig. 7. Cave tomb, Jericho WH1 (Kenyon 1965: fig. 254)

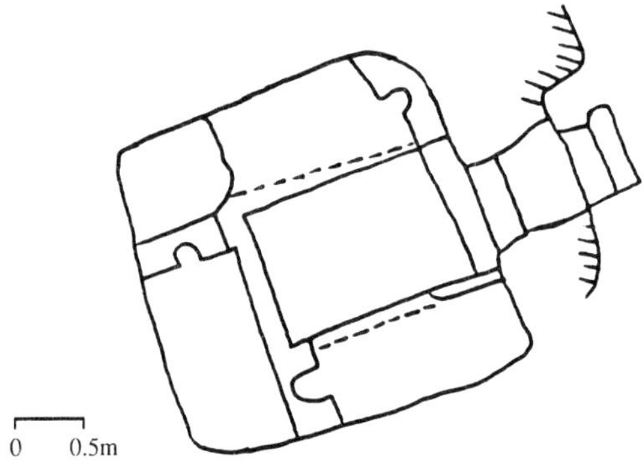

Fig. 8. Bench tomb, Gibeon Tomb 8 (Eshel 1987: fig. 9)

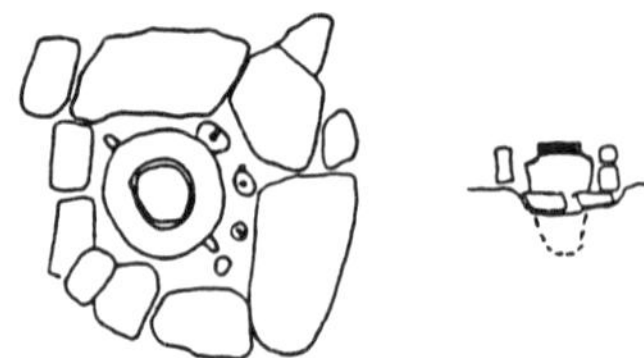

Fig. 9. Cremation Burial, Azor D63 (M. Dothan, field notes)

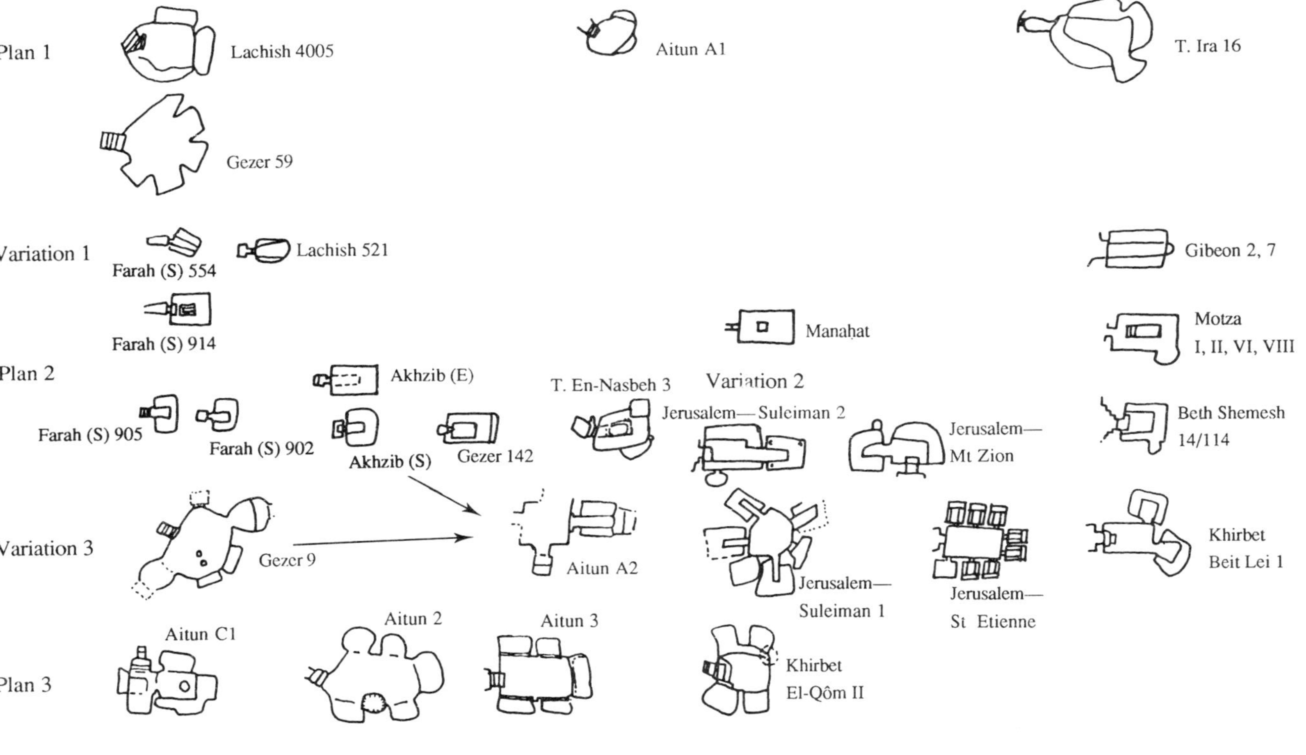

Fig. 10. Development of the Bench Tomb

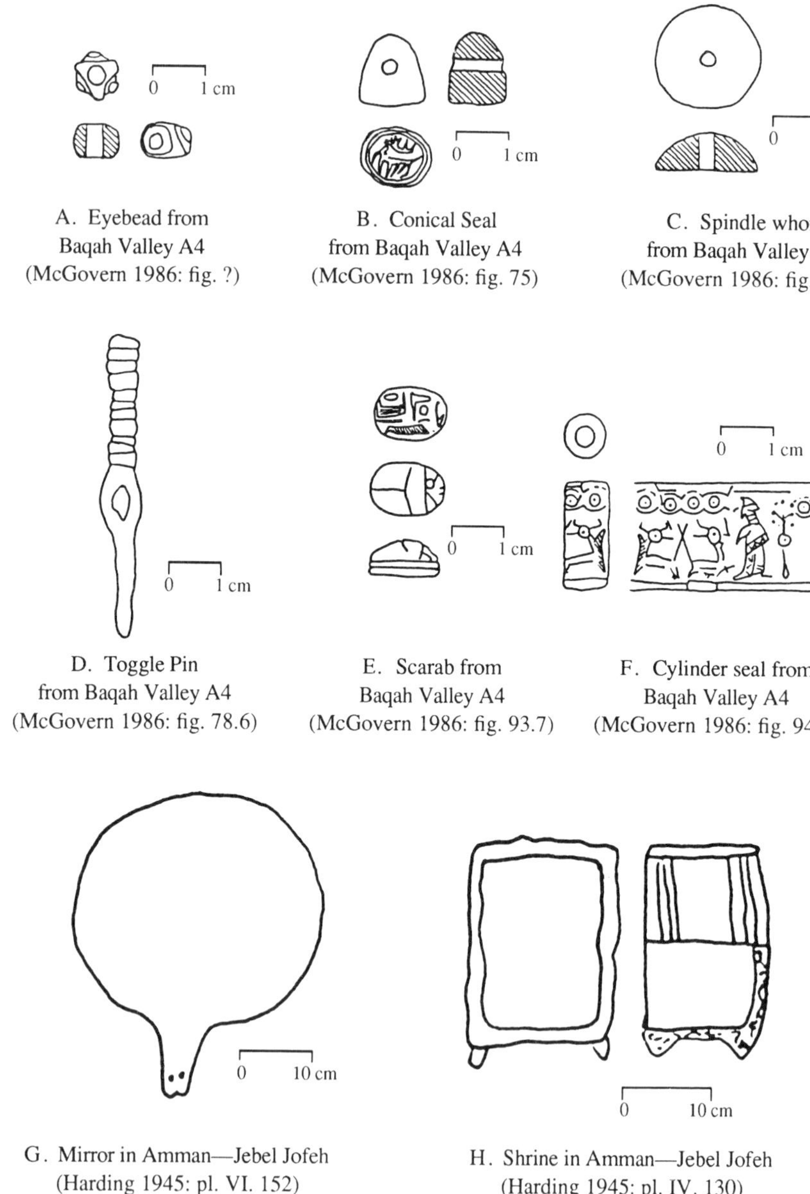

A. Eyebead from Baqah Valley A4 (McGovern 1986: fig. ?)

B. Conical Seal from Baqah Valley A4 (McGovern 1986: fig. 75)

C. Spindle whorl from Baqah Valley A4 (McGovern 1986: fig. 76.

D. Toggle Pin from Baqah Valley A4 (McGovern 1986: fig. 78.6)

E. Scarab from Baqah Valley A4 (McGovern 1986: fig. 93.7)

F. Cylinder seal from Baqah Valley A4 (McGovern 1986: fig. 94.6)

G. Mirror in Amman—Jebel Jofeh (Harding 1945: pl. VI. 152)

H. Shrine in Amman—Jebel Jofeh (Harding 1945: pl. IV. 130)

Fig. 11. Objects provided in burials—eyebead, conical seal, spindle whorl, toggle pin, scarab, cylinder seal, mirror, shrine

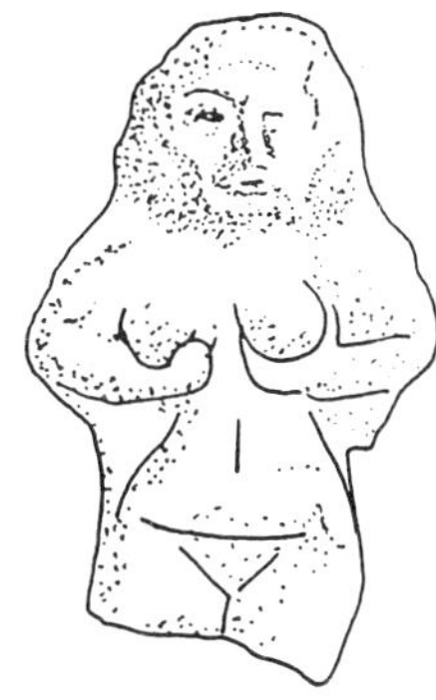

A. Female plaque figurine from Tell Zeror V (Ohatta 1967: pl. XLVII.3)

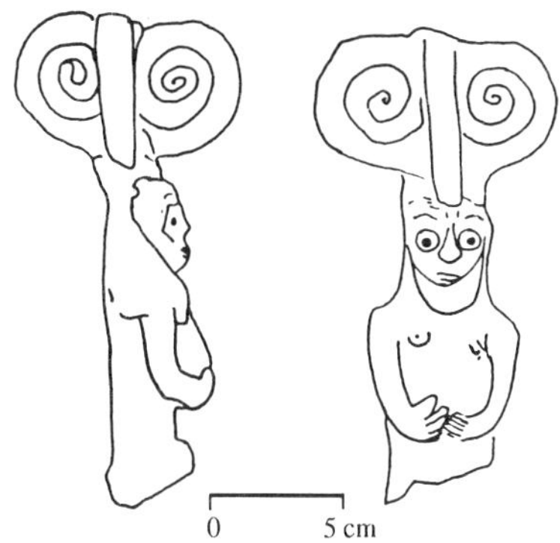

B. Hermaphrodite figurine from Amman (Hading 1951: pl. XIV)

C. Fertility goddess with sheep (?) rom Madeba (Thompson 1984: fig. V. 24)

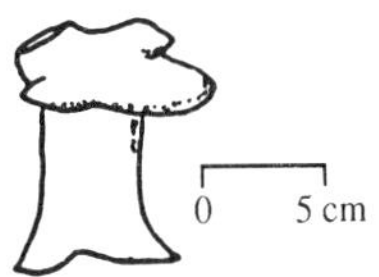

D. Bird figurine from Gezer 28 (Macalister 1912: pl. LXXIII.14)

E. Horse and rider figurine from Lachish 1002 (Tufnell 1953: pl. 29.18)

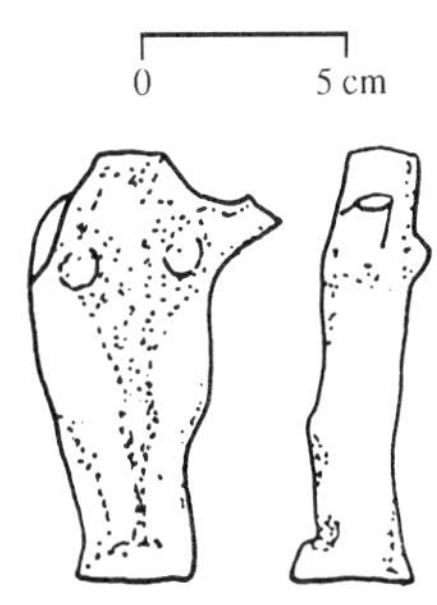

F. Mycenaean female figurine from Beth Shan (Oren 1973: fig. 50.12)

Fig. 12. Figurines provided in burials—female plaque figurine, hermaphrodite figurine, fertility goddess with sheep (?) figurine, bird figurine, horse and rider figurine, Mycenaean female figurine

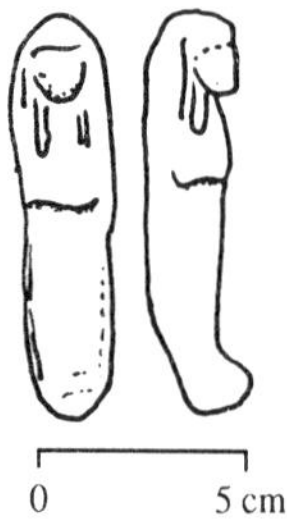

A. Ushwabti figurine from Beth Shan (Oren 1973: 50.13)

B. Bes figurine from Deir el-Balah (T. Dothan 1979: fig. 204)

C. Wedjet eye from Beth Shan (James 1966: fig. 113.15)

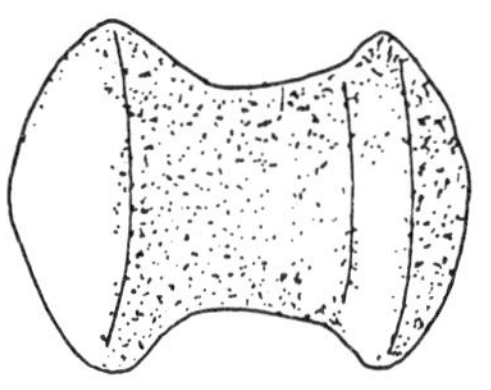

D. Rattle from Lachish 120 (Tufnell 1953: pl. 27.9)

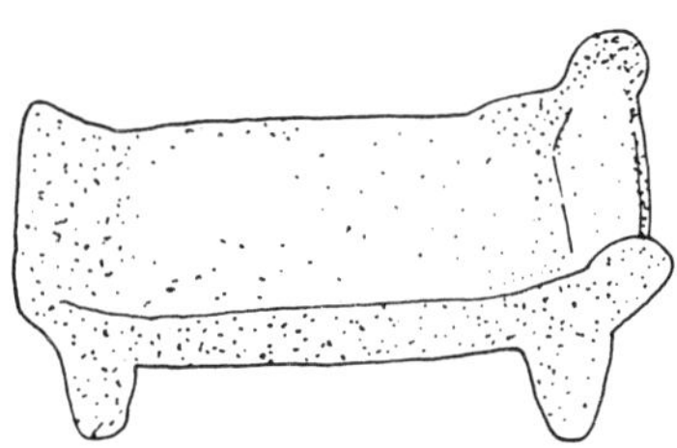

E. Model bed from Lachish 1002 (Tufnell 1953: pl. 29.21)

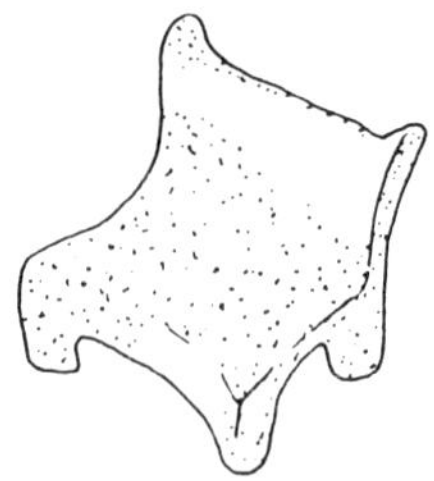

F. Model chair from Lachish 1002 (Tufnell 1953: pl. 29.22)

Fig. 13. Objects provided in burials—Ushwabti figurine, Bes figurine, Wedjet eye, rattle, model bed/couch, model chair/throne

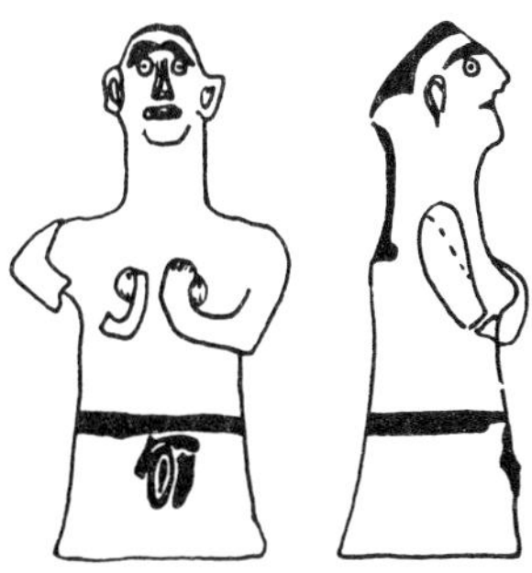

A. Female figurine from Enkomi (Courtois 1984L fig. 26.1)

B. Goddess with Tambourine from Mt Nebo (Saller 1966: fig. 28.2)

C. Female pillar figurine with moulded head from Lachish 1002 (Tufnell 1953: pl. 28.10)

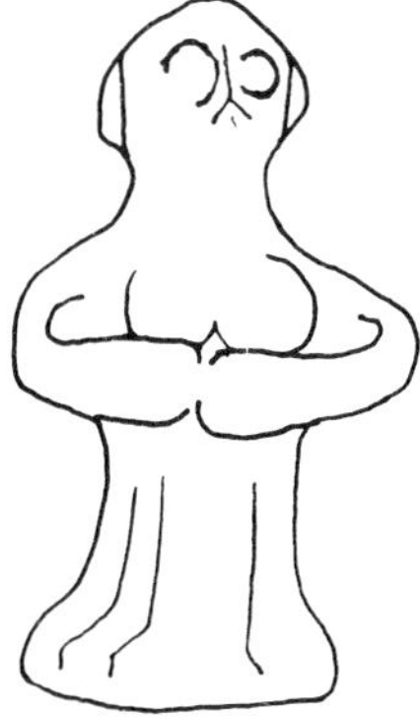

D. Female pillar figurine with beak face from Lachish 1002 (Tufnell 1953: pl. 28.14)

Fig. 14. Female figurines—Cypriot female pillar figurine, goddess with tambourine (?) figurine, female pillar figurine with moulded head, female pillar figurine with beak face

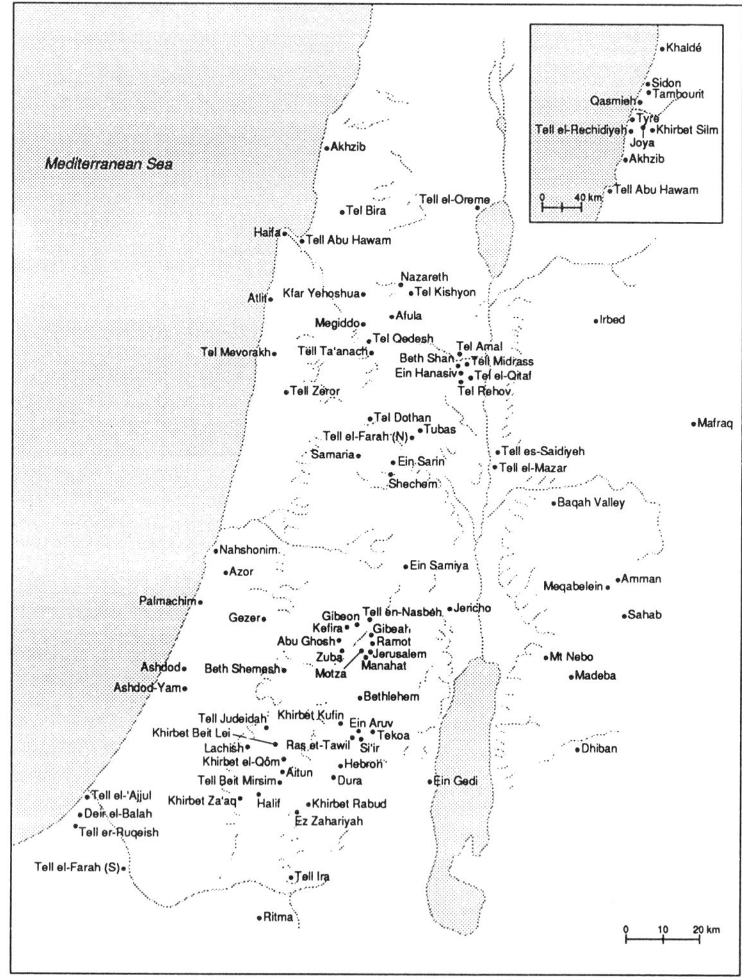

Figure 15. Sites with Iron Age burials

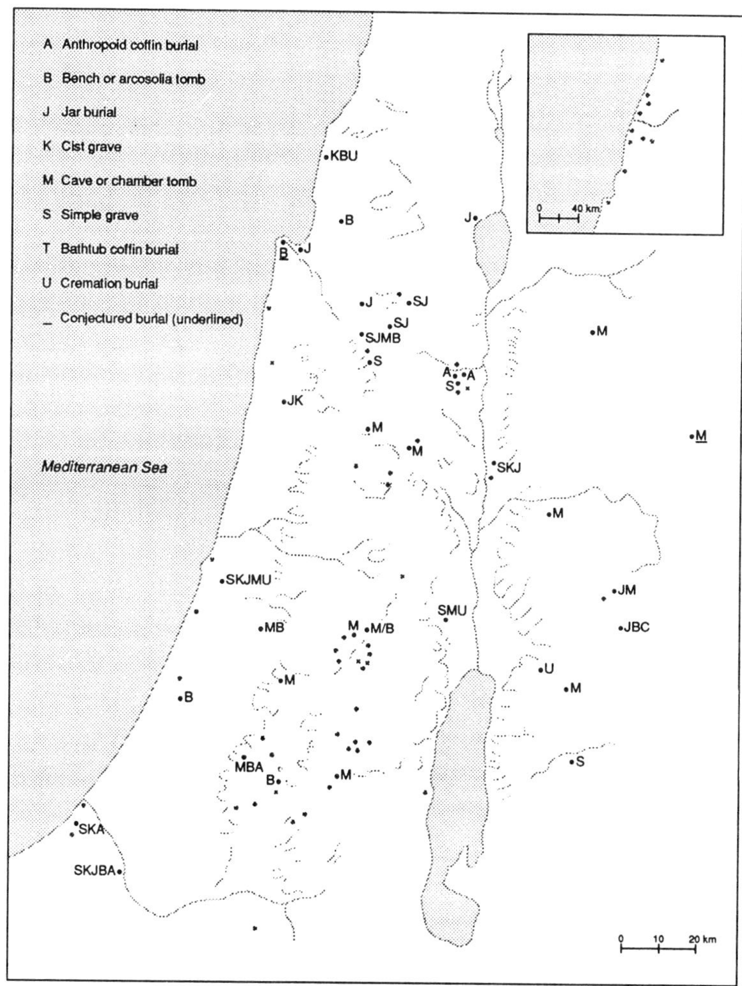

Figure 16. Distribution of twelfth- and eleventh-century BCE burial types

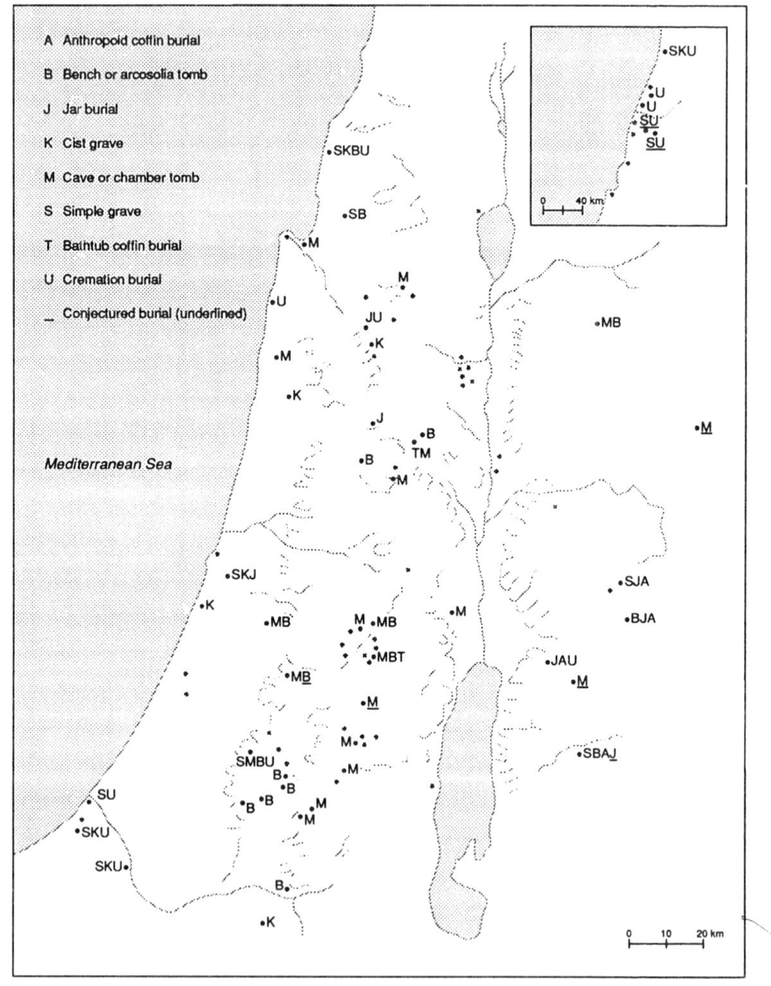

Figure 17. Distribution of tenth- through third quarter eighth-century BCE burial types

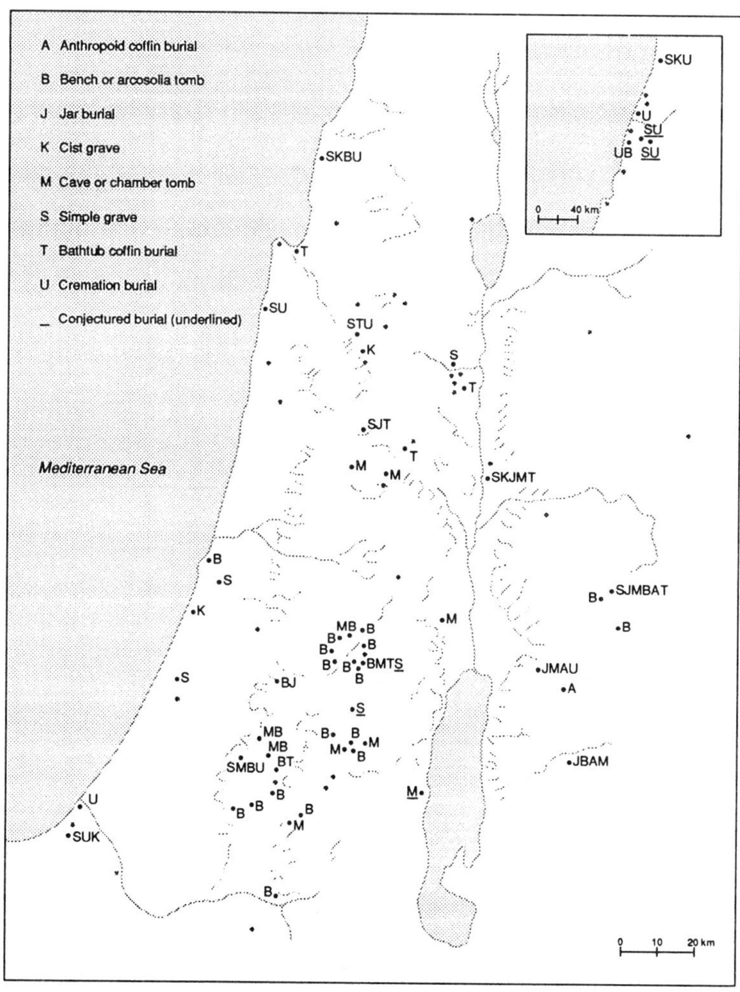

Figure 18. Distribution of last quarter eighth- through first quarter sixth-century BCE burial types

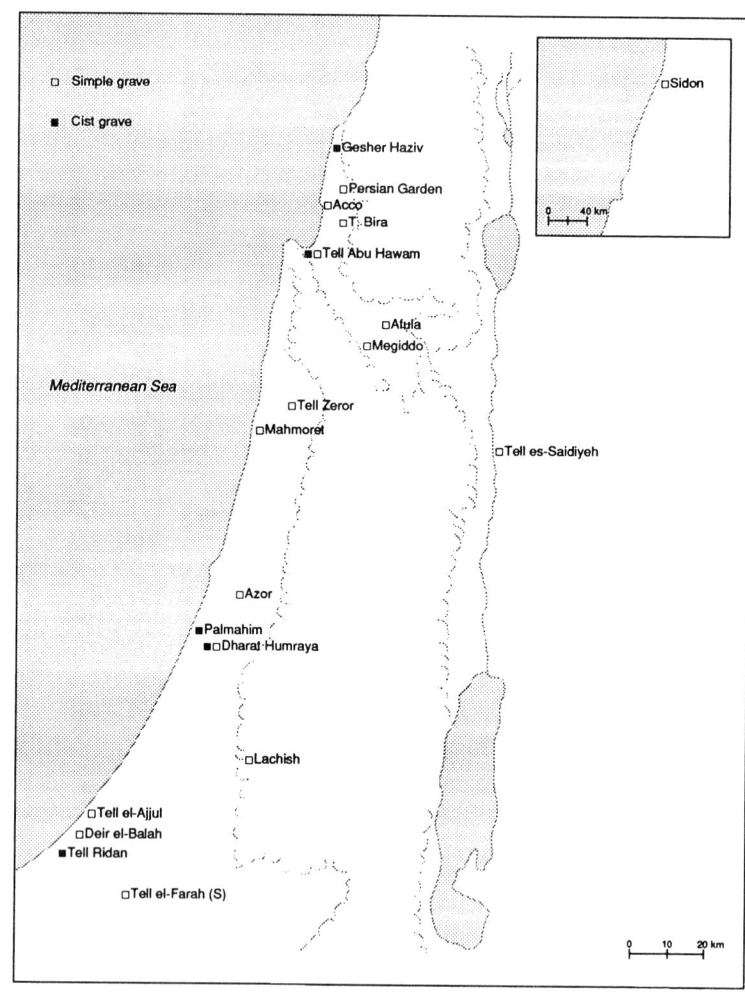

Figure 19. Distribution of Late Bronze Age simple and cist burials (translated into English from Gonen 1979: Map 1)

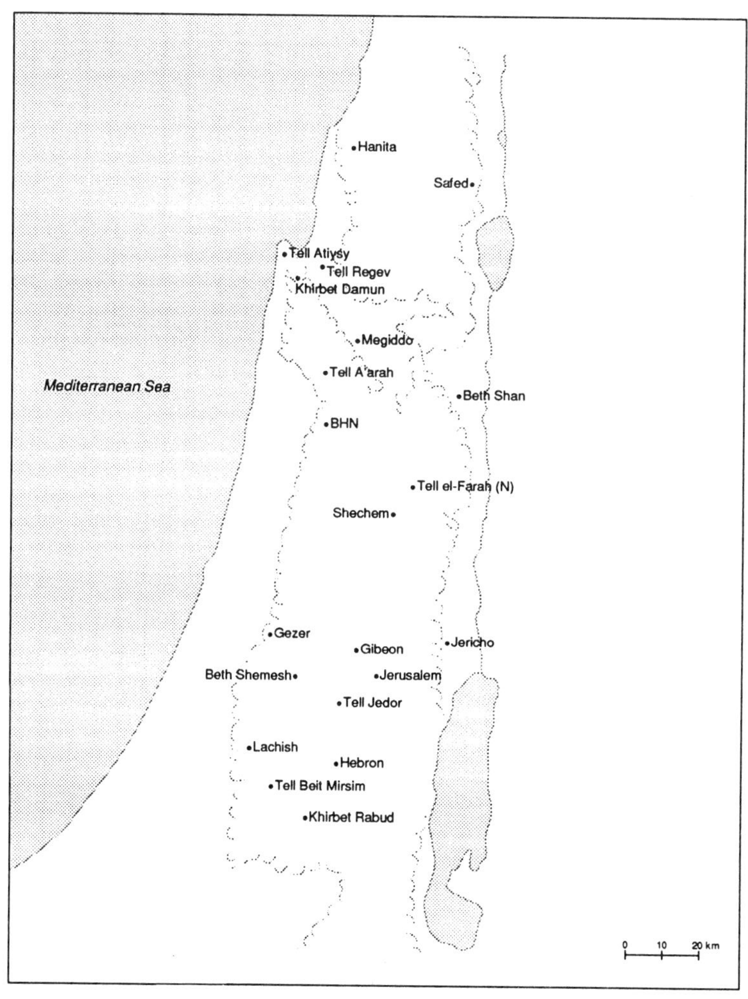

Figure 20. Distribution of Late Bronze Age multiple burials in caves (translated into English from Gonen 1979: Map 2)

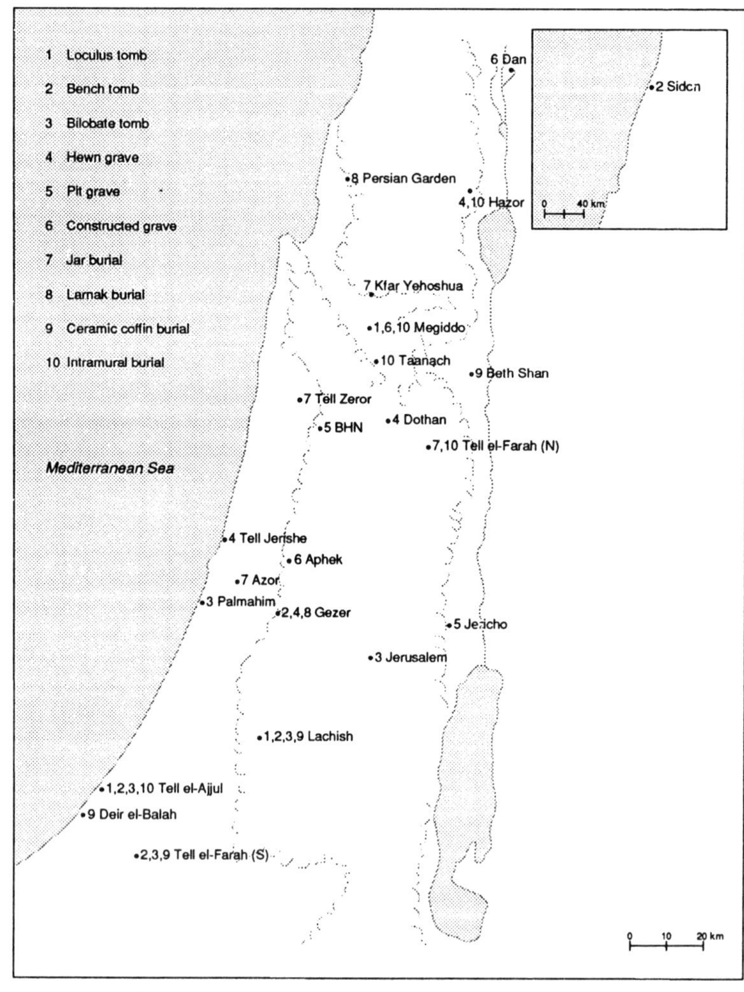

Figure 21. Distribution of various Late Bronze Age burial types (translated into English from Gonen 1979: Map 3)

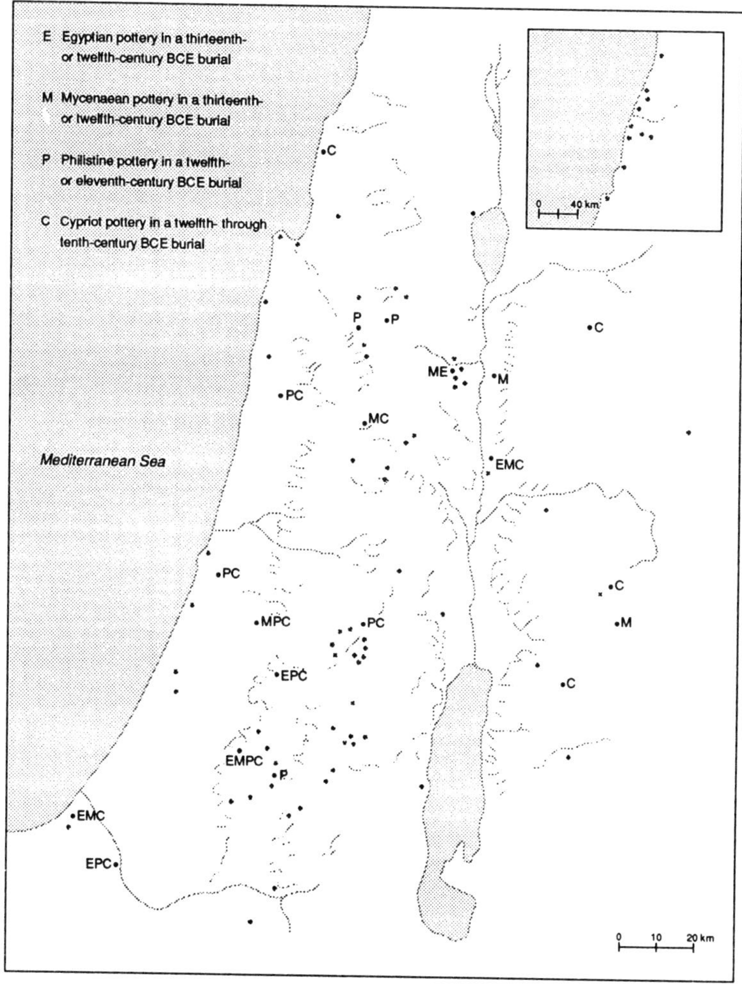

Figure 22. Distribution of imported pottery in burials dating between the thirteenth and the tenth centuries BCE

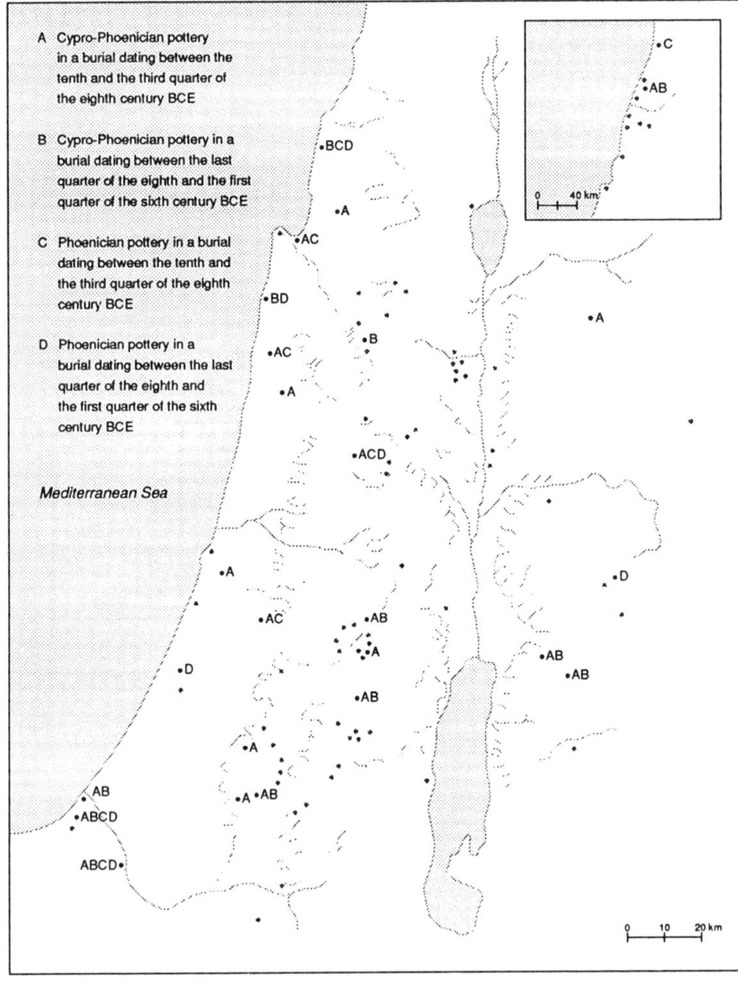

Figure 23. Distribution of Phoenician and Cypro-Phoenician imported wares in burials dating between the tenth and the seventh centuries BCE

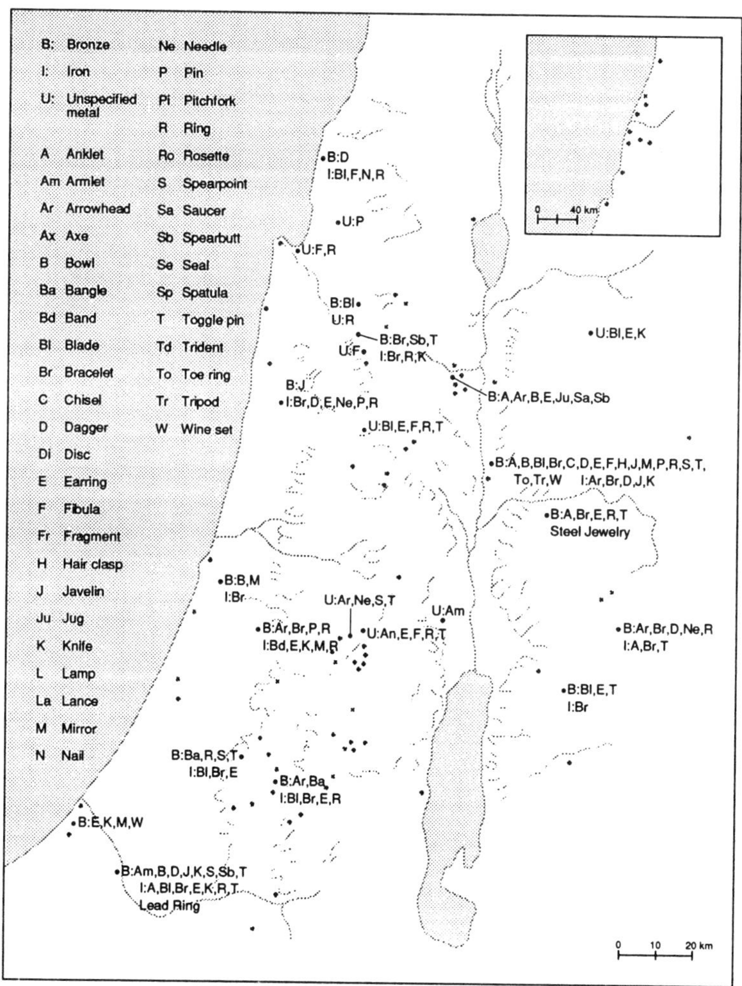

Figure 24. Metal artifacts in burials dating between the twelfth and the eleventh centuries BCE

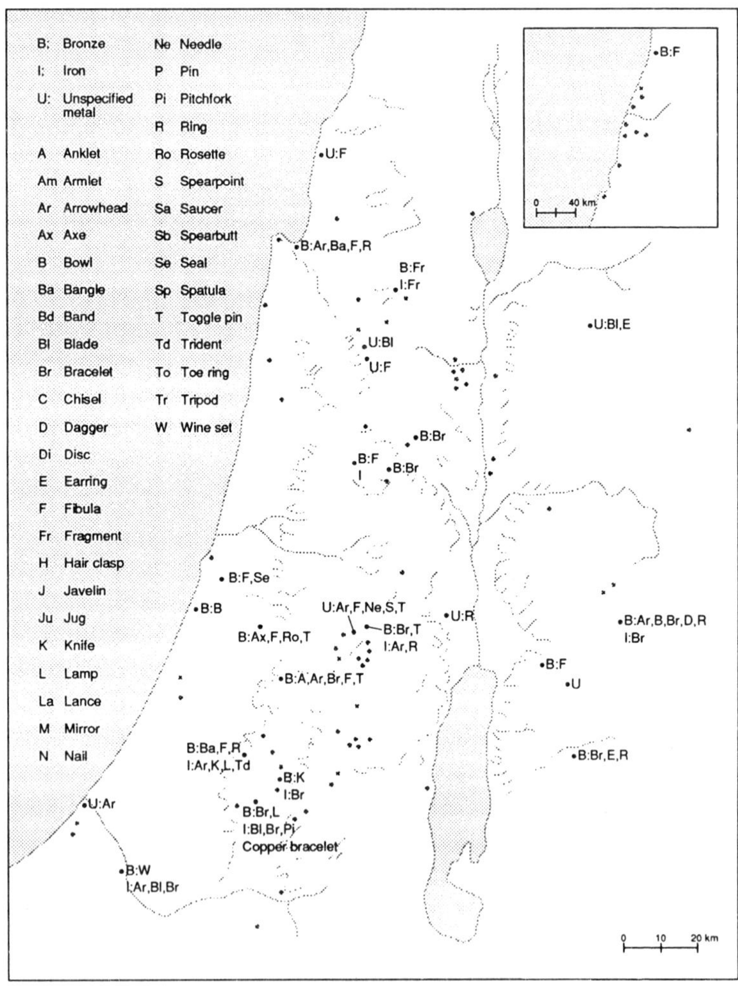

Figure 25. Metal artifacts in burials dating between the tenth and the third quarter of the eighth century BCE

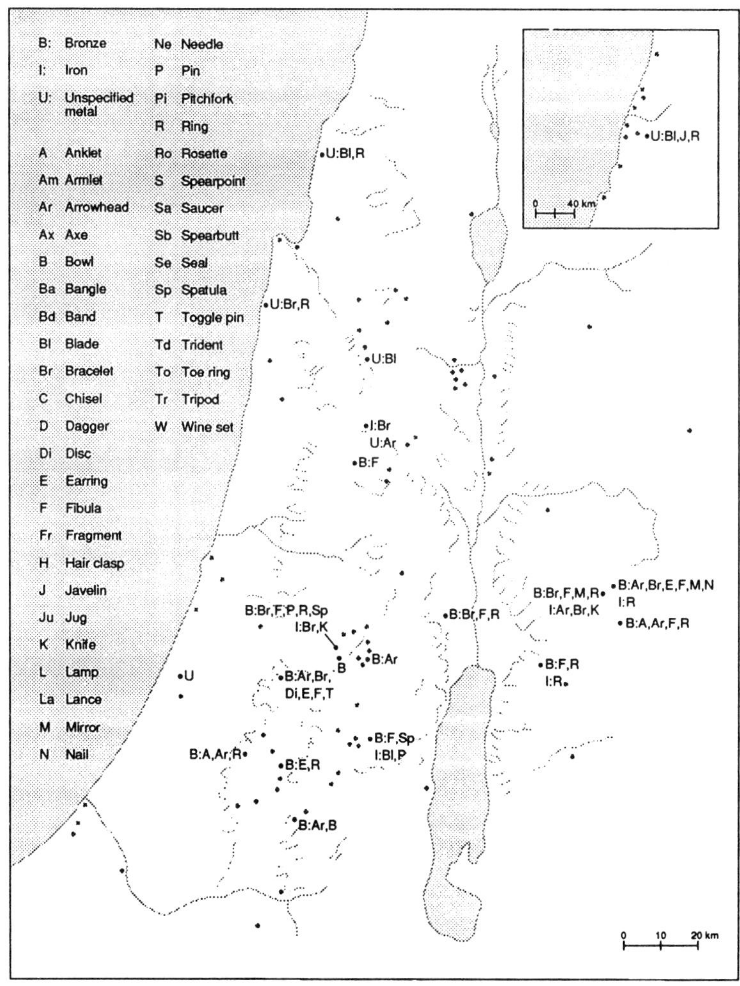

Figure 26. Metal artifacts in burials dating between the third quarter of the eighth and the first quarter of the sixth century BCE

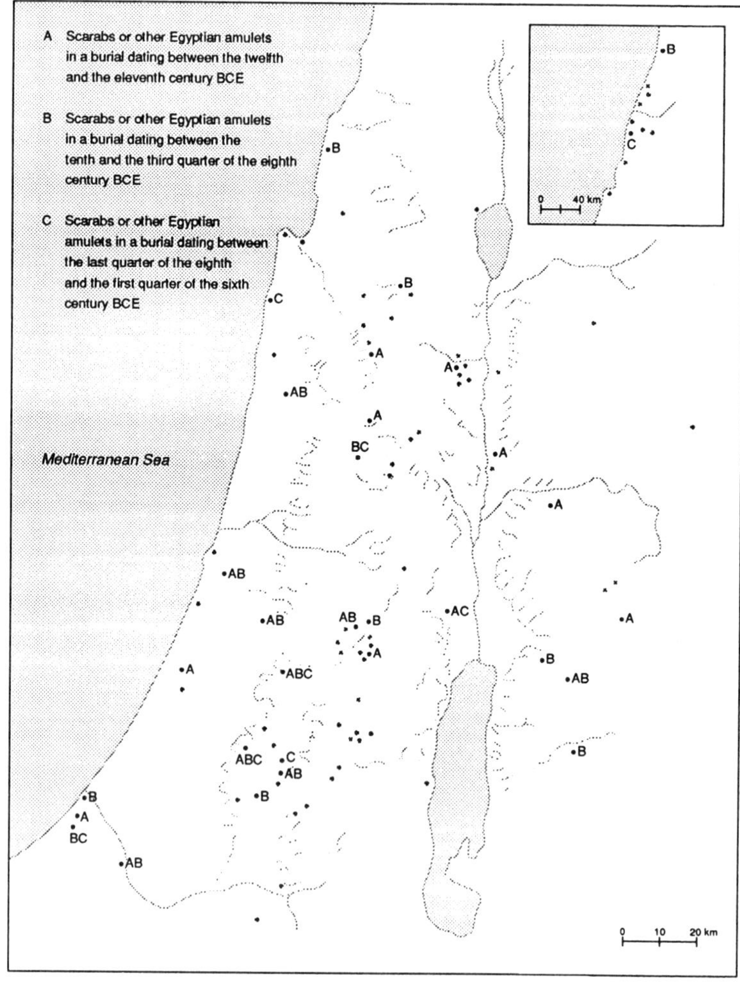

Figure 27. Scarabs and other Egyptian amulets in Iron Age burials

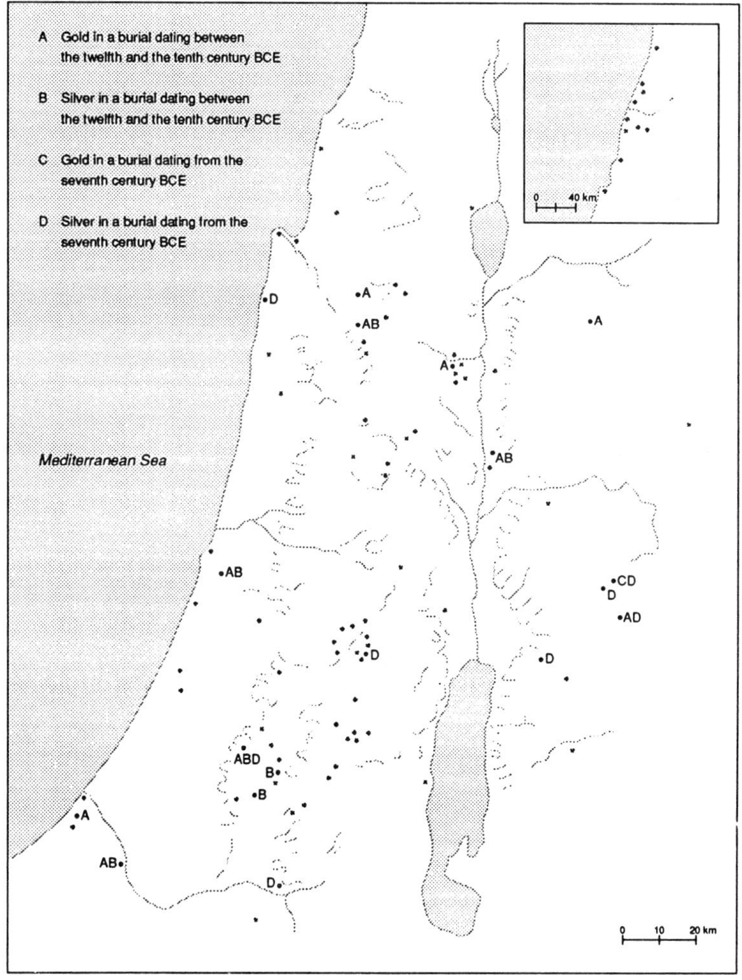

Figure 28. Gold and silver in Iron Age burials

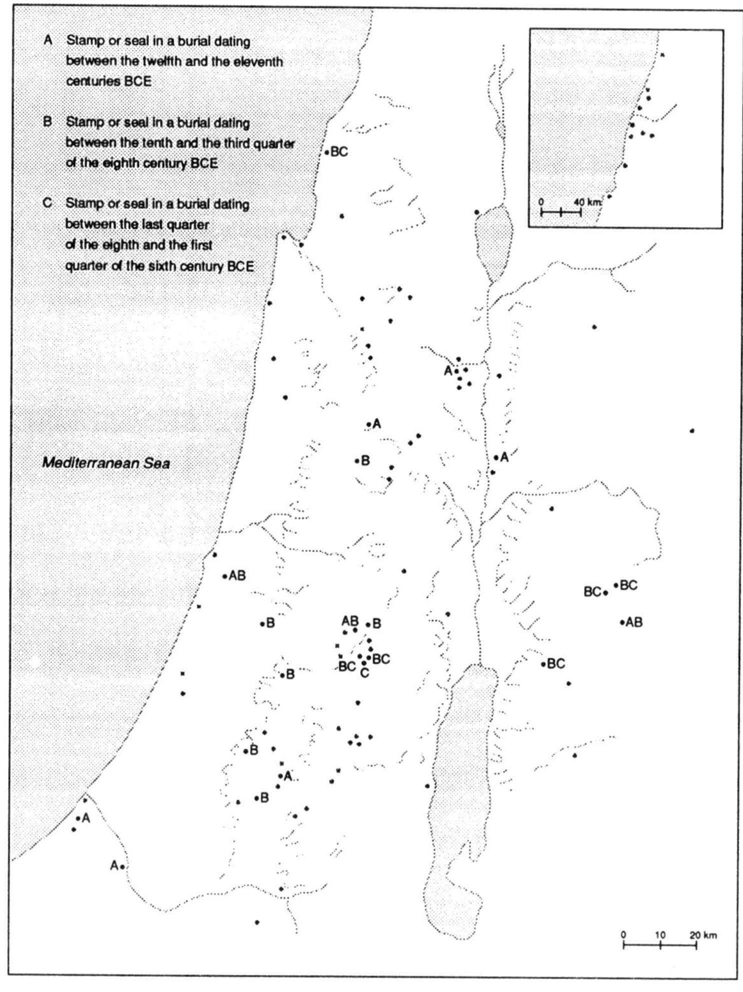

Figure 29. Stamps and seals in Iron Age burials

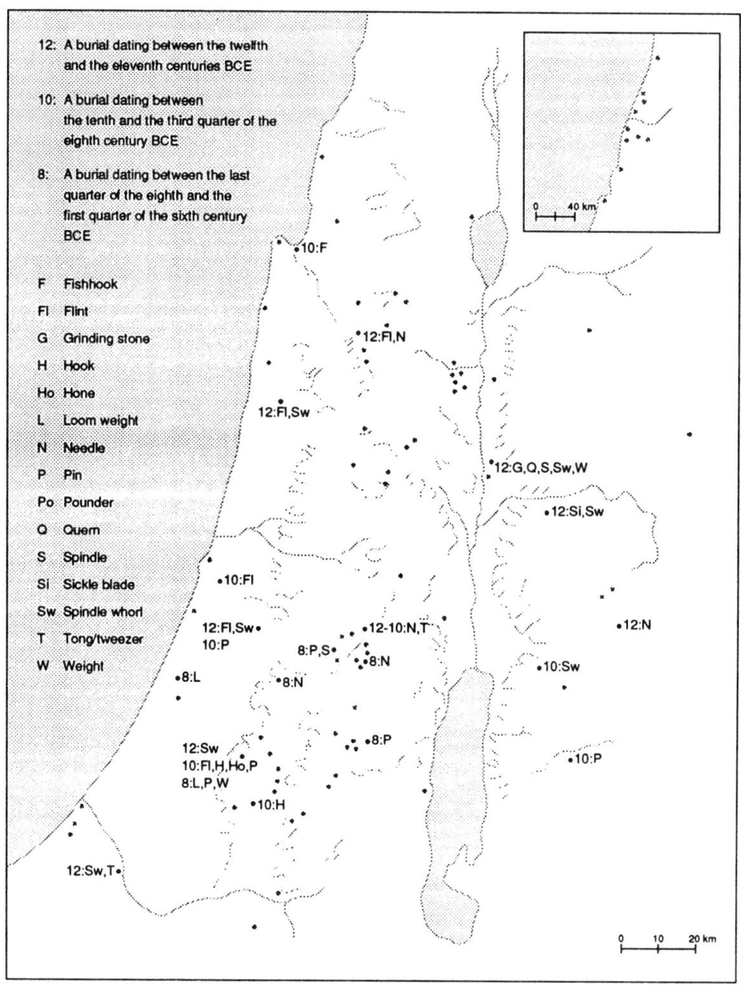

Figure 30. Houshold articles in Iron Age burials

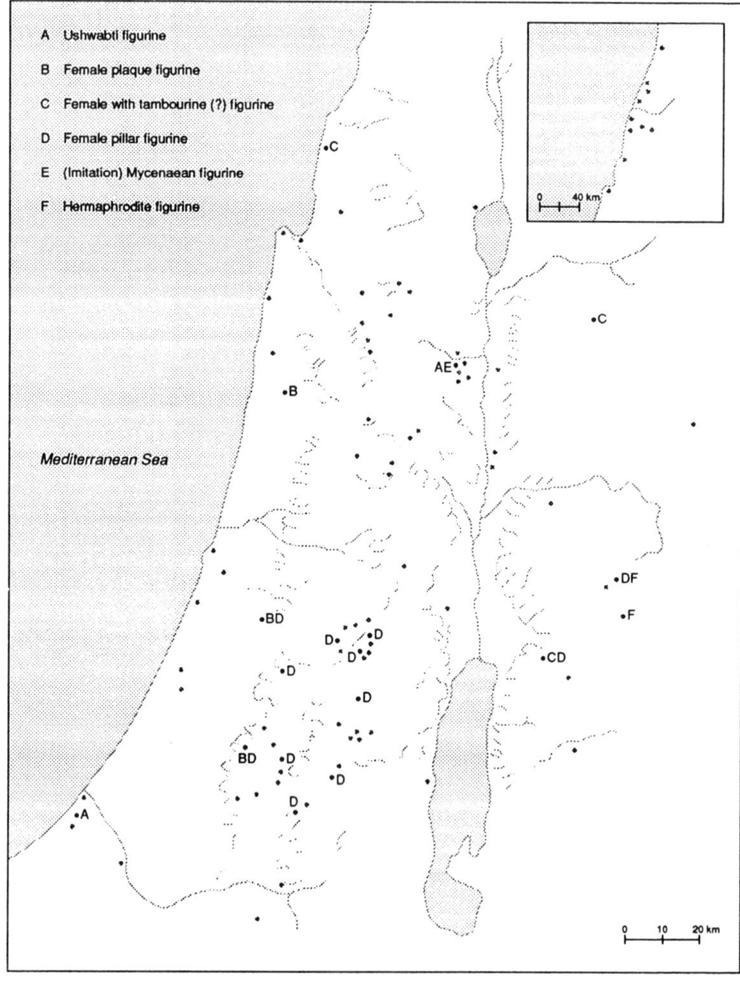

Figure 31. Anthropomorphic figurines in Iron Age burials

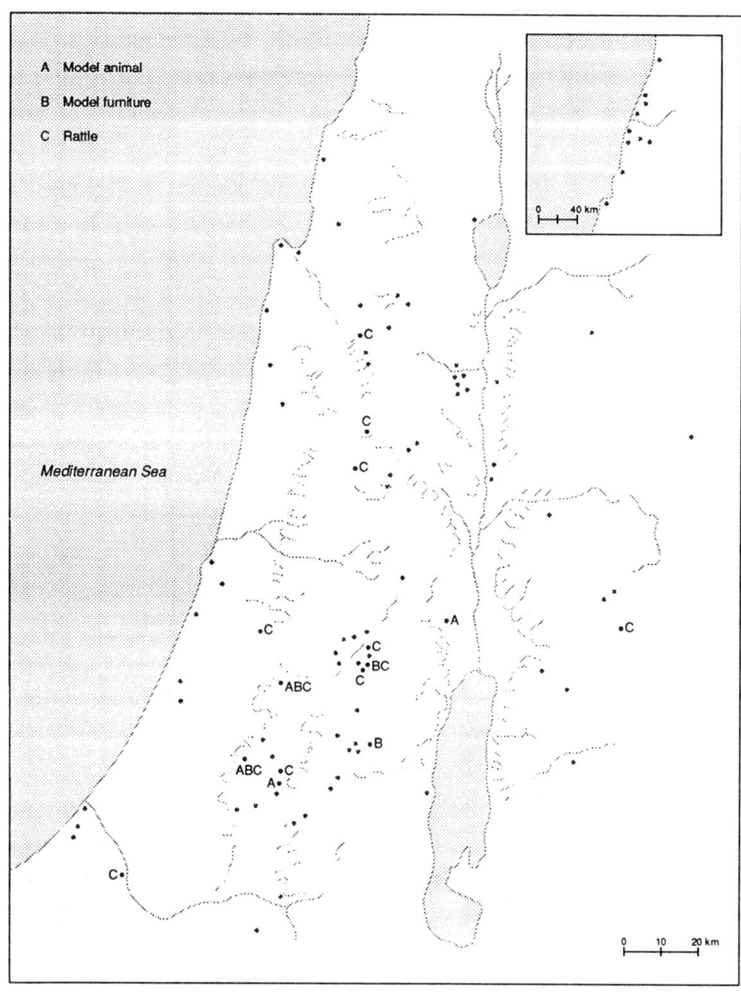

Figure 32. Model animals, model furniture and rattles in Iron Age burials

Bibliography

Abel, F.M.

1921 'Découverte d'un tombeau antique a Abou-Ghôch'. *RB* 30: 97-102.

Abercrombie, J.R.

1979 'Palestinian Burial Practices from 1200 to 600 BCE'. PhD dissertation, University of Pennsylvania.

1984 'A Short Note on a Siloam Tomb Inscription'. *BASOR* 254: 61-62.

Ackerman, S.

1987 'Syncretism in Israel as Reflected in Sixth-Century Prophetic Texts'. PhD dissertation, Harvard University.

Ackroyd, P.R.

1981 'The Death of Hezekiah—A Pointer to the Future?'. In *De la Tôrah au Messie: Mélanges Henri Cazelles*, 219-26. Ed. M. Carrez, J. Doré and P. Grelot. Paris: Desclée.

Aharoni, Y.

1967 *The Land of the Bible: A Historical Geography*. Trans. A.F. Rainey from Hebrew, 1962. Philadelphia: Westminster Press.

1975 *Investigations at Lachish: The Sanctuary and the Residency (Lachish V)*. Tel Aviv: Gateway.

Ahlström, G.W.

1982 'Where did the Israelites Live?'. *JNES* 41: 133-38.

1984 'An Archaeological Picture of Iron Age Religions in Ancient Palestine'. StudOr 55.3: 117-45.

1986 *Who were the Israelites?* Winona Lake, IN: Eisenbrauns.

Ahlström, G.W., and D. Edelman

1985 'Merneptah's Israel'. *JNES* 44: 59-61.

Albright, W.F.

1923a 'The Ephraim of the Old and New Testament'. *JPOS* 3: 36-40.

1923b 'Interesting Finds in Tumuli near Jerusalem'. *BASOR* 10: 2-3.

1932 'An Anthropoid Clay Coffin from Saḥâb in Transjordan'. *AJA* 36: 295-306.

1939 'Astarte Plaques and Figurines from Tell Beit Mirsim'. In *Mélanges Syriens offerts à René Dussaud*, I, 107-20. Institut Français D'archéologie de Beyrouth. Bibliothèque Archéologique et Historique, 30. Paris: Paul Geuthner.

1942 *Archaeology and the Religion of Israel*. Baltimore: Johns Hopkins University Press.

1943 'Soundings at Ẓâherîyeh in 1932'. *AASOR* 21-22: 155-60.

1947 'The Phoenician Inscriptions of the Tenth Century from Byblus'. *JAOS* 67: 153-60.

1957 'The High Place in Ancient Palestine'. In *Volume du Congrès International pour l'Etude de l'Ancien Testament*, 242-58. VTSup, 4. Leiden: Brill.

Alfrink, B.

1948 'L'expression "ne'esap 'el 'ammāyv" '. *OIS* 5: 118-31.

Alt, A.

1968 *Essays in Old Testament History and Religion*. Trans. R.A. Wilson from German, 1953, 1959, 1964. Anchor Books. Garden City, NY: Doubleday.

Amiran, D.H.K., J. Elster, M. Gilead, N. Rosenan, N. Kadmon and U. Paran

1970 *Atlas of Israel*. Jerusalem: Survey of Israel, Israel Ministry of Labor; Amsterdam: Elsevier.

Amiran, R.

1956 'Two Tombs in Jerusalem from the Period of the Kings of Judah'. *BIES* 20.3-4: 173-79 (Hebrew).

1957 'Two Tombs in Jerusalem from the Period of the Kings of Judah'. In *Judah and Jerusalem*, 65-72. Jerusalem: Israel Exploration Society (Hebrew.)

1957–58 'A Stone Bowl of the Later Assyrian Period from Tell el-Qitaf in the Beth Shan Valley'. *'Atiqot* 2 (Hebrew series): 116-18 (Hebrew).

1958 'The Tumuli West of Jerusalem: Survey and Excavations, 1953'. *IEJ* 8: 205-27.

1970 *Ancient Pottery of the Holy Land: From its Beginnings in the Neolithic Period to the End of the Iron Age*. Jerusalem: Massada.

Amiran, R., and C. Cohen

n.d. 'Tel Kishyon'. Israel Antiquities Authority Files.

Amman—Jabal el-Qusur

1966 *ADAJ* 11: 103.

'Amr, A.-J.

1988 'Ten Human Clay Figurines from Jerusalem'. *Levant* 20: 185-96.

Anati, E.

1959 'Excavations at the Cemetery of Tell Abu Hawam (1952)'. *'Atiqot* 2: 89-102.

Arensburg, B.

1973 'The People in the Land of Israel from the Epipaleolithic to Present Times'. PhD dissertation, Tel Aviv University.

Arensburg, B., and Y. Rak

1985 'Jewish Skeletal Remains from the Period of the Kings of Judah'. *PEQ* January–June: 30-34.

1958 *The Assyrian Dictionary of the Oriental Institute of the University of Chicago*. Ed. A. Leo Oppenheim. E. Vol. 4. Chicago: Oriental Institute; Glückstadt: J.J. Augustin.

1971 *The Assyrian Dictionary of the Oriental Institute of the University of Chicago*. Ed. A. Leo and Erica Reiner. K. vol. 8. Chicago: Oriental Institute; Glückstadt: J.J. Augustin.

Attridge, H.W. and R.A. Oden.

1976 *The Syrian Goddess (De Dea Syria): Attributed to Lucian*. Missoula, MT: Scholars Press.

1981 *The Phoenician History: Philo of Byblos*. CBQMS, 9. Washington, DC: Catholic Biblical Association of America.

Avigad, N.

1947 'Architectural Observations on some Rock-cut Tombs'. *PEQ*: 112-22.

1953 'The Epitaph of a Royal Steward from Siloam Village'. *IEJ* 3: 137-52.

1954 *Ancient Monuments in the Kidron Valley*. Jerusalem: Bialik Institute (Hebrew).

1955 'The Second Tomb Inscription of the Royal Steward'. *IEJ* 5: 163-66.

1970 'Excavations in the Jewish Quarter of the Old City of Jerusalem, 1969/70'. *IEJ* 20: 1-8, 129-40.

Badè, W.F.

1931 *Some Tombs of Tell en-Nasbeh Discovered in 1929*. Palestine Institute Publication, 2. Berkeley, CA: Pacific School of Religion Palestine Institute.

Bagatti, B.

1947 *I monumenti di Emmaus El-Qubeibeh dei Dintorni*. Pubblicazioni dello Studium Biblicum Franciscanum, 4. Jerusalem: Tipografia dei padri francescano.

1965 'Bethléem'. *RB* 72: 270-72.

1977 'Nazareth'. In *Encyclopedia of Archaeological Excavations in the Holy Land*, III. Ed. M. Avi-Yonah and E. Stern. Englewood Cliffs, NJ: Prentice–Hall.

Bailey, L.R.

1979 *Biblical Perspectives on Death*. Philadelphia: Fortress Press.

Baly, D.

1957 *The Geography of the Bible: A Study in Historical Geography*. New York: Harper & Brothers.

Barag, D.

1970 'Note on an Inscription from Khirbet el-Qôm'. *IEJ* 20: 216-18.

Baramki, D.C.

1934–35 'An Early Iron Age Tomb at Eẓ Ẓahiriyye'. *QDAP* 4: 109-10.

1956–58 'A Late Bronze Age Tomb at Sarafend, Ancient Sarepta'. *Berytus* 12: 129-42.

Barkay (Barkai), G.

1975 'Memorial Sites for the Kings of Judah'. In *Third Archaeological Congress in Israel, 12–13 March, 1975, Congress Abstracts*, 13. N.p. (Hebrew).

1977 'The Problem of the Burial of the Later Kings of the House of David'. In *Between Hermon and Sinai: Memorial to Amnon (Binyaminovits)*, 75-92. Ed. M. Broshi. Jerusalem: N.p. (Hebrew).

1983 'Excavations on the Hinnom Slope in Jerusalem'. *Bamahaneh* Oct. 12: 33-42 (Hebrew).

1984 'Excavations on the Hinnom Slope in Jerusalem'. *Qadmoniot* 17: 94-108 (Hebrew).

1986a 'The Garden Tomb: Was Jesus Buried Here?' *BARev* 12.2: 40-57.

1986b *Ketef Hinnom: A Treasure Facing Jerusalem's Walls*. Jerusalem: Israel Museum.

1988 'Burial Headrests as a Return to the Womb—A Re-Evaluation'. *BARev* 14: 48-50.

Barkay, G., and A. Kloner

1976 'Burial Caves North of Damascus Gate, Jerusalem'. *IEJ* 26: 55-57.

1986 'Jerusalem Tombs from the Days of the First Temple'. *BARev* 12.2: 22-39.

Barkay, G., A. Mazar and A. Kloner

1975 'The Northern Cemetery of Jerusalem in First Temple Times'. *Qadmoniot* 8: 71-76 (Hebrew).

Barnett, R.D.

1951 'Four Sculptures from Amman'. *ADAJ* 1: 34-36.

1966 *Illustrations of Old Testament History*. London: Trustees of the British Museum.

Baron, A.G.

1987 'The Tombs at Tel 'Ira'. Unpublished manuscript.

Barrick, W.B.

1975 'The Funerary Character of "High-Places" in Ancient Palestine: A Reassessment'. *VT* 25: 565-95.

Bartel, B.

1982 'A Historical Review of Ethnological and Archaeological Analyses of Mortuary Practice'. *JAJ* 1.1: 32-58.

Bayliss, M.

1973 'The Cult of Dead Kin in Assyria and Babylonia'. *Iraq* 35: 115-25.

Beck, P.

1982 'The Drawings from Ḥorvat Teiman (Kuntillet 'Ajrud)'. *Tel Aviv* 9.1: 3-68.

Beit-Arieh, I.

1985a 'Further Burials from the Deir el-Balah Cemetery'. *Tel Aviv* 12.1: 43-53.

1985b 'Tell Ira—A Fortified City of the Kingdom of Judah'. *Qadmoniot* 18: 17-25 (Hebrew).

Bianchi, R.S.

1983 'Skarabäus'. In *Lexikon der Ägyptologie*, cols. 967-82. Ed. W. Helck and W. Westendorf. Wiesbaden: Otto Harrassowitz.

Bieńkowski, P.A.

1982 'Some Remarks on the Practice of Cremation in the Levant'. *Levant* 14: 80-89.

Binford, L.R.

1971 'Mortuary Practices: Their Study and their Potential'. In *Approaches to the Social Dimensions of Mortuary Practice*, 6-29. Ed. J.A. Brown. Memoirs of the Society for American Archaeology, 25. Washington: Society for American Archaeology.

Bin-Nun, S.R.

1968 'Formulas from Royal Records of Israel and of Judah'. *VT* 18: 414-32.

Biran, A.

1974 'Tell er-Ruqeish to Tell er-Ridan'. *IEJ* 24: 141-42.

Biran, A., and R. Gophna

1965 'Tel Ḥalif'. *IEJ* 15: 255.

1969 'An Iron Age Burial Cave at Tel Ḥalif'. *Eretz Israel* 9: 29-39 (Hebrew).
1970 'An Iron Age Burial Cave at Tel Ḥalif'. IEJ 20: 151-69.

Bird, P.
1990 'Gender and Religious Definition: The Case of Ancient Israel'. *Harvard Divinity Bulletin* 20.2: 12-13, 19-20.

Bliss, F.J., and R.A.S. Macalister
1902 *Excavations in Palestine during the Years 1898–1900*. London: Palestine Exploration Fund.

Bloch, M.
1971 *Placing the Dead: Tombs, Ancestral Villages and Kinship Organization in Madagascar*. New York: Seminar Press.
1982 'Death, Women and Power'. In *Death and the Regeneration of Life*, 211-27. Ed. M. Bloch and J. Parry. New York: Cambridge University Press.

Bloch, M., and J. Parry
1982 'Introduction'. In *Death and the Regeneration of Life*, 1-44. Ed. M. Bloch and J. Parry. New York: Cambridge University Press.

Boling, R.G.
1975 *Judges*. AB. Garden City, NY: Doubleday.

Bordreuil, P.
1977 'Epigraphe d'amphore phénicienne du 9e siècle'. *Berytus* 25: 159-61.

Bordreuil, P., and D. Pardee
1982 'Le rituel funéraire ougaritique RS 34.126'. *Syria* 59: 121-28.

Borghouts, J.F.
1973 'The Evil Eye of Apopis'. *JEA* 59: 114-50.

Braun, E.
1982 'Tell Beit-Mirsim'. *Hadashot Arkhiologiyot* 80-81: 37 (Hebrew).

Brichto, H.C.
1973 'Kin, Cult, Land and Afterlife—A Biblical Complex'. *HUCA* 44: 1-54.

Brink, E.C.M. van den
1982 *Tombs and Burial Customs at Tell el-Dab'a*. Veröffentlichungen der Institut für Afrikanistik und Ägyptologie der Universität Wien, 23. Beiträge zur Ägyptologie, Band 4. Vienna: Afro-Pub.

Broshi, M., G. Barkai and S. Gibson
1983 'Two Iron Age Tombs below the Western City Wall, Jerusalem and the Talmudic Law of Purity'. *Cathedra* 28: 17-32 (Hebrew).

Brown, P.
1981 *The Cult of the Saints: Its Rise and Function in Latin Christianity*. Chicago: University of Chicago Press.

Brunner-Traut, E.
1975 'Farben'. In *Lexikon der Ägyptologie*, II, cols. 118-27. Ed. W. Helck and W. Westendorf. Wiesbaden: Otto Harrassowitz.

Budge, E.A.W.
1961 *Amulets and Talismans*. New York: University Books.

Bull, R.J., J.A. Callaway, E.F. Campbell, Jr, J.F. Ross and G.E. Wright
1965 'The Fifth Campaign at Balâṭah (Shechem)'. *BASOR* 180: 7-41.

Bull, R.J., and E.F Campbell, Jr
1968 'The Sixth Campaign at Balatah (Shechem)'. *BASOR* 190: 2-41.

Callaway, J.A.

1963 'Burials in Ancient Palestine: From the Stone Age to Abraham'. *BA* 26.3: 74-91.

Canaan, T.

1927 *Mohammedan Saints and Sanctuaries in Palestine*. London: Luzac.

Carroll, R.P.

1986 *Jeremiah*. OTL. Philadelphia: Westminster Press.

Chambon, A.

1984 *Tell el-Far'ah I: L'âge du fer*. Editions Recherche sur les Civilisations 'Memoire', 31. Paris: Editions Recherche sur les Civilisations et CNRS.

Chapman, R.W., and K. Randsborg

1981 'Approaches to the Archaeology of Death'. In *The Archaeology of Death*, 1-24. Ed. R. Chapman, I. Kinnes and K. Randsborg. Cambridge: Cambridge University Press.

Chapman, S.V.

1972 'A Catalogue of Iron Age Pottery from the Cemeteries of Khirbet Silm, Joya, Qrayé and Qasmich of South Lebanon'. *Berytus* 21: 55-194.

Charles, R.H.

1913 *The Apocrypha and Pseudepigrapha of the Old Testament*. 2 vols. Oxford: Clarendon Press.

Chéhab, M.

1940 'Tombes phéniciennes: Majdalouna'. *Bulletin du Musée de Beyrouth* 4: 37-53.

1970–71 'Observations au sujet du sarcophage d'Ahiram'. *Mélanges de l'Université St Joseph*, XLVI. Mélanges Maurice Dunand, 2. Beirut: Impremerie Catholique, 105-17.

Clements, R.E.

1965 'Deuteronomy and the Jerusalem Temple Cult Tradition'. *VT* 15: 301-12.

Clermont-Ganneau, M.C.

1869 *Archaeological Researches in Palestine During the Years 1873–1874*, I. London: Palestine Exploration Fund.

1871 'Notes on Certain New Discoveries at Jerusalem'. *PEFQS*: 103.

1882 *Une Mission en Palestine et en Phénicie, 1881*. Paris: Imprimerie Nationale.

Cogan, M., and H. Tadmor

1988 *II Kings*. AB. Garden City, NY: Doubleday.

Cohen, H.R.

1978 *Biblical Hapax Legomena in the Light of Akkadian and Ugaritic*. SBLDS, 37. Missoula, MT: Scholars Press.

Cohen, R.

1980 'The Iron Age Fortresses in the Central Negev'. *BASOR* 236: 61-78.

Cole, D.P.

1978 'Tel Ḥalif (Lahav), 1977'. *IEJ* 28: 119-21.

Conder, C.R., and H.H. Kitchener

1883 *The Survey of Western Palestine*, III. London: Committee of the Palestine Exploration Fund.

Contenson, H. de, J.-C. Courtois, E. Lagarce, J. Lagarce and R. Stucky
1974 'La XXXIVe campagne de fouilles a Ras Shamra en 1973 rapport préliminaire'. *Syria* 51: 1-30.

Cooke, F.T.
1925 'The Site of Kirjath-jearim'. *AASOR* 5: 105-20.

Cooley, R.E.
1968 'The Contribution of Literary Sources to a Study of the Canaanite Burial Pattern'. PhD dissertation, New York University.
1983 'Gathered to his People: A Study of a Dothan Family Tomb'. In *The Living and Active Word of God: Studies in Honor of Samuel J. Schultz*, 47-58. Ed. M. Tuchand and R. Youngblood. Winona Lake, IN: Eisenbrauns.

Cooper, A.
1981 'Divine Names and Epithets in the Ugaritic Texts'. In *Ras Shamra Parallels: The Texts from Ugarit and the Hebrew Bible*, III, 333-469. Ed. S. Rummel. Rome: Pontifical Biblical Institute.

Courbin, P.
1977 'Une pyxis géométrique argienne (?) an Liban'. *Berytus* 25: 147-57.

Courtois, J.-C.
1974 'Ugarit Grid, Strata, and Find-Localization: A Re-assessment'. *ZDPV* 90: 97-114.
1984 *Alasia III: Les objets des niveaux stratifiés d'Enkomi fouilles C.F-A. Schaeffer (1947–70)*. Editions recherche sur les civilisations mémoire, 32. Paris: ADPF.

Cross, F.M.
1956 'The Boundary and Province Lists of the Kingdom of Judah'. *JBL* 75: 202-26.
1970 'The Cave Inscription from Khirbet Beit Lei'. In *Near Eastern Archaeology in the Twentieth Century: Essays in Honor of Nelson Glueck*, 299-306. Ed. J.A. Sanders. Garden City, NY: Doubleday.
1973 *Canaanite Myth and Hebrew Epic: Essays in the History of the Religion of Israel*. Cambridge, MA: Harvard University Press.
1974 'Leaves from an Epigraphist's Notebook'. *CBQ* 36: 486-90.

Cross, F.M., and G.E. Wright
1956 'The Boundary and Province Lists of the Kingdom of Judah'. *JBL* 75: 202-26.

Crowfoot, G.M.
1932 'Pots, Ancient and Modern'. *PEFQS*: 179-87.

Crowfoot, J.W., and G.M. Crowfoot
1938 *Early Ivories from Samaria*. London: Palestine Exploration Fund.

Crowfoot, J.W., G.M Crowfoot and K.M. Kenyon
1957 *The Objects from Samaria*. London: Palestine Exploration Fund.

Crowfoot, J.W., K.M. Kenyon and E.L Sukenik
1942 *The Buildings at Samaria*. London: Palestine Exploration Fund.

Culican, W.
1973 'The Graves at Tell er-Reqeish'. *AJBA* 2.2: 66-105.

1982 'The Repertoire of Phoenician Pottery'. In *Phönizier im Westen*, 45-82. Ed. H.G. Niemeyer. Mainz am Rhein: Philipp von Zabern.

Dagan, Y.

1982 *The Judean Shephelah*. Israel: Kibbutz Movement Publications for the Knowledge of the Land (Hebrew).

Dahood, M.

1966 *Psalms*, I. AB. Garden City, NY: Doubleday.

1968 *Psalms*, II. AB. Garden City, NY: Doubleday.

1970 *Psalms*, III. AB. Garden City, NY: Doubleday.

Dajani, A.K.

1951 'Discoveries in Western Jordan, 1949–1950'. *ADAJ* 1: 47-48.

1953 'An Iron Age Tomb at al-Jib'. *ADAJ* 2: 66-74.

Dajani, R.W.

1964 'Iron Age Tombs from Irbed'. *ADAJ* 8- 9: 99-101.

1966a 'Four Iron Age Tombs from Irbed'. *ADAJ* 11: 88-101.

1966b 'An Iron Age Tomb from Amman'. *ADAJ* 11: 41-47.

1966c 'Jabal Nuzha Tomb at Amman'. *ADAJ* 11: 48-52.

1970 'A Late Bronze–Iron Age Tomb Excavated at Sahab, 1968'. *ADAJ* 15: 29-34.

Dales, G.F.

1960 'Mesopotamian and Related Female Figurines: Their Chronology, Diffusion and Cultural Functions'. PhD dissertation, University of Pennsylvania.

Damian of the Cross, Sister (Eugenia Nitowski)

1986 'The Field and Laboratory Report of the Environmental Study of the Shroud in Jerusalem'. Unpublished manuscript.

Davies, N.A.

1938 'Some Representations of Tombs from the Theban Necropolis'. *JEA* 24: 25-40.

Davis, D., and A. Kloner

1978 'A Burial Cave from the End of the Period of the First Temple on the Slopes of Mt. Zion'. *Qadmoniot* 11: 16-19 (Hebrew).

Davis, J.J.

1974 'Tekoa Excavations: Tomb 302'. *Bulletin of the Near East Archaeological Society* NS 4: 27-49.

Derekh Ḥebron

1975 *Hadashot Arkhiologiyot* 53: 22 (Hebrew).

Dethlefsen, E., *et al.*

1977 'Social Commentary from the Cemetery'. *Natural History* 86: 32-39.

Dever, W.G.

1970 'Iron Age Epigraphic Material from the Area of Khirbet el-Kôm'. *HUCA* 40: 139-204.

1976 'Gezer'. In *Encyclopedia of Archaeological Excavations in the Holy Land*, II, 428-43. Ed. M. Avi-Yonah. Englewood Cliffs, NJ: Prentice–Hall.

1978 'Khirbet el-Qôm'. In *Encyclopedia of Archaeological Excavations in the Holy Land*, IV, 976-77. Ed. M. Avi-Yonah and E. Stern. Englewood Cliffs, NJ: Prentice–Hall.

1984 'Asherah, Consort of Yahweh? New Evidence from Kuntillet 'Ajrud'. *BASOR* 255: 21-38.

Dever, W.G., H.D. Lance and G.E. Wright
1970 *Gezer I: Preliminary Report of the 1964–66 Seasons*. Jerusalem: Hebrew Union College Biblical and Archaeological School.

Donner, H., and W. Röllig
1971 *Kanaanäische und aramäische Inschriften*. I. *Texte*. Wiesbaden: Otto Harrassowitz.

Dornemann, R.H.
1983 *The Archaeology of the Transjordan in the Bronze and Iron Ages*. Milwaukee: Milwaukee Public Museum.

Dorsey, D.A.
1981 'The Roads and Highways of Israel during the Iron Age'. PhD dissertation, Dropsie University.

Dothan, M.
1955 'The Excavations at 'Afula'. *'Atiqot* 1: 19-70.
1958 'Azor'. *IEJ* 8: 272-74.
1960 'Azor'. *IEJ* 10: 259-60.
1961a 'An Inscribed Jar from Azor'. *'Atiqot* 3: 181-84.
1961b 'Excavations at 'Azor, 1960'. *IEJ* 11: 171-75.
1961c 'Ḥafirot 'Azor, 1960'. *BIES* 25: 224-30 (Hebrew).
1964 'Ashdod: Preliminary Report on the Excavations in Seasons 1962/1963'. *IEJ* 14: 79-95.
1971 'Ashdod II–III: The Second and Third Seasons of Excavations, 1963, 1965, Soundings in 1967'. *'Atiqot* 9-10. Jerusalem: Department of Antiquities and Museums in the Ministry of Education and Culture, and Hebrew University Department of Archaeology.
1972 'Ashdod—Seven Seasons of Excavation'. *Qadmoniot* 5.1: 2-13 (Hebrew).
1975 'Azor'. In *Encyclopedia of Archaeological Excavations in the Holy Land*, I, 144-47. Ed. M. Avi-Yonah. Englewood Cliffs, NJ: Prentice–Hall.

Dothan, T.
1969 'A Female Mourner Figure from the Lachish Region'. *Eretz Israel* 9: 43-46 (Hebrew).
1972 'Anthropoid Coffins from a Late Bronze Age Cemetery near Deir el-Balaḥ'. *IEJ* 22: 65-72.
1973 'Anthropoid Clay Coffins from a Late Bronze Age Cemetery near Deir el-Balaḥ'. *IEJ* 23: 129-46.
1979 *Excavations at the Cemetery of Deir el-Balah*. Qedem, 10. Jerusalem: Institute of Archaeology, Hebrew University of Jerusalem.
1982 *The Philistines and their Material Culture*. New Haven: Yale University Press.

Douglas, M.
1973 *Natural Symbols: Explorations in Cosmology*. London: Barrie & Jenkins.

Douglass, W.A.
1969 *Death in Murelaga: A Funerary Ritual in a Spanish Basque Village*. Seattle, WA: University of Washington Press.

Driver, G.R.
1962 'Plurima Mortis Image'. In *Studies and Essays in Honor of Abraham A. Neuman*. Ed. M. Ben-Horin, B.D. Weinryb and S. Zeitlin. Leiden: Brill.

Druks, A.
1966 'A "Hittite" Burial near Kefar Yehoshua'. *BIES* 30.3-4: 213-20 (Hebrew).

Durkheim, E.
1915 *The Elementary Forms of the Religious Life: A Study in Religious Sociology*. Trans. J.W. Swain from French, 1912. London: George Allen & Unwin.

Edelstein, G.
1968 'A Philistine Jug from Tell 'Aitun'. *Qadmoniot* 1.3: 100 (Hebrew).
n.d. 'Tell Aitun Tomb C1'. Unpublished manuscript.

Edelstein, G., and Y. Glass
1973 'The Uniqueness of Philistine Ceramics in Light of Petrographic Analysis'. In *Excavations and Studies in Honor of Shmuel Yeivin*, 125-31. Ed. Y. Aharoni. Jerusalem: Kiryath Sepher (Hebrew).

Edelstein, G., D. Ussishkin, T. Dothan and V. Tzaferis
1971 'The Necropolis at Tell 'Aitun'. *Qadmoniot* 4.3: 86-90 (Hebrew).

Ein Aruv
1968 *Hadashot Arkhiologiyot* 27: 20 (Hebrew).

Ein Samiyeh
1971 *Hadashot Arkhiologiyot* 37: 23 (Hebrew).

Engle, J.R.
1979 'Pillar Figurines of the Iron Age and Asherah/Asherim'. PhD dissertation, University of Pittsburgh.

En Hanaziv
1972 *Hadashot Arkhiologiyot* 44: 10 (Hebrew).
1981 *Hadashot Arkhiologiyot* 76: 14 (Hebrew).
1983 *Hadashot Arkhiologiyot* 82: 15-16 (Hebrew).

Erikson, J.M.
1969 *The Universal Bead*. New York: Norton.

Eshel, H.
1987 'The Late Iron Age Cemetery of Gibeon'. *IEJ* 37.1: 1- 17.
1989 'A *lammelek* Stamp from Bethel'. *IEJ* 39.1-2: 60-62.

Fagan, B.
1972 'Ingombe Ilede: Early Trade in South Central Africa'. *Addison–Wesley Modular Publication* 19: 1-34.

Ferembach, D.
1961 'Les restes humains des tombes Philistines du cimetière d'Azor'. *Bulletin de la Société d'Anthropologie* 9: 83-91.

Finkel, I.L.
1983 'Necromancy in Ancient Mesopotamia'. *AfO* 29: 1-17.

Finkelstein, I.
1983 'The 'Izbet Ṣarṭah Excavations and the Israelite Settlement in the Hill Country'. PhD dissertation, Tel Aviv University (Hebrew).
1986a *The Archaeology of the Period of Settlement and Judges*. Israel: Hakibbutz Hameuchad Publishing House (Hebrew).

1986b 'The Iron Age Sites in the Negev Highlands—Military Fortresses or Nomads Settling Down?'. *BARev* 12: 46-53.

1988 *The Archaeology of the Israelite Settlement*. Jerusalem: Israel Exploration Society.

Finkelstein, J.J.

1966 'The Genealogy of the Hammurapi Dynasty'. *JCS* 20: 95-125.

Flannery, K.

1972 'The Origins of the Village as a Settlement Type in Mesoamerica and the Near East: A Comparative Study'. In *Man, Settlement and Urbanism*, 23-54. Ed. P.J. Ucko, R. Tringham and G.W. Dimbleby. London: Gerald Duckworth.

Fleming, A.

1972 'Vision and Design: Approaches to Ceremonial Monument Typology'. *Man* 7: 57-73.

1973 'Tombs for the Living'. *Man* 8: 177-93.

'Flowers on Graves Don't Mean Much'.

1986 *Missionaries of Africa Report*. N.p.

Fowler, M.D.

1982 'The Israelite *bāmâ*: A Question of Interpretation'. *ZAW* 94: 203-13.

Frankfort, H.

1970 *The Art and Architecture of the Ancient Orient*. London: Penguin Books.

Free, J.P.

1954 'The Second Season at Dothan'. *BASOR* 135: 14-20.

1955 'The Third Season at Dothan'. *BASOR* 139: 3-9.

1956 'The Excavation of Dothan'. *BA* 19.2: 43-48.

1959 'The Sixth Season at Dothan'. *BASOR* 156: 22-29.

1960 'The Seventh Season at Dothan'. *BASOR* 160: 6-14.

Friedman, R.E.

1979-80 'The MRZḤ Tablet from Ugarit'. *Maarav* 2: 187-206.

Frost, S.B.

1972 'The Memorial of the Childless Man'. *Int* 26: 437-50.

Gal, Z.

1982 'The Lower Galilee in the Iron Age'. PhD dissertation, Tel Aviv University (Hebrew).

Gallery Book: Iron Age.

1940 Jerusalem: Palestine Archaeological Museum.

Galling, K.

1936 'Die Nekropole von Jerusalem'. *PJ* 32: 73-101.

Garstang, J.

1932 'Jericho: City and Necropolis'. *Liverpool Annals of Archaeology and Anthropology* 19: 35-54.

1933 'Jericho: City and Necropolis'. *Liverpool Annals of Archaeology and Anthropology* 20: 3-42.

Gaster, T. (ed.)

1968 *The New Golden Bough: A New Abridgement of the Classic Work by Sir James Frazer*. New York: Phillips.

1973 'A Hang-Up for Hang-Ups'. *BASOR* 209: 18-26.

Gennep, A. van

1960 *The Rites of Passage*. Trans. M. Caffee and G. Caffee from French, 1908. Chicago: University of Chicago Press.

Germer-Durand, J.

1906 'Découvertes archéologiques à Aboughoch'. *RB* 3: 286-87.

Gibson, J.C.L.

1971 *Textbook of Syrian Semitic Inscriptions*. I. *Hebrew and Moabite Inscriptions*. Oxford: Clarendon Press.

Gifford, E.S.

1958 *The Evil Eye*. New York: Macmillan.

Goldstien, L.

1981 'One-Dimensional Archaeology and Multi-Dimensional People: Spatial Organization and Mortuary Analysis'. In *The Archaeology of Death*, 53-69. Ed. R. Chapman, I. Kinnes and K. Randsborg. Cambridge: Cambridge University Press.

Gonen, R.

1979 'Burial in Canaan of the Late Bronze Age as a Basis for the Study of Population and Settlements'. PhD dissertation, Hebrew University (Hebrew).

1984–85 'Regional Patterns of Burial Customs in Late Bronze Age Canaan'. *Bulletin of the Anglo-Israel Archaeological* Society 4-5: 70-74.

Goodman, A.H., and G.J. Armelagos

1989 'Infant and Childhood Morbidity and Mortality Risks in Archaeological Populations'. *World Archaeology* 21: 225-43.

Goody, J.

1962 *Death, Property and the Ancestors: A Study of the Mortuary Customs of the Lodagaa of West Africa*. Stanford: Stanford University Press.

Gophna, R., and D. Meron

1970 'An Iron Age I Tomb between Ashdod and Ashkelon'. *'Atiqot* 6: 1-5, *1 (Hebrew).

Grant, E.

1929 *Beth Shemesh: Progress of the Haverford Archaeological Expedition*. Biblical and Kindred Studies. Haverford, PA: Haverford College Press.

1931 *Ain Shems Excavations 1928–1931*. Part I and II. Biblical and Kindred Studies, 3 and 4. Haverford, PA: Haverford College Press.

1934 *Rumeileh being Ain Shems Excavations*. Part III. Biblical and Kindred Studies, 5. Haverford, PA: Haverford College Press.

Grant, E., and G.E. Wright

1939 *Ain Shems Excavations (Palestine)*. Parts IV and V. Biblical and Kindred Studies, 8. Haverford, PA: Haverford College Press.

Greenfield, J.C.

1973 'Un rite religieux araméen et ses parallèles'. *RB* 80: 46-52.

Guide Book to the Palestine Museum of Antiquities

1924 Jerusalem: Department of Antiquities.

Guy, P.L.O.

1924 'Mt Carmel: An Early Iron Age Cemetery Near Haifa, Excavated September, 1922'. *Palestine Museum Bulletin* 1: 47-55.

1938 *Megiddo Tombs*. University of Chicago Oriental Institute Publications, 33. Chicago: University of Chicago Press.

Haas, N.
1963 'Human Skeletal Remains in Two Burial Caves'. *IEJ* 13: 93-96.
1971 'Anthropological Observations on the Skeletal Remains Found in Area D (1962–3)'. *'Atiqot* 9-10: 212-14.

Hadidi, A.
1987 'An Ammonite Tomb at Amman'. *Levant* 19: 101-20.

Hadley, J.M.
1987 'The Khirbet el-Qom Inscription'. *VT* 37: 50-62.

Haifa—Newe Yosef
1978 *Hadashot Arkhiologiyot* 65-66: 11-12 (Hebrew).

Halevi, B.
1975 ' '*qbwt nwspym lpwlḥn 'bwt*'. *Beth Mikra* 64.1: 101-17 (Hebrew).

Halpern, B.
1981 'Sacred History and Ideology: Chronicles' Thematic Structure—Indications of an Earlier Source'. In *The Creation of Sacred Literature: Composition and Redaction of the Biblical Text*, 35-54. Ed. R.E. Friedman. Berkeley, CA: University of California Press.

Hamilton, R.W.
1933 'Tall Abū Hawam'. *QDAP* 3: 74-80.
1935 'Excavations at Tell Abu Hawām'. *QDAP* 4: 1-69.

Hanauer, J.E.
1889 'Curious Cave at Saris'. *PEFQS*: 184-85.
1890 'Cave at Sarîs'. *PEFQS*: 71-72.

Handcock, P.S.P.
1916 *The Archaeology of the Holy Land*. New York: Macmillan.

Hanson, P.D.
1975 *The Dawn of Apocalyptic*. Philadelphia: Fortress Press.

Haran, M.
1969a *'Zebaḥ Hayyamîm'*. *VT* 19: 11-22.
1969b *'Zbḥ Ymm in the Karatepe Inscription'*. *VT* 19: 372-73.
1971 'Holiness Code'. *EncJud*, VIII, cols. 819-25.
1978 *Temples and Temple-Service in Ancient Israel: An Inquiry into the Character of Cult Phenomena and the Historical Setting of the Priestly School*. Oxford: Clarendon Press.

Harding, G.L.
1937 'Some Objects from Transjordan'. *PEQ*: 253-55.
1945 'Two Iron Age Tombs from 'Amman'. *QDAP* 11: 67-80.
1947 'An Iron-Age Tomb at Sahab'. *QDAP* 13: 92-102.
1950 'An Iron-Age Tomb at Meqabelein'. *QDAP* 14: 44-48.
1951 'Two Iron Age Tombs in Amman'. *ADAJ* 1: 37-40.
1953 *Four Tomb Groups from Jordan*. Palestine Exploration Fund Annual, 6. London: Palestine Exploration Fund.

Healey, J.F.
1977 'Death, Underworld and Afterlife in the Ugaritic Texts'. PhD dissertation, University of London.

1984 'The Immortality of the King: Ugarit and the Psalms'. *Or* 53: 245-54.

Hebron

1966 *Hadashot Arkhiologiyot* 18-19: 27 (Hebrew).

Heidel, A.

1946 *The Gilgamesh Epic and Old Testament Parallels*. Chicago: University of Chicago Press.

Heider, G.C.

1985 *The Cult of Molek: A Reassessment*. JSOTSup, 43. Sheffield: JSOT Press.

Hertz, R.

1960 *Death and the Right Hand*. Trans. R. Needham and C. Needham from French, 1909. Glencoe: Free Press.

Herzog, G.

1983 'Enclosed Settlements in the Negeb and the Wilderness of Beer-Sheba'. *BASOR* 250: 41-49.

Hestrin, R.

1987a 'The Cult Stand from Ta'anach and its Religious Background'. In *Phoenicia and the East Mediterranean in the First Millennium BC: Proceedings of the Conference Held in Leuven from the 14th to the 16th of November 1985*, 61-72. Ed. E. Lipiński. Studia Phoenicia, 5. Orientalia Lovaniensia Analecta, 22. Leuven: Peeters.

1987b 'The Lachish Ewer and the 'Asherah'. *IEJ* 37: 212-23.

Hestrin, R., and M. Dayagi-Mendels

1979 *Inscribed Seals*. Jerusalem: Israel Museum.

1983 'Another Pottery Group from Abu Ruqeish'. *Israel Museum Journal* 2: 49-57.

Hillers, D.R.

1970 'The Goddess with the Tambourine: Reflections on an Object from Taanach'. *CTM* 41: 606-19.

Hodder, I.

1982 *Symbols in Action: Ethnoarchaeological Studies of Material Culture*. Cambridge: Cambridge University Press.

Holladay, J.S., Jr

1971 'Khirbet el-Qôm'. *IEJ* 21: 175-77.

1976 'Of Sherds and Strata: Contributions toward an Understanding of the Archaeology of the Divided Monarchy'. In *Magnalia Dei: The Mighty Acts of God*, 253-93. Ed. F.M. Cross, W.E. Lemke and P.D. Miller. Garden City, NY: Doubleday.

Holland, T.A.

1975 'A Typological and Archaeological Study of Human and Animal Representations in the Plastic Art of Palestine During the Iron Age'. DPhil dissertation, University of Oxford.

1977 'A Study of Palestinian Iron Age Baked Clay Figurines, with Special Reference to Jerusalem: Cave 1'. *Levant* 9: 121-55.

Horn, S.H.

1971 'Three Seals from Sahab Tomb "C"'. *ADAJ* 16: 103-106.

Horwitz, L.K.
1987 'Animal Offerings from Two Middle Bronze Age Tombs'. *IEJ* 37: 251-55.

Huntington, R., and P. Metcalf
1979 *Celebrations of Death: The Anthropology of Mortuary Ritual*. Cambridge: Cambridge University Press.

Iakovidis, S.P.E.
1966 'A Mycenaean Mourning Custom'. *AJA* 70: 43-50.

Ibrahim, M.M.
1972 'Archaeological Excavations at Sahab, 1972'. *ADAJ* 17: 23-36.
1975 'Third Season of Excavations at Sahab, 1975'. *ADAJ* 20: 69-82.

Illman, K.-J.
1979 *Old Testament Formulas about Death*. Meddelanden Från Stiftelsens för Åbo Akademi Forskningsinstitut, 48. Åbo: Åbo Akademi.

Irwin, W.H.
1967 ' "The Smooth Stones of the Wady"? Isaiah 57,6'. *CBQ* 29: 31-40.

Isserlin, B.J.
1953 'Notes and Comparisons'. *Palestine Exploration Fund Annual* 6: 34-47.

James, F.
1966 *The Iron Age at Beth Shan: A Study of Levels VI–IV*. Philadelphia: University Museum.

Jameson, M.H.
1989 'Sacrifice and Ritual: Greece'. In *Civilizations of the Ancient Mediterranean: Greece and Rome*, 959-79. Ed. M. Grant and R. Kitzinger. New York: Charles Scribner's Sons.

Japhet, S.
1985 'The Historical Reliability of Chronicles: The History of the Problem and its Place in Biblical Research'. *JSOT* 33: 83-107.

Jerusalem
1938 *QDAP* 7: 58.

Jerusalem—Shimon Hazadik St.
1977 *Hadashot Arkhiologiyot* 61-62: 29 (Hebrew).

Jerusalem City Museum
n.d. *Finds from the Archaeological Excavations near the Temple Mount*. Jerusalem: Israel Exploration Society.

Johns, C.N.
1932 'Excavations at 'Atlīt (1930–1): The South-Eastern Cemetery'. *PEQ* 2: 41-104.
1933 'Excavations at Pilgrim's Castle 'Atlīt (1932): The Ancient Tell and the Outer Defenses'. *PEQ* 3: 145-64.
1936–37 'Excavations at Pilgrim's Castle, 'Atlīt (1933): Cremated Burials of Phoenician Origin'. *PEQ* 6: 121-52.
1975 ' 'Atlit'. *Encyclopedia of Archaeological Excavations in the Holy Land*, I, 130-44. Ed. M. Avi-Yonah. Englewood Cliffs, NJ: Prentice–Hall.

Kenna, M.E.
1976 'Houses, Fields, and Graves: Property and Ritual Obligation on a Greek Island'. *Ethnology* 15.1: 21-34.

Kennedy, C.A.

1983 'Tartessos, Tarshish and Tartarus: The Tower of Pozo Moro and the Bible'. Society of Biblical Literature Meeting in Spain. Unpublished manuscript.

1989 'Isaiah 57.5-6: Tombs in the Rocks'. *BASOR* 275: 47-52.

Kenyon, K.M.

1965 *Excavations at Jericho*. II. *The Tombs Excavated in 1955-58*. London: British School of Archaeology in Jerusalem.

1974 *Digging up Jerusalem*. London: Ernest Benn.

1981 *Excavations at Jericho*. III. *The Architecture and Stratigraphy of the Tell*. London: British School of Archaeology in Jerusalem.

Khirbet el-Kôm

1968 *Hadashot Arkhiologiyot* 25: 27 (Hebrew).

Khirbet Za'aq

1976 *Hadashot Arkhiologiyot* 59-60: 42-43 (Hebrew).

Kloner, A.

1982–83 'Rock-Cut Tombs in Jerusalem'. *Bulletin of the Anglo-Israel Archaeological Society* 2–3: 37-40.

1983 'Burial Cave from the First Temple Period at Zova'. *Hadashot Arkhiologiyot* 78-79: 71-72 (Hebrew).

Knohl, I.

1987 'The Priestly Torah versus the Holiness School: Sabbath and the Festivals'. *HUCA* 58: 65-117.

Kochavi, M.

1973 'Khirbet Rabud—Ancient Debir'. In *Excavations and Studies (in Honor of S. Yeivin)*, 49-76. Ed. Y. Aharoni. Jerusalem: Kiriat Sefer (Hebrew).

1974 'Khirbet Rabûd = Debir'. *Tel Aviv* 1: 2-32.

1978 'Tel Zeror'. In *Encyclopedia of Archaeological Excavations in the Holy Land*, IV, 1223-25. Ed. M. Avi-Yonah and E. Stern. Englewood Cliffs, NJ: Prentice–Hall.

Kochavi, M. (ed).

1972 *Judea, Samaria and the Golan: Archaeological Survey 1967–68*. Jerusalem: Carta (Hebrew).

Kôm Abou Billou

1971 *Or* 40: 227-28.

Kuechler, S.

1983 'The Melangan of Nombowai'. *Oral History* 11: 65-98.

Lagrange, M.-J.

1894 *Saint Etienne et son sanctuaire a Jérusalem*. Paris: Alphonse Picard et fils.

Lance, H.D.

1971 'The Royal Stamps and the Kingdom of Josiah'. *HTR* 64: 315-32.

Lang, B.

1983 *Monotheism and the Prophetic Minority*. The Social World of Biblical Antiquity Series, 1. Sheffield: Almond Press.

1988 'Life after Death in the Prophetic Promise'. In *Congress Volume, Jerusalem 1986*, 144-56. Ed. J.A. Emerton. VTSup, 40. Leiden: Brill.

Lapp, P.W.
1964 'The 1963 Excavation at Ta'annek'. *BASOR* 173: 4-44.
1966 *The Other Mirzbaneh Tombs*. New Haven: American Schools of Oriental Research.

Leach, E.
1977 'A View from the Bridge'. In *Archaeology and Anthropology: Areas of Mutual Interest*, 161-76. Ed. M. Spriggs. British Archaeological Reports Supplementary Series, 19. Oxford: British Archaeological Reports.

Leclant, J.
1971 'Fouilles et travaux en Egypt et au Soudan', 1969–70;. *Or* 40: 224-64.

Lees, G.R.
1892 'Notes by G. Robinson Lees, F.R.G.S'. *PEFQS*: 196-98.

Lemaire, A.
1976 'Prières en temps de crise: Les inscriptions de Khirbet Beit Lei'. *RB* 83: 558-68.

Lemke, W.E.
1976 'The Way of Obedience: 1 Kings 13 and the Structure of the Deuteronomistic History'. In *Magnalia Dei: The Mighty Acts of God*, 301-26. Ed. F.M. Cross, W.E. Lemke and P.D. Miller. Garden City, NY: Doubleday.

Levine, B.A., and J.-M. de Tarragon
1984 'Dead Kings and Rephaim: The Patrons of the Ugaritic Dynasty'. *JAOS* 104: 649-59.

Levy, S.
1962 'Tel 'Amal'. *IEJ* 12: 147.

Levy, S., and G. Edelstein
1972 'Tel 'Amal (Nir David)'. *RB* 79: 232-43.

Lewis, T.J.
1986 'Cults of the Dead in Ancient Israel and Ugarit'. PhD dissertation, Harvard University.
1987 'Death Cult Imagery in Isaiah 57'. *Hebrew Annual Review* 11: 267-84.
1989 *Cults of the Dead in Ancient Israel and Ugarit*. HSM, 39. Atlanta: Scholars Press.

Lichty, E.
1971 'Demons and Population Control'. *Expedition* 13.2: 22-26.

Lieberman, S.
1965 'Some Aspects of After Life in Early Rabbinic Literature'. In *Sefer Ha-Yovel li-kbod Tsevi Wolfson [Harry A.] Wolfson Jubilee Volume*, II, 495-532. New York: American Academy for Jewish Research.

Liverani, M.
1973 'The Amorites'. In *Peoples of Old Testament Times*, 100-30. Ed. D.J. Wiseman. Society for Old Testament Studies. Oxford: Clarendon Press.

Lods, A.
1932 *Israel: From its Beginnings to the Middle of the Eighth Century*. New York: Knopf.

Loffreda, S.

1965–66 'Il Monolita di Siloe'. *SBFLA* 16: 85-126.

1968 'Iron Age Rock-Cut Tombs in Palestine'. *SBFLA* 18: 244-87.

1973 'The Late Chronology of Some Rock-Cut Tombs of the Selwan Necropolis, Jerusalem'. *SBFLA* 23: 7-36.

Ma'ayeh, F.S.

1960 'Recent Archaeological Discoveries in Jordan'. *ADAJ* 5: 114-16.

Macalister, R.A.S.

1900 'The Rock-Cut Tomb in Wâdy er-Rababi, Jerusalem'. *PEFQS*: 225-48.

1901 'The Rock-Cut Tomb in Wâdy er-Rababi, Jerusalem'. *PEFQS*: 145-58.

1902 'The Sculptured Cave at Sarîs'. *PEFQS*: 125-29.

1912 *The Excavation of Gezer 1902–1905 and 1907–1909*, I-III. London: Palestine Exploration Fund.

1915 'Some Interesting Pottery Remains'. *PEFQS*: 35-37.

1925 *A Century of Excavation in Palestine*. London: Religious Tract Society.

McCarter, P.K., Jr

1980 *I Samuel*. AB. Garden City, NY: Doubleday.

McClellan, T.L.

1979 'Chronology of the "Philistine" Burials at Tell el-Far'ah (South)'. *Journal of Field Archaeology* 6.1: 57-73.

McCown, C.C.

1947 *Tell en-Nasbeh*. Berkeley: Palestine Institute of Pacific School of Religion; New Haven: American Schools of Oriental Research.

Macdonald, E., J.L. Starkey and G.L. Harding

1932 *Beth-Pelet II*. London: British School of Archaeology in Egypt and Bernard Quaritch.

McGovern, P.E.

1980 'Ornamental and Amuletic Jewelry Pendants of Late Bronze Age Palestine: An Archaeological Study'. PhD dissertation, University of Pennsylvania.

1981 'Baq'ah Valley Project 1980'. *BA* 44: 126-28.

1982a 'Baq'ah Valley Project 1981'. *BA* 45: 122-24.

1982b 'Exploring the Burial Caves of the Baq'ah Valley in Jordan'. *Archaeology* 35.5: 46-53.

1986 *The Late Bronze and Early Iron Ages of Central Transjordan: The Baq'ah Valley Project, 1977–1981*. University Museum Monograph, 65. Philadelphia: University of Pennsylvania, University Museum.

McKane, W.

1986 *Jeremiah*. ICC. Edinburgh: T. & T. Clark.

Mackenzie, D.

1911 'The Excavations at Ain Shems, 1911'. *Palestine Exploration Fund Annual* 1: 41-94.

1912–13 'Excavations at Ain Shems (Beth Shemesh)'. *Palestine Exploration Fund Annual* 2.

Macridy, T.

1904 'Caveaux de Tell el-Rachédieh, a Tyr'. *RB* 564-70.

Makhouly, N.
1941 'Achzib/ez-Zib'. British Mandate Period Palestine Department of Antiquities Files.

Malamat, A.
1968 'King Lists of the Old Babylonian Period and Biblical Genealogies'. *JAOS* 88: 163-73.

Margueron, J.
1977 'Ras Shamra 1975 et 1976: Rapport préliminaire sur les campagnes d'automne'. *Syria* 54: 151-88.
1981 'Ras Shamra: Nouvelles perspectives des fouilles'. In *Ugarit in Retrospect*, 71-80. Ed. G.D. Young. Winona Lake, IN: Eisenbrauns.

Martin-Achard, R.
1960 *From Death to Life: A Study of the Development of the Doctrine of the Resurrection in the Old Testament*. Trans. J.P. Smith from French, 1956. London: Oliver & Boyd.

Maxwell-Hyslop, K.R.
1971 *Western Asiatic Jewellery c. 3000–612 BC*. London: Methuen.

May, H.G.
1935 *Material Remains of the Megiddo Cult*. Oriental Institute Publications, 26. Chicago: University of Chicago Press.

Mayes, A.D.H.
1977 'The Period of the Judges and the Rise of the Monarchy'. In *Israelite and Judean History*, 285-331. Ed. J.H. Hayes and J.M. Miller. Philadelphia: Westminster Press.

Mazar, A.
1976 'Iron Age Burial Caves North of the Damascus Gate, Jerusalem'. *IEJ* 26: 1-8.

Mazar (Maisler), B.
1946 'Canaan and the Canaanites'. *BASOR* 102: 7-12.
1976 'The Archaeological Excavations near the Temple Mount'. In *Jerusalem Revealed: Archaeology in the Holy City 1968–1974*, 25-40. Ed. Y. Yadin. New Haven: Yale University Press.

Mazar, B., and M. Ben-Dov
n.d. *Excavations near the Temple Mount*. Jerusalem: Jerusalem City Museum.

Mazar, B., T. Dothan and I. Dunayevsky
1966 'En Gedi: The First and Second Seasons of Excavations 1961–1962'. *'Atiqot* 5. Jerusalem: Department of Antiquities and Museums in the Ministry of Education and Culture, and Hebrew University Department of Archaeology.

Mazor, G.
1983 'Mt Scopus, Burial Cave'. *Hadashot Arkhiologiyot* 82: 45 (Hebrew).

Meggitt, M.J.
1965 'The Mae Enga of the Western Highlands'. In *Gods, Ghost and Men in Melanesia*, 105-31. Ed. P. Lawrence and M.J. Meggitt. New York: Oxford University Press.

Meshel, Z.
1965 'Tel Ritma'. *Hadashot Arkhiologiyot* 9: 20 (Hebrew).
1974 'History of the Negev in the Time of the Kings of Judah'. PhD dissertation, Tel Aviv University.
1976 'Kuntillat Ajrud—An Israelite Site from the Monarchial Period on the Sinai Border'. *Qadmoniot* 9: 118-24 (Hebrew).
1979 'Who Built the "Israelite Fortresses" in the Negev Highlands'. *Cathedra* 11: 4-28 (Hebrew).

Metcalf, P.
1981 'Meaning and Materialism: The Ritual Economy of Death'. *Man* 16: 563-78.

Meyers, C.L.
1991 'Of Drums and Damsels: Women's Performance in Ancient Israel'. *BA* 54: 16-27.

Meyers, E.M.
1970 'Secondary Burials in Palestine'. *BA* 33: 2-29.

Milgrom, J.
1976 'First Born'. In *IDBSup*, 337-38. Ed. K. Crimm *et al.* Nashville: Abingdon Press.

Millard, A.R.
1973 'The Canaanites'. In *Peoples of Old Testament Times*, 29-52. Ed. D.J. Wiseman. Society for Old Testament Studies. Oxford: Clarendon Press.

Morgenstern, J.
1966 *Rites of Birth, Marriage, Death and Kindred Occasions among the Semites.* Cincinnati: Hebrew Union College.

Morris, I.
1987 *Burial and Ancient Society: The Rise of the Greek City-State.* Cambridge: Cambridge University Press.

Mosca, P.G.
1975 'Child Sacrifice in Canaanite and Israelite Religion: A Study in MULK and MLK'. PhD dissertation, Harvard University.

Müller, V.
1929 *Frühe Plastik in Griechenland und Kleinasien.* Augsburg: Dr Benno Filser.

Myers, J.M.
1965 *II Chronicles.* AB. Garden City, NY: Doubleday.

Naḥshonim
1961 'A Burial Cave at Naḥshonim'. *Hadashot Arkhiologiyot* 1: 7-8 (Hebrew).

Naveh, J.
1963a 'Hebrew Inscription in a Cave Tomb from the Period of the First Temple'. *BIES* 27: 235-56 (Hebrew).
1963b 'Old Hebrew Inscriptions in a Burial Cave'. *IEJ* 13: 74- 92.
1968 'A Paleographic Note on the Distribution of the Hebrew Script'. *HTR* 61.1: 68-74.
1979 'Graffiti and Dedications'. *BASOR* 235: 27-30.

Nazareth
1973 *Hadashot Arkhiologiyot* 46: 3 (Hebrew).

Negbi, O.
1963 'Mevasseret Yerushalayim'. *IEJ* 13: 145.
1964 'Tombs near Manahat South-West of Jerusalem'. *IEJ* 14: 114.
1970 'The Cemetery of Biblical Moza'. In *Sefer Shmuel Yeivin*, 358-70. Ed. S. Abramsky and Y. Aharoni. Israel Society for Biblical Research. Jerusalem: Kiryath Sepher (Hebrew).
1974 'The Continuity of the Canaanite Bronzework of the Late Bronze Age into the Early Iron Age'. *Tel Aviv* 1: 159-72.
1976 *Canaanite Gods in Metal*. Tel Aviv: Tel Aviv University Institute of Archaeology.

North, R.
1973 'Ugarit Grid, Strata and Find-Localizations'. *ZDPV* 89: 113-60.

Noth, M.
1965 *Leviticus: A Commentary*. Trans. J.E. Anderson from German, 1962. OTL. London: SCM Press.
1968 *Numbers: A Commentary*. Trans. J.D. Martin from German, 1966. OTL. London: SCM Press.

O'Callaghan, R.T.
1952 'A Statue Recently Found in 'Amman'. *Or* NS 21: 184-93.

Ohata, K. (ed).
1966 *Tel Zeror*, I. Tokyo: Society for Near Eastern Studies in Japan.
1967 *Tel Zeror*, II. Tokyo: Society for Near Eastern Studies in Japan.
1970 *Tel Zeror*, III. Tokyo: Society for Near Eastern Studies in Japan.

Olyan, S.A.
1988 *Asherah and the Cult of Yahweh in Israel*. SBLMS, 34. Atlanta: Scholars Press.

Openheim, A.L.
1969 'Babylonian and Assyrian Historical Texts'. In *Ancient Near Eastern Texts Relating to the Old Testament*, 265-317. Ed. J.B. Pritchard. Princeton, NJ: Princeton University Press.

Oren, E.D.
1973 *The Northern Cemetery of Beth Shan*. Leiden: Brill.

Oren, E., N. Fleming, S. Kornberg, R. Feinstein and P. Naḥshoni
1986 'A Phoenician Emporium on the Border of Egypt'. *Qadmoniot* 19.3-4: 83-91 (Hebrew).

Orni, E., and E. Efrat
1971 *Geography of Israel*. Jerusalem: Keter Publishing House.

Ory, J.
1948 'A Bronze-Age Cemetery at Dhahrat el Humraiya'. *QDAP* 13: 75-89.

Other Discoveries: 1 July 1938 to 30 June 1940
1940 *QDAP* 10: 201-207.

Palmahim
1973 *Hadashot Arkhiologiyot* 46: 19 (Hebrew).

Patrick, D.
1985 *Old Testament Law*. Atlanta: John Knox.

Pedersen, J.
1926 *Israel: Its Life and Culture*. London: Oxford University Press.

Petrie, W.M.F.
1914 *Amulets: Illustrated by the Egyptian Collection in University College, London*. London: Constable.
1928 *Gerar*. London: British School of Archaeology in Egypt and Bernard Quaritch.
1930 *Beth-Pelet I*. London: British School of Archaeology in Egypt and Bernard Quaritch.
1932 *Ancient Gaza II*. London: British School of Archaeology in Egypt and Bernard Quaritch.

Piccirillo, M.
1975 'Una tomba del ferro IA Madaba (Madaba B—Moab)'. *SBFLA* 25: 199-224.
1976 'Una tomba del ferro IA Mafraq (Giordania)'. *SBFLA* 26: 27-30.

Piggott, S.
1969 'Conclusions'. In *The Domestication and Exploitation of Plants and Animals*, 555-60. Ed. P.J. Ucko and G.W. Dimbley. London: Gerald Duckworth.

Pipano, S.
1984 'Azor'. *Excavations and Surveys* 3: 6-7.

Pitard, W.
1979 'The Ugaritic Funerary Text RS 34.126'. *BASOR* 232: 65-75.

Platt, E.E.
1972 'Palestinian Iron Age Jewellery from Fourteen Excavations'. PhD dissertation, Harvard University.
1978 'Bone Pendants'. *BA* 41: 23-28.

Pope, M.H.
1972 'A Divine Banquet at Ugarit'. In *The Use of the Old Testament in the New and Other Essays: Studies in Honor of Wm. F. Stinespring*, 170-203. Ed. M. Efird. Durham, NC: Duke University Press.
1977a 'Notes on the Rephaim Texts from Ugarit'. In *Essays on the Ancient Near East*, 163-82. Ed. M. de Jong Ellis. Memoirs of the Connecticut Academy of Arts and Sciences, 19. Hamden, CT: Archon Books.
1977b *Song of Songs*. AB. Garden City, NY: Doubleday.
1981 'The Cult of the Dead at Ugarit'. In *Ugarit in Retrospect*, 159-79. Ed. G.D. Young. Winona Lake, IN: Eisenbrauns.

Porada, E.
1973 'Notes on the Sarcophagus of Ahiram'. *JANESCU* 5: 355-72.

Porath, P.
1985 ''En ha-Naṣiv, 1982–1985'. *IEJ* 35: 193-94.

Porath, Y.
1973 'En Ha-Naṣiv'. *IEJ* 23: 259-60.

Prausnitz, M.W.
1959 'Achzib'. *IEJ* 9: 271.
1960 'Achzib'. *IEJ* 10: 260-61.
1962 'Tell Bir el-Gharbi (Yas'ur)'. *IEJ* 12: 143.
1963 'Achzib'. *IEJ* 13: 337-38.
1965 'Achzib'. *IEJ* 15: 256-58.

1966 'A Phoenician Krater from Akhzib'. *OrAnt* 5: 177-88.

1969 'Burial Rites at Akhzib'. In *Proceedings of the Fifth World Congress of Jewish Studies*, I, 85-89. Jerusalem: World Union of Jewish Studies.

1970 'Genesis 10:15, Canaan Became the Father of Sidon, his First-Born, Then Heth'. In *Sefer Shemuel Yeivin*, 375-79. Ed. S. Abramsky and Y. Aharoni. Israel Society for Biblical Research. Jerusalem: Kiryath Sepher (Hebrew).

1975a 'Accho, Plain of'. In *Encyclopedia of Archaeological Excavations in the Holy Land*, I, 23-25. Ed. M. Avi-Yonah. Englewood Cliffs, NJ: Prentice–Hall.

1975b 'Achzib'. In *Encyclopedia of Archaeological Excavations in the Holy Land*, I, 26-30. Ed. M. Avi-Yonah. Englewood Cliffs, NJ: Prentice–Hall.

1982 'Die Nekropolen von Akhziv und die Entwicklung der Keramik von 10. bis zum 7. Jahrhundert v. Chr. in Akhziv, Samaria und Ashdod'. *Madrider Beiträge* 8: 31-44.

Pritchard, J.B.

1943 *Palestinian Figurines in Relation to Certain Goddesses Known through Literature*. AOS, 24. New Haven: American Oriental Society.

1962 *Gibeon, Where the Sun Stood Still*. Princeton, NJ: Princeton University Press.

1964 'Excavations at Tell es-Sa'idiyeh'. *ADAJ* 8-9: 95-98.

1965 'The First Excavations at Tell es-Sa'idiyeh'. *BA* 28: 10-17, 126-28.

1980 '*The Cemetery at Tell es-Sa'idiyeh, Jordan*'. University Museum Monograph, 41. Philadelphia: University Museum.

Provan, I.

1988 *Hezekiah and the Book of Kings*. Berlin: de Gruyter.

Rad, G. von

1961 *Genesis: A Commentary*. Trans. J.H. Marks from German, 1956. OTL. Philadelphia: Westminster Press.

Radcliffe-Brown, A.R.

1922 *The Andaman Islanders*. Cambridge: Cambridge University Press.

Rahmani, L.Y.

1981 'Ancient Jerusalem's Funerary Customs and Tombs: Part Two'. *BA* 44: 229-35.

Rainey, A.F.

1963 'A Canaanite at Ugarit'. *IEJ* 13: 43-45.

Ramot

1971 *Hadashot Arkhiologiyot* 40: 21 (Hebrew).

Ras et-Tawil

1974 *Hadashot Arkhiologiyot* 50: 17 (Hebrew).

Ratosh, J.

1971 '"'*br*" *bmqr' 'w 'rṣ h'brym*'. *Beth Mikra* 47: 549-68 (Hebrew).

Redmount, C.A.

1989 'On an Egyptian/Asiatic Frontier: An Archaeological History of the Wadi Tumilat'. PhD dissertation, University of Chicago.

Reed, W.L.

1952 'Report of the Director of the School in Jerusalem'. *BASOR* 128: 4-7.

1957 'A Recent Analysis of Grain from Ancient Dibon in Moab'. *BASOR* 146: 6-10.

Reich, R.

1990 'Tombs in the Mamilla Street Area, Jerusalem'. In *Highlights of Recent Excavations*, 16-17. Jerusalem: Israel Antiquities Authority.

Reifenberg, A.

1948 'A Newly Discovered Hebrew Inscription of the Pre-Exilic Period'. *JPOS* 21: 134-37.

Reiner, E.

1971 'Akkadian Treaties from Syria and Assyria'. In *Ancient Near Eastern Texts Relating to the Old Testament*, 531-41. Ed. J.B. Pritchard. Princeton, NJ: Princeton University Press.

Renfrew, C.

1978 'Varna and the Social Context of Early Metallurgy'. *Antiquity* 52: 199-203.

Reynolds, F.E., and E.H. Waugh (eds.)

1977 *Religious Encounters with Death*. Pennsylvania: Pennsylvania State University Press.

Ribar, J.W.

1973 'Death Cult Practices in Ancient Palestine'. PhD dissertation, University of Michigan.

Ribichini, S., and P. Xella

1979 'Milk'aštart, *mlk(m)* e la tradizione siropalestinese sui Refaim'. *Rivista di Studi Fenici* 7: 145-58.

Riis, P.J.

1949 'The Syrian Astarte Plaques and their Western Connections'. *Berytus* 9: 69-90.

Rosenbaum, J.

1979 'Hezekiah's Reform and the Deuteronomistic Tradition'. *HTR* 72: 23-43.

Rosenberg, R.

1980 'The Concept of Biblical Sheol within the Context of Ancient Near Eastern Beliefs'. PhD dissertation, Harvard University.

Rothschild, N.A.

1979 'Mortuary Behavior and Social Organization at Indian Knoll and Dickson Mounds'. *American Antiquity* 44: 658-75.

Rouillard, H., and J. Tropper

1987a '*Trpym*, rituels de guérison et culte des ancêtres d'apres 1 Samuel XIX 11-17 et les textes parallèles d'Assur et de Nuzi'. *VT* 37: 340-61.

1987b 'Von kanaanäischen Ahnenkult zur Zauberei: Eine Auslegungsgeschichte zu den hebräischen Begriffen 'WB und YD'NY'. *UF* 19: 235-54.

Rowe, A.

1930 *The Topography and History of Beth-Shan*. Philadelphia: University of Pennsylvania Press.

1940 *The Four Canaanite Temples of Beth-Shan*. Philadelphia: University of Pennsylvania Press.

Rupp, D.W.

1985 'Prolegomena to a Study of Stratification and Social Organization in Iron Age Cyprus'. In *Status, Structure and Stratification: Current Archaeological*

Reconstructions, 119-30. Ed. M. Thompson, M.T. Garcia and F.J. Keene. Calgary: Archaeological Association of the University of Calgary.

Saggs, H.W.F.
1974 ' "External Souls" in the Old Testament'. *JSS* 19: 1-12.

Saidah, R.
1966 'Fouilles de Khaldé: Rapport préliminaire sur la première et deuxième campagnes (1961–1962)'. *Bulletin du Musée de Beyrouth* 19: 51-90.
1967 'Chronique: Fouilles de Khaldé'. *Bulletin du Musée de Beyrouth* 20: 165-68.
1969 'Archaeology in the Lebanon 1968–69'. *Berytus* 18: 119-42.
1977 'Une tombe de l'age de fer à Tambourit (région de Sidon'). *Berytus* 25: 135-46.

Saliby, N.
1979-80 'Une tombe d'Ugarit découverte fortuitement en 1970'. *Les annales archeologiques arabes Syriennes* 29-30: 105-39.

Saller, S.J.
1966 'Iron Age Tombs at Nebo, Jordan'. *SBFLA* 16: 165-298.
1968 'Iron Age Remains from Bethlehem'. *SBFLA* 18: 153-80.

Samaria
1967 *Hadashot Arkhiologiyot* 24: 42 (Hebrew).

Sauer, J.A.
1979 'Babylonian-Persian Cemetery at Tell el-Mazar'. *BA* 42.2: 71-72.

Saxe, A.A.
1970 'Social Dimensions of Mortuary Practices'. PhD dissertation, University of Michigan.

Schaeffer, C.F.-A.
1929 'Les fouilles de Minet-el-Beidha et de Ras Shamra'. *Syria* 10: 285-97.
1931 'Les fouilles de Minet-el-Beidha et de Ras Shamra: Deuxième campagne (Printemps 1930)'. *Syria* 12: 1-14.
1932 'Les fouilles de Minet-el-Beidha et de Ras Shamra: Troisième campagne (Printemps 1931)'. *Syria* 13: 1-24.
1933 'Les fouilles de Minet-el-Beidha et de Ras Shamra: Quatrième campagne (Printemps 1932)'. *Syria* 14: 93-127.
1934 'Les fouilles de Minet-el-Beidha et de Ras Shamra: Cinquième campagne (Printemps 1933)'. *Syria* 15: 105-31.
1935 'Les fouilles de Minet-el-Beidha et de Ras Shamra: Sixième campagne (Printemps 1934)'. *Syria* 16: 141-76.
1937 'Les fouilles de Minet el-Beidha et de Ras Shamra-Ugarit: Huitième campagne (Printemps 1936)'. *Syria* 18: 125-54.
1938 'Les fouilles de Minet el-Beidha et de Ras Shamra-Ugarit: Neuvième campagne (Printemps 1937)'. *Syria* 19: 193-255, 313-34.
1954 'Les fouilles de Ras Shamra-Ugarit: Quinzième, seizième et dix-septième campagnes (1951, 1952 et 1953)'. *Syria* 31: 14-67.

Schaeffer, C.F.-A., and F. Armand
1929 'Les fouilles de Minet el-Beidha et de Ras-Shamra (campagne du printemps 1929): Rapport Sommaire'. *Syria* 10: 285-97.

1951 'Reprises des recherches archéologiques à Ras Shamra-Ugarit: Sondages de 1948 et 1949, et campagne de 1950'. *Syria* 28: 1-21.

Schick, B.C.
1885 'Neu aufgedeckte Felszisternen und Felsgemächer in Jerusalem'. *ZDPV* 8: 42-45.

Schumacher, G.
1908 *Tell el-Mutesellim*, I. Leipzig: Haupt.

Seger, J.D.
1972 'Tel Ḥalif'. *IEJ* 22: 161.

Seger, J.D. *et al.*
1978 Lahav Research Project 1977 Season Part 1. Unpublished manuscript.

Seligson, M.
1951 *The Meaning of* נפש מת *in the Old Testament.* StudOr, 16.2. Helsinki: Societas orientalis fennica.

Sellin, E., and C. Watzinger
1913 *Jericho: Die Ergebnisse der Ausgrabungen.* Leipzig: J.C. Hinrichs.

Shanklin, W.M., and M.K. Ghantus
1966 'A Preliminary Report on the Anthropology of the Phoenicians'. *Bulletin du Musée de Beyrouth* 19: 91-94.

Shay, T.
1985 'Differentiated Treatment of Deviancy at Death as Revealed in Anthropological and Archaeological Material'. *Journal of American Anthropology* 4: 221-41.

Shennan, S.
1975 'The Social Organization at Branč'. *Antiquity* 49: 279-88.

Si'ir
1978 *Hadashot Arkhiologiyot* 67-68: 76 (Hebrew).

Sinclair, L.A.
1976 In 'Gibeah'. In *Encyclopedia of Archaeological Excavations in the Holy Land*, II, 444-46. Ed. M. Avi-Yonah. Englewood Cliffs, NJ: Prentice–Hall.

Smith, M.S.
1984 'The Magic of Kothar, the Ugaritic Craftsman God, in KTU 1.6 VI 49-50'. *RB* 91: 377-80.
1988 ' "Seeing God" in the Psalms: The Background to the Beatific Vision in the Hebrew Bible'. *CBQ* 50: 171-83.
1990 *The Early History of God: Yahweh and the Other Deities in Ancient Israel.* San Francisco: Harper & Row.

Smith, M.S., and E. Bloch-Smith
1988 'Death and Afterlife in Ugarit and Israel'. *JAOS* 108: 277-84.

Smith, R.H.
1962 *Excavations in the Cemetery at Khirbet Kūfīn, Palestine.* London: Bernard Quaritch.
1973 'A Sarcophagus from Pella: New Light on Earliest Christianity'. *Archaeology* 26: 250-56.

Soggin, J.A.

1972 *Joshua: A Commentary*. Trans. R.A. Wilson from French, 1972. OTL. Philadelphia: Westminster Press.

1987 *Judges: A Commentary*. OTL. London: SCM Press. 2nd edn.

Speiser, E.A.

1964 *Genesis*. AB. Garden City, NY: Doubleday.

Spronk, K.

1986 *Beatific Afterlife in Ancient Israel and in the Ancient Near East*. AOAT, 219. Neukirchen–Vluyn: Neukirchener Verlag; Kevelaer: Butzon & Bercker.

Stager, L.E.

1983 'The Finest Olive Oil in Samaria'. *JSS* 28: 241-45.

1985a 'The Archaeology of the Family in Ancient Israel'. *BASOR* 260: 1-35.

1985b 'Merenptah, Israel and Sea Peoples: New Light on an Old Relief'. *Eretz Israel* 18: *56-64.

Stager, L.E., and S.R. Wolff

1984 'Child Sacrifice at Carthage—Religious Rite or Population Control?'. *BARev* 10.1: 30-51.

Steele, R.

1977 'Death, Dying and Bereavement among the Maya Indians of Mesoamerica: A Study in Anthropological Psychology'. *American Psychologist* 32: 1060-68.

Stern, E.

1968 'Tel Qedesh'. *IEJ* 18: 193-94.

1969 'Excavations at Tel Qadesh (Tell Abu Qudeis)'. *Qadmoniot* 2.3: 95-97 (Hebrew).

1977 'Tel Mevorakh'. In *Encyclopedia of Archaeological Excavations in the Holy Land*, III, 866-71. Ed. M. Avi-Yonah and E. Stern. Englewood Cliffs, NJ: Prentice–Hall.

1982 *Material Culture of the Land of the Bible in the Persian Period 538–332 BC*. Warminster: Aris & Phillips.

Stern, E., and I. Beit Arieh

1979 'Excavations at Tel Kedesh (Tell Abu Qudeis)'. *Tel Aviv* 6.1-2: 1-25.

Stiebing, W.H.

1970 'Another Look at the Origins of the Philistine Tombs at Tell el-Far'ah (S)'. *AJA* 74: 139-43.

Sukenik, E.L.

1931 'The Funerary Tablet of Uzziah'. *PEQ*: 217-21.

1940 'Arrangements for the Cult of the Dead in Ugarit and Samaria'. In *Mémorial Lagrange*, 59-65. Ed. J. Gabalda *et al.* Paris: Gabalda.

1947 'The Earliest Records of Christianity'. *AJA* 51: 351-65.

1948 'Archaeological Investigations at 'Affūla'. *JPOS* 21: 1-79.

Tadmor, M.

1982 'Female Cult Figurines in Late Canaan and Early Israel: Archaeological Evidence'. In *Studies in the Period of David and Solomon and Other Essays*, 139-73. Ed. T. Ishida. Tokyo: Yamakawa-Shuppansha.

Tanakh—The Holy Scriptures
1988 Philadelphia: Jewish Publication Society.

Taylor, J. du Plat
1957 *Myrtou-Pigadhes: A Late Bronze Age Sanctuary in Cyprus*. London: Department of Antiquities Ashmolean Museum.

Taylor, J.G.
1989 'Solar Worship in the Bible and its World'. PhD dissertation, Yale University.

Tel 'Aitun
1968 *IEJ* 18: 194-95.

Tel Kishyon
1982 *Hadashot Arkhiologiyot* 78-79: 18 (Hebrew).

Tel Rehob
1972 *Hadashot Arkhiologiyot* 44: 11 (Hebrew).

Tell er-Reqeish
1940–42 *QDAP* 10: 205.

Tell Kadesh
1968 *Hadashot Arkhiologiyot* 27: 27 (Hebrew).

Tell Ruqeish
1974 *Hadashot Arkhiologiyot* 48-49: 3-6 (Hebrew).

Thompson, H.O.
1984 'Madaba—An Iron Age Tomb'. In *The Answers Lie Below: Essays in Honor of Lawrence Edmund Toombs*, 147-83. Ed. H.O. Thompson. New York: University Press of America.

Toorn, K. van der
1990 'The Nature of Biblical Teraphim in the Light of Cuneiform Evidence'. *CBQ* 52: 203-22.

Tromp, N.J.
1969 *Primitive Conceptions of Death and the Nether World in the Old Testament*. Rome: Pontifical Biblical Institute.

Tsori, N.
1975 'Middle Bronze I and Early Iron I Tombs Near Tel Rehov in the Beth-Shean Valley'. *Eretz Israel* 12: 9-17 (Hebrew).

Tubas
1971 *Hadashot Arkhiologiyot* 38: 13-14 (Hebrew).

Tubb, J.N.
1980 *An Iron Age II Tomb Group from the Bethlehem Region*. British Museum Occasional Papers, 14. London: British Museum.
1988 'Tell es-Sa'idiyeh: Preliminary Report on the First Three Seasons of Renewed Excavations'. *Levant* 20: 23-88.

Tufnell, O.
1953 *Lachish III: The Iron Age*. London: Oxford University Press.
1958 *Lachish IV: The Bronze Age*. London: Oxford University Press.

Turner, V.
1977 'Death and the Dead in the Pilgrimage Process'. In *Religious Encounters with Death*, 24-39. Ed. F. Reynolds and E. Waugh. Pennsylvania: Pennsylvania State University Press.

Tushingham, A.D.

1954 'Excavations at Dibon in Moab, 1952–53'. *BASOR* 133: 6-26.

1972 *The Excavations at Dibon (Dhībân) in Moab: The Third Campaign 1952–53*. AASOR, 40.

Tzaferis, V.

1982a 'A Burial Cave in Ramot'. *'Atiqot* 8: 11 (Hebrew).

1982b 'Iron Age II Tombs at Tell 'Eitun'. *'Atiqot* 8: 7-10 (Hebrew).

Ucko, P.J.

1962 'The Interpretation of Prehistoric Anthropomorphic Figurines'. *Journal of the Royal Anthropological Institute of Great Britain and Ireland* 92: 38-54.

1968 *Anthropomorphic Figurines of Predynastic Egypt and Neolithic Crete with Comparative Material from the Prehistoric Near East and Mainland Greece*. Royal Anthropological Institute Occasional Paper, 24. London: Andrew Szmidla.

1969 'Ethnography and Archaeological Interpretation of Funerary Remains'. *World Archaeology* 1: 262-80.

Ussishkin, D.

1970 'The Necropolis from the Time of the Kingdom of Judah at Silwan, Jerusalem'. *BA* 33: 34-46.

1973 'Tombs from the Israelite Period in Tell 'Eitun'. In *Excavations and Studies*, 31-47. Ed. Y. Aharoni. N.p. (Hebrew).

1974 'Tombs from the Israelite Period at Tel 'Eton'. *Tel Aviv* 1: 109-27.

1978 'Excavations at Tel Lachish—1973–1977, Preliminary Report'. *Tel Aviv* 5.1: 1-97.

1982 *The Conquest of Lachish by Sennacherib*. Tel Aviv: Tel Aviv University Institute of Archaeology.

1985 'Levels VII and VI at Tel Lachish and the End of the Late Bronze Age in Canaan'. In *Palestine in the Bronze and Iron Ages: Papers in Honour of Olga Tufnell*, 213-30. Ed. J.N. Tubb. Institute of Archaeology Occasional Publication, 11. London: Institute of Archaeology.

1986 *The Village of Silwan: The Necropolis from the Period of the Judean Kingdom*. Jerusalem: Yad Ben-Tzvi and the Society for the Exploration of the Land of Israel and her Antiquities (Hebrew).

Vaughan, P.H.

1974 *The Meaning of 'Bāmâ' in the Old Testament*. Cambridge: Cambridge University Press.

Vaux, L. de

1888 'Fouilles entreprises par les R.P. Dominicains: Dans leur domaine de Saint-Etienne, pres de la porte de Damas, a Jérusalem'. *RArch* 12: 32-60.

Vaux, R. de

1958 'Les sacrifices de porcs en Palestine et dans l'Ancien Orient'. In *Von Ugarit nach Qumran*, 250-65. BZAW, 7. Berlin: Töpelmann.

1965a *Ancient Israel*. I. *Social Institutions*. Trans. J. McHugh from French, 1958. New York: McGraw–Hill.

1965b *Ancient Israel*. II. *Religious Institutions*. Trans. J. McHugh from French, 1960. New York: McGraw–Hill.

1968 'Le Pays de Canaan'. *JAOS* 88: 23-30.

Vaux, R. de, and A.M. Steve
1950 *Fouilles à Qaryet el-'Enab Abu Gôsh.* Paris: Gabalda.

Vincent, H.
1911 *Underground Jerusalem: Discoveries on the Hill of Ophel (1909–11).* London: Horace Cox.

Vincent, H., and A. Steve
1954 *Jérusalem de l'Ancien Testament.* Paris: Gabalda.

Vriezen, K.J.H.
1975 'Ḫirbet Kefīre—Eine Oberflächenuntersuchung'. *ZDPV* 19: 133-58.

Waldbaum, J.C.
1966 'Philistine Tombs at Tell Fara and their Aegean Prototypes'. *AJA* 70: 331-40.

Weill, R.
1920a *La Cité de David: Campagne de 1913–1914.* Paris: Paul Geuthner.
1920b 'La Cité de David, compte rendu des fouilles exécutées à Jérusalem, sur le site de la ville primitive (campagne de 1913–1914)'. *REJ* 71: 1-45.
1920c 'La Cité de David, compte rendu des fouilles exécutées à Jérusalem, sur le site de la ville primitive (campagne de 1913–1914)'. *REJ* 70: 149-79.
1947 *La Cité de David: Campagne de 1923–24.* Institut français d'archéologie de Beyrouth. Bibliothèque archéologique et historique, 44. Paris: Paul Geuthner.

Weinfeld, M.
1985 'The Emergence of the Deuteronomic Movement: The Historical Antecedents'. In *Das Deuteronium: Entstehung, Gestalt und Botschaff,* 76-98. Ed. N. Lohfink. Leuven: Leuven University Press, Peeters.

Wente, E.F.
1982 'Funerary Beliefs of the Ancient Egyptians: An Interpretation of the Burials and the Texts'. *Expedition* 24.2: 17-26.

Westendorf, W.
1977 'Horusauge'. In *Lexikon der Ägyptologie,* III, cols. 48-51. Ed. W. Helck and E. Otto. Wiesbaden: Otto Harrassowitz.

Western Galilee
1967 *Hadashot Arkhiologiyot* 21: 18 (Hebrew).

Wilkinson, A.
1971 *Ancient Egyptian Jewellery.* London: Methuen.

Williamson, H.G.M.
1977 *Israel in the Books of Chronicles.* Cambridge: Cambridge University Press.

Wilson, J.A.
1971 'Egyptian Hymns and Prayers'. In *Ancient Near Eastern Texts Relating to the Old Testament,* 365-81. Ed. J.B. Pritchard. Princeton, NJ: Princeton University Press.

Wilson, R.R.
1980 *Prophecy and Society in Ancient Israel.* Philadelphia: Fortress Press.

Wilson, V.
1975 'The Iconography of Bes with Particular Reference to the Cypriot Evidence'. *Levant* 7: 77-103.

Winnett, F.V., and W.L. Reed
1964 *The Excavations at Dibon (Dhībân) in Moab.* AASOR, 36-37. Missoula, MT: Scholars Press.

Wold, D.J.
1979 'The Kareth Penalty in P: Rationale and Cases'. In *SBLSP*, I, 1-45. Ed. P.J. Achtemeier. Atlanta: Scholars Press.

Wright, G.E.
1948 'Review of *Tell en-Nasbeh I and II*'. *AJA* 52: 470-72.

Yassine, K.N.
1975 'Anthropoid Coffins from Raghdan Royal Palace Tomb in Amman'. *ADAJ* 20: 57-68.
1983 'Social-Religious Distinctions in Iron Age Burial Practices in Jordan'. In *Midian, Moab and Edom: The History and Archaeology of Late Bronze and Iron Age Jordan and North-West Arabia*, 29-36. Ed. J.F.A. Sawyer and D.J.A. Clines. JSOTSup, 24. Sheffield: JSOT Press.
1984 *Tell el Mazar I: Cemetery A.* Amman, Jordan: University of Jordan.

Yasur
1970 *Hadashot Arkhiologiyot* 36: 8 (Hebrew).

Yeivin, Z.
1976 'Ein Samiya and Dhahr Mirzbaneh'. In *Encyclopedia of Archaeological Excavations in the Holy Land*, II, 357-58. Ed. M. Avi-Yonah. Englewood Cliffs, NJ: Prentice–Hall.

Zayadine, F.
1968 'Une tombe du fer II a Samarie-Sébaste'. *RB* 75: 562-85.
1973 'Recent Excavations on the Citadel of Amman'. *ADAJ* 18: 17-35.

Zevit, Z.
1984 'The Khirbet el-Qom Inscription Mentioning a Goddess'. *BASOR* 255: 39-47.

Zimhoni, O.
1985 'The Iron Age Pottery of Tel 'Eton and its Relation to the Lachish, Tell Beit Mirsim and Arad Assemblages'. *Tel Aviv* 12.1: 63-90.

INDEXES

INDEX OF REFERENCES

OLD TESTAMENT

INDEX OF SITE NAMES

Index of Authors

JOURNAL FOR THE STUDY OF THE OLD TESTAMENT

Supplement Series

33 LAW AND THEOLOGY IN DEUTERONOMY
J.G. McConville
34 THE TEMPLE SCROLL:
AN INTRODUCTION, TRANSLATION & COMMENTARY
Johann Maier
35 SAGA, LEGEND, TALE, NOVELLA, FABLE:
NARRATIVE FORMS IN OLD TESTAMENT LITERATURE
Edited by George W. Coats
36 THE SONG OF FOURTEEN SONGS
Michael D. Goulder
37 UNDERSTANDING THE WORD:
ESSAYS IN HONOR OF BERNHARD W. ANDERSON
Edited by James T. Butler, Edgar W. Conrad & Ben C. Ollenburger
38 SLEEP, DIVINE AND HUMAN, IN THE OLD TESTAMENT
Thomas H. McAlpine
39 THE SENSE OF BIBLICAL NARRATIVE II:
STRUCTURAL ANALYSES IN THE HEBREW BIBLE
David Jobling
40 DIRECTIONS IN BIBLICAL HEBREW POETRY
Edited by Elaine R. Follis
41 ZION, THE CITY OF THE GREAT KING:
A THEOLOGICAL SYMBOL OF THE JERUSALEM CULT
Ben C. Ollenburger
42 A WORD IN SEASON:
ESSAYS IN HONOUR OF WILLIAM MCKANE
Edited by James D. Martin & Philip R. Davies
43 THE CULT OF MOLEK:
A REASSESSMENT
G.C. Heider
44 THE IDENTITY OF THE INDIVIDUAL IN THE PSALMS
Steven J.L. Croft
45 THE CONFESSIONS OF JEREMIAH IN CONTEXT:
SCENES OF PROPHETIC DRAMA
A.R. Diamond
46 THE BOOK OF JUDGES: AN INTEGRATED READING
Barry G. Webb
47 THE GREEK TEXT OF JEREMIAH:
A REVISED HYPOTHESIS
Sven Soderlund

48 TEXT AND CONTEXT:
OLD TESTAMENT AND SEMITIC STUDIES FOR F.C. FENSHAM
Edited by W. Claassen

49 THEOPHORIC PERSONAL NAMES IN ANCIENT HEBREW:
A COMPARATIVE STUDY
Jeaneane D. Fowler

50 THE CHRONICLER'S HISTORY
Martin Noth
Translated by H.G.M. Williamson with an Introduction

51 DIVINE INITIATIVE AND HUMAN RESPONSE IN EZEKIEL
Paul Joyce

52 THE CONFLICT OF FAITH AND EXPERIENCE IN THE PSALMS:
A FORM-CRITICAL AND THEOLOGICAL STUDY
Craig C. Broyles

53 THE MAKING OF THE PENTATEUCH:
A METHODOLOGICAL STUDY
R.N. Whybray

54 FROM REPENTANCE TO REDEMPTION:
JEREMIAH'S THOUGHT IN TRANSITION
Jeremiah Unterman

55 THE ORIGIN TRADITION OF ANCIENT ISRAEL:
1. THE LITERARY FORMATION OF GENESIS AND EXODUS 1–23
T.L. Thompson

56 THE PURIFICATION OFFERING IN THE PRIESTLY LITERATURE:
ITS MEANING AND FUNCTION
N. Kiuchi

57 MOSES:
HEROIC MAN, MAN OF GOD
George W. Coats

58 THE LISTENING HEART:
ESSAYS IN WISDOM AND THE PSALMS
IN HONOR OF ROLAND E. MURPHY, O. CARM.
Edited by Kenneth G. Hoglund, Elizabeth F. Huwiler, Jonathan T. Glass and Roger W. Lee

59 CREATIVE BIBLICAL EXEGESIS:
CHRISTIAN AND JEWISH HERMENEUTICS THROUGH THE CENTURIES
Edited by Benjamin Uffenheimer & Henning Graf Reventlow

60 HER PRICE IS BEYOND RUBIES:
THE JEWISH WOMAN IN GRAECO-ROMAN PALESTINE
Léonie J. Archer

61 FROM CHAOS TO RESTORATION:
AN INTEGRATIVE READING OF ISAIAH 24–27
Dan G. Johnson

62 THE OLD TESTAMENT AND FOLKLORE STUDY
Patricia G. Kirkpatrick

63 SHILOH:
A BIBLICAL CITY IN TRADITION AND HISTORY
Donald G. Schley

64 TO SEE AND NOT PERCEIVE:
ISAIAH 6.9-10 IN EARLY JEWISH AND CHRISTIAN INTERPRETATION
Craig A. Evans

65 THERE IS HOPE FOR A TREE: THE TREE AS METAPHOR IN ISAIAH
Kirsten Nielsen

66 SECRETS OF THE TIMES:
MYTH AND HISTORY IN BIBLICAL CHRONOLOGY
Jeremy Hughes

67 ASCRIBE TO THE LORD:
BIBLICAL AND OTHER STUDIES IN MEMORY OF PETER C. CRAIGIE
Edited by Lyle Eslinger & Glen Taylor

68 THE TRIUMPH OF IRONY IN THE BOOK OF JUDGES
Lillian R. Klein

69 ZEPHANIAH, A PROPHETIC DRAMA
Paul R. House

70 NARRATIVE ART IN THE BIBLE
Shimon Bar-Efrat

71 QOHELET AND HIS CONTRADICTIONS
Michael V. Fox

72 CIRCLE OF SOVEREIGNTY:
A STORY OF STORIES IN DANIEL 1–6
Danna Nolan Fewell

73 DAVID'S SOCIAL DRAMA:
A HOLOGRAM OF THE EARLY IRON AGE
James W. Flanagan

74 THE STRUCTURAL ANALYSIS OF BIBLICAL AND CANAANITE POETRY
Edited by Willem van der Meer & Johannes C. de Moor

75 DAVID IN LOVE AND WAR:
THE PURSUIT OF POWER IN 2 SAMUEL 10–12
Randall C. Bailey

76 GOD IS KING:
UNDERSTANDING AN ISRAELITE METAPHOR
Marc Zvi Brettler

77 EDOM AND THE EDOMITES
John R. Bartlett

78 SWALLOWING THE SCROLL:
TEXTUALITY AND THE DYNAMICS OF DISCOURSE
IN EZEKIEL'S PROPHECY
Ellen F. Davies

79 GIBEAH:
THE SEARCH FOR A BIBLICAL CITY
Patrick M. Arnold, S.J.

80 THE NATHAN NARRATIVES
Gwilym H. Jones

81 ANTI-COVENANT:
COUNTER-READING WOMEN'S LIVES IN THE HEBREW BIBLE
Edited by Mieke Bal

82 RHETORIC AND BIBLICAL INTERPRETATION
Dale Patrick & Allen Scult

83 THE EARTH AND THE WATERS IN GENESIS 1 AND 2:
A LINGUISTIC INVESTIGATION
David Toshio Tsumura

84 INTO THE HANDS OF THE LIVING GOD
Lyle Eslinger

85 FROM CARMEL TO HOREB:
ELIJAH IN CRISIS
Alan J. Hauser & Russell Gregory

86 THE SYNTAX OF THE VERB IN CLASSICAL HEBREW PROSE
Alviero Niccacci
Translated by W.G.E. Watson

87 THE BIBLE IN THREE DIMENSIONS:
ESSAYS IN CELEBRATION OF FORTY YEARS OF BIBLICAL STUDIES
IN THE UNIVERSITY OF SHEFFIELD
Edited by David J.A. Clines, Stephen E. Fowl & Stanley E. Porter

88 THE PERSUASIVE APPEAL OF THE CHRONICLER:
A RHETORICAL ANALYSIS
Rodney K. Duke

89 THE PROBLEM OF THE PROCESS OF TRANSMISSION
IN THE PENTATEUCH
Rolf Rendtorff
Translated by John J. Scullion

90 BIBLICAL HEBREW IN TRANSITION:
THE LANGUAGE OF THE BOOK OF EZEKIEL
Mark F. Rooker

91 THE IDEOLOGY OF RITUAL:
SPACE, TIME AND STATUS IN THE PRIESTLY THEOLOGY
Frank H. Gorman, Jr

92 ON HUMOUR AND THE COMIC IN THE HEBREW BIBLE
Edited by Yehuda T. Radday & Athalya Brenner

93 JOSHUA 24 AS POETIC NARRATIVE
William T. Koopmans

94 WHAT DOES EVE DO TO HELP? AND OTHER READERLY QUESTIONS
TO THE OLD TESTAMENT
David J.A. Clines

95 GOD SAVES:
LESSONS FROM THE ELISHA STORIES
Rick Dale Moore

96 ANNOUNCEMENTS OF PLOT IN GENESIS
Laurence A. Turner
97 THE UNITY OF THE TWELVE
Paul R. House
98 ANCIENT CONQUEST ACCOUNTS:
A STUDY IN ANCIENT NEAR EASTERN AND BIBLICAL HISTORY WRITING
K. Lawson Younger, Jr
99 WEALTH AND POVERTY IN THE BOOK OF PROVERBS
R.N. Whybray
100 A TRIBUTE TO GEZA VERMES:
ESSAYS ON JEWISH AND CHRISTIAN
LITERATURE AND HISTORY
Edited by Philip R. Davies & Richard T. White
101 THE CHRONICLER IN HIS AGE
Peter R. Ackroyd
102 THE PRAYERS OF DAVID (PSALMS 51–72):
STUDIES IN THE PSALTER, II
Michael Goulder
103 THE SOCIOLOGY OF POTTERY IN ANCIENT PALESTINE:
THE CERAMIC INDUSTRY AND THE DIFFUSION OF CERAMIC STYLE
IN THE BRONZE AND IRON AGES
Bryant G. Wood
104 PSALM STRUCTURES:
A STUDY OF PSALMS WITH REFRAINS
Paul R. Raabe
105 ESTABLISHING JUSTICE
Pietro Bovati
106 GRADED HOLINESS:
A KEY TO THE PRIESTLY CONCEPTION OF THE WORLD
Philip Jenson
107 THE ALIEN IN THE PENTATEUCH
Christiana van Houten
108 THE FORGING OF ISRAEL:
IRON TECHNOLOGY, SYMBOLISM AND TRADITION IN ANCIENT SOCIETY
Paula M. McNutt
109 SCRIBES AND SCHOOLS IN MONARCHIC JUDAH:
A SOCIO-ARCHAEOLOGICAL APPROACH
David Jamieson-Drake
110 THE CANAANITES AND THEIR LAND:
THE TRADITION OF THE CANAANITES
Niels Peter Lemche
111 YAHWEH AND THE SUN:
THE BIBLICAL AND ARCHAEOLOGICAL EVIDENCE
J. Glen Taylor

112 WISDOM IN REVOLT:
METAPHORICAL THEOLOGY IN THE BOOK OF JOB
Leo G. Perdue

113 PROPERTY AND THE FAMILY IN BIBLICAL LAW
Raymond Westbrook

114 A TRADITIONAL QUEST:
ESSAYS IN HONOUR OF LOUIS JACOBS
Edited by Dan Cohn-Sherbok

115 I HAVE BUILT YOU AN EXALTED HOUSE:
TEMPLE BUILDING IN THE BIBLE IN THE LIGHT OF MESOPOTAMIAN AND NORTH-WEST SEMITIC WRITINGS
Victor Hurowitz

116 NARRATIVE AND NOVELLA IN SAMUEL:
STUDIES BY HUGO GRESSMANN AND OTHER SCHOLARS 1906–1923
Translated by David E. Orton
Edited by David M. Gunn

117 SECOND TEMPLE STUDIES:
1. PERSIAN PERIOD
Edited by Philip R. Davies

118 SEEING AND HEARING GOD WITH THE PSALMS:
THE PROPHETIC LITURGY FROM THE SECOND TEMPLE IN JERUSALEM
Raymond Jacques Tournay
Translated by J. Edward Crowley

119 TELLING QUEEN MICHAL'S STORY:
AN EXPERIMENT IN COMPARATIVE INTERPRETATION
Edited by David J.A. Clines & Tamara C. Eskenazi

120 THE REFORMING KINGS:
CULT AND SOCIETY IN FIRST TEMPLE JUDAH
Richard H. Lowery

121 KING SAUL IN THE HISTORIOGRAPHY OF JUDAH
Diana Vikander Edelman

122 IMAGES OF EMPIRE
Edited by Loveday Alexander

123 JUDAHITE BURIAL PRACTICES AND BELIEFS ABOUT THE DEAD
Elizabeth Bloch-Smith